SEMIOSIS

in the Postmodern Age

SEMIOSIS

in the Postmodern Age

Floyd Merrell

Purdue University Press
West Lafayette, Indiana

99   98   97   96   95   5   4   3   2   1

The paper used in this book meets the minimum requirements of American National Standard for Information Sciences—Permanence of Paper for Printed Library Materials, ANSI Z39.48-1984.

Printed in the United States of America
Design by Anita Noble

Library of Congress Cataloging-in-Publication Data
Merrell, Floyd, 1937–
    Semiosis in the postmodern age / Floyd Merrell.
       p.   cm.
    Includes bibliographical references and index.
    ISBN 1-55753-055-6 (cloth : alk. paper)
    1. Semantics (Philosophy) 2. Peirce, Charles S. (Charles Sanders), 1839–1914.
    3. Postmodernism. I. Title.
    B840.M47 1995
    121'.68—dc20   94-21557
                                                 CIP

Contents

List of Figures

Preface

Some four years into my professional career, after a brief stint teaching chemistry and physics in public schools followed by an interdisciplinary degree in Iberoamerican studies, I began dabbling in Peirce, then I read the *Collected Papers* from cover to cover. And I was hooked on signs. The radically crossdisciplinary trail I followed in my pursuit of the evasive sign was not without its perils and pitfalls, however. It eventually led me to the conviction that semiotics cannot be that great pretender offering a science of science, a theory to end all theories, the ultimate method and set of analytical tools. It seemed that such pretension could not but end in sham.

Theories, methods, and analytical techniques cannot hope to become paradise regained, for they are more often than not predicated on the assumption that borders must be staked out and defended to the hilt. However, like signs in general, the procreation and practice of theories, methods, and analytical techniques cannot carve out distinct borders for all time, for these very activities are themselves processual, *semiosic.* The signs they propagate spread, amoebalike, to absorb their neighbors; they appear from nowhere only to disappear further downstream; they slip and slide along the precarious slopes of history, always becoming something other than what they were; they interpenetrate, diverging and converging, in a massive tangled web that ultimately defies all description and all comprehension. Benoit Mandelbrot, inventor of fractals, hit the nail on the head: Mountains are not triangular and clouds are not round, and to conceive of them as such is a terribly distorted hyperabstraction, a purely artificial construct. Likewise, theories, methods, and analytical techniques that are artificially extracted from the flow, like all borders, limns, taxonomies, typologies, delineations, and pigeonholes, are invariably the product of futile exercises.

Indeed, if we reflect on Peirce sufficiently—as well as on process philosophy and the general mood among leading scientists of this century—we will find ourselves leaning toward the conclusion that no corpus of thought, or the road leading to it, can be registered by clear and distinct areas. It is we humans that think we are capable of perceiving and conceiving sharpness between categories. But thoughts—themselves signs, *thought-signs*—never merely tread water. They move to and fro at variable speeds, changing places with one another, inviting interpenetration and disclosing only their surfaces, whose shapes vary according to the angles at which they are approached. The same applies to *sign-events* "out there"—I write "events," for signs are not rock-hard entities; they do not imply some sort of permanence but come into view at the same time that they are passing on.

Moreover, only the most presumptuous of minds operate on the premise that thinking is identifiable with a determinate object to which it refers, as though the gap between thought-signs and the world's furniture could ever be closed, as if the mind could push thought-signs beyond the limitations of infinitely deferred time and infinitely pliable space, as if the mind were capable of grasping the essence of things in one gulp. The river of time exists within the enduring curvatures of space, both of which rush thought-signs and sign-events along, reducing the amnesic mind to useless attempts at identifying ideas and things. But the mind cannot expect to triumph in a free-for-all with the incessant emanation of semiotic entities.

The best we can do, I would submit, is grope around in the stream, catching a few slithering signifying events—if not to say signs—here and there, with the hope that we can somehow put together a family of them that we might be able to grasp conceptually. We are helpless in our efforts to penetrate the flow to its depths, for we are always caught within it, without sextant or anchorage. In fact, the very story I have to tell in this volume illustrates how all narratives, discourse, and conceptual schemes cannot help but begin in midstream, and they cannot hope to reach a determinate ending but are destined merely to suffer more or less arbitrary cuts at points along the way. As Robert Frost once put it, "Ends and beginnings—there are no such things." Why should we, narratives (i.e., signs) that we are, that are us, expect our condition to be otherwise? What are we to suppose we are capable of comprehending the world of which we are a part, and what is the world to suppose it can be understood by us, minuscule and insignificant spatiotemporal warps contained within it? We are ephemeral eddies in the stream, originating somewhere, occasionally fancying that we have altered the current somewhat, quickly passing away somewhere else. And all remains as it was, but not quite.

So also with writing, the premier medium for telling stories in our pumped-up academic world. Belief in a legitimate beginning entails one's presuming to be "outside," surveying the vast expanse, then selecting a spot where the first cut will be enacted. But there is no "outside." And to pretend one can reason toward and reach a determinate ending is to presume knowledge of what lies "beyond," such that at the most propitious spot one can draw the diverse lines of narrative together and neatly tie them. But there is no "beyond." Beginning and ending, outside and beyond, presuppose a pattern of timeless, absolute reference, representation, and knowledge. Without this pattern, we have only that Faustian quest, the cataclysms and triumphs, of modernity. So in the final analysis, we are left with no more than the panting, the heaving, the inhalation and expiration of words, much in the style of Samuel Beckett's *How It Is,* the stuttering, uncertain fits and starts of *Molloy, Malone Dies,* and *The Unnamable,* the perpetual oscillation of *Waiting for Godot.*

My own words somehow begin, in the Introduction, with postmodernism. But I subscribe neither to the delirious proclamations of pop postmodernists that the problems of elitism, of "highbrow" culture, can at long last be assigned to the past, nor to a contempt for "mass culture" that falls under the sway of that other strain of postmodernism, which is an extension of traditional norms rather than something new. In other words, I subscribe neither to Norman O. Brown, Leslie Fiedler, Buckminster Fuller, Susan Sontag, and Ihab Hassan, nor to Herbert Marcuse, Marshall McLuhan, Terry Eagleton, Andreas Huyssen, and Fredric Jameson. My concerns are not throwaway pop culture but hopefully something worth holding on to; not uncurbed consumption of words and things but ecological engagement; not here again, gone tomorrow, but persistence, even obsession, with the captivating issues at hand; not anti-intellectualism but an effort to think things out with acknowledgment that there can be no endgame.

In other words, I would wish to capture the spirit of Charles Sanders Peirce, whose own incessant ransacking through the rubble of human thought in pursuit of the sign evinces that Faustian brand of modernity with which we are all too familiar, though his refusal to concede to determinate beginnings, endings, and centers of foci falls in line with the postmodern temper. As a caveat, however, it behooves me to mention that I am not always faithful to Peirce's writings: I often use him as a point of departure. After this confession, many Peirce purists will immediately sound the alarm. Yet I hold fast to my position. The contemporary relevance of Peirce does not stem from the letter of his tripartite sign but from the spirit that made it possible in the first place: an open-ended mode of inquiry eventually destined to push beyond Peirce himself, which, I imagine, he would welcome.

To get down to specifics, in the first three chapters of this volume, I dwell on the elusiveness of the sign, following my general thesis that we are always somewhere in the flow. In chapters Four and Five, my description of the comings and goings of signs might appear to render them virtually intangible. Yet we can hardly expect things to be otherwise, since our conscious awareness of what we are doing is but the tip of an iceberg, the bulk of our knowledge remaining tacit, below the surface. In chapters Six, Seven, and Eight, I address myself directly to Peirce's sign types, which, one naturally assumes, should belong at the beginning of an inquiry on signs. I suggest that there is method in my madness, however, motivated by an effort properly to till the ground before sowing time. Then, if in chapters Nine and Ten, attention seems to rest more on the "semiotics" of physicist John Archibald Wheeler than on Peirce—a strange sort of "quantum-theoretical" disquisition on signs—it is because I believe all theories merge into, and at times give way to, successor theories. And at this moment in history, I happen to find the quantum turmoil captivating, a worthwhile game to play.

Finally, I take Jean Baudrillard to task in Chapter Eleven. But I do so at a rather abstract level, quite divorced from the nitty-gritty of everyday life, upon which Baudrillard's work rests. This final chapter returns us to the beginning, whenever and wherever that was, but, I would hope, from a somewhat different slant on the "semiotic object" as always and invariably something other than the "real," whatever that is. Indeed, in a previous book, *Signs Becoming Signs: Our Perfusive, Pervasive Universe* (Merrell 1991a), stress generally rests on Firstness, the possibility of signs' emergence into our "semiotic world." The present inquiry is rather more attuned to what I term the "semiotically real," the domain of Secondness. Yet another volume, entitled *Signs Grow: Semiosis and Life Processes* (Merrell 1994), rounds out what I would like to consider a trilogy of sorts. As would be expected, this third inquiry approaches Thirdness; it focuses more directly than the other two volumes on the ongoing stream of signification within which we are immersed in our everyday living. Though I can hardly garner any expectations of having delivered in these three books a theory to end all theories or the ultimate analytical toolkit with which to engage in the practice of semiotics, I hope at least to have addressed myself to the proper problems, raised the relevant questions, and provided a scattering of insights here and there.

A final word. To the obvious question, "Who are you, with no formal training in many of the disciplines into which you exercise forays, to be writing this book?" my only excuse is that nobody else happened to be writing one with this particular focus: not semioticians, not Peirce specialists, not philosophers or philosophers of science, not anthropologists or sociologists, not literary or culture critics. So I gave it a try.

Acknowledgments

I would like to thank Tom Sebeok, as I have numerous times in the past, for his continued support. Myrdene Anderson, Terry Prewitt, and Joe Ransdell gave me valuable input. Lucia Santaella and her vivacious group of associates at São Paulo, Brazil, lent a willing ear to my oral and gesticulatory ramblings in a seminar I gave in the summer of 1992, some of which found its way into this volume. During that same year, a miniseminar presented at Montevideo, Uruguay, at the invitation of Fernando Andacht also allowed me to air out a few ideas, as did conferences in Buenos Aires and Rosario, Argentina. I wish to express my appreciation to former students at Purdue University, that for a few fleeting moments I was able to trap within the confines of some drab classroom or other and mumble a few soporific nothings: they are by no means faceless, though their number does not allow mention of particular individuals here. Thanks to Margaret Hunt, Susan Y. Clawson, and Anita Noble for their editing and design work; they are always a pleasure to work with. Finally, to Araceli.

Parts of chapters Six and Seven were previously published in *Semiotica* and *Signa* and appear in this volume with the permission of the editors.

The Semiosic Cascade

> This world: a monster of energy, without beginning, without end; . . .
> a sea of forces flowing and rushing together, eternally changing, eternally
> flooding back, with tremendous years of recurrence, with an ebb and a
> flood of its forms. . . . [T]his, my Dionysian world of the eternally self-
> creating, the eternally self-destroying, this mysterious world of the twofold
> voluptuous delight, my "beyond good and evil," without goal, unless the
> joy of the circle is itself a goal.
>
> —FRIEDRICH NIETZSCHE

To begin, then, *in medias res,* a few words on postmodernism.

Although lingering guardians of good taste and an often recalcitrant but heterogeneous coterie of true believers would like us to forget about postmodernism altogether, it can hardly be overlooked. This emerging cultural paradigm, this index of decadence or ephemeral fad, depending upon the eye of its beholder, is forbidding, a bewilderingly variegated bag of tricks—one encounters virtually as many postmodernisms as there are postmodernists these days.[1]

To be sure, definition of the term "postmodernism" has suffered from rampant inflation. To make matters worse, rather than aiding and abetting social and political commitment, postmodernism has been branded "more of a program developed by theorists than the common reality of contemporary society and culture" (Kuspit 1990, 54). Indeed, the baffling postmodern milieu with which numerous scholars have become obsessed prompts Linda Hutcheon (1988a, 1) to pen the question, "Why has post-modernism been both acclaimed and decried by both ends of the political spectrum?" The most obvious answer, she concludes, is "that everyone is talking about different cultural phenomena— which they all label as post-modern."[2] And the Sturm-und-Drang debates over the banes and beauties of this new furor continue.[3]

Aware of postmodernism's defense tactics against any and all theoretical or conceptual grasps, in this introduction I nonetheless wish at least to evoke a feel for the postmodern age we have entered. In fact, the best I can hope to do is evoke some sort of feel. Indeed, it is my intention to resist, insofar as that may be possible, the modernist illusion of one's always being able self-critically to transcend oneself. According to most postmodern tenets, one cannot transcend the past, let alone the present, in order to exercise a break with conventions handed down by tradition and thereby step outside the sphere of language into the diaphanous midday of innocence. Postmodernism places in question the capacity of language (even, and especially, critical language) to render "truths" about the world or forms of language objective and transparent.

Indeed, a chief characteristic of postmodernism is the conviction that we are finally able to divest ourselves of that presumptuous aura of self-presence predicated on the primacy of the *eikon* and its referentialist representationalism. That Platonic conception of immobile being in the form of *eidos* (*idea*), which raises itself up in all its brilliant splendor to be grasped by the cogitating mind—a rationally intuiting individual standing aloof from the world—has faded. The autonomous, contemplating soul, whose function was mimetically to reveal the nature of the world like a mirror—a microcosm reduplicating the macrocosm—yielded no faithful representation at all but at best a false sense of *re-presentation*. That is to say, for modernism, what was presumably presented somewhere in the remote past can now, with proper means and methods, be presented anew (re-collected in the venerable Platonic tradition). In contrast, postmodernism tells us that there will always be an inevitable tinge of difference: Nothing is exactly what it was but always something else with each iteration (or repetition, following Kierkegaard's invectives against Platonism). Moreover, there is not, nor can there be, any subject standing over and against the object. The postmodern subject is not that fleshless, bloodless, decentered semiological variety. Nor is there any inner self in direct contrast to the outer world. There is, rather, a fusion of all such distinctions. Subject and object become both actors in, and spectators of, the drama being played out on nature's stage.

However, the picture remains confusing. This catchall term, "postmodernism," has been hailed by many observers as new and refreshing. In this guise, it entices anxious academicians—from the untenured young to midlife commissars of proper methods and tastes, and finally to preretirement seniors seeking an injection of new life—to thrust boldly into the hitherto uncharted territory of popular culture (Collins 1989; Fiedler 1975). As a result, the impending state of affairs occasionally approaches academic anarchy. Postmodernism has consequently been at one and the same time characterized as a questioning of totalizing, hierarchized systems—though it remains incapable of destroying them (Hutcheon 1988b; Lyotard 1984); intellectual containment limiting openness (Connor 1989); an end to rugged individualism (via the "death of the subject") (Foucault 1970); and an intersection, even a fusion, of scientific, artistic, and academic attitudes (Hassan 1987). It has been branded a failure of commitment (Howe 1970); the ultimate extension of capitalist, consumerist societies (Jameson 1983, 1984a); a form of commercial or coopted capitalism (Kroker and Cook 1986); a "neoconservative" reaction curtailing the "unfinished project" of Enlightenment-modernist thought and reason (Habermas 1983, 1985); and either a break with, or an intensification of, certain characteristics of modernism (Foster 1983; Kaplan 1988).[4]

This perplexing drift, postmodernism, is also disparately defined, regarding its radical break with totalizing postures and grand logical systems, as a suspension of logocentric discourse of identity, presence, and certainty in favor of pluralism, discontinuity, and indeterminacy (C. Scott 1990). At the same time, it has been hailed as a return to the yesteryear of cosmological visions arising out of the "new physics" of interconnectedness (Griffin 1988; Toulmin 1982a).[5] Furthermore, it is variously modeled on architecture (Jencks 1977); parody and paradoxes of literary form (Hutcheon 1988b); local narratives, which will ultimately triumph over monolithic grand narratives (Lyotard 1984); pragmatically designed communities of interlocutors (Rochberg-Halton 1986); and the sign's elevation to the status of "hyperreality," whereby it becomes more "real" than the "real" (Baudrillard 1983a). It has even been seen to mirror the decline of Western civilization (Toynbee 1954), thus presenting virtually nothing new (Graff 1979). And at the furthest stretch, we have Charles Newman (1985, 17) sardonically characterizing postmodernists as "a band of vainglorious contemporary artists following the circus elephants of Modernism with snow shovels."

Such wrangling might prompt one to throw in the towel. But there is no call for either despair or apocalyptic premonitions; a thread does link the convoluted, convergent, and divergent postmodernist views. Postmodernists are generally willing to concede, apparently without regrets, that discord arising from the contradictions of thought and everyday practice is as healthy as it is inevitable and, indeed, a necessary condition for individual, social, and cultural experience (Hutcheon 1988a, 7). On the other hand, attempting to stash any and all conflicts of postmodernism away in the closet and pretend they do not exist would be myopic, though occasionally this has been the immediate response from certain humanist enclaves taking upon themselves the responsibility of safeguarding the cherished canons of their cultural heritage.

In spite of this reigning state of confusion, it is tentatively possible to distinguish between two general thrusts of postmodernist theory, which focus on: (1) narratives that reveal the emergence of a Nietzschean negation of the "real" and the absence of univocal, unequivocal meaning in the world of art and culture and that thus tend to break down the familiar separations of art/life, science/nonscience, literature/history, practice/theory, fiction/nonfiction, and sentiment/reason (de Laurentis 1985, 16);[6] and (2) the appearance of new social, political, and economic trends that place classical theories of production

3

and consumption, authority and knowledge, and dominance and subservience in question (Huyssen 1986). These thrusts, customarily labeled "postmodernism" and "postmodernity," respectively, have traveled along routes now diverging, now converging, but always interrelated.

In what appears to be their most common denominator, postmodernism and postmodernity are a special *attitude toward* our radically transient contemporary culture. Postmodernism produces narratives and other forms of expression in response to the overwhelming complexities, quandaries, and vicissitudes of contemporary life. Postmodernity, a reaction to the apparent monotony of modernism's positivistic, technocratic vision of the world—with its belief in linear progress, absolute truth, the standardization of knowledge and production, the rational planning of social orders, and the good life for all—tends to generate politically *engagé* discourse. It is a mind-set governing either a direct or a tangential critique of culture.

To be sure, both postmodernism and postmodernity, in narrative and through radical critique, favor heterogeneity, difference, fragmentation, and indeterminacy as liberating forces.[7] The rediscovery of pragmatism; the new philosophy of science; the various expressions of poststructuralism and culture criticism; and new developments in mathematics, physics, and biology emphasizing catastrophe and chaos theory, dissipative structures, and fractal geometry mark a profound shift in the nature of reason and madness, logic and nonsense, experience and sentiment (Harvey 1989, 10–65).[8] In Terry Eagleton's (1987) somewhat cynical words, today we are "in the process of wakening from the nightmare of modernity, with its manipulative reason and fetish of the totality, into the laid-back pluralism of the postmodern, that heterogeneous range of lifestyles and language games which has removed the nostalgic urge to totalize and legitimate itself."

Apart from their most obvious reflection of the arts, popular culture, and social, political, and economic institutions, postmodernism and postmodernity have played a role in giving rise to revisionist historicism and "archaeology";[9] notions of all aspects of everyday life as tacit, collective practices;[10] rejuvenated literary theory and general cultural critique;[11] science as a community-oriented attitude;[12] and culture as dialogic, polyphonic interaction.[13] It is becoming increasingly apparent that this trend is not to be defined in relation to a given medium or merely as a critique of social classes, conventions, and institutions but rather as an elaborate set of operations on an apparently discordant corpus of cultural terms: both postmodernism and postmodernity are consequently textual through and through (Foster 1983).

In this light, a brief account of the decline of modernism and the surfacing of postmodernism is in order before turning to the latter's cultural-texturing facet.

In essence, modernism was a troubled and ambiguous response to the milieu
created by modernity, itself the product of modernization. The general conception of modernity falls in line with the traditional term "modern philosophy,"
which originated with Descartes, gained an overwhelming head of steam with
Newtonian mechanics, and perpetuated itself well into the twentieth century.
The concerns of modernism are thus rooted in a foundationalism seeking to
acquire knowledge based on a turn to the inner sanctum of the knowing subject's
mind and a faithful representation of the objective world "out there." Indeed,
modernist representation was marked not only by the emergence of the de-   5
tached subject as spectator and by science, the ground lending it support, but
also by a redistribution of the authority of science—now constituted via a faith
more dogmatic than the religious faith of prior epochs, according to Alfred North
Whitehead (1925)—by the powers of an absolute state, and by a reconception
of the nature of the arts (Cascardi 1988). There appeared to be no limits.

Yet modernism's push for totalization was Janus-faced. As early as
the 1860s, Baudelaire dubbed modernism "the transient, the fleeting, the contingent; it is the one half of art, the other being the eternal, and the immutable"
(quoted in Harvey 1989, 10). The history of modernism, especially in its aesthetic role, has zigzagged between this dual formulation, at times exercising
violent swings rendering it virtually the opposite of what it was. In Marshall
Berman's (1982, 15) words:

> To be modern is to find ourselves in an environment that promises
> us adventure, power, joy, growth, transformation of ourselves and
> the world—and, at the same time, that threatens to destroy every-
> thing we have, everything we know, everything we are. Modern
> environments and experience cut across all boundaries of geogra-
> phy and ethnicity, of class and nationality, of religion and ideology;
> in this sense, modernity can be said to unite all mankind. But it is a
> paradoxical unity, a unity of disunity: it pours us all into a mael-
> strom of perpetual disintegration and renewal, of struggle and con-
> tradiction, of ambiguity and anguish. To be modern is to be part of
> a universe in which, as Marx said, "all that is solid melts into air."

Intellectuals of all stripes have attempted to confront this disconcerting collision of opposites that fosters a perplexing sense of fragmentation,
ephemerality, chaotic change, and a strange new experience of time and space
as fleeting and arbitrary—some of them, as mentioned, dubbing this milieu the
logical extension of modernism, while others saw it as the announcement of
postmodernism.[14] This baroque concoction of unified contraries, of discordant
harmony, led many thinkers to recognize that the only security is to be found
in insecurity. Within such a gyrating centrifuge of change, there could be no

respect for the past or for any premodern notions of social order, ethical norms, aesthetic recipes, metaphysical doctrines, or scientific prescriptions. Perpetual transitoriness canceled historical continuity; internal ruptures and fragmentation demanded ruthless breaks with preceding historical conditions. Hence all conventions and norms, myths and misplaced religious beliefs, were to be creatively destroyed. Yet the eternal and immutable was thought somehow to lurk within this buzzing confusion: There must be some essential character to the dizzying sequence of events, this delirious scrapbook of images.

Jürgen Habermas (1983, 1987) tells us that the "project of modernity" is a "rational response" to this perplexing *mise-en-scène*. He endows Enlightenment thought with the task of developing an objective science and universal codes of ethics, morality, and law, with art standing outside as an autonomous purveyor, via its own inner logic, of some set of immutable aesthetic values. In Habermas's vision, all individuals, making up the whole of society, each according to his/her capacity and talents, would work freely and creatively to bring about the accumulation of knowledge founded on the bedrock of "reason" in the pursuit of human emancipation, the enrichment of everyday life, and the scientific and technological taming of nature in order to abolish scarcity and natural calamities and to satisfy needs and desires. The good life would be just around one of the gently sloping curves along the road toward indefinite progress.

Yet the inner conflict tormenting the modern mind persists, and it has resurfaced in postmodernism. This conflict is perhaps most readily apparent in the now celebrated, now maligned rift between the so-called two cultures, modern art and modern science. Generally speaking, modernist aesthetics culminated in the assurance that (1) the artistic medium is a transparent mediator between the work and its meaning; (2) the artist is a *sujet fondateur,* an isolated individual and the sole source of the aesthetic object; (3) for a given culture, there is a "center," a "master pattern," or "model" constituting a set of timeless universal values from which aesthetically legitimate works arise and against which their value can be measured; (4) given the existence of a "center," a fixed meaning of the work is possible and within reach of the privileged, knowing subject to the exclusion of all other, lesser individuals; and (5) the audience of authentic art is enlightened, while mass culture, numbed by the simplicity, predictability, and stultifying sameness of the art it consumes, is unable to step outside its sphere of ignorance. It seemed to follow, according to the venerable authorities of the day, that a boundary must be established between "highbrow" and "lowbrow" art, the former evincing novelty of form, the latter remaining undifferentiated, the product of assembly-line means, methods, and ends. Consequently, the role of the critic as knowing subject must be to defend the canons handed down by tradition in order to safeguard the "master pattern" against the barbarous threat of an unenlightened public (Collins 1989, 7–16).[15]

In view of these imperatives, from the turmoil at the opening of this century to the period immediately preceding the emergence of postmodernism during the latter 1950s and early 1960s, it came to be widely agreed, quite notably among New Critics in the United States, that the ideal work should be: (1) autonomous, thus maintaining its pristine purity by avoiding contact with culturally blemished forms; (2) self-referential—the product of a hyper-conscious, detached spirit—with a liberal dose of irony, ambiguity, and paradox proper to an alienated citizen in a debasing society; (3) the result of an exploration of the medium of which the work is composed, with an accompanying disparagement of content and a foregrounding of form; and (4) removed from the age-old axioms mandating that "representation" and "realism" be propagated as the prime functions of art; rather, art exists for its own sake, it is its own medium and must be negotiated from within the parameters it sets for itself (Huyssen 1986, 44–62). Experimentalism was thus favored, kitsch was condemned. One encountered only language directly rather than the world or culture. And a work was conceived to be the heroic product of the artist's rigorous asceticism, abstention, and resistance to, and suppression of, the ways of the world. The work existed at the edge of time, on the margins of history. It was otherworldly rather than worldly, an aborted effort to present the unpresentable (see Lyotard 1984).

And here we encounter the notorious breach between modernist aesthetics and science.[16] Romanticism had replaced Descartes's "I think therefore I am" with "I feel therefore I am," signaling a radical departure from an explicitly rational and instrumentalist strategy to a more consciously subjectivist one for achieving Enlightenment goals. Kant also recognized that aesthetic judgment should be distinguished from practical moral judgment and scientific knowledge, with aesthetics forming a necessary, albeit problematic bridge between morals and science. The foregrounding of aesthetics as distinct from cognition was most decidedly a nineteenth-century affair, motivated by the confrontation with "exotic" cultures, present and past. It also resulted from the difficulty in applying Enlightenment principles of reason and scientific knowledge to moral, social, and political principles. Finally, toward the end of the nineteenth century, Nietzsche, among others, planted a bombshell in the grand scientistic-Enlightenment project, thus widening the gap between the two cultures, with his assertion that art and aesthetics are capable of projecting beyond good and evil and beyond traditional conceptions of truth and falsity.

Another tug-of-war arose out of the opposition between, on the one hand, the modern mind's concern with order versus disorder and its seeking to bring everything under its control and, on the other hand, nature, which pays these concerns hardly any attention. The modern mind seeks the elation derived from mastery over the world, whereas nature offers it the sublime resignation that accompanies an undifferentiated participation with the whole of things. The mind seeks self-sufficiency; nature offers it relationship. And the mind desires invulnerability, while nature serves as a constant reminder that it is bonded to all things. This tension continued unabated throughout the reign of modernity.[17]

8   During the early years of this century, movements such as dadaism, cubism, and surrealism marked a partial breakdown of this world-in-conflict and the ushering in of something at least different, if not exactly new. Yet postmodernism continued to evince certain commonalities with early twentieth–century avant-garde movements of high modernism (Hassan 1982, 139), though in its early stages it experienced a sense of new frontiers. That is, postmodernism has not (yet, at least) parted ways with modernism regarding the Nietzschean negation of representation and the Derridean-Lacanian proclamation that the existence of the "trace" marks the absence of determinable meaning. Nor was there (yet) any issue such as that which was later revealed in the modernist-postmodernist debate between Habermas and Jean-François Lyotard—or Marxism and neo-Nietzscheanism—the former inscribing a metanarrative with precise values and premises, and the latter placing in jeopardy both the product and process of inscription.

These problems were not scheduled to arrive on the scene until around the later 1960s and early 1970s. With their advent, other inevitable contradictions soon arose. Postmodern optimism regarding electronics, video, TV, and other marvels of technology tended to validate popular culture, which had been the focus of modernism's derision.[18] An indirect response to this contradiction surfaced in the guise of poststructuralism, deconstruction, the new American pragmatism—a facet of postmodernism to which Habermas attached the notorious epithet "neoconservatism"—and other ardent practices. The earlier, wide-eyed sense of contemporary culture and possibilities for the future now began to wane, as did the postmodern neoromantic image—actually a holdover from modernism—of the artist as an anxiety-ridden, hypersensitive, and alienated outsider. Certain postmodernists now countered modernism with a robust anti-intellectualism, an antipathy toward institutional practices, and a litany of "death to the subject," while the majority began working toward new modes of speaking and listening, writing and reading, acting and viewing (Huyssen 1986, 213–16).

Concomitantly, notions of inner self, other self, and social other gained attention as postmodernism began in earnest to negotiate between modernism's dichotomies of high art and mass culture, the sublime and the mundane, subjectivity and objectivity, sentiment and reason (Collins 1989; Conner 1989, part 2). As a result, postmodernism abandoned the modernist search for inner meaning, asserting a broader, synthetic base with a quite disparate juxtaposition of past and present models and modalities, and of collective practices (Harvey 1989, 83). In Fredric Jameson's (1984a) encapsulation, postmodern aesthetic persuasion gravitates—again revealing contradictory practices—toward: (1) a focus on surface events, (2) the historicist effacing of history, (3) a decentering of the self, (4) a sense of rootlessness—deterritorialization, in Gilles Deleuze and Félix Guattari's (1983) terms—and (5) an abolition of the dream of critical distance (Donougho 1989). Dichotomies are thus presumably diffused. Everything merges with everything else, and shamanic voices tell the story of an end to any and all metanarratives. In short, since it is impossible to step outside postmodern narratives, postmodernism itself remains implicated in the values it chooses to contest.

9

Even here, problems of demarcation remain, however. For example, Marike Finlay argues throughout *The Potential of Modern Discourse* (1990) that Musil, Peirce, and the Copenhagen interpretation of quantum mechanics—particularly its expression through Heisenberg—reveal our contemporary quandaries to be not postmodernist at all but instead deeply rooted in modernism. I would contend, rather, that whether they are modern or postmodern in their ways depends on the observer's way of taking them (and admittedly, my statement is itself postmodern, or perhaps modern, depending on one's way of taking it). I will adopt the view, while conceding to its inevitable touch of prejudices and presuppositions, that much of Peirce's writings—and those of his contemporaries such as Nietzsche—in certain respects *were* postmodern. Heisenberg, Bohr, Schrödinger, and some of the quantum physicists were, at the fringe of their thought, postmodern. The works of Picasso, Braque, Duchamp, Apollinaire, Pirandello, and other avant-garde artists bordered on postmodernism. But I do not wish to wage an extended critique of, or enter into the problematics of, classifying and periodizing. Rather, throughout this inquiry, I shall attempt to chisel out the hypothesis that Peirce was painfully aware of the problems inherent in what are on the current scene labeled metanarrative infinite regresses as well as the notions of foundationalism, precise values and premises, and ultimate determinations of truth.[19] Nevertheless, at this juncture a few words are in order concerning the enticement of, and inevitable pitfalls in, any and all taxonomic schemes, particularly in view of the overriding emphasis that modernism has traditionally placed on them.

To be sure, many observers have contended that postmodern thought can ill afford dualistic or taxonomic thinking, and that indeed, the critique of such thought must be our chief "intellectual imperative, since the hierarchical opposition of marked and unmarked terms . . . is the dominant form both of representing difference and justifying its subordination in our society" (Owens 1983, 62). Programmatic edicts customarily fall short of desired goals, however. The attempt to eschew and dissolve all dichotomies of mind and matter that inevitably breed priorities and erect hierarchies does not by that mere fact abolish distinctions once and for all (Hutcheon 1988a, 61). As a case in point, Ihab Hassan (1982, 267–68; 1987, 91–92) constructs two towers of opposition in his effort to foreground "certain schematic differences" between modernism and postmodernism. In passing I list a smattering of them, which is an appropriate move, I believe, since they will occasionally be placed in the spotlight as future chapters unfold:

MODERNISM	POSTMODERNISM
Form (conjunctive, closed)	Antiform (disjunctive, open)
Purpose	Play
Design	Chance
Hierarchy	Anarchy
Art Object/Finished Work	Process/Performance/Happening
Distance	Participation
Centering	Dispersal
Root/Depth (vague)	Rhizome/Surface (general)
Origin/Cause	Difference-Différance/Trace
Determinacy	Indeterminacy
Transcendence	Immanence

At the outset, Hassan's dichotomies may strike one as mere caricatures, though David Harvey (1989, 44)—quite correctly, I believe—observes that "there is scarcely an arena of present intellectual practice where we cannot spot some of them at work." To Hassan's credit, he takes pains to impress upon the reader that his apparent proliferation of opposites bears witness to the fact that there is no absolute break between modernism and postmodernism: history, he writes, is a palimpsest, and culture is permeable regarding past, present, and future. The seductive power of Hassan's model and his effort to avoid rigid application do not escape prioritization, however. Dark clouds hover over the left side of his scheme, while the right side smacks suspiciously of a chant over all that is good about the world. Modernism is rigid and potent; postmodernism is supple yet wily. Modernism is patriarchal, domineering, and authoritarian; postmodernism is matriarchal and egalitarian. Modernism stultifies, hence it must be pushed into the musty closet of forgotten relics; postmodernism, in contrast, opens out to a brave new world, joyously strutting its gala colors. The masculine left-brain is at long last giving ground to right-brained feminism, obviously the wave of the future. And we are experiencing the liberating effects of a shift from the dichotomy of self and other and its accompanying language of alienation to a process of decentering (*différance,* dissemination, dispersal). That coveted (logo)center of modernism, functioning as a fulcrum affording leverage to exhibit the privileged side of self/other, male/female, mind/body, objectivity/subjectivity, and so on, is now doomed, we are told.

Hassan, one of the most influential early postmodern theorists, apparently continues to nurture a rather aggressive, aggravatingly unpostmodern penchant for constructing diametrically opposed modern and postmodern attitudes while revealing his preference for the latter. This lingering remnant of Cartesian either/or hierarchical thinking suggests a deluded resolution of what Hutcheon (1988a, 49) considers to be an unresolvable contradiction within postmodernism itself: 11

> I would see [either/or thinking] less as a case of postmodern play versus modernist purpose. The same is true of all [Hassan's] oppositions: postmodernism is the *process* of making the *product;* it is *absence* within *presence,* it is *dispersal* that needs *centering* in order to *be* dispersed; it is the *ideolect* that wants to be, but knows it cannot be, the *master code;* it is *immanence* denying yet yearning for *transcendence.*

In other words, Hutcheon goes on to argue, postmodernism should evince a logic of "both/and" rather than "either/or." It comes as no surprise that those who in one way or another tend to privilege, in contrast, the modern over the postmodern—Eagleton (1985), Gerald Graff (1979), Habermas (1983, 1985), Newman (1985), and to a degree Jameson (1983, 1988)—by and large construct a hierarchy of terms rather complementary with those of Hassan. Hassan tells us that in order to promote his "postmodern logic," which presumably would oppose binary logic, he has no recourse but to rely on binary logic, especially regarding the notions of displacement and difference. True to form, he contrasts difference and origin, irony and metaphysics, and so on, in an attempt to demonstrate that his twin towers of cultural symptoms could be extended indefinitely, while the modernism/postmodernism opposition that sustains them remains intact.

Even Jean Baudrillard (1981, 1983a, 1988a)—on occasion considered one of the supreme propagators of the postmodern mind-set, and at times exercising a move "beyond" it—repeatedly lapses into his own binaries: production/seduction, reality/appearance, depth/surface, irreversibility/reversibility, and law/game. Baudrillard also succumbs to the temptation of privileging one term while denigrating the other, which prompts Douglas Kellner (1989, 178–80) rather disparagingly to remark:

> Such binary thinking and conceptualization is highly problemati-
> cal, . . . and should be deconstructed. It is curious that Baudrillard,
> at one time a thoroughgoing deconstructionist, is not more
> deconstructive himself. . . . Like all metaphysicians, Baudrillard
> has thus constituted the world to his own measure and tastes. His
> metaphysics is a subjective construct, a projective machine which
> projects favorite categories into the being of the world.

Granted. Poststructuralism and other current fashions tend to propagate difference, which, in the French intellectual milieu, became a rallying cry
for new critical practices. Difference evokes plurality, nonlinear propagation,
multiplicity, heterogeneity—in short, polyphony rather than dichotomies. Consequently, whatever meanings can then be generated—if meanings there be at
all—are not hierarchically structured but horizontally spread out. They depend
on the way of their making, for they can be made in myriad ways. Thus depth
gives way to breadth, profundity to surface, the essence of things to network
series of events. And the grand dichotomies of Cartesian reason can finally be
shunted aside in favor of more characteristically human and—presumably—
more enlightened concerns. This is postmodernism at its best, we are told.

On the other hand, Richard Rorty (1989, 208) has confessed that he finds
"the knee-jerk suspicion of binary oppositions" among deconstructionists—and,
in this context, poststructuralists in general, and certain postmodernists—baffling.
To dictate that the prioritized term of a dichotomy presupposes the other term is
within the reach of common sense, but such reciprocal definability does not
necessarily cast doubt on a given dichotomy's utility within a particular context. What is worse, such definitions potentially open the floodgates to an overwhelming array of unruly possibilities, which is what the ballyhoo regarding
difference is all about. That is to say, just as Nelson Goodman (1976), among
others, argues convincingly that anything can resemble anything else in myriad
ways, given the confounding range of possible contexts, and just as for Peirce
(CP, 2.247), anything, "be it a quality, existent individual, or law, is an icon of
anything, in so far as it is like that thing and is used as a sign of it," so also the
inverse can hold: anything can differ from anything else—even from itself,
with time—and from some possible perspective it can always be contrasted
with something else.

Moreover, since resemblances, differences, and oppositions are invariably construed within particular contexts, when the context is switched,
that which is privileged may become the object of contempt, the superordinate
may become subordinate, the victimized may become the victimizer. Rhetorical and paralogical ingenuity can always serve to recontextualize any conceptual scheme so as to place its validity in doubt. If such recontextualization is
indeed indeterminate and boundless, as Jacques Derrida and many of his co-

horts proclaim, then, Rorty (1989, 208–9) asks, how is it possible to grasp the conditions of possibility of any and all possible contexts? What is the context in which the notion of a potentially infinite range of contexts can be propagated? Where is the vantage point from which it can be dogmatically proclaimed that these are oppositions, these are differences, and those merely resemblances? One has hardly any alternative, it would appear, but to engage in a rather irresponsible happy-go-lucky flitting in and out of whatever context happens to be at hand, a Nietzschean joyous affirmation, a full-blown epistemological anarchy beyond Paul Feyerabend's wildest musings.

13

Another point that some deconstructors neatly miss, and that is given brief passing by Rorty (1989, 211), is Derrida's inclusion of such categories of writing as algebraic, scientific, legal, anthropological, and historical within the general category of texts. Contrary to the notion one garners after reading most commentaries on Derrida, the literary text is in no form or fashion unduly privileged by this master of liminal metaphysics. All texts should therefore fall into that most general category, *writing,* which includes speech, discourse, and narrative in the broadest possible sense. In fact, as we shall note, commensurate with Peirce's semiotic, all texts belong equally to the category of signhood: all signs merge into all other signs in a regressive and progressive stream—*semiosis*—that cannot be halted by Cartesian intuition or introspection, that is, by the interpreter in order that it stand for something to her in place of something else in some predetermined or determinate respect or capacity. As soon as she attempts to grasp the *interpretant* (roughly, meaning) of the sign, like Merlin the Magician it has transmuted into something else, though not without leaving a "trace" of what it was. In other words, the Peircean interpretant is incessantly and inexorably different and deferred: it is always already something other than what it was.

Peirce, of course, engaged in a constant struggle against the West's most-coveted dichotomies. They cannot but be constantly mediated, he argued time and again, as they ride the lulls, the eddies, and the waves along the vast stream of *semiosis.* Peirce believed the importance of his concept of semiosis to lie in the growth and development of signs, knowledge of which is at least partly available by means of what he calls concrete reasonableness rather than by progressive analytical moves toward parsimony and abstraction. In accordance with postmodernism, Peirce dwelled not merely on certainty, balance, harmony, equilibrium, and symmetry but also on indeterminacy, tension, a struggle of divergent forces, disequilibrium, irreversibility, nonlinearity, and asymmetry. His philosophy, we shall observe, represents a thoroughgoing attempt to undercut the bifurcating tendencies of modernism with a theory of the sign that includes, in addition to abstract thought, the role of volition and feeling in the generation of meaning. Reflecting the postmodern attitude, Peirce held that the world does not contain some "reality" mysteriously hidden underneath surface manifestations of signs, whether of the mind or in the "real" world. Rather, the universe is a "perfusion of signs," and the minuscule portion of its myriad possibilities that we can know constitutes our "semiotically real" world, at least for now, since later it will be something else, in spite of our efforts to halt it. Transcendental deduction is neither possible nor necessary, for a given "semiotically real" world is *our* "real" world. It is without any "center" or "underlying causal forces" that are to be disinterred—according to modernist dreams—by those privileged few possessing some mysterious and sufficient perspicuity of mind. Rather, it is constructed by us from somewhere within the stream.

14

As would be natural, in this regard Peirce was not accustomed to sounding the alarm whenever an intellectual quandary or a presumably intransigent dyad threatened to bound onto center stage. His undying fascination with Zeno's prioritizing discontinuity over continuity and his own dissolution and reversal of this priority attest to his willingness to confront apparent irresolvables head on. He neither discounted them without further ado, nor was he so presumptuous as to believe he could merely dissolve them or rationalize them away once and for all. His concrete reasonableness—which falls in line, Eugene Rochberg-Halton (1986) takes pains to argue, with postmodernism tenets—entails attention both to commonsense beliefs, many of them concealing irresolvables, and critical intelligence. Belief and reason should not be irreconcilably opposed, as the nature-versus-culture dichotomists proclaim. Rather, natural tendencies can find expression and refinement by becoming a play of the imagination, which can then act on the process of rational thought and conduct. The *semiosic* flow is thus radically contextualized: sentiment tempers reason, and reason tempers sentiment, while allowing the individual to get on with the game of sign pro-creation and interpretation. Indeed, as will become evident, Peirce's call for intellectual modesty is a far cry from modernism's ambitious commitment to totalizing theories, to metanarratives with which to give account of linguistic phenomena and the physical world. Like Peirce, postmodernism, in Eagleton's (1987) words, "signals the death of . . . 'meta-narratives' whose secretly terroristic function was to ground and legitimate the illusion of a 'universal' human history."

On the other hand, unlike many postmodernists, Peirce always recognized the existence, as an ultimate potentiality, of truth, though he conceded that it can be no more than a theoretical ideal and incompatible with the kingdom of our finite existence. For Peirce, thought tends to follow a pathway toward increasing generality, toward universals. Yet the very existence of thought is dependent upon the particulars of concrete everyday life. Consequently, his concept of sign holds broad possibilities for the postmodern venture.[20] But in order for this characteristic of the sign to become manifest, it must emancipate itself from those semioticians who are still to a greater or lesser extent enraptured with illusions of classical scientism, whose writings at times reveal the latest incarnation of modern rationalism, and who have somewhat unfortunately placed Peirce in a pigeonhole with logical positivism (Morris 1938; Posner 1981, 1986), artificial intelligence and the philosophy of language (Eco 1976, 1984), Saussurean semiology (Eco 1976; Giraud 1975; MacCannell and MacCannell 1982), and information theory in various semblances (Bense 1969; Eco 1976; Jakobson 1960), or who have presented structuralism in the guise of semiotics (Hawkes 1977). From diverse angles, Peirce has also been at times packed into a form of "pop semiotics" (Berger 1989; Blonsky 1985), and semiotics has been euphorically viewed as some sort of panacea with which to uncover what others cannot see (Jack Solomon 1988), to taxonomize the universe (Deely 1982, 1990), or to create new languages and reform old ones (Sless 1986).[21]

But, I must admit, these charges are unduly harsh, for, given our inherent limitations, we can hardly expect to do more than pick up the pieces left by our predecessors, put them back together however we can within a different context, and hope for the best. Peirce was keener on this idea than most of his contemporaries, hence he never fled from the inevitable quirks and quandaries of human thought. Following his example, why should I not openly concede to my own hankering, in spite of my best intentions, for some elusive set of squeaky-clean equations? In fact, why not disclose my own inclinations—insofar as I am aware of them—toward a tenuous collection of polarized terms? Perhaps I can then go about my task of illustrating that they need not necessarily be construed as classical categories of thought at all but rather *complementarities* mediated by Peirce's triadic *semiosis*. Thus I chisel out:

Linear/Nonlinear

Boolean/Non-Boolean

Context-Free/Context-Dependent

Binary/Complementary

Discontinuous/Continuous

Seeing *As-That*/Merely Seeing

Knowing *That*/Knowing *How*

Consciousness/Tacitness

Explicitness/Implicitness

Generality/Vagueness

Breadth/Depth

Incompleteness/Inconsistency

These dichotomies are, of course, quite familiar. Some of them have already made their appearance in this introduction. And they will often be evoked during the course of this study, which will serve to add fuel to the perpetual Heraclitean fire conjoining and fusing—whether we like it or not—any and all dichotomous terms dear to metaphysicians, as once proud crystalline symmetries tend to become diffuse fractals, structures dissipate, and discontinuities begin sublimating into continuities. In other words, the dichotomies that I have listed serve as a backdrop for the development of an appropriately Peircean triadic perspective.

It has, I assume, become sufficiently obvious that the style of postmodernism that I wish to evoke is not that shallow pop variety. Rather, I shall attempt to outline the Peircean semiosic process by which postmodernism, as an outgrowth or a break with modernism, was made possible in the first place. Nor do I sympathize with those frivolous excesses of postmodernism that evade confrontation with the dangers of cooptation and the suicidal push of consumerism. Postmodernism, I submit, must be critical of its historical predecessors at the same time that it maintains a self-critical stance. Those happy-go-lucky junkies who continue to snort precipitates from decadent modernist meaning and representation masquerading as a postmodern free play of signifiers should thus come clean and admit themselves to a detoxification program of self-critique. There can legitimately be neither smug complacency nor reverie in kitsch, for too much is at stake.[22]

Now that we have things properly in the open, I will pull anchor and set sail anew. Yet lingering questions remain. How to begin? If there has been some sort of beginning, how to go on? By design, or merely to ward off boredom? If it is not possible not to go on, then must tedium not surely be imminent, anyway? And if so, how can we call that going on? Once on the uncertain path, how to end, if there can be no closure? If one begins wherever one is, is one not destined to end up suspended in midair? How is it possible to escape these ubiquitous aporias?

But . . . we cannot tarry, the current continues to whisk us along . . .

PART
One

Awakening from the Dreams of Reason

The Dialogical Turn

Recently the postmodern idea has been bantered about in anthropological circles, spawning a special hybrid of what usually goes by the name of ethnography. Occasionally dubbed the "writing of culture," ethnography pervades a variety of fields traditionally focusing on cultural phenomena.[1] Indeed, the rise of ethnography is accompanied by a crisis among those disciplines treasuring overspecialized myopia, coveted academic real estate surveyed and staked out by tradition, and customary territorialized genres of discourse. Boundaries are becoming "blurred," as Clifford Geertz (1983, chap. 1) puts it. A threshold has been reached from whence it appears that the only open pathways lead either to a new form of disordered order or to terminal burnout.

It is not surprising, in view of this turn of the screw, that anthropology and certain other disciplines have been converging on literary theory. The shift from functionalism, structuralism, and other sundry social theories, to culture-, history-, society-, and even science-as-dialogic-text, now appears in many circles to be a *fait accompli*.[2] According to the typical argument, just as it is now conceived that literature is itself a transient phenomenon capable of contributing to a given society's storehouse of knowledge, so nonliterary texts share certain essential qualities with literature.

This is quite a radical turnabout, especially in view of certain observations in the Introduction of this book. Literature, of course, has not always enjoyed a favorable nod from the intelligentsia that be. After the hard-hat Baconian methodology of modern science replaced the "soft," "hermaphrodite" sciences of alchemists and hermeticists, literature was categorically excluded from the circle of respectable accounts of the world and of people due to its purported sentimental, speculative nature and its lack of the desired univocity believed to be available to scientific discourse. By the nineteenth century, literary writing, and more specifically prose fiction, had evolved as a bourgeois institution, taking its place alongside the other arts. It was now viewed as nonutilitarian, though culturally necessary for its aesthetic appeal, its experimental transgressions, its constant questioning of tacitly presupposed cultural values, and, quite frankly, its utility, within the rising bourgeois class, as a pastime for the emerging consciousness of Victorian homemakers while their husbands were out struggling to survive in the brave new dog-eat-dog world of the Industrial Revolution.

After the turn of the century, declarations such as Gottlob Frege's that literature offers no truth value and Bertrand Russell's that fictional reference is "empty" served further to demean the gentle art of writing. The height of embarrassment came with the rise of logical positivism and its general consensus that literature, the arts, the humanities, metaphysics, and all such nonscientific activities were to be tossed into the bin along with other frivolous and impractical concerns. Language, we were told, must be under the control of rational, scientific, logical discourse. And literature simply was not up to the task.[3] The problem is that the more language came under the control of science in order to justify the proof of its own assertions, the more the justification of its proof depended on a controlled language—yet at the same time the more language became uncontrollable. But I am getting ahead of myself; back to literature.

In spite of attacks from the Genghis Khans of logical positivism, there seemed to be a smidgen of saving grace for the tender of mind. The predominant view regarding literature, it appeared, could rather efficiently fall in step to the tune of the modernist bandwagon. Resting somewhat comfortably at the other—albeit subservient—side of the object/subject, science/aesthetics, reason/sentiment, true-false/meaningless divides, it was now conceived that *literateurs* might take their rightful place as complements to their macho knowledge-grinding counterparts. Literature might even be defended as aesthetically, if not epistemologically, meaningful. The goal of literature thus became that of freeing the so-called signifier—it is more appropriate to use semiological rather than Peircean terminology here—from an economy of discourse mandating that it be determined by one-to-one linear sequentiality, the nature of the signified, and the writer's intention. It was generally conceded that though narrative could by no stretch hope to reflect the "real" world, when on its best behavior, it might at least stand a chance of mirroring diverse subjective worlds—those of the reader's immediate experience—in addition to mirroring the aesthetic sensitivities of the time.

Ultimately, as a consequence, the literary text's project became that of addressing itself to itself, of engaging in self-referential navel-gazing. The inevitable outcome was the notion of a work as outlined above: the autonomous product of a hyperconscious poet privy to intuitive insights unavailable to common folk and of a totalizing quest for meaning—the Grand Symbol—in the work arising from some primordial verbal icon. What over the long haul ensued, however, was an awe of, but inability effectively to deal with, such discomforting uncertainties as indeterminacy, ambiguity, irony, paradox, vagueness, and other ills that had been banned from the positivist's Garden of Eden (Hutcheon 1988a, 30).

This was not so tragic, however. If one lends a credulous ear to the "new philosophers of science," especially the outspoken Feyerabend (1975, 1987), one cannot help but incline toward the idea that science has hardly been less caught up with myth and rhetoric, fads and fashions, power plays and hero worship, than have been literature and the arts—and the practices of all social institutions, for that matter. As Vladimir Nabokov once put it, "[t]here is no sci- 21 ence without fancy, no art without facts" (in Appel 1967, 140–41). The science/ nonscience division never really existed in the first place. Western science has been foisted onto a gullible public in a coat of many attractive colors. In order to bring this massive campaign to fruition, science over the years saw fit to engage in diverse "styles of reasoning," to use Ian Hacking's (1982) intriguing phrase. In fact, throughout this disquisition I shall hammer at the idea that diverse styles of reasoning (signifying modes resulting from particular community-shared conventions coloring the range of perspectival fields) do not confront the "real" but rather particular "semiotic realities." Indeed, it now appears that the business of "redescribing what 'reason' means and of liberating it from metaphysics and dogmatism is beginning to catch on" (Caputo 1987, 210).

By "reasoning," Hacking does not mean "logical reasoning" but the very opposite, for logic is the instrument for preserving truth according to particular traditions. Styles of reasoning, in contrast, at least create the *possibility* of truth, while deduction and induction merely preserve it. In a capsule, Hacking argues that:

1. There are different styles of reasoning, which emerge at definite points and have distinct trajectories of maturation: some die out while others are still going strong.

2. Propositions of the sort that necessarily requires reasoning to be substantiated possess truth values only in consequence of the styles of reasoning in which they occur.

3. Many categories of possibility, of what may be classified as true or false, are contingent upon historical events, namely, the development of certain styles of reasoning.

4. There will always be other categories of possibility than those that have emerged in a given tradition.

5. Therefore we cannot reason without a shadow of a doubt as to whether alternative systems of reasoning are better or worse than ours; the propositions to which we reason get their sense only from the method of reasoning that we employ.

It is not that Hacking wishes to toss reason into the circular file. Rather, he is against the modernist compulsion toward mastery, against its claim to found and ground all truth in reason and all reason in truth: *our* reason and *our* truth. There is actually nothing wrong with reason within its proper sphere of influence, we are told. But that sphere is severely limited. Hacking does not slip into the mire of totally relativized reason or of radically subjectivized historical notions of truth and falsity. He distinguishes between commonsensical reasoning, which is not stringently linked to logical procedures, and reasoning in the formal disciplines. However, the formal disciplines cannot entirely escape cultural and historical contextualization; even here one must concede to a diversity of styles of reasoning and methods. Hacking grants that on occasion problems have been solved and truths established. But this does not warrant a unified image of ultimate truth, he writes, and he thus proposes a sort of Feyerabendian pluralism that keeps as many options open as possible.

Hacking openly admits that the very word "style" is suspect, and for good reason. Pilfered from art and literary criticism, where it never evolved into the crisp method long sought by philosophers and scientists—though, to repeat, many have recently been drawn to the idea that actually there never was any general, permanent method to be had—"style" was normally deemed incompatible with proper reasoning. Nevertheless, despite Hacking's reservations, he chooses to appropriate the term for use in a historical analysis of science, while remaining cognizant that when he does this, his own style of reasoning will develop as the story he tells unfolds. Hacking is also rather perturbed by apparent relativist trappings inherent in his posture. As a countermeasure, he expatiates on what he calls "arch-rationalism," a nonrelativism capable of embracing diverse styles of reasoning. Arch-rationalism, he argues, is derived from what is generally termed "rationality." This is not the result of a confrontation between science and alien cultures, for it has emerged from within the scientific tradition itself. In other words, the implication is that whether a statement, *p,* is true or false depends upon its author's capacity to reason about it in a particular manner that suits her mode of reasoning. For her, thinking about *p* anchors its meaning within a given context, the nature of which is determined by, and dependent upon, her particular style of thinking and reasoning. Hacking's worry is that the meaning of *p* hinges on the style of reasoning appropriate to *p* from a particular vantage point, hence that style cannot be criticized as a road to the truth or falsity of *p* because its truth value is simply determined in the way that it is determined, nothing more, nothing less.[4] Such circularity apparently leads one into that blind alley where truth and falsehood have no existence independently of the style of reasoning used to arrive at what is to be considered true or false—which, as we shall note, often plagued Peirce's thought.

Hacking (1982, 51) observes further that, much like Thomas Kuhn's "paradigms," the idea of "style" serves as a tool with which the new philosophers and historians of science can "point to something general in the history of knowledge." Even though historians will surely not agree on how to carve history up according to styles—just as literary critics enjoy nary a chance of agreeing on style and genre—they will at least find a diversity of styles throughout. Thus arch-rationalism, we are told, is "informed by a proper respect both for history and for the idiosyncrasies of ourselves and others" (Hacking 1982, 52).[5] Arch-rationalism, then, helps bridge the long-standing putative gap between hard-nosed thinking and tender-minded concerns. 23

And the *concrete situatedness* that is characteristic of the postmodernist mind-set—which, as we shall note in Chapter Three, is also prevalent in Peirce's semiotic—forces its way onto the scene. To this topic I now turn.

Is the Very Idea of a Postmodern Science Heretical?

Certain historians, literary theorists, and philosophers have recently been telling us that no theory is immune to amendments, deletions, and eventual rejection. There is no warrant for the belief that the scientist is privy to a "master plan" with which to account for the universe, that there can be a privileged knowing subject, or that science enjoys undeniable priority over any other means of understanding.

This tenuous nature of science is dramatically portrayed in a juxtaposition of two observations by Whitehead. In 1939 he wrote, "I was taught science and mathematics by brilliant men and . . . since the turn of the century I have lived to see every one of the basic assumptions of both set aside. . . . And yet, in the face of that, the discoverers of the new hypotheses in science are declaring, '*Now at last, we have certitude*'—when some of the assumptions which we have seen upset had endured for more than twenty centuries" (Whitehead 1956, 109). A few years later, he had this to say: "I have been fooled again, . . . Einstein is supposed to have made an epochal discovery. I am respectful and interested, but also skeptical. There is no reason to suppose that Einstein's relativity is anything final. . . . The danger is dogmatic thought; it plays the devil with religion, and science is not immune from it" (Whitehead 1956, 277).

Actually, it was the philosophers who insisted on mummifying science in the first place. We have on the one hand Bacon, whose dispassionate number-crunching scientist was to construct, brick by brick, the everlasting edifice of knowledge, and on the other Descartes, whose solitary thought-mongering, word-grinding philosopher, stepmother to the scientist, disregarded everything that tradition handed down and drove straight to the cornerstone of the edifice to get things right. According to both accounts, legitimate scientific knowledge would be here to stay, unalterable and unshakable. The pie in the sky was *episteme,* in contrast to what was conceived to be the quivering gelatin of mere opinion, or *doxa.* Then, when philosophers finally discovered that science is in constant flux, they solemnly declared that there was a crisis of "reason."

On the other side of the ledger, during a specific moment in philosophy, those supreme theorophiliacs, the logical positivists, made mush of both metaphysics and narrative. Then finally, after certain upstarts and a few erstwhile positivists and analytic philosophers discovered that philosophy actually lacked the sharp cutting edge long presumed to be its forte, it was declared to be, in Rorty's (1982) view, "just another kind of writing"—though not a small number of hard-liners continued to operate under the illusions of yesteryear. Rhetoric was now foregrounded, with the ensuing debate over whether literature is itself just another kind of knowledge taking its place beside philosophy and, by extension, over whether metaphors and other tropes really are frivolous embellishments or whether they are essential to cognitive advances.

It is now becoming increasingly apparent that *figurative* style as a style of reasoning, which in modernist circles is supposedly reserved for literary writing, is, after all is said and done, the only possible style. Simple, direct, or scientific style, as rhetoric states, is now increasingly considered to be, in Gérard Genette's (1982, 47) words, "merely a less decorated style, . . . and it, too, like the lyric and the epic, has its own special features." A growing medley of philosophers, scientists, critics, and writers tends to agree.

In fact, it is becoming increasingly evident that the natural sciences, like the arts, the humanities, and the human or social sciences, are, and have actually been all along, hermeneutical through and through, as witnessed by Kuhn's (1977, xiii) oft-cited passage: "What I as a physicist had to discover for myself, most historians learn by example in the course of professional training. Consciously or not, they are all practitioners of the hermeneutic method" (see also Rosen 1987, chap. 4). And in *The Structure of Scientific Revolutions* Kuhn (1970, 158) writes: "The man who embraces a new paradigm at an early stage must . . . have faith that the new paradigm will succeed with the many large problems that confront it, knowing only that the older paradigm has failed with a few. A decision of that kind can only be made on faith." It is not mere happenstance that after Kuhn published his celebrated and at times maligned book, he began referring to the entire scientific enterprise as "hermeneutical." Kuhn and the new philosophers of science have demonstrated not only that science must be understood as just another way of interpreting the world but also that it is a far from objective description. As we shall note in Chapter Two, the way the scientist sees the world by and large determines what the world he sees *is,* and what science *says* of the world is dependent not simply on the way things are in themselves but on the way the scientist sees them through the tainted spectacles of a particular theory or model. Scientific knowledge is no passive copy or mirror of the world but an active construction of it. Just as artistic media are no longer viewed as a transparent mediator between the work and its meaning, so also a scientific theory is no longer a neutral bystander mediating between the world and the scientist.

One is inclined to agree with Rorty's (1979, 315) estimation, however, that hermeneutics is not a discipline or method for reaching the goals that remain beyond epistemology's grasp. On the contrary. It is "an expression of hope that the cultural space left by the demise of epistemology will not be filled." Nevertheless, there does appear to have been a general slippage from the conception of science in the pursuit of epistemic finality to one of science swimming along the current of cultural customs and conventions, fads and fashions. For instance, in support of Kuhn, we have Mary Hesse's (1980, 167–86) vivid juxtaposition, masterfully contextualized in analytic philosophical discourse by Richard Bernstein (1983, 30–34), of five characteristics usually attributed to the natural sciences (*Naturwissenschaften*) (hereafter NS) and the human sciences (*Geisteswissenschaften*) (hereafter HS):

1. NS experience is objective, testable, and independent of theories; HS data is not detachable from theories.

2. NS theories are a priori artificial hypothetical-deductive constructs, to be connected a posteriori to the facts; HS theories are vague, mimetic (re)constructions of the facts, hence blemished with preconceptions.

3. NS's lawlike relations, derived from experience, are detached from both the data and the investigator; HS relations, derived from experience, are dependent upon human categories of understanding.

4. NS language is exact; HS language is irreducibly equivocal, continually adapting itself to particulars.

5. NS meanings of terms are separate from the facts; HS meanings of terms constitute the facts—they are inexorably subjective.

Though these contrasts have not always been explicitly stated, Hesse (1980, 171–72) sets them up to support her argument that in the relevant literature in philosophy of science the five points regarding HS have recently been made about NS, and that the traditional empiricist view is "almost universally discredited." She concludes that when NS is redefined according to the new philosophy of science, it cannot help but fall within the scope of HS. NS is, and has been all along, just another language game that humans play. It is, to be sure, no idle speculative game but one of far-reaching consequences for reorganizing humans' modes of existence within the world.

According to Charles Taylor (1980, 26), Rorty (1979) has also effectively and cogently argued for a "new thesis of the unity of science," to wit, that HS and NS are methodologically one, "not for the positivist reason that there is no rational place for hermeneutics; but for the radically opposed reason that all sciences are equally hermeneutic." This is indeed an extraordinary reversal, and it marks a definite turn in the history of hermeneutical thought. The Diltheyan distinction between NS and HS dissolves. The priests and priestesses of traditional hermeneutics, having defended the priority and purity of their sacred path to insights presumably unavailable to their epistemological sausage-grinding scientific counterparts, now find themselves without an adversary against which to rant. Epistemology loses in the final round to hermeneutics, if only by a split decision.

Actually, what is at issue here is a "new-look hermeneutics." Philosopher of "postmodern" science Stephen Toulmin (1982a, 99–l00) observes that the traditional dichotomy which hermeneuticists held between NS and HS "has done us a disservice . . . because it does not recognize any comparable role for interpretation" in NS, and in this way sharply separates the two branches of scholarship and experience. Consequently, "the central truths and virtues of hermeneuticists have become encumbered with a whole string of false inferences and misleading dichotomies." Toulmin concludes that "critical judgment" in NS

> is not geometrical, and critical interpretation in the humanities is not whimsical. In both spheres, the proper aims should be the same—that is, to be perceptive, illuminating, and reasonable. In the sciences, formal rigor is not the same as rational soundness; in the humanities, idiosyncrasy is not the same as originality. In either case, a successful interpretation will combine *soundness and centrality* in its general approach with *relevance* and *sensitivity* in its specific details. (Toulmin 1982a, 117)

The world of post-Renaissance natural philosophy, which was rent asunder by the mind/matter, reason/emotion, and culture/nature splits placing a premium on objective knowledge and the knower as a detached, passive spectator, is suffering from terminal burnout (Toulmin 1982b, 242–43).[6] In this case, a dovetailing of subjectivities between distinct human traditions appears quite feasible, though a certain unbreachable gap between human patterns of perception and conception will undoubtedly remain.

Hans-Georg Gadamer is generally construed as one of the foremost proponents of the new hermeneutics.[7] In *Truth and Method* (1975), he raises the question of interpretive decidability, whether we are speaking of literary, scientific, or other texts, or of the world as text. The hermeneutical tradition up to and including Dilthey was guided by faith in a naive sort of objectivism: texts had unique meanings subject to interpretations that are ultimately both determinable and decidable. Gadamer's view, in contrast, is at least in this respect in tune with the contemporary "postpositivist" turn. It rejects the promise of empirical certainty via the "correspondence theory" and embraces something rather akin to a constructivist posture (Connolly and Keutner 1988, 16).

According to the general tenets of constructivism, it is not that the one and only true interpretation has not yet been found but rather that there is no final interpretation. That is to say, regarding a text, as Gadamer would have it, the nonselective domain consists of the range of all possible interpretations, one or more of which can be selected from within a given context of reading by a particular interpreter. Placing the text in another context inevitably alters the possibilities for selection, and consequently another interpretation arises. And so on, with no end in sight. There can be no meaning-mongers standing above and beyond the text extracting Truth in all its pristine clarity but rather merely human beings striving to cope a bit more effectively with the text they are (de)(re)constructing, the text they are in. Once again, the subject/object and truth/falsity dichotomies of modernism collapse, this time in line with the most progressive recent forays into metaphysics by natural scientists such as David Bohm, Ilya Prigogine, and John Wheeler, as well as with those of earlier physicist-philosophers, most notably Niels Bohr, Louis de Broglie, Arthur Eddington, Werner Heisenberg, and Erwin Schrödinger.

It is now increasingly acknowledged that the subject/object distinction was actually no more than a charming eighteenth-century rationalist dream appropriated, given a different twist, and propagated by nineteenth-century romantics.[8] Certain American New Critics and others who continued to nurture faith in this senile distinction believed that they effectively rejected subjectivity in practicing their craft, as did the logical positivists with respect to their conception of science. But with the turn in hermeneutical theory, postanalytic and postpositivist movements, the emergence of deconstruction, and other various practices, traditional notions of objectivity are being questioned, put to the test, and found wanting in both NS and HS. To the chagrin of many observers, this has occasionally led to a rather helplessly paradoxical theory of relative truth. Nevertheless, skepticism regarding any and all dogmas, doctrines, theoretical postures, and methodological practices is in the air: a return to yesteryear's naiveté seems unlikely, though a clear-cut consensus has not yet appeared on the horizon.[9]

In this light, there is a dilemma threatening to blow a cylinder in Gadamer's bandwagon, in spite of his reputed constructivism. Indeed, in certain respects, Gadamer's thought remains fossilized: he still maintains NS and HS in separation; his Baconian view of scientific method as monolithic, homogeneous, and fixed for all time is out of fashion; and he tends to privilege NS.

Method in NS, Gadamer writes, "is everywhere one and the same, and only displays itself in an especially exemplary manner." In contrast, HS has "no special method" (Gadamer 1975, 9). Joel Weinsheimer (1985, 4), on the other hand, argues that method has actually varied greatly among the diverse branches of NS, hence the distinction between HS and NS becomes even "less categorical than it often appears in *Truth and Method*." If Weinsheimer's exposition is not sufficiently convincing, an exploration into the new sociologists of science should remove any lingering nostalgia for positivist-empiricist objectivity.[10] It appears, then, that Gadamer would like to stake out a special piece of turf for HS in order to separate it from NS, but he is still caught in an outmoded conception of NS.

The present conception of science as hermeneutic and of scientific and narrative rhetoric as merely different styles of reasoning aside, we are told by those of postmodern bent that the modernist dream of ultimate foundations, of representation, and of the power of signs to mirror the world has been an illusion all along. Modernism's notion of representation—or modernism as the age of representation in Heidegger's conception—is the venerated mirror held up to the world. This entails the utopian dream of a transparent, zero-degree language capable of transforming the world into a picture and the observer into a fleshless, detached, passive recipient of "facts" through the senses. Modernist time is reduced to mathematical and geometrical constructs, and space to a mere receptacle containing the furniture of the world: a convenient fairy tale fading away along with the grand myth of reason.

During the latter part of the nineteenth century, Peirce, Michael Faraday, James Maxwell, Ludwig Boltzmann, Jules-Henri Poincaré, Nietzsche, and others followed Kant's initial frontal attack against the West's faith in its capacity to know the world "out there" with their own offensive. Now, after relativity and quantum theory, cutting-edge science generally concedes that whatever "real" world happens to be commonly embraced by a particular community is an elaborate construct rather than a faithful representation: it is a fiction, or fable, as Nietzsche (1968b, 24) trenchantly put it. Science on the inevitable road to truth, as a result, is being replaced with the emerging postmodernist view that any and all descriptions, explanations, interpretations, and even perceptions are indelibly conditioned by language, culture, the dominant worldview, personal idiosyncrasies and beliefs, and by interests based on race, gender, and social class. The very meaning of truth itself is coming to be seen as largely context-dependent, if not thoroughly constructivist—which, quite unfortunately, has led some self-proclaimed postmodernists to acquiesce and accept modernity as just another form of life.

Nevertheless, the age-old dream of an objective world "out there" lingers on. Jacques Monod (1971, 21), for one, tells us that the "cornerstone of the scientific method, is the postulate that nature is objective. . . . There is no way to be rid of it, even tentatively or in a limited area, without departing from the domain of science itself." Monod insists that any view of the world accommodating the observer in such a way that she is made to feel "at home" in nature is "fundamentally *hostile* to science." In contrast, the postmodern age is that of relative frames of reference, quantum uncertainty-complementarity, Gödelian undecidability, and perspectivism, conventionalism, and constructivism, as well as the radical turnabout in twentieth-century hermeneutics, phenomenology, and especially the demise of logical positivism.[11] The postmodernist subject simply cannot be severed from her everyday life, her cultural and intellectual activities, her language, and what is most crucial, from her world. In this light, Monod's pure scientist as a cold, passive spectator of the world's drama can no longer be defended.

29

Toulmin (1982b, 255) is quite clear on this point. He writes that "the expansion of scientific inquiry into the human realm is compelling us to abandon the Cartesian dichotomies and look for ways of 'reinserting' humanity in the world of nature."[12] Indeed, on calling for a return to the ancient practice of thinking about the universe in terms of cosmos, of a single integrated system, Toulmin's human community is an immanent part of the object of knowledge.[13] We are told that

> our own contemporary scientific picture of the world is, . . . a historical—more particularly, an evolutionary—picture, above all else. In this respect, it shares more with the natural philosophy of the Epicureans than it does with the other major systems of Greek antiquity. . . . If the catch-words of the classical cosmology were "cosmos" and "order" and those of the seventeenth-century world picture were "harmony" and "design," the central themes of our twentieth-century world picture are, accordingly, "evolution" and "adaptation." The world of nature is the place where, as members within the larger evolutionary scheme of things, human beings are "well adapted," and so "at home"; where they have the power to *make* themselves "at home." (Toulmin 1982b, 259–60)

In short, there is no one and only style of reasoning. The long-cherished gap between NS and HS was in large part a convenient fiction, and Cartesian objectivity, by a bizarre twist elevated to its extreme expression in the "human sciences" in the name of structuralism and culminating in the "death of the subject," is overturned, lock, stock, and barrel.

Can There Be a Language of What Is?

Like postmodernism, postclassical quantum physics rebels at the very idea of something independent of someone and of language. Physics, like language, is only indirectly about the stuff of the world. Directly, it is talk about experimental arrangements and observations as well as talk about talk, which seems clear enough. What muddies the waters is *how* the physicist describes and explains the results of her activity. She is apparently caught up in that labyrinth common to all languages, whether formal or natural. In a sense, one can hardly doubt the existence of a world "out there," Zeno's paralyzed arrow, Bishop Berkeley's omniscient God, and J. M. E. McTaggart's and Francis Bradley's frozen universes notwithstanding. Yet, if one pays heed to the new physics, one walks away shaking one's head, for there simply is no one and only "real world."

Peirce also remained quite firm in this respect. The obstinate domain of existents, which we must confront daily, is inescapable. We sense it as what Peirce calls Firstness (feeling), and we engage in an incessant struggle with it as Secondness (what *is,* brute fact). Our interaction with our world either at mindless levels—in a manner akin to the instinctive responses of other organisms—or consciously—a practice at which the human animal is most adept—appears quite direct and relatively untroublesome. A cloud of unknowing enshrouds us and begins to thicken, however, after we enter into the arena of Thirdness, the center of attraction of which is language.

When we begin using symbols (language) to talk about our otherwise quite familiar world, it suddenly becomes transfigured, something other than what it was, in spite of our obstinate desire to halt, by the use of language, the becoming of its beingness, or the beingness of its becoming. The world is no longer the concrete world of our immediate sensations. It is now a domain of "trees," "cars," "landfills," "Gallup polls," "bacteria," "weather forecasts," "neurons," "VCRs," "Dow Jones averages," "quarks," and "quasars." It is as if language were a great seducer disguising "reality," or as if it went on vacation when we most desperately needed it. Specifically regarding the language of physics, Bruce Gregory (1988, 184) writes:

> A physicist's world is made up of leptons and quarks because physicists talk about their experiments in terms of leptons and quarks. In the same way, the mathematician's world is made up of imaginary numbers and infinite sets because imaginary numbers and infinite sets are an essential feature of the discussions of contemporary mathematicians; an economist's world includes markets, supply, and demand for a similar reason. The word *real* does not seem to be a descriptive term. It seems to be an honorific term that we bestow on our most cherished beliefs—our most treasured ways of speaking.

Awareness of this talking game physicists play is chiefly a product of the turmoil surrounding quantum theory of the 1920s and 1930s. Of the physicist-titans clashing in debate over the nature of the world, perhaps nobody gave more thought to the implications of the language of quantum theory than Bohr, Einstein, Heisenberg, and Schrödinger—though they strongly disagreed on many issues. For Bohr the problem was more semantic than ontological. Caught between classical descriptions (subatomic phenomena as "particles") and nonvisualizable quantum descriptions (subatomic phenomena as "waves") that remain well-nigh ineffable in natural language, he once observed that "[w]e are suspended in language in such a way that we cannot say what is up and what is down" (in Petersen 1963, 10). He was keen on the idea that "reality" does not lie behind, nor is it more fundamental than, language, and hence it cannot legitimately be the focus of the physicist's epistemological aspirations. The duty of physics is not to discover the nature of nature but rather only what can be said about nature. That is, the language of physics is not talk about "nature in itself" but talk about talk, about experimental arrangements, observations, models, equations, *Gedanken* experiments, theories, in short, about the physicist's "method of questioning nature" (Heisenberg 1958, 58).

But is this not as it should be? Language, whether we know it or not and whether we like it or not, is incessantly used and abused, modified and hammered into new forms in order that it fit the standards of new world-images. Feyerabend (1975, 257) writes that it is essential for the scientist "to learn talking in riddles" rather than driving for instant clarity. In fact, new perspectival frameworks and conceptual schemes, when endowed with linguistic window dressing, invariably resemble riddles and require some time to become part of everyday working knowledge. Classical logic was born only after rhetoric was sufficiently developed so as to serve as a starting point. Arithmetic was developed before a clear understanding of number could exist. Full comprehension of the Copernican universe required a couple of centuries—in fact, the Copernican model was called "Copernicus's paradox" for generations after its author's death. The idea that a stone does not fall "straight down" when dropped but follows a long trajectory in harmony with the earth's rotation remained a difficult pill to swallow for some time after Galileo. There is yet no clear-cut consensus on the second law of thermodynamics, and relativity and quantum theory continue to remain enigmatic. Were there, during each of these transition periods, a demand for instant clarity, science would have been virtually paralyzed—and it hardly needs saying that such a demand for everyday language in the arts would be absolutely stultifying.

Friedrich Waismann (1952) discusses the scientist's undue fear of vagueness and of speaking in circles. Eventually she becomes tongue-tied, continually asking herself whether what she is doing makes sense. However,

31

Waismann observes, if the pioneers of science had demanded iron-clad pre-
ciseness at every step, it would have been the surest means of sapping any
creative power. Surely the scientist should not cease striving for clarity; it should
at times, though not always, be her primary consideration. Yet an initial effort
toward the best possible answer, if given a vague, ambiguous, or even paradoxical formulation, has the most likely chance of leading to unexpected consequences and perhaps an entirely new conception of nature. Vague beginnings
can also place the scientist in hot water: when she believes she has hit upon a
solution and attempts to communicate it to her colleagues, she is often met with
suspicion, bemused cynicism, disinterest, or even sheer incredulity. Effective
communication of her idea invariably requires time—in fact, Max Planck once
cryptically observed that a theory's acceptance is often not forthcoming until
"its opponents eventually die, and a new generation grows up that is familiar
with it" (in Kline 1980, 160).

Much the same can be said of the initial response to departures from
the beaten path in literature and the arts in general. "Random music," which is
to all appearances totally indeterminate and hence hardly subjected to critical
discussion, let alone analysis, seemed to the ears of its early listeners devoid of
all significance. It was simply nonsensical. Yet it eventually compelled its public to make explicit their convictions, prejudices, and doubts; only then was it
appropriately perceived. In literature, writers like William Burroughs created
images by cutting up their texts and recombining them in random or near-ran-
dom fashion, which was at the outset considered incomprehensible by readers
accustomed to thinking in purely linear terms. Today's aware readers, in contrast, are familiar with these methods and encounter little difficulty absorbing
such texts. And in painting, the strange works of Jackson Pollock are simply
there; there is no depth, no space, no indication of a temporal sequence during
the original creation or upon viewing the canvas. What appears to the senses is
no more than a static, seemingly random present. Yet these works eventually
became commonplace in many circles.[14]

Another problem with the ordinary conception of language is the lingering modernist faith, which emerged especially during the heyday of logical
positivism, in the existence of a metalanguage with which to verify a conceptual scheme or theory and adjudicate between it and competing ones. In contrast, as I mentioned in the Introduction, philosophers of language, the new
philosophers of science, avant-garde historiographers and ethnographers, literary theorists, and Continental thinkers of a poststructuralist bent are now eager
to point out that the very idea of a metalanguage is muddled at best, and at
worst it allows for illusions of epistemological grandeur. All languages and all
terms, be they abstract or concrete, formal or everyday, are flattened to take
their place in a linguistically democratic domain—a *semiocracy,* if you will.

Language is a motley hodgepodge. It cannot be conveniently packed into a precise hierarchy of sets and classes.[15]

This notion throws modernist considerations of reference into confusion. Tradition has usually held that behind language there is univocal meaning: here the word and there the meaning, which can be disclosed to the mind with proper training and insight. Now, whether we are speaking of scientific or any other discourse, it appears that nothing is to be expected beyond language, that is, words. As Bruce Gregory observes of physics talk, there is no direct relationship between words and things "out there." And as we shall note in greater detail below, physics, like semiotics—or semiotics, like physics or any other focus of inquiry, for that matter—is not about the world but about contextualized signs. And there is no meaning until signs are interpreted by communally shared theories, assumptions, conventions, and a general worldview. Thus "dogs," "electrons," or whatever is "real" because a particular community mandates it. But presumably not "unicorns," in our contemporary world at least. The "unreality" of "unicorns" is dependent upon the community's holding virtually no expectations that any flesh-and-blood unicorns, living or dead, will pop up in the "real" world; they exist solely in myth and such. Most likely "unicorns" will not in the foreseeable future acquire "reality" status, though if they were subjected to the same discursive contexts as "UFOs," "Bigfoot," the "Loch Ness monster," "phlogiston," the "ether," the "Piltdown man," and other such oddities, they might stand a chance of becoming "real," for certain crowds at least.

Quite conceivably, the use of "quarks" in everyday physics talk could well commit physicists eventually to their indubitable existence, even though they might not yet have been verified by empirical evidence. On the other hand, a particular aspect of past talk in physics might be taken as categorically "false" when juxtaposed with its "true" counterpart in current talk guided by a radically distinct style of reasoning. However, even this apparent surety can be illusive. Today, for example, the proclamation of the fifth–century B.C. philosopher Heraclitus that everything consists of fire might be looked upon as mere poetic license or sheer nonsense. Yet Heisenberg (1958, 43) observes that contemporary physics "is in some way extremely near to the doctrines of Heraclitus. If we replace the word 'fire' by the word 'energy' we can almost repeat his statements word for word from our modern point of view."[16] The way of one's talk dictates the way of one's world. Very slowly it is becoming possible to appreciate what Bohr meant when he once quipped that "if anybody says he can think about quantum problems without getting giddy, that only shows that he has not understood the first thing about them" (in B. Gregory 1988, 200).

While Bohr attended to language, Einstein focused on the mind. Unlike Bohr, he was committed to certain concepts, such as observer-independent "reality," strictly deterministic laws, and local causes for all events. His scientific concepts, hypotheses, and theories, even those closest to experience, are, from the point of view of logic, "freely chosen conventions" (Einstein 1949a, 13). "Being," he believed, "is always something which is mentally constructed by us, that is, something which we freely posit (in the logical sense). The justification of such constructs does not lie in their derivation from what is given by the senses . . . [but] in their quality of making intelligible what is sensorily given" (Einstein 1949b, 699). Since Heisenberg (1971, 77) has Einstein saying that it is "theory that decides what we can observe," it seems only fitting that though "sense experiences are the given subject matter," the "theory that shall interpret them is man made" and "the result of an extremely laborious process of adaptation: hypothetical, never completely final, always subject to question and doubt" (Einstein 1950, 98). According to Einstein's radical constructivism it seems that what there is, is in large part mind-dependent, in contrast to Bohr's radically language-dependent world. Combining the two notions yields roughly the view—to be developed in chapters Eight, Nine, and Ten—of our perfusive universe of signs, including ourselves, as a vast bootstrapping operation.

The general epistemological turmoil exemplified by the Einstein-Bohr conflict in large part has its origins in Heisenberg's *uncertainty principle.* Dugald Murdoch (1987) maps out the events leading from initial disappointments during the early days of quantum theory to Heisenberg's profound account of quantum uncertainty, which is, in essence, a consequence of the undecidability of a particle's mass and momentum at any given moment. On the other hand, Bohr's uncertainty, which led to his *complementarity principle,* was a reflection of conceptual inadequacy: no classical space-time description of the behavior of microphysical particle events is permitted. That is to say, quantum theory entails a single framework incorporating apparently incompatible classical and nonclassical considerations. Bohr's move was to consider the particle/wave, and momentum/mass pairs to be complementary rather than contradictory, allowing for classical descriptions, though they must ipso facto remain limited. From a given perspective, no more than a partial picture of the whole affair would be possible. But the bottom line, Bohr could not overemphasize, was linguistic:

> [T]he difficulties of the quantum theory are connected with the concepts, or rather with words, which are used in the ordinary description of nature, and which all originate in the classical theories. These concepts just give us the choice between Scylla [waves] and Charybdis [particles] according as we direct our attention to the continuous or to the discontinuous side of the description. We feel at the same time, however, that the hopes conditioned by our own habits lead us into temptation here, as it has so far always

been possible for us to keep swimming between the realities as long as we are prepared to sacrifice all our customary wishes. The very fact that the limitation of our concepts coincides so exactly with the limitation of our powers of observation allows us, as Heisenberg stresses, to avoid contradictions. (in Murdoch 1987, 52)

In passing one might note that Bohr's "swimming" reminds one of Peirce's rather dark idea that we are always "swimming" in a continuum—i.e., the doctrine he termed *synechism* (CP, 6.169; see Almeder 1980, 1983). Bohr advocates a medley of choppy, discontinuous butterfly strokes when considering the grainy world of particles and smooth, continuous breast strokes when wave mechanics comes into the picture. Peirce's notion of the continuum consists of the range of *possibilia* within which actualized signs intermittently emerge into existence and fade out again. Bohr, in apparent contrast to Peirce, asks us to discard, once and for all, our intuitive desire for continuity, since matter and energy are not unequivocally either corpuscular or undulatory. According to this view, natural language, "which is designed for the organization of our ordinary sensory experience, presupposes continuity; hence, when this presupposition fails, ordinary language, including the models in terms of which we interpret physical theory, becomes not-well-defined, or 'ambiguous' as Bohr puts it" (Murdoch 1987, 73). In contrast, Peirce's thought, understandably imbued with nineteenth-century classical overtones, inclined toward continuity, although he by no means discounted the actual world of signification, the grainy *this-hereness* of signs (Murphey 1961). The upshot is that, whether speaking of Peirce's *synechism* or quantum undulations or of his mediately—never immediately—available sign instantiations or the scintillating coming into, and going out of, existence of quantum particles, we are speaking of events that lie "outside the domain of our ordinary experience and which present difficulties to our accustomed forms of perception" (Bohr 1934, 5).

Seeing without Talking and Talking without Seeing

Bohr, to the consternation of many of his colleagues, believed quantum quandaries, although linguistic paradoxes, are deeply rooted in nature: if paradox is endemic in nature, then nature must be "schizophrenic" through and through.[17]

One important aspect of quantum "schizophrenia" bearing on the focus of this inquiry entails the inherent limitations of our capacity for visualization, which throws the ocular metaphor of modernity for a loop.[18] Bohr and, in general, those who embraced the Copenhagen interpretation of quantum phenomena were privy to this severe stricture. The nonvisualizable can be modeled mathematically, and it can be presented through parables, Zen koans, chants, rituals, and drug, sexual, and other ecstasies. On the other hand, attempts to express the nonvisualizable in natural language invariably run into a brick wall.

This dilemma raises its ugly head in response to the most fundamental questions regarding the nature of matter, light, and energy. Heisenberg's matrix mechanics calls for a stark, absolutely formal exercise, which does not lend itself to physical models in the least, and Schrödinger's wave mechanics uses nonvisualizable imaginary numbers. Both notions, Bohr believed, make purely symbolic use of classical concepts. Bohr did not hold that the symbol world conjured up by the physicist's equations admits of a univocal, realist interpretation. Rather, he found in the relation between the wave and particle interpretations an expression of the limitations of classical theory and the nonvisualizability of it all. Classical models afford concrete pictures, but quantum formulations are purely symbolic (neither iconic nor indexical, since reference is never direct but tangential).

The concept of matter waves, or "wavicles," is applicable only in circumstances where a quantum event must be taken into account outside the domain of classical causality and the customary ways of speaking about matter, light, and energy. Consequently, phrases such as "the corpuscular nature of light and the wave nature of electrons" are contradictory, since "corpuscle" and "wave" are well-defined only within the scope of classical physics, where light and electrons are electromagnetic waves and material corpuscles, respectively.[19] Time and again Bohr reminded his colleagues of the crucial distinction between unambiguous classical descriptions of material objects and electromagnetic fields and ambiguous quantum theoretical descriptions of subatomic particles and electron waves. Descriptions of electrons as waves shunt space-time location aside; descriptions of electrons as particles prohibit any account of field. Combinations of the two descriptions do not resemble anything familiar or imaginable, much less sensorily available. Yet if electrons were not particles, it would be impossible to explain how a TV set works, and if they were not also waves, quantum action at a distance would be virtually inconceivable.

The applicability of quantum descriptions is limited to cases in which, due to quanta of action, it is not possible to consider the phenomena observed as independent of the instruments of observation and of the observer. Thus the entire field is all-important; the individual quantum event is relatively unimportant. Regarding the language describing them, whether elegantly formal or clumsily natural, the context is crucial; the definition of isolated terms is relatively unimportant. Neither definitions nor reference as a one-to-one correspondence determine meaning; rather, the linguistic context assigns meaning to the terms, and the context is given implicitly in the physicist's comprehension of her theoretical scheme as a whole. In other words, a particular statement or formula is embedded in the language used by the physicist, who assumes that the general community of physicists will adequately understand it within the context of their shared conventions of discourse (Weizsäcker 1980, 49–63).

Another aspect of Bohr's quantum "schizophrenia" ultimately involves the general idea—to be fleshed out in detail below—of our everyday "semiotically real" world and its incessant clashes and occasional close encounters with the "real." In order effectively to deal with the "world" at all, we talk about it. What is for *us* "real"—that is, semiotically real—*is* what we can *say* about it. And so we (think we) see it. But our seeing can never be so innocent. A frog, as we shall note in Chapter Two, senses moving dots, lashes out its tongue, and eats them. A bat senses sonar waves and at the propitious moment opens its mouth and consumes them. A tick senses olfactory signs from a mammal's sweat glands, drops on its prey, and after a few more signs have been properly detected, settles down for a meal. These creatures' worlds are semiotically real, not "real" *an sich.* So also is our world. Consequently, if frogs, bats, and ticks could talk, as Wittgenstein (1953, 223e) says of a lion, we would not be able to understand them. Of course, the world we *say* is exceedingly more variable than that of our cousins, the inarticulate organisms. On the one hand, our having been thrown into language affords us a head start, and on the other, it marks our expulsion from that Paradise of the Eternal Now. To repeat, the minute we begin talking about *our* world, it changes. This is because it is already delimited by language, a powerful language capable of creating worlds and of destroying them.

For example, the world of Einstein's language superseded that of Newton's language in theory talk. Then, after Eddington's experiment demonstrating that the sun's gravity bends photons of light, Einstein's language was adapted to experiment talk as well. The space-time manifold has not yet become embedded in everyday talk, but it may win out in the long run. Moreover, each new language—as well as the world it creates—discloses previous ignorance more than it unveils new knowledge; it says what was "false" more adequately than it can reveal what is unequivocally "true." Einstein's theory did not match up with what the physicists knew but revealed what they did not know. Cervantes's *Quixote* did not merely paraphrase what everyone knew—the novels of chivalry—but revealed what hitherto had remained concealed. Renaissance art did not portray what everyone saw in painting but what had not yet been depicted on canvas. The story is endless. And it reveals the overriding *power of language,* whether speaking of formal or natural language or the language of art. Language, in this fashion, constructs no more than semiotically real worlds. These include the mathematically real world of the physicist, which, though "real" in its own right, is not necessarily any more "real" than the "reality" of a Goethe or a Berkeley in his argument against the classical paradigm, nor is it necessarily more "real" than a canvas by Picasso, a novel by Kafka, a

37

play by Pirandello, a story by Borges, or our everyday world of auditory, olfactory, visual, gustatory, and haptic sensations. All are semiotically real within their proper context.

Quite unfortunately, modernity's myth of indubitable exactitude in the hard sciences has colored the talk and, indeed, the general *modus operandi* of humanists and social scientists. As a case in point, during a typical congress of humanists, a paper is read, word-for-word, from a meticulously prepared manuscript, every phrase of which has been carefully weighed and secured against possible misunderstandings. The only freedom that the participant permits himself consists of occasional voice modulations and a few quips. After reading the final word and appropriately thanking his public, polite applause is forthcoming, then a few questions, perhaps even a half-hearted debate, and off to the cash bar for some serious socializing. A typical lecture by a physical scientist consists of her referring to an experiment, whether real or imaginary, or to some symbols she has written on the blackboard. She addresses her audience in a more or less lackadaisical manner, referring to the blackboard with the words "now if you will consider this formula," or to the experiment, with "and then such and such usually occurs." After she finishes, a heated argument ensues.

There are, of course, exceptions to these two hyperbolic examples. Nonetheless, C. F. von Weizsäcker (1980, 48) observes, regarding the two types of scholars, that

> the presentations of natural scientists are characterized by a certain nonchalance and by the influx of non-linguistic elements. The claim that, on the face of it, the language of physics is particularly exact is surely an exaggeration. . . . [T]he physicist can afford a certain inexactness in his language because of the very exactness of physics itself. It is not necessary for the physicist to say exactly what he means to communicate, because in his field nuances are less likely to lead to misunderstandings. He can afford being rather sloppy since, thanks to their common understanding of the subject matter, those who understand him at all can easily see past his sloppy manner of expression.

In physics and the other natural sciences, a relatively exact language, mathematics, is available. However, this exact science expressed in an exact language "can never under any circumstances do without its link to what we call natural or everyday language" (Weizsäcker 1980, 49). The physicist must perpetually engage in acts of transformation from the formal but nonvisualizable and ambiguous proclivities of a precise language to the cloudy, mundane language of ordinary talk. So the conception of a single pristine language for describing the physical world is pure fiction. Weizsäcker (1980, 49) concludes that perhaps "one can always increase the exactness, but I wouldn't even know whether that would mean one is approaching 'absolute exactness' conceived of as an ideal; it is probably impossible to define such a limit." I, of course, have implied much the same regarding the distinction between the "real" and the merely semiotically real. There is, consequently, no such thing as an exact natural science in the modernist conception of the phrase. On the other hand, the new-look hermeneutical thrust regarding natural science and the semiotically real upon which it focuses is, as I shall argue below, quite close to the mark.

39

Admittedly, Weizsäcker's words are heady. And they are themselves formulated in a rather vague fashion—which is perhaps most appropriate, given the tenor of his message. Moreover, if true, they must also apply to themselves, thus placing their author in a self-referential quandary. This is to be expected, however, since Weizsäcker's talk is merely about talk. Why should we suppose the role of language could ever be otherwise? The history of a given technical term—Weizsäcker (1980, 50–63) discusses "potential energy"—is invariably caught up in so many levels of embedment in our language, given its Judeo-Christian, Greek, Sanskrit, Roman, Arabic, Egyptian, and what not heritage, that one cannot separate words about things from words about themselves. And the possibility of words absolutely defining themselves is also out of the question, a point that Karl Popper (1974) forcefully argues. Definitions are only roughly decidable from within the linguistic contexts that assign meaning to them, and the context is given only implicitly. Consequently, in actual practice, whether in the humanities, physical sciences, or everyday talk, we tend to muddle through, assuming that our fellow interlocutors will understand us, and get on with the game.

And one should never be so presumptuous as to believe that the game corresponds in any form or fashion to "reality" as it is, or that physics talk can be made commensurate with any other sort of talk. Physics can describe light in terms of the spectrum of frequencies and wavelengths, but it would be absurd to try using these symbols to describe the world of economics or politics. "Reality" is not made up of supply and demand, profit and loss, rising expectations and repression, democracy and tyranny. Neither is it made up of leptons and quarks, imaginary numbers, mathematical groups, and infinite sets. Words and other signs are merely ways of qualifying experience in our aborted efforts to know what the world is like outside language altogether—nothing more, nothing less. All descriptions are thus *façons de parler,* stories. It is not a matter of language capturing a world independent of it but rather of language as a way of coming to grips with diverse aspects of the world from diverse perspectives and conceptual schemes. When a misanthrope meets a saint, he later describes him in terms of distrust and contempt; when the hunter fails to slay a fleeing buck, he later recalls not the graceful elegance of nature's creation but the absent trophy on the wall of his den.

What I am speaking of is the notion of *complementary perspectives* expressed by means of styles of reasoning and modes of discourse. Complementarity, according to my understanding of Bohr's formulation—which he did not limit to quantum events—is quite closely patterned in contemporary postmodern culture through juxtaposed discordant modes of *feeling* (Peirce's Firstness), *perception* (Secondness), and *conception* (Thirdness) that might well be labeled, in terms of Hutcheon's (1985) postmodernist poetics, *irony.* The very notion of complementarity—the fusion of otherwise incompatibles, conceptual vagueness, the generality of the whole squeezed from inconsonant parts, the apparent harmony bred from syncopation—is postmodernist to the core. There is no modernist center or bedrock of fixed meanings, no comfort in plunging to the depths, no promise of ultimate truth or a master pattern springing forth from the inner sanctum where the privileged guru-mathematicians, scientists, philosophers, and artists dwell, no mirror reflecting the world "out there." Nor do language, logical categories, and figures of thought exist outside and independent of history and society as neutral tools to be utilized for critical purposes without affecting those purposes.

The upshot is that what the physicist—and we mere mortals as well— talks and writes about is her semiotically real world, which takes its place alongside all other possible and actual semiotic worlds, the sum of which is one. Change her language, and her semiotic world is transmuted accordingly, for better or for worse. There is no guarantee that she or her collaborators—or those who try to discredit her as well as multitudinous disinterested bystanders—will ever know what the "real" would be like from some absolute point of view, which is to say from no point of view. They all more or less know only what *their* semiotic world looks like. Language is a contextualized, community-oriented human activity. It is a shifting riverbed, not solid bedrock, and semiotic reality is what our equally shifty, and at times exceedingly fickle, minds can make of it.

So, according to the postmodern perspective, one can no longer enjoy the smug positivist confidence that language can be molded to suit one's epistemological purposes and prejudices. Language, in collaboration with the knowing subject, does its own thing, for it is the mouthpiece of the community opinion: give-and-take *doxa,* not authoritarian *episteme.* The flow of signs, in the final analysis, is all we have. There is no perception, conception, or thought behind signs. Thinking and speaking and writing themselves exist within the general semiosic process. In this vein, Thomas Sebeok (1979, xii) writes that "people, animals, plants, bacteria, and viruses—are only a sign's way of making another sign." And Peirce often mused that a sign's *interpretant* (that is, its meaning) is its way of knowing what a sign is.[20]

This is postmodernism at its best. Each and every semiosic system, from quark to quasar, from amoeba to Einstein, is part of a magnificently interwoven flux of signs becoming signs. There are no hooks out there with which to anchor the whole concoction, nor is there any outside fulcrum from which to budge it. The individual and the community get along as best they can wherever they find themselves, over time enjoying a virtually infinite array of possible sign-states, each as ephemeral in one sense as it is persistent in another.

41

Text, Textuality, Texture: World

This 180-degree turn regarding language, especially in scientific discourse, has inspired Hassan (1987, 62), among other postmodernists, to euphoric proclamations such as "relativity, uncertainty, complementarity, and incompleteness are not simply mathematical idealizations; they are concepts that begin to constitute our cultural languages; they are part of a new order of knowledge founded on both indeterminacy and immanence."

Though Hassan stretches his terms beyond the limits for which they were originally intended, the message at least serves to slap one out of one's poststructuralist-semiological somnambulism. The carnivalesque dance of *semiosis* throws the sobriety of Saussure's *langue* into havoc. It mocks those totalizing efforts of modernity, which aims to stop signs dead in their tracks in the name of order, progress, organization, efficiency, and parsimony. Kinesis takes over where form had slipped into lethargic bliss. Chance and change obviate the necessity of permanence. Static, spatialized forms give way to temporal flow. Signs dissolve that once proud philosopher's stone labeled "representation," and commensurately, the cipher and static writing become language unfolding.

By and large, within our cultural milieu we are inexorably suspended in a fabric of signification, of kinetic textuality, rather than being able to exercise, after the proper apprenticeship, a God's-eye gaze on an ideal set of crystalline texts or the ideal, unmoving, *text of the world*. Ethnography becomes perhaps the most adequate expression from the human sciences of the postmodernist thrust. Ethnography construes the whole of culture as textuality, the ethnographer's task being that of foregrounding hitherto unnoticed connections, thus revealing the subtle reverberations in the rituals, metaphors, and meanings of everyday life.

Kinetic textuality in the sense of the term used here is quite comparable to Calvin Schrag's "middle term," "texture," lying between "text" and "textuality." "Texture" implies a primacy neither of the text nor of perception nor of action. Rather, it "gathers the display of meanings within the text of everyday speech and the text of the written word, and in addition it encompasses the play and display of meanings within the field of perception and the fabric of human action" (Schrag 1986, 30). Of course, the book or text as metaphor of the universe is nothing new. It gained respectability in the modern scientific sense in the writings of Paracelsus and other alchemists, and from perhaps its keenest expression in the work of Galileo. In contemporary times, the notion of textuality as everything and everything as textuality is propagated by the likes of Derrida (1974, 1978) and a diverse host of poststructuralists. Textuality, texture, the weave of signs, are, they tell us, polyvocal to the extreme. By a similar token, among certain ethnographers the idea of culture as textuality turns out to be ambiguous through and through—if not undecidable—thus allowing for multiply variegated readings.

42

However, there are imminent danger signs regarding this posture. Roger Keesing (1987, 162) warns that cultural meanings may be read too deeply: worldviews and philosophies that appear to be implied by folk usage may not exist until the ethnographer creates them. The ethnographer's own text risks being made to appear to refer to a "real" cultural world, yet that world consists of layer upon layer of textual conventions serving to guide ethnographic writing itself. That apparent "reality" consequently must be judged by readers in comparison with other texts, with a potentially infinite profusion of texts. The world in this sense legitimately—albeit artificially—becomes itself "texture"—the ethnographer's counterpart to Borges's notorious Library of Babel.

This is good news as well as bad. The bad news—at least for some—is that language is neither properly presentational nor representational but rather lies outside traditional scientific knowledge. The good news is that the postmodern view privileges dialogue over writing—which is traditionally conceived as monologue (solitary writers and readers hermetically doing their own thing.[21] Stephen Tyler, one of the foremost proponents of this shift, denigrates monologic writing in the modernist sense in favor of the postmodernist view of writing, which highlights speech:

> Postmodern experiments in ethnographic writing are the inverse of the modernist experiment. Where modernists sought by means of ideographic method to reveal the inner flow of thought hieroglyphically—as in Joyce or Pound, for example—postmodern writing focuses on the outer flow of speech, seeking not the thought that "underlies" speech, but the thought that is speech. Where modernists sought an identity between thought and language, postmodernists seek the "inner voice" that is the equivalent of thinking and speaking. Modernists sought a form of writing more in keeping

with "things," emphasizing, in imitation of modern science, the
descriptive function of writing. (Tyler 1987, 197)

Textuality (texture) as dialogic in nature places the spotlight not only
on the interaction between reader (ethnographer) and text (informant) but, in
addition, between reader and cultural texture, and, as Peirce puts it, between
the self(reader) of one moment and the emerging self(reader) of the next. There
is no Infallible Pen, no Great Patriarchal Tongue, no Superreader or Superwriter,
but merely the self interacting with its other self, people interacting with people,
signs interacting with signs.

43

Language is thus forcefully returned to its original immanence to complete the radical program of deconstructing the world's furniture as objects of
perception in the physical sciences, and of deconstructing the primacy of the
self—the perceiving subject—in the social sciences. It is now conceded—though
reluctantly in some quarters—that both subject and object, knower and known,
are mediated by language. Classical categorical splits must therefore go the
way of the heliocentric universe, phlogiston, the ether, the human animal as a
pleasure-pain machine, social Darwinism, rat psychology, the brain as nothing
but a computer, and other such catchalls. "Seeing is always mediated by saying," Tyler (1987, 171) declares, from within a framework reminiscent of
Norwood Hanson's (1958, 1969) contention—following Wittgenstein—that
seeing is always already interpreted (a topic I will take up in the next chapter).

One might be tempted, in this context, to rephrase Wittgenstein's pro-
nouncement in the *Tractatus* (1961, 1), "The world is all that is the case," to
yield "The sign is all that is the case." And "The world is the totality of facts,
not of things" (1961, 1.1) might be restated as "The sign is the totality of events,
not of things." Wittgenstein (1961, 1.12) goes on to assert that the world is
constituted by facts, for "the totality of facts determines what is the case, and
also whatever is not the case." Thus the totality of sign events determines the
semiotic world, that is, what is the case as defined by the exigences of a given
Umwelt. This totality also determines what is *not* the case due to the sign's
ability to refer back in time to something else, since human semiotic is grounded,
as Eco (1976, 6–8; 1984, 177–82) effectively reveals, in the capacity to generate falsity, or to lie.

However, unlike the early Wittgenstein's "facts," "what is the case,"
and "world," the sign, within its semiosic process—and indeed the semiotic
agent interpreting the sign as well—remain, in line with postmodernist tenets,
immanent. There is no ladder with which to climb up and over the whole confusing, labyrinthine hodgepodge. In this light, Peirce puts into question the
very network of many of the interconnected terms traditionally associated with
modernity: autonomy of the subject, transcendence, determinacy, Cartesian

authority, totalization, universalization, hierarchy, closure, origin, and finality. Just as there can be no Cartesian meditator capable of spouting out Truth from the depths of her soul, so there can be no Grand Transcendental Index pointing to Truth, and so also no Immaculate *Eidos,* that ultimate image in the form of an ocular icon, "out there" to be discovered once and for all. All signs are intertwined with their users.

This general notion bears on an important facet of the present inquiry: Peirce's unmitigated struggle against excessive abstractions.[22] It is most unfortunate that one of Peirce's early interpreters, Charles Morris (1938), placed semiotics within a positivist context, which is actually diametrically opposed to Peirce's call for concrete reasonableness and the battles he constantly waged against the Cartesian analytic framework.[23] In contrast to Morris, I shall attempt to illustrate that *semiosis,* as creative and as evolutionary—through Peirce's biological-organic view ("my language is the sum total of myself" [CP, 5.314])—provides a fruitful vision of ongoing *sign generativity.*[24] This vision aids in bridging the gap between postmodern free-wheeling play and modern purpose, between chance and design, disorder and order, anarchy (or heterarchy) and hierarchy, absence and presence, mediacy and immediacy—or, to use semiological terminology, between metonymy and metaphor, combination and selection, signifier and signified. Those cherished dichotomies of reason, which are occasionally employed even by the staunchest propagators of the postmodern perspective, are thus deflated, perhaps beyond repair.

I raise the above issues in this chapter for the purpose of placing them, throughout the remainder of my disquisition, within the context of Peirce's semiotic to illustrate that the universe *is semiosis,* a veritable perfusion of signs. What for a given community is taken to be the semiotically real is not, nor can it ever be in the finite world of finite beings, coterminous with the actually real. On the contrary. A given semiotic reality is generated by the *Umwelt* of a particular species—*Homo semeioticus* in this case—with which, by way of "mind" (i.e., emergent body and brain functions), to map the world. In this sense, *semiosis,* as it is ordinarily perceived, conceived, and expressed from the fast but myopic track of natural language use, is, from the big view of things, the whole of the universe as sign.

I now turn to further consideration of our semiotically real world.

Undoing Knowing

An Inexorable Element of Chimera?

As discussed in Chapter One, postmodernism has it that those who desire to proceed on the straight and narrow road to truth must eventually come face-to-face with the cold realization that there are many "straight and narrow roads to truth." Indeed, if one follows the labyrinthine paths from phenomenology to deconstruction, structuralism to poststructuralism, analytic philosophy to its recent neopragmatist offshoots, mathematical confidence-building programs to Gödelian undecidability, classical physics to relativity and recent strains in quantum theory, positivist science to hermeneutical science, and finally, from modernism to postmodernism, one is forced to conclude with Eddington (1935, 292), one of the early bearers of tenuous tidings, that there is no purely objective world. Eddington opens *New Pathways in Science* (1935, 1) with a quotation from Henri Poincaré: "What we call 'objective reality' is, strictly speaking, that which is common to all." That is, "objective reality" is actually intersubjective through and through. It is the product of a community enterprise (see especially the argument in Eddington 1958a).

When we contemplate these words sufficiently, they indeed become intoxicating. In physics, where mathematics reigns supreme—though, as Eugene Wigner (1969) points out, perhaps physicists do not deserve such a gift—Hermann Minkowski's "block universe" rendition of Einstein's theory of relativity, according to which everything is always already there, might presumably be such common ground. The "block" is there, irrespective of any and all semiotic agents. That is to say, it is the same with respect to all possible observers, though it remains independent of any collection of actual observers. Eddington's physics-inspired conception probes deeper; it includes the collective community mind as well as individual consciousness. He recognized—before cognitive science, computer models of the brain, recent hermeneutics, and poststructuralism—that "the only subject presented to me for study is the content of my consciousness." He continues:

> Accordingly my subject of study becomes differentiated into the
> contents of many consciousnesses, each content constituting a *view-
> point*. There then arises the problem of combining the view-points,

> and it is through this that the external world of physics arises. Much
> that is in any one consciousness is individual, . . . but there is a
> stable element which is common to other consciousness. . . . This
> common element cannot be placed in one man's consciousness
> rather than in another's; it must be in neutral ground—an external
> world. (Eddington 1958b, 283–84)

In short, the postulate of a "real" world "out there" is viable only when it is the means of bringing together the worlds of many minds sharing some common viewpoint. The synthesis or "joint product" of all possible points of view constitutes the scientific concept of "reality" (Eddington 1958b, 284).

The "real" as our construct is not the only possible "real" world. In other times and places, myriad "realities" have come and are yet to come into existence. Other perspectives than the human one yield yet other "realities," and even a purely ideal world independent of the composite of our finite and fallible perspectives might conceivably exist. It follows, ultimately, that there is no absolute guarantee that a given appearance or perspective is necessarily more "real" than any other, for "reality is only obtained when all conceivable points of view have been combined" (Eddington 1920, 182). Thus any and all "reality" constructs can be no more than semiotically real singularities existing along space-time coordinates. And the actually real must be defined as the product of a synthetic merging of all possible points of view from which the particular and the collective can be sifted out. (As we shall observe, Eddington's common area shared by a given set of individuals falls comfortably in line with Peirce's truth as the consensus that a community of knowers will finally arrive at in the theoretical long run, and with Wheeler's idea that "reality" is the joint product of the community of participant-observers.)

Given this constructivist notion of meaning, knowledge, and "truth" as the joint product of an ideal community's dialogic activity, if one ponders over the plethora of scientific, mythical, cosmological, and commonsensical theories of "reality," past, present, and future, one is forced to realize that meaning, knowledge, and "truth" have repeatedly been divided and subdivided into domain after domain of conceptual schemes and experience, some of them almost identical, others radically distinct, and still others well-nigh irreconcilable with one another. Considering science—that venerable storehouse of presumably "objective knowledge"—the terms "fire," "air," "earth," and "water" once organized the world into a particular conceptual and perceptual framework that allowed for a quite effective domain of experience. In recent times, "mass," "position," and "velocity" call for one set of observables, while "electrons," "photons," "neutrinos," and "quarks" pertain to another domain. And from yet another vantage point, "temperature," "pressure," "free energy," and "entropy" are fundamental to the definition of the thermodynamic universe.[1]

As Hanson (1958, 1969) trenchantly puts it, Kepler saw the sun "at rest," while Tycho Brahe saw it "in motion"; Kepler construed the earth to be "in motion," while for Tycho it was "at rest." To the question, Did they both see the same sun? any traditional answer that is meticulously dusted off and spit polished to account for a precise difference in their "seeing" becomes problematic. It can safely be said that the two astronomers saw the same thing if, when oriented in the same direction under the same conditions, similar areas of their retinas were affected in roughly the same way. That is, they had fundamentally the same visual impressions when radiation in the form of light of comparable frequency produced similar electrochemical changes in their neural receptors, their rods, and their cones.

47

However, "seeing" the sun is not seeing retinal pictures of a brilliant yellow-white patch in a blue expanse. The raw retinal images that Kepler and Tycho experienced were for practical purposes identical: two in number, inverted, and quite tiny. Such reactions are strictly physical, a mere photochemical excitation. They do not constitute an *experience*. People *see*, not retinas; cameras and eyeballs are blind—a point keenly illustrated by Julio Cortázar's short story "Blow Up." Attempts to locate *seeing* the sun either as "stationary" or "mobile" in the organs of sight are futile. So while it is correct that Kepler and Tycho saw the same physical object, the joint product of their *seeing* is not supported by reference to retinas, optical nerves, or visual cortices. It is reasonably safe to say, however, that their virtually identical visual experiences in a certain manner of speaking constituted their *seeing* the same sun, for, we must suppose, each could have understood most of the other's statements about it.

On the other hand, when it is a matter of *seeing* the "sun in motion" or the "sun at rest," problems arise reminiscent of Wittgenstein's drawing, borrowed from psychologist Joseph Jastrow, who once studied with Peirce, *seen* either as a "duck" or a "rabbit"—to which Hanson also refers repeatedly in his argument. Wittgenstein (1953, 212) asks, regarding his ambiguous figure, "Do I really see something different each time, or do I only interpret what I see in a different way?" He answers: "I am inclined to say the former. But Why? To interpret is to think, to do something; seeing is a state." Take another Wittgensteinian example: the Necker cube. It can be *seen* as a cube from above or from below, as a polygonally cut gem, a crisscross of lines on a two-dimensional plane, a wire construction, or a block of ice. Do all these accounts refer to the same thing? If so, how can the differences be accounted for? If not, in what sense are they the same? Once again, Wittgenstein (1953, 200) asks: "But how is it possible to *see* an object according to an *interpretation?* The question represents it as a queer fact; as if something were being forced into a form it did not really fit. But no squeezing, no forcing took place here." Hanson's answer, following Wittgenstein, is that there are different interpretations of what various observers see in common. The observers' retinal responses to the lines on paper can be virtually identical, since their empirical content is fundamentally the same. Yet one observer interprets them as a cube-up, and another observer as a cube-down.[2]

This process appears to entail two Peircean operations: retinal stimulation (immediate) and interpretation (mediated). Immediacy is *feeling* (Firstness), the *might be* of a possibility; mediacy is *intellection* (Thirdness), a synthesis of feeling and the *effect* (Secondness) of something "out there" on the sensory organs. Merely feeling a bombardment of photons on the retina is not *seeing*, as one might expect.[3] Hanson (1969, 93) offers the example of having his right hand on a stove and his left hand in the refrigerator, then plunging both hands into a basin of tepid water. He would get a familiar variable reaction: his hands *felt* different things. But it is not a matter of one hand feeling the water as "hot" and the other feeling it as "cold." There is not yet any distinction between what one hand feels and what the other feels, though different sense-data would be associated with each hand. Likewise, the bare sensation (feeling) of a rabbit-duck drawing is not yet acknowledgment of either one or the other. It is the sensation of both its aspects, for at this stage of Firstness, there is no more than a rabbit-duck superposition. Nothing has been actualized for someone in some respect or capacity.

It can be said that the drawing contains, as a superposed set of possibilities, two or more contradictory interpretations, one of which at a given instant can be actualized. If one observer sees the drawing and reports "duck," and another sees it and says it is a "rabbit," the differences they see are not due to differences in *what* they see. They saw the same thing, though their reports differed. And if suddenly the "duck" gazer says she was mistaken, for it is actually a "rabbit," the shift in interpretation might have occurred without her actively "thinking" about or forcing it. She simply saw the drawing differently and changed her report. In other words, as a superposed set of two possibilities before either a "rabbit" or a "duck" was actualized in the mind of its contemplator, it was both a "rabbit" and a "duck," or, if you will, neither a "rabbit" nor a "duck." We are here speaking of mere seeing, feeling, and sensing, not seeing something *as* something and *that* it is such-and-such, which is another issue entirely.

When a vague feeling of the rabbit-duck sign is actualized in consciousness, the phenomenon is then seen *as* a particular item—say, a "duck"—at some space-time juncture. Seeing *as,* in Peircean terms, is the force (Secondness) of the "real" world "out there" on the senses of something. To see *as* is to set something apart and identify it, and identification is the product of past events stored in the memory. Raw seeing is merely seeing, but to see *as* is to see some object ordinarily labeled a bicycle, Dustin Hoffman, an X-ray tube, Max Headroom, a cube with its face up, or a rabbit. Seeing in this manner—in contrast to seeing in the sense-datum (or oculist's-office) manner—involves a recollection of some past events and a reaction to a "clash" of the "real" on the senses. Thus the dyadic relation of Secondness.

Seeing *that* (Thirdness), in addition to seeing the Necker drawing *as* an ice cube, a transparent box, or a wire-framed block of glass, entails seeing *that* it is six-faced, twelve-edged, and eight-cornered, *that* all the corners are at right angles rather than as they are presented on the two-dimensional plane, *that* it is in a solid rather than liquid or gaseous state, *that* in its three-dimensional embodiment it occupies space, *that* it is located at some particular spot, *that* it is static rather than mobile, and so on. Seeing *that* demands knowledge about boxes. It calls for interpretation and the generation of an interpretant, the third leg of Peirce's sign tripod, which also includes a sign (*representamen*) and an object. Interpretation involves relations inherent in the triad of sign components (CP, 3.415–16). As such, when something is seen, knowledge is usually there, in the seeing, not an adjunct of the seeing, for we never or rarely catch ourselves adjoining bits and pieces of knowledge to what we see. We simply do it as a matter of course. In Hanson's (1969, 115) words:

> You see a person standing there . . . as solid, tangible, but not as bilaterally symmetrical (in the sense that he would present the same facade to you if he rotated through 180°). Of course, if he were to turn out to be shaped like one of Aristophanes' primeval men, if you were to see him rotate half a turn only to exhibit the same front view, you would say that you did not believe your eyes. But of course it isn't your eyes that would be lying. It would be the *seeing as* and the *seeing that* components of your seeing that would have got jarred up through such an experience.

So in what seems to be an instant, Wittgenstein's "rabbit" may be re-interpreted as a "duck," the observer suddenly having seen *that* it is something other than what she previously thought it to be. This act of constructing a successive sign of Thirdness serves as mediator between the previous *representamen* (sign) and its object, "rabbit." There was no forcing, no squeezing. Everything was there in the seeing, for all intents and purposes as if the raw seeing, the seeing *as,* and the seeing *that* had occurred without the subject's being actively aware of it: an interpretation.

At the outset, both juxtaposed possibilities were available to our observer, for she was familiar with rabbits and ducks. In contrast, the inhabitant of a world with ducks but no rabbits could not see the drawing's ambiguity. We are generally capable of seeing only what we know, but this is not the whole picture. We are also capable of seeing anew in the sense that what we thought

49

we knew turns out to be something other than what we suddenly feel, see, or think. Conjuring tricks are made possible by our seeing something *as* related to what we know without realizing that it should have been related to something else. The sleight-of-hand artist gets our minds and eyes moving in one direction in order to force us into seeing what we expected to see, though it could have, and should have, been seen otherwise. Peirce often insisted, like Hanson, that "[i]f one *sees* [*as*], one cannot avoid the percept; and if one *looks* [*sees that*], one cannot avoid the perceptual judgment. Once apprehended, it absolutely compels assent" (CP, 7.627; see also 5.302–3).[4] The obvious conclusion—Nietzsche knew it well—is that "perception is interpretation" (CP, 5.184).[5] In Joseph Agassi's (1981, 11) words, we tend "to see facts as if they prove us right and ignore the same facts when they prove us wrong." The distinction between experience and knowledge has thus been closed, modernity's empiricist biases to the contrary (Connor 1989, 33).

However, all interpretations remain inexorably incomplete—according to Peirce's generality principle—since our observer could also have seen the drawing as a wire contraption, a block of ice, and so on. And the Necker cube as a superposition, in line with Peirce's vagueness principle, implies that hitherto unforeseen consequences of *semiosic* activity always exist as unactualized possibilities (to be discussed in chapters Five, Six, and Eight). Hence, to the question, Can an observer simultaneously slap both the cube-up and cube-down interpretations on the drawing when she takes a gander at it? the answer is generally no, according to most current studies in psychology and to Bohr's complementarity principle as outlined in Chapter One above. She can only see *that* it is now a cube-up, now a cube-down. Then did she intentionally interpret it when she saw *that* it was a cube-up? No also. At the moment of seeing it *as* a cube and *that* it was in such-and-such a position, she was immediately aware of no intentionality, though mediately she could have become aware of her perceptual judgment.

In short, there is no clear-cut three-step sequence consisting of an optical pattern created by the subject's consciousness, then soaked up by her, and then interpreted. Interpretation is not made up of three separable components: seeing (Firstness), seeing *as* (Secondness), and seeing *that* (Thirdness). The cube is simply—and apparently automatically—identified *as* a cube *that* has certain characteristics. A few moments later, it may flip-flop into its enantiomorphic twin to become something else. The operation is processual rather than digital and sequential. What is ordinarily construed as seeing is constituted by those inseparable partners—Firstness, Secondness, and Thirdness—flowing along the stream of *semiosis*. This inseparability of raw seeing and seeing *as-that* renders perception a perpetual bedfellow to interpretation.

A Word Can Procreate a Thousand Pictures

Hanson is by no means tied to the "picture theory" of language, according to which the nature of language is to be found in its likeness to the features of theories (*theoros,* sight), formal isomorphisms, linguistic displays, mirror reflections, photographs, paintings, and maps. It is now quite apparent that this theory is an impoverished account of the "real."

Hanson (1969, 121) does believe that we tend to "see things sententially, almost always," though there is "nothing sentential or linguistic about the picture formed in our eye or in our mind's eye"—recall our observations on physics as talk, and talk about talk, in Chapter One. Knowledge, as well, Hanson tells us, is largely—though by no means exclusively—sentential. To see the sun *as* the "sun" either "at rest" or "in motion" is to be able to say a great deal. Without language it is hardly conceivable that the human community could have evolved to the point of taking on a particular perspective, developing a theory and belief system regarding the way things are, and communicating theories and beliefs to others. An important facet of a given collection of sentences expressing knowledge of theories and beliefs is that, like the field of *semiosis,* it is alinear: weblike and even fabriclike rather than chainlike.

This most properly entails a holistic view of cognition, of which Pierre Duhem was one of the foremost early proponents. Duhem (1954, 218) once put the matter thus:

> Enter a laboratory; approach the table crowded with an assortment of apparatus, . . . [and ask the physicist] what he is doing. Will he answer "I am studying the oscillations of an iron bar which carries a mirror"? No, he will answer that he is measuring the electric resistance of the spools. If you are astonished, if you ask him what his words mean, *what relation they have with the phenomena he has been observing and which you have noted at the same time as he,* he will answer that your question requires a long explanation and that you should take a course in electricity.

The physicist must teach his visitor everything he knows before he can show her what she should be seeing. Only then will she be sufficiently privy to the intellectual context so as to see those aspects of the cluster of objects before her eyes that the physicist over the years has learned to take as a matter of course. At the outset, the curious onlooker can see the objects, and she can even identify some of them. But she cannot yet see *that* their function is such-and-such and know *how* to operate them. Following the postmodern tenets outlined above, explicit knowledge *that*—of objects, acts, and events seen *as* cultural artifacts when properly contextualized—is, when made explicit, more textual than picturable, more linguistic sounds or marks than sight or images, and there is a vast logical distinction between language and pictures. Seeing is much more than merely what meets the eye, or even the "mind's eye." There is no innocent eye; what is seen is always already interpreted, and to an extent always already textual.

There is an all important linguistic component to seeing *that,* which is a giant logical remove from mere picturing. Language—deficient though it may be, and inexorably divorced from the "real"—can to a greater or lesser degree encapsulate, from within a semiotically real domain, smiles *and* the sense of friendship, a cake *and* its taste, sounds *and* a musical score, a silk scarf *and* its tactile qualities. In contrast, pictures, qualitative and quantitative analyses, amplifiers, and sensitometers, can reveal no more than happy faces, the chemical composition of pastry, frequency patterns, and reflection and refraction of light. That is, visual images, molecular structure, sound waves, and the color spectrum embody certain properties analogous to, isomorphic with, or related in one form or another to, the original itself. Sentences, on the other hand,

> do not stand for things in virtue of possessing properties of the original; . . . They can state what is, or could be, the case [i.e., Secondness and Thirdness]. They can be used to make assertions, convey descriptions, supply narratives, accounts, etc., none of which depend on the possession of some property in common with what the statement is about. (Hanson 1958, 27–28)

Language is no mere copy. Neither does it show what it says in the naive picture theory sense, nor is it capable of exhausting a community's storehouse of knowledge. It states what it can and leaves the rest to intuition, disposition, premonition, feeling, gut reaction, and the realm of the ineffable. I must emphasize that I am speaking of the aspect of knowing which by means of language can largely be made explicit. Unless one's knowledge can (with varying degrees of efficacy) be expressed in books, journals, lectures, speeches, street talk, or whatever, one cannot very well communicate the most important aspects as well as the subtle nuances of one's knowledge to others. This is not to say that one does not rely on implicit knowing *how,* which entails a "feel" for things that takes on paramount importance in the arts and everyday living and plays a crucial role in scientific endeavors. Yet precisely for this reason, the imponderables in one's activities have relatively little effect on the general corpus of knowledge as it exists in the laboratory, the library, the gallery, the museum, and cultural forms of life in general, which are chiefly, though not wholly, in the form of sentences (Hanson 1969, 126). These sentences include a rough to relatively precise account of seeing *as* and seeing *that* in the good Peircean dialogic mode—as we shall observe further in Chapter Eight. In our quest to know—not in the sense of *episteme* but *doxa*—dialogue is made possible by the community opinion concerning what is good and what is bad, what is true and what is false, what works and what does not. Visual images, sounds, and gustatory, olfactory, and tactile sensations are hardly by themselves capable of adjudicating between what the community prefers and what not. That must be left primarily to the arena of dialogue.

So immediate appearances, according to the eye, dictate either that the sun moves and the earth stands still, or vice versa. But in order for these divergent phenomena to be incorporated into worlds, worlds must be constructed, and world constructs, for the human semiotic animal, are generally more textual than sensorial. They are frequently learned as much—and with formal education, even more—by explicit instruction (knowing *that,* seeing *that*) as by example (knowing *how*)—though I by no means wish to ignore the importance of this second component of knowing, which will be taken up in later sections. Galileo and Bruno made the earth rotate and the sun stop, not by the physical force of Secondness but chiefly by imagination (Firstness) and verbal invention (Thirdness). Paintings, music, and culinary fashions are what they are in other respects than mere sight, sound, and taste. They are the product of textuality, of texture, both linguistic and otherwise. They are endowed with value primarily insofar as they are embodied in language.

Yet who can effectively contest the preponderance—even the imperious tyranny—of the eye, the icon, the image, *eidos: eidola* all? How can the Necker cube be articulated in one primal scream or holophrastic evocation as it is grasped in an apparently instantaneous perceptual gulp? Each glance at the figure entails a particular "cube world," and each can be at a given moment "true" for its contemplator, though the two possible "cube worlds" are in conflict. The point remains, however, that in addition to context, each of the two cube worlds' coming into existence depends in large part upon textuality (texture), upon their possibility for being endowed with linguistic (semiotic) garb. As Nelson Goodman (1978, 1–22) puts it, we can have words without worlds but no world without words and other symbols.

In spite of the differences between Peirce and Goodman, both place emphasis on language, that which endows *Homo semeioticus* with a distinctive signifying capacity—though at its root level the difference between human and nonhuman is most likely of degree rather than kind.[6] In order to illustrate this language emphasis, let me begin with Peirce's *pragmatic maxim,* a sentential method *par excellence* for knowledge acquisition.[7] Peirce held that before we can know what the world is, we must know what the propositions presumably saying something about that world mean. To that end, he provided his maxim:

53

"Consider what effects, that might conceivably have practical bearings, we conceive the object of our conception to have. Then our conception of these effects is the whole of our conception of the object" (CP, 5.402). This veritable mind-twister in essence affords us the promise that the meaning of any proposition is to be found in another proposition, and the meaning of that one in yet another, and so on, such that the general description of all the conceivable practical bearings or effects of a proposition can be made available by seeing how it works in the semiotically real world.[8] For example, the meaning of "Sodium produces a yellow flame" is obtained by translating the expression into a set of conditional statements such as "If a wire were dipped in an NaCl solution and subjected to a Bunsen burner flame, a yellow hue would be produced." So we put the conditional to the test, and if the predicted result ensues, that's that.

But life is not so easy. In order to reach the final interpretant—the proposition's univocal meaning—we must run the test on other solutions, such as Na_2SO_4 and Na_2CO_3, just to be sure nature has not slipped one over on us. And given the holistic character of knowledge and the sentences conveying it, these tests ultimately concern the nature of halogens and of salts, of valences, electron shells, chemical composition, spectroscopic analysis, and so on, which in turn solicit regard for the relation between sodium and the other elements in the periodic table. And to top it all off, each proposition must be put to the test. There is no end in sight. The range of possible conditional statements and their implied propositions is open-ended. Hence Peirce's *indeterminacy principle of meaning.*

On the one hand, if all the possible conditional statements were taken spatially as an indefinite range of superposed variables rather than a diachronic sequence of actualized propositions, tests, and their practical consequences, some of them converging and some diverging, the pragmatic maxim in its ultimate extension would hold these possibilities in check (i.e., in superposition). The whole concoction, this holistic fabric, composes an exceedingly complex sign of Firstness, a *monad,* parts of which can be subject to successive actualizations (into Seconds) through time and thus potentially yield meaning (interpretants, Thirds). The problem is that when so taken in spatial, synchronic terms, the validity of Peirce's pragmatic maxim paradoxically depends itself on the pragmatic maxim—in addition to the fact that this whole is inaccessible to the finite individual knower and even to an entire community of knowers. It implies all propositions that, if true, must ultimately apply to themselves, and what it implies of these propositions must also be applied to itself. This situation is tantamount to the *tu quoque* argument, that *bête noire* of rationalism: he who believes in reason must have at some point taken an irrational leap of faith landing him squarely in reason, *his* reason.

On the other hand, regarding a given community's holistic fabric of signs, there is no simple linear, time-dependent sequence beginning with a presuppositionless given and ending in truth. Everything is there, all at once, *en bloc* as it were. A given individual's finite, fallible awareness of this whole can be only piecemeal at best, and her ability to use the signs that the whole offers up depends upon her knowledge of it in its entirety. Understanding chess entails not the ability to follow a mere sequence of moves but a grasp, however vague and incomplete, of the entire system; likewise, understanding a mathematical proof entails a grasp of the series of equations as a whole. Chess and mathematics enjoy explicitly specifiable rules and a generally agreed-upon set of strategies. In contrast, the community's shared *semiosic* fabric—a form of life entailing multiply variegated language-games—offers only fuzzy contours, vague borders, cloudy distinctions, and no clearly perceptible outlines. The final semiotic reach of Peirce's maxim is thus a receding horizon. So the question remains: Is its validity simply undecidable?

Undecidability might bring Kurt Gödel to mind. Although the pragmatic maxim and the *semiosic* fabric to which it refers are hardly comparable to formal axioms and their proofs, in both cases self-reference and an infinite regress inhere. Moreover, given the impossibility of exhausting the maxim's practical effects, it also shares a self-negating characteristic with Gödelian sentences. In this vein, consider J. Findlay's (1942, 262) natural-language rendition of a Gödelian sentence—and pardon my evoking what at the outset must surely appear to be hopelessly recondite, but I believe the thrust of my argument will eventually become evident: "We cannot prove the statement which is arrived at by substituting for the variable in the statement form 'we cannot prove the statement which is arrived at by substituting for the variable in the statement form the name of the statement form in question' the name of the statement form in question." Substituting *Y,* a variable, for "the name of the statement form in question" quickly reveals that the statement refers to its own undecidability as a whole. It asserts that it is *not* provable by referring back to itself, thus creating a paradox. It is true, though its truth cannot be demonstrated or effectively given sentential garb.

We might be prone to counter that, by analogy, the pragmatic maxim's validity, like that of any such all-embracing, self-referring proposition, is undecidable; hence, even though one cannot reason oneself into it, it can at least be embraced by a leap of faith. According to the maxim, the possible conceivable effects of the object of one's conception make up the whole of one's possible conception of the object. Since the *n*-dimensional dissemination of all possible propositions leading from the original proposition regarding the object of conception includes a virtually unlimited web of sentences, even though one's conception of all the possible effects composes the whole of one's conception of the object in a positive, not a negative, sense—thus avoiding paradox—it cannot be grasped *in toto,* given our inherent limitations. Consequently, the effects of the initial proposition as well as the maxim itself must remain to a degree indeterminate, undecidable.

It is as if the maxim were to say to us: "I bear no determinable meaning for you, when you are considering the totality of all possible effects that might conceivably have practical bearings on *your* conception of the object of which I am a predication." If this statement is itself determinably meaningful, then it must be false, and if false, then it must be determinably meaningful, but if so, then it is false. If solid ground there be regarding the maxim, it appears to be of that merely hoped-for variety resulting from an act of faith rather than from there being any firm grasp of a preordained and rationally constructed axiom. Ultimately, the maxim must be embraced on faith.

Things are rarely as cut-and-dried as our leaps of faith—acts of Firstness—apparently are when considering the give-and-take of everyday language use. Our embracing the maxim is a good case in point. Upon a casual reading by an unlicensed logician—the way we most often read a text—the meaning of Findlay's sentence comes through about as clear as mud, for it is difficult to hold the totality to which it refers in check. Even after a close reading, one may fail to make head or tail of it. Although the sentence is a well-formed and intelligible syntactic string, semantically it presents an almost insurmountable challenge, for it demands comprehensive, not atomistic, understanding. The key unlocking the door to such understanding is not at hand; one requires an "Open Sesame" entailing a well-nigh impossible grasp of the whole of things. Such also is the understanding of, say, Joyce's *Finnegan's Wake,* Picasso's *Guernica,* or a Bach fugue.

Thus the ultimate import of Peirce's maxim, like that of Findlay's sentence, is that it somehow squeezes the entire fabric of knowledge, of signs, into its purview. It resembles more a baroque Gordian knot than Renaissance bits and bites cumulated linearly. At the level of the whole—and with a polite nod to Hanson's sentential thesis regarding knowledge—such understanding is largely tacit: sensed (Firstness) more than cognized (Thirdness), felt more than known explicitly, intuited more than the product of abstract reason, which calls on concrete reasonableness for tenuous, uncertain guidance. In this fashion, the maxim stipulates an overwhelming set of interconnected sentences and the conditions of their use. If a given proposition is taken in one massive dose as "true," according to the maxim one cannot expect to hold the entire set of sentences interrelated with that proposition in a tight embrace. One can at most exercise a partly to almost wholly tacit grasp of a limited number of them, each of which is no more than a peephole to the whole. "The sun moves" and "The sun is stationary" imply contradictory holistic worlds, though each can be considered as "true" and viable, according to the maxim, in its own right and within the context of a limited set of sentences implied by it as a consequence. "The earth moves relative to the sun, and vice versa" is yet another world, as are "The earth is flat," "sits on a turtle's back," "consists of three continents," "is inanimate matter," "possesses a spirit," and "The sun is a flat disk," "a life-giving god," and so on.

Given the virtual impossibility in a finite world of exhausting the range of sentences implied by the maxim, each and every sentence is, and will remain, *incomplete,* though it may be adequately—that is, pragmatically—understood against the holistic background of one's cultural knowledge and one's conceptual scheme. Concocting, by way of the maxim, a coherent set of such fragmented statements into an agglutinated whole can serve to create a compound world, while concocting an incoherent set of them creates a mélange of worlds in conflict. But no matter how complex the set of concocted worlds, it can never stand a chance of becoming The Complete World in the finite domain of finite beings. Peirce and Goodman would agree on this point, if on few others. 57

An agglutinated world of conflicting world versions is ordinarily held in repugnance according to the rational priorities of modern Western discourse. Indeed, our penchant for order seems to cry out for rejection of such an unruly swamp. Yet when all is said and done, no single world version has weathered, and in the future none is likely to weather, the test of time. The Necker cube-up at some indeterminable moment will flip-flop: Herbert Spencer's social Darwinism turned out to be a nightmare, the dream of logical atomism never materialized, behaviorism was eventually seen as a crass oversimplification, the parameters of Newtonian mechanics proved to be more restrictive than Einsteinian relativity, and atoms have become penetrable and indeterminately divisible rather than solid spheres. Every "true" world has had a telltale contradictory sign hidden away somewhere in the closet. When it was found, that world began to procreate an unwanted family of anomalies, until it finally collapsed *in toto.* So, in Goodman's terms, if there is any world at all, there are many worlds, for in every "true" world somewhere there are conflicting versions that cannot both be "true" in the same world. And all these worlds in their turn, or even concurrently if the context is able to withstand the stress and strain, can be at some point in time "actual." If the notion of multiple and conflicting "actual" worlds is unpalatable, it is certainly less intolerable than the alternative of a world, The Complete World, in which all possible versions are simultaneously "true" from one perspectival framework or another.[9]

Since many "truths" conflict—the earth as standing still and the sun as moving, or vice versa—no system is guaranteed to be true for all time. How is it possible, then, to accommodate "truths" in conflict while holding onto the difference between "truth" and "falsity" for dear life? Goodman suggests that we treat different world versions as merely "true" in different worlds: "Versions not applying in the same world no longer conflict; contradiction is avoided by segregation. A true version is true in some worlds, a false version in none. Thus the multiple worlds of conflicting true versions are actual worlds, not the merely possible worlds or nonworlds of false versions" (Goodman 1984, 31).

58

That is to say, the ink flowing from Peirce's pen would construct the notion of multiple worlds contained within the realm of possibilities (Firsts) that are not necessarily either "true" or "false" or not both "true" and "false" but merely possibles existing in the realm of pure chance. Actualized worlds (Seconds) are drawn from this realm and, given certain hypothetical conditions—and complying with the maxim—can potentially become construed (in the realm of Thirds) as either "true" or "false," depending upon particular habits, expectations, conventions, and beliefs. In other words, the realm of possibilities is *vagueness,* pure undecidability, utter chance (where everything is superposed). The world of actualities consists of a collection of what is deemed either "true," "false," or "fictive" in a particular *here-now.* And the realm of potentiality is a mediator and moderator of the other two. Its task is to extract the juice of knowledge from the pulp of actuals and the essence of unborn qualities. For this reason, in its ultimate extrapolation, Thirdness is *generality.*

Goodman's nominalist, yet constructivist, view does not have many worlds traveling along different highways. Space-time is ordered within each specific world without the possibility of an Einsteinian or Everettian sort of cosmic space-time manifold enveloping all worlds.[10] Neither are worlds distinguished by an all-inclusive metalanguage from a metamanifold or some transcendental God's-eye perspective but rather by the points of conflict between them (CP, 5.289–91). This is because Goodman's worlds come in whole packages: for every world, a cosmos—presumably an orderly, harmonious system. There are many different stars, books, events, and pebbles near the sea, but worlds are surely inclusive and self-sufficient entities. As totalities, they can differ from one another, but there can be, for us, no comprehensive whole encompassing all of them, or any complete and consistent embrace of any of them. If the notion of the sun or its lack thereof differs in different worlds, each of these worlds cannot be part of something bigger—a world containing both the sun at rest and the sun in motion, for example. Each self-contained world is a set containing its own myriad parts, but there is no possible set of all sets that contains itself. In Peirce's terms, this is to say that the ultimate extension of the maxim demands the "real" as a generality, though it is unavailable to a given individual or community of knowers.

From a Peircean nonnominalist, yet constructivist, framework, there *is* a domain capable of including any and all contradictory entities, or contradictory worlds containing contradictory entities in superposition—to be discussed further in chapters Six and Eight. This domain is precisely that of *vagueness,* where the contradictory range of all possibilities lurks. Once a world has been actualized, with time many other competing and conflicting worlds can be actualized. As worlds proliferate, a wily nominalist might claim the ability to leap nimbly from world to world, shifting at will between points of view and frames of reference, from stationary sun to ambulating sun, from space and time to space-time, from people as inherently good to people as pleasure-pain machines, from organisms taxonomized and fixed for all time to organisms evolving, from the earth as a few thousand years old to the earth of a few billion years of age. Such schizophrenic dancing between conceptual schemes promises a free-wheeling relativism welcomed by some as refreshing and liberating but striking a note of fear for others. And a joyous Dionysian nihilistic dance (Eros, deconstruction), a morbid sort of nihilism (thanatos, destruction), or sheer (Faustian) despair can ensue. This is perhaps inevitable, given the idea that either one world becomes a plethora of worlds or the concoction of all possible worlds becomes—for the finite human semiotic animal—no world at all but chaos.

Seeking another alternative, one may cling to the elusive hope that in the most *general* of spheres, everything can eventually be discovered. But this everything becomes at the same time an empty sort of monism. In Goodman's (1984, 32–33) words, "When we undertake to relate different [world] versions, we introduce multiple worlds. When that becomes awkward, we drop the worlds for the time being and consider only the versions. We are monists, pluralists, or nihilists not quite as the wind blows but as befits the context." In light of above observations, an argument for this intriguing but aggravating plurality postulate—or, if you wish, monistic postulate—is perhaps most adequately found, if at all, within the broadest possible historical context. Other peoples have alternate worlds: Zande witchcraft, Aztec cosmology, the Upanishads, the pre-Socratics, Medieval faith in the unknown, Renaissance astrology, Zen Buddhism, the way of Tao. The bizarre categories developed by alchemy waver between the ludicrous and the exotic, whether from the modern or the postmodern view. Claude Lévi-Strauss's (1966) "savage mind" carves up his world "metaphorically," whereas Western science does so "metonymically." B. L. Whorf's (1956) Zuni perceives something akin to space-time, while we perceive space and/or time. Jacob Bronowski (1978, 80) once mused that flowers could quite effectively have been classified according to their colors and hues, shapes, or size. And, of course, to top it off, we have Borges's (1964, 103) strange Chinese encyclopaedia (cited in Chapter Four).

There appears, in the final analysis, no absolute sense in which something belongs to a particular category; it is we humans who put things into categories, into worlds of our own making.

To the Pith of the Matter

60 Pluralism, in the final analysis, seems to be the order of the day. From the vantage point of "postmodern science," as noted in the Introduction, there is no one and only description of the "real," any more than there is a singular work of art to be sculptured from a block of marble. The question, What is the ultimate work to be chipped from this piece of stone? is meaningless. A work's shape will be whatever it will be shaped into. One shape is potentially as valid as the next from within one of a vast number of particular temporal and spatial contexts—though, admittedly, there is probably some nebulous set of universal givens regarding the value of a work. By a comparable token, until the present century, scientists asked of a theory: "Is it true or false?" In contrast to this overzealous query, the notion has gradually gained ascendancy, reaching its apogee in postmodern science, that any and all absolute criteria of truth eventually fall into bankruptcy. Nowadays, "we do not ask whether a given concept is true or false. We ask: Is it convenient or inconvenient; is it useful or not" (Rashevsky 1956, 142). Or, consonant with the Copenhagen interpretation of quantum mechanics, one might simply say: "Does it work or not? And if it does, don't mess with it."

Postmodern science neither propagates nor pursues "truth" as it is traditionally conceived. It recognizes that the way of all interpretations and even perceptions is to a large extent conditioned by language and by styles of reasoning. Thus the concern for "truth," its meaning, and the criteria for arriving at it are radically context-dependent. Modernity's scientific but imperialist ambitions to achieve power over nature ultimately ended in power for its own sake, not "truth," as its aim. The postmodernist, in contrast, has learned to live, is striving to live, without the illusion of a transcendental science. If modern science entailed the dream of transcendence opening the pearly gates to "reality," postmodern science entails the possibility of making many worlds by the exercise of sheer imagination, which allows its citizens to find a "home" in "their world" (Toulmin 1982b, 244–45).

The science of postmodernism, like the thrust of Peirce's philosophy, does not categorically place form over feeling or standards of objectivity over sentiment and subjectivity. On the other hand, its enthusiastic adoption of pluralism appears anti-Peircean: the spectre of pluralism ultimately satisfied neither his head nor his heart (CP, 8.262). Yet Peirce never ceased to admire those with the ability to free themselves from the trammels of totalitarian system-building intrepidly to forge ahead, uncommitted to their own past assertions. While modern science in the guise of logical positivism was a suspicion of metaphysics, infatuation with that hoped-for demarcation between science and nonscience, and emphasis on testability of concepts and propositions, postmodernism is suspicion of totalization and loss of faith in the possibility of demarcations, neutral "data," and metalanguages with which to adjudicate between theoretical languages and observation languages. In fact, according to postmodern science, whatever "world" might have ascended to prominence during a particular time has depended in large part upon the wizardry of its propagators rather than upon purely objective methods.[11]

61

It is no longer a matter of "truth" or "falsity" or of the absolute science/nonscience distinction of modernity. Belief in such is adoption of the criterion according to which science brings about definable cultural achievements or technological advances through the ability to control and predict, while nonscience does not. In contrast, the pragmatic, postmodern notion of cultural *and* technological development is at certain points in tune with what Peirce had in mind for his "economy of research" program (see Rescher 1978). It also avoids the logical positivists' idea of a monolithic "unified science" as well as such conundrums embodied in the questions, What method of investigation unites ethnology and chemistry, and biology and nuclear physics? and Can the human sciences—or, of all things, semiotics—become scientific like the natural sciences? These outdated springboards for inquiry are no more and no less muddled than the classical notions of control and prediction. Indeed, the fracas caused by Feyerabend, Kuhn, and others has served effectively to undermine the old Platonic distinction between *episteme* and *doxa* such that both "science" and "nonscience"—that is, culture in general—are conceived of as a vast interconnected fabric of signification. Peirce's pragmatic "unification" of intellectual endeavors falls squarely under this nonmodern umbrella rather than under that of positivism, a point that Morris neatly failed to see.[12]

Peirce's idea of a dialogical "fabric of signification" implies a multiplicity of semiotic realities—worlds of our own making. Of course, this range of semiotically real worlds is not exactly unlimited; that is, it is not wholly arbitrary in the nominalist (or semiological) sense. A statue cannot be sculptured that is taller than the block of marble, and the strength, texture, and durability of the material to an extent dictates the degree of detail and definition of the sculpture. Limitations on alternate semiotically real worlds, whether human or animal, are mandated by beliefs, habits, and conventions, as well as perceptual and conceptual faculties. In addition, any and all semiotic worlds are constructed with the "real"—the force of Secondness—looking over the constructor's shoulder, suggesting a few additions here, mandating some deletions there, and forcibly opening occasional new pathways, but in general allowing the game to go on.

We must entertain the idea, then, that a given semiotically real domain cannot be coterminous with, though it is dependent upon and at the same time complementary with, the "real."

Other Minds, Other Worlds

Getting outside One's Own Conceptual Skin: An Impossible Dream?

Cognizant of the difficulty of leaping from one conceptual scheme, with its accompanying perceptual mode, into another one, Alex Comfort (1984) calls for the painful process of developing a sense of *empathy* with the emerging twentieth-century model of the universe in order to discard what has for centuries been conceived of as the cold, impersonal universe of classical mechanics.[1]

The Cartesian-Newtonian paradigm of the corpuscular-kinetic machine was not embraced in one fell swoop; the Occidental mind only very slowly came to empathize with it. Once firmly entrenched, it then reigned for generation after generation finally to become deeply embedded in Western thought; it became a *cognitive map,* so to speak—not in terms of the mind as a mirror of nature but in terms of a conceptual framework, a diagrammatic (indexical) indicator of a particular semiotic world. Such maps are working models that pattern selected events and processes within semiotic realities. A new world image capturing the empathy of a particular human community can thus never become a taken-for-granted "reality" without the prior embedment and embodiment of such a cognitive map. The question is, Once a particular semiotically real world has become entrenched by way of a cognitive map, how can one then swim against the current of one's entire cultural heritage in order to become aware of a radically distinct semiotic world? (see CP, 6.327–28).

Interestingly enough, at the same time Einstein was struggling with a new world image, C. H. Hinton (1887, 1904), one among a diverse collection of scholars scattered throughout Europe and the United States obsessed with otherworldly models, was attempting to get a feel for and even create a mental image depicting the fourth dimension. The results are fascinating, the mental navigation, by sheer intellection, of a free spirit into waters hitherto uncharted—at least within Hinton's cultural milieu. Whether or not Hinton was actually able to understand, let alone perceive—as he claimed—objects in a four-dimensional world is relatively unimportant. Rather, focus must rest on the excruciating Faustian effort expended: it allows a glimpse into the very act of world making. Like Douglas Hofstadter (1979) and his dialogical method of exposition appropriated from Lewis Carroll, Comfort engages in what he dubs "demonics":

imaginary incursions into how a being outside our time-bound, three-dimensional universe might possibly perceive and conceive of things. Comfort's trek into the wilderness is even more fascinating than Hinton's, especially since it is cleverly couched in terms of our contemporary postmodern scene. He leads one to the compelling notion that, somehow, dissonant gaps between worlds can at least partly be closed by wild leaps of the imagination.

But a further question lingers: When attempting to cognize the hitherto uncognizable, how can one resist the compulsion to anthropomorphize the whole account? Are we inexorably limited to human models? Perhaps *Umwelt*-generated world maps of other human cultures and especially other organisms are of a subtlety beyond ordinary human perception, conception, and even imagination. Nevertheless, Thure von Uexküll's (1982, 1989) account of the *Umwelt*-theory of his father, Jakob, takes the notion of the perennially inaccessible "real" and the inevitability of the semiotically real—which is, ipso facto, *Umwelt*-generated—to its extreme articulation. Thure reports on Jakob's celebrated "functional circle" of semiotic transmission from an organism's (1) receptor picking up potential information from an object "out there" to (2) perceptual mechanism and interpreter to (3) effector and (4) "out there" again in the process of generating its semiotically real world. Thure argues that for the "lower" organisms there is no object of perception in the classical human sense. Rather, the sensation of an object oscillates in and out again in the course of the *semiosic* process.

Jakob von Uexküll's example (Uexküll 1957), a tick, remains motionless on the underside of a branch in readiness to respond to three signals: (1) an olfactory sign caused by the beta oxybutyric acid from the sweat of a warm-blooded animal, (2) a tactile sign, after the insect, if lucky, has dropped onto the hairy covering of the mammal of its choice, and (3) heat signs produced by the skin area of the mammal toward which the tick gravitates in search of a bare spot promising a meal. One sign's phasing in marks another's phasing out in what, as far as we are concerned, is a continuous process. But for the tick it is not. More purely a nominalist than the most exacting of humans, the tick simply takes its signs as they come, as discontinuous packets of signification. Thus the tick's semiotic object, Jakob argues, differs fundamentally from the presumably static objects that we perceive. An unwary animal passing under the tree where the tick is hanging is ordinarily seen by us as a permanent object "with identical spatio-temporal appearance throughout the process of observation" (T. von Uexküll 1989, 137; see also Jerison 1973).

Of course, as Nietzsche properly warned us, anthropomorphism in this and other such imaginary ventures into the semiotic world of nonhuman organisms always threatens to run roughshod over our best intentions. Thure is painfully aware of this problem, as evidenced by his admonition that

> the difficulty of identifying the object of a biosemiosis in terms of
> the expectations inherent in the semiotics of human sign processes
> . . . draws attention to the fact that is easily overlooked in semiotic
> concepts: the object, which is defined as a significatum, only exists
> in the human mind as a coherent whole distinctly definable in space
> and time—i.e., it is an abstraction. (Uexküll 1989, 138)[2]

I will highlight the idea of the semiotic object along with Thure's subject-object relationship, while leaving the concept of "openness" for a later section. Drawing from Jakob's observations, Thure posits a semiotic object that, in the signifying process, is correlated with the *functional circle* by the structure of the interrelations making up a context of interpretation. The interpreting subject inhabits a subjective universe whose objective counterpart is represented by the context—described as "a section of nature which provides the resources essential for a living being or a species to survive and reproduce and in which dangers are kept within tolerable limits" (Uexküll 1989, 139). Thure then evokes the term "autonomy" to qualify *habituated action* (Peirce's Thirdness) on the part of the subject, as opposed to brute *physical reaction* (Secondness), which is characteristic of inanimate objects. Autonomy implies at least a minimal degree of selfhood. Even the relatively simple cell is capable of responding to its environment in somewhat autonomous rather than heteronomous fashion, which endows it with certain ego-qualities. Jakob thus "explained a phenomenon which in modern science is described as the capability of living systems to distinguish between 'self' and 'non-self' or, in other words, to respond to the quality of 'non-self' in a 'self-preserving' manner" (T. von Uexküll 1989, 140).

This all seems fine and dandy. An aggravating problem remains, however: the *human* observer as interpreter of *animal* sign processes. To be sure, Thure judiciously warns that, in good Peircean fashion, all interpretations are in the final analysis interpretations of other interpreters' interpretations. And he concludes:

> A science of general semiotics in which the language is only one
> of the myriad sign systems in a semiotic universe has to relativize
> the examples used in the textbooks and treatises on sign processes.
> . . . Thus, for instance, the classic example of "smoke signifies fire"
> has to be relativized considering the fact of what smoke and fire
> mean in the subjective worlds of the bat or the tick, etc.—whether
> anything like "smoke" exists in them at all and what "fire" could
> look like as a "semiotic object" in their subjective worlds. (T. von
> Uexküll 1989, 155)

The message is that we should never forget that we cannot simply step out of our conceptual skin and abandon our position as outside observers. We inexorably remain trapped within our own subjective universe when observing the objective effects of the subjective universe of another organism. There simply is no absolutely determinable demarcation between subject and object.

In this respect, both Uexkülls are in tune with recent findings from quantum physics, biology, and anthropology. As Thure (1989, 147) puts it, Jakob's fundamental premise accords with the principles of contemporary physics insofar as he "emphasized the fact that the natural sciences are, in reality, never concerned with the objects of their concepts, but always merely with their concepts of objects." The presumed objective reality of the sciences is drawn from a long line of metaphors enabling and abetting logocentric interpretations of so-called empirical evidence from "hard data" that is ultimately derived from the experience of a solitary cogitating self, the scientist. As I outlined above, this "objectivity" never existed in the first place. Rather, theories are the product of free-wheeling constructs of the mind. Heisenberg (1958, 81), describing this fundamental shift from classical to new physics, observes that natural science "does not simply describe and explain nature; it is a part of the interplay between nature and ourselves; it describes nature as exposed to our method of questioning." And elsewhere, in a vein reminiscent of Peirce, he writes: "The same organizing forces that have shaped nature in all her forms are also responsible for the structure of our minds" (Heisenberg 1971, 101).

As a consequence of this inevitable epistemological merry-go-round, anthropomorphism—let alone logocentrism—tends to run rampant, from our conception of quarks and quasars to DNA, cells, ticks, bats, primates, and other human cultures. In essence, Einstein anthropomorphically imagined what it would be like if he were a photon, then asked himself what it meant to say that two events are "simultaneous." Once the question was brought into sharp focus, the classical edifice began to tumble. To speak of two events occurring at the same instant when they are nearby does not apply to events in distant places, he reasoned, and the meaning of "simultaneous" from that point onward changed radically. The inevitable occurred, however: both meanings were to a degree anthropomorphized by the general public, since we persist in our pig-headed notion of things as permanent and change as things moving from one spot to another or from one time to another. Given our inclination to follow pathways of least linguistic and conceptual resistance, humankind will most likely require decades, perhaps even centuries to gain legitimate empathy for the universe suggested by the new physics (Comfort 1984).

Einstein's notorious instance of anthropomorphism involves human subjectivities and their confrontation with what is taken to be the objectively real world. Let us now switch the focus back to subjectivities regarding other subjectively real worlds in order to return to the central issue of the present chapter from a different vantage point. Thomas Nagel (1974) once queried,

"What is it like to be a bat?" concluding that the bugbear rests in matching subjectivities between our experience and the bat's, which are intrinsically different. Spatial and temporal perception, concepts of inside and outside, above and below, to the right and to the left, here and there, moving and stationary, and so on, are problematic at best regarding the distinction between human and bat semiotically real worlds. No mere addition or subtraction of perceptual and conceptual features can guarantee a transformation of our experience into the bat's. To Nagel's credit, toward the end of his provocative paper he hints at the possibility of constructing an objective phenomenon to attempt a description of the subjective character of experience in a form comprehensible to other organisms incapable of these particular experiences. Unlike Jakob von Uexküll, however, he does not attempt to outline a project for such a construction (but see Pugmire 1989; Tilghman 1991).

67

As a physiological counterpart to Nagel's philosophical ruminations on a bat's world, Warren McCulloch (1965) and his associates demonstrated that a frog's eye communicates information to its brain about a "reality" well-nigh incompatible with ours. The frog, simply put, does not "see" the same world we do. His eyes do not move; if his body changes position, his entire vision is changed with it. He has no fovea, or region of greatest acuity upon which he can center part of his vision. He has only a single visual system; his retina is uniform throughout. In other words, the frog's vision is specifically adapted for detecting small dark objects that enter his receptive field and move about intermittently in stroboscopic fashion. Consequently, he is not concerned with the detail of stationary parts of the world around him. He builds for himself a "frog map" of the universe, which is quite efficient for catching air-born bugs and eluding storks. He makes biological sense of the information he receives, thus increasing his chances for survival.

However, if suddenly confronted with a hostile world in which he is surrounded by immobile food—dead flies—he will starve to death. The fault lies not in his brain but in his eyes, however, for they speak to the brain "in a language already highly organized and interpreted, instead of transmitting some more or less accurate copy of the distribution of light on the receptors" (McCulloch 1965, 251). That is to say, the frog's eyes abstract from the physical world, and consequently what the brain "sees" is the result of what has been abstracted a priori (see also McFarland 1985, 232–33).

To demonstrate further how the frog's perceptive abilities differ from those of humans, Roger W. Sperry (1956) cut the optic nerve of a frog, turned its eyeball upside down, and then reconnected it (while acknowledging the barbarity of this act, I choose not to dwell on the issue here). The frog was able to regenerate his vision, but for the remainder of his life, he struck out for food in the wrong direction. If a fly was moving at the top of his vision, he responded

by striking downward. The hapless creature was never able to modify his behavior. He lacked the innate intelligence to adapt to his crossed wiring, though
he obviously received all the information he needed for survival. Humans, in
contrast, are able to adjust to such an inverted perception of things. Numerous
inverted goggle experiments have demonstrated that the upside-down world is
reinverted after a few clumsy days.

It seems that an organism's world map develops in tandem with the
evolution of its brain. At each stage of evolution, an organism develops its own
map, which is, in John Z. Young's (1978) term, its "cosmology," the degree of
sophistication of which corresponds to the stage of its evolution (see also Jerison
1973). The evolutionary trail from the frog's world to the space and time of
Newton and Einstein, Monet and Rembrandt, Vivaldi and Beethoven, Cervantes
and Balzac, is long and arduous. Humans not only perceive objects in space
and time in exceedingly sophisticated ways; they also construct signs representing those objects—language being the prime example—in order to reflect
on them and communicate thoughts about them. In semiotic terms, such reflection, especially self-reflection, mediates between the more direct signifying
modes of iconicity and indexicality, thus fostering the creation of an overwhelming variety of signs and their interpretations—recall the above discussion of
postmodern and modern science.

Perhaps we need not look as far as Nagel, McCulloch, Uexküll, and
others for the intrigues and enigmas of alien semiotic worlds. Rather, they can
be found in subjectivities commonly thought to be compatible in their most
basic form: divergent "worlds" held by distinct human communities. After all,
did not the Ptolemaic and the Copernican scientists see the "same" sun in terms
of streams of photons bombarding their retinas? Then how is it that they "saw"
and described "different" suns? Did not Einstein's relativity and classical physics refer to the same external world? Wittgenstein (1969, 80e) presents the problem and hints at the impossibility of a determinate solution:

> Is it wrong for me to be guided in my actions by the propositions of
> physics? Isn't precisely this what we call a "good ground"?
>
> Supposing we met people who did not regard that a telling
> reason. Now, how do we imagine this? Instead of the physicist,
> they consult an oracle. (And for that we consider them primitive.)
> Is it wrong for them to consult an oracle and be guided by it?—if
> we call this "wrong" aren't we using our language-game as a base
> from which to *combat* theirs?

In addition to evoking the trials, tribulations, and trepidations that
have long plagued anthropologists, Wittgenstein, it appears, in somewhat

Kuhnian fashion avers that ordinarily the physicist can do no more than engage in a verbal jousting match with the oracle-scientists. She cannot reason with them, nor they with her, in whatever style of reason each uses. They will simply talk past each other from within their own particular conceptual schemes. On the other hand, Wittgenstein seems to suggest that, when in the proper frame of mind, we *can* learn different language games that more adequately enable us to get on with the business of living, and with greater or lesser degrees of success, we can somehow learn to live within the language games of other communities. However, in general, Wittgenstein sends the message that in practical, everyday affairs our knowledge is superior to the reasons we can offer in support of it. In other words, we usually know more than we can tell, for a large part of our knowledge is invariably embedded (implicit, tacit). Hence cognitive leaps between conceptual schemes are relatively few and far between.

Peirce labeled such tacit knowledge *habit.* In contemporary dress, a comparable notion sports the name of *convention.* In either case, whatever we can come to know of the world, our knowledge can do no more than refer to our particular semiotic reality rather than the world *an sich.* Semiotically real worlds, in view of the *Umwelt* theory, vary from species to species. All living creatures need to perceive and be aware of their environment, and different species do so in different ways. However, since their knowledge of the external world is always selective, through the sense organs and by way of a given *Umwelt,* it can never be complete. For example, a particular species may emphasize smell over sight such that the olfactory sensations it picks up take priority over visual sensations. The working model created by this particular process is a radically simplified and specialized version of the "real" thing. But this is necessary, for only thus is the organism able to make some sort of sense out of an overwhelming barrage of incoming data and carry on with its daily affairs. A semiotically real world can in this manner be defined in much the same way that Jakob von Uexküll defines "biological reality": a particular map of the world that "the brain of a given species is able to build" (T. von Uexküll 1982, 56).

This is constructivism in its most cardinal form. It maintains that human communities are distinctive because semiotically real worlds can diverge radically from one generation to another, from one culture to another, and at times even from one mind to another. What is more, if the *Umwelt* hypothesis regarding human communities is capable of producing infinitely variable and indefinitely differentiated world constructs presenting intractable barriers against intercommunication, then the distinction between human semiotically real worlds and those of other organisms is even more impenetrable. From human to tick, we begin to sense the magnitude of the perplexity.[3]

How Many Possible Answers to the Riddle?

Though empathy has by and large fallen from grace in anthropological circles, the notions of textuality (texture), and especially intertextuality, dear to the postmodern mind, resurrect certain vestiges of that well-worn term. Both empathy and intertextuality involve the problems and pitfalls of human-human communication: modes of understanding across radically distinct cultures, and the process of acquiring a feel for new world models and constructing radically different cognitive maps. If we toss the *Umwelt* hypothesis into the picture, we have, in addition, the problem of empathizing with other creatures. Empathy, as Comfort uses the term, does not entail a conscious and intentional program but by and large a tacitly assimilated feel for things. As such, *Umwelt*-generated "realities" are in part the very product of empathizing. A chief distinction between human and nonhuman *Umwelten* is that the former are accompanied in one form or another by greater awareness of that which is empathized, and hence the possibility exists for a given human world map to be altered at will.

As a further illustration of the limits of anthropomorphism that may nonetheless aid us in coming to grips with the semiotic import of the *Umwelt* concept, some years ago in *Punch* a cartoon appeared depicting a kingfisher perched on a limb spying a fish in the water below and thinking to herself: "$\mu = \sin\varnothing/\sin\theta$" (see also the discussion in Boden 1984). George Snell's equation for the diffraction of light when passing from air to water is hardly less intelligible for the kingfisher than a set of formulas in another cartoon I once saw in a mathematics journal was for me. It consisted of a chalkboard full of equations and two mathematicians, one leaning against a desk and pointing to the board, the other rolling on the floor while holding his belly, and both completely overcome with laughter. As far as I could tell, the marks on the board may as well have been from an undecipherable code in ancient Martian. Yet the punch line, I must presume, was perfectly intelligible to the experts in question.

The point involves the now familiar two pairs of terms (which, unfortunately, I find most convenient to mark with that bête noire of binarist thinking, the virgule): seeing/seeing *as-that,* and knowing *how*/knowing *that.*[4] According to the above discussion, seeing is unmediated; seeing *as* and seeing *that* are mediated. Knowing *how* (i.e., actions that can be made only partially explicit) is foregrounded by postmodernism; exclusively and explicitly knowing *that* (i.e., Hanson's sentential knowledge entailing the capacity by and large to explicate and expound on one's actions) is the age-old imperialist quest, that obsession with power, of modernity. Tacit knowing, or behavioral know-*how,* is the competence to perform. It is passive understanding—whether instinctual or through embedded, habitual practices—in contrast to active understanding. Knowing *how* is both the enemy and the ally of knowing *that.* It can be: (1) linked to instinct, (2) former explicit knowing *that* which has submerged into nonconsciousness to become a pathway of least mental resistance, or (3) the possible source of new modes of knowing *that,* through abduction.

Habit by instinct, needless to say, lies by and large beyond conscious control. Knowing *how,* in the sense of (2), is a readiness to act governed by expectations rendering the conscious subject either oblivious or receptive to surprises. It is knowledge that has become automatized, mechanized, habitualized. This noninstinctual habit includes actions, often highly complex, that, as a result of repetition, are performed routinely and without the need of conscious attention, such as speaking, playing a piano, and driving a car (see Merrell 1991a). What we do by knowing *how* to do it is what we do most naturally, without thinking. It *"diminishes the conscious attention with which our acts are performed"* (James 1950, 1:114).[5] The beauty is that it relieves us of having to think about the innumerable linear acts in which we are engaged. We simply do what we do mindlessly, acting and reacting in terms of wholes of experience. Consequently, the greater the number "of the details of our daily life we can hand over to the effortless custody of automation, the more our higher powers of mind will be set free for their own proper work" (James 1950, 1:122). Thus the dialectic between habit and consciousness, between knowing *how* and knowing *that,* and thus the dialogic between the self and its inner other.[6]

Our kingfisher sees the fish and without further ado tacitly knows *how* to travel the shortest path between herself and her prey, thus abiding by Snell's law. Seeing *as-that* and knowing *that,* in contrast, entail propositional and computational language unavailable to the kingfisher.[7] Though Snell could give his feathered friend a lesson on the altered velocity of light through different media, the kingfisher would most likely respond that it is all quite interesting but she has no need of such hows and whys, thank you. The proof of the test is in knowing *how* to snatch a quick meal and simply doing it rather than jawing interminably about *how* it is done and why.

The terms "propositional" and "computational" in contemporary cognitive psychology come to us from AI-inspired computer modeling—to be taken up in another context in Chapter Eleven.[8] Two root assumptions lurk behind much AI research: (1) what can be understood is algorithmic and can be programmed, hence it is computable; and (2) what is computable is determinate, complete, and precise. Regarding (1), Marvin Minsky (1980) has suggested that ultimately it is possible to write programs capable of producing art and music, and subsequently, for understanding them. This assertion carries with it the implication that the programmer writing the program for understanding a symphony understands the symphony, so his own understanding can by a 180-degree turn be programmed into a computer, which demands that the programmer understand his understanding of the symphony, and an unending sequence of steps begins. Computation of understanding, in this fashion, cannot reach ultimate completeness. Regarding (2), AI workers continue painstakingly to separate the wheat of computability from the unwanted, noncomputable chaff, a task they and only they claim to be capable of performing, since theories proposed in psychology, philosophy, linguistics, and related disciplines, they tell us, are too incomplete and too vaguely articulated to be realized in computational terms (Winston and Brady 1971).

The link between AI's computational thesis and cognitive psychology has its roots in Kenneth Craik's assumption in *The Nature of Explanation* (1943) that the mind serves to translate percepts from the external world into internal representations—somewhat reminiscent of Jakob von Uexküll's functional circle. These representations yield others, and, when needed, they can be translated back into behavior. An organism's entire set of representations makes up its (*Umwelt*-generated) model of the world. In the act of intercommunication, it is necessary that the addressee construct a hypothetical model of the addresser's representation—a representation of a representation—and map that model onto her own in order to generate an interpretation—an interpretation of an interpretation. Thus we have a model embedded within a model—much like the map paradox—and the beginning of another regress without end. This is the first nesting implied by the computational model. The second nesting is derived from the computational thesis of self-consciousness: the idea of a program, or automaton, that can print out a complete description of itself. This nimble computing beast would supposedly be aware of itself—of its own computations—since it is able to describe itself, and hopefully, to reprogram itself. It would be consistent and complete, the stuff modernity's dreams are made of.

Unfortunately, we humans are not as mentally spry as are our hardwired counterparts: they would have little patience with our torpid computational powers. Nevertheless, in addition to being able to construct models based on our understanding of the external world, and unlike machines as they have been developed up to now, we can construct models—however incomplete and inconsistent—of the workings of our own mind. Self-consciousness depends on our capacity to observe ourselves observing or acting on the world. Whether or not machines are potentially capable of such a feat, whatever is embedded within the mind at a given moment can be no more than an incomplete representation of the mind sufficient for constructing an indirect, and mediate, subjective sense of self-awareness. Peirce would undoubtedly agree on this point.

In the second place, the brain-mind combination is not a mere logic machine but a medium for knowing *how* in addition to knowing *that*. With knowing *how* to do something and doing it, an immense corpus of implicit knowledge is called into activity, all of which occurs in such brief intervals of time that most of it remains outside the level of awareness. Conscious deliberation and inferential reasoning is but a tiny tip of the knowledge iceberg, for "our logically controlled thoughts compose a small part of the mind, the mere blossom of a vast complexus" (CP, 5.212).[9] Cognitivist Ulric Neisser (1980) points out—and I argued earlier—that when a complex new mental or physical skill is internalized, it is then performed chiefly without thinking, leaving the conscious mind free to attend to more immediate matters. Conscious activity and tacit activity take place for all intents and purposes in parallel, as mind, body, and signs move along, doing their thing. Consequently, there is hardly any procedure for defining the capacities of the brain-mind because they never stand still long enough for their limits to be determined. In fact, the brain-mind is a hopeless muddle compared to a computer. The brain-mind's knowing *how* is nonlinear rather than linear, multiply parallel rather than serial, partly non-Boolean rather than strictly Boolean. Boolean logic works as it ideally should only if the information being processed is complete and consistent. For better or for worse, in contrast, one of these two requirements is always unfulfilled regarding the affairs of the brain-mind (see Campbell 1989; Layzer 1990; Penrose 1989).

73

The fundamental nature of human understanding as well as the distinction it implies between knowing *that* and knowing *how* forces itself onto the scene at this juncture. Gödel's proof of the undecidability of mathematical statements by means of some preassigned set of precise formal rules and procedures particularly applies to machines. It demonstrates that there is no programmable, automatic, algorithmic method for generating true and nothing but true propositions from within a formal system. Most likely, humans doing mathematics are also limited to Gödel's strictures. Yet it is indeed remarkable that Gödel's very argument offers up to the mathematician's gaze a specific arithmetical proposition whose truth she, following the argument, can see, intuit, and understand, even though she may not be capable at each stage of simultaneously holding every aspect of the argument in her mind—recall Findlay's sentence, a natural-language embodiment, though much less complex, of a Gödelian sentence.[10] "But why," Roger Penrose (1987, 270) asks,

> can one not simply get a computer also to follow this Gödel argument and itself "see" the truth of any new Gödel proposition? The catch lies in "seeing" that the Gödel argument, in any specific realization, has actually been correctly applied. The trouble is that the computer does not have a way of judging truth; it is only following rules. It does not "see" the validity of the Gödel procedure—or, indeed, to *see* the validity of *any* mathematical procedure—one must be conscious. One can follow rules without being conscious,

but how does one *know* that those rules are legitimate rules to follow
without being, at least at some stage, conscious of their meaning?[11]

Minsky's computer hardware that enjoys artistic, philosophical, and
everyday commonsensical sensibilities is thus placed in question. Humans, to
be sure, are capable of embedded, automatized activity, mindlessly following
rules according to an inflexible algorithmic program. Our hard-wired counterpart, the machine, can do us better in this regard by an exponential factor, however. On the other hand, understanding, artistic appraisal, and judgment of truth
all require—in addition to propositional-computational knowing *that*—knowing *how,* which somehow entails a sense of the whole of things. Such comprehension solicits the aid of intuition and sentiment rather than mere automatic
response; tacit perceptual judgment and inferential reasoning rather than mindlessly following rules; understanding of the whole rather than programmed,
linear accumulation of bits and pieces of information; and moral, aesthetic, and
ethical assessment rather than algorithmic generativity (Dreyfus and Dreyfus
1986).[12]

This is certainly not to say that our kingfisher, who mindlessly obeys
the dictates of her instincts, is merely a Cartesian machine in contrast to humans. Although she exercises neither conscious control of her range of responses
nor the inferential reasoning processes available to her *Homo sapiens* neighbors, she nonetheless possesses a remarkable capacity to handle her environment and to survive. She is no mere machine but possesses her own sensibilities,
which, radically distinct from those of humans, endow her with her own semiotic
capabilities.

Besides, humans depend more on knowing *how* than we would like to
admit—even when taking Hanson's thesis into due consideration—which accounts for expansive common ground between ourselves and other semiotic
organisms. Consequently, our verbal explanations, which draw from knowing
that—explicit knowledge (the tip of the iceberg)—are often unreliable because
a large part of our knowing is left tacit. Whitehead, coauthor of the *Principia
Mathematica* (1910), later conceded that underneath what appears to be the
stark simplicity of ordinary language lies a wealth of implicit knowledge unavailable to ordinary formal rules and strategies—and he subsequently left logic
for good. Our tacit background knowledge of rabbits, for example, is virtually
endless, ranging from molecular biology to zoology to ecology and animal hus-
bandry, and from Walt Disney cartoons to *Alice in Wonderland* to Easter com-
mercialism to *Playboy* magazines to Australia, the American West, hunting,
and culinary habits, not to mention the rabbit's relation to ducks—following
Wittgenstein's example—and so on. Given the pragmatic maxim, that is, the
holistic nature of language, the univocal or ultimate meaning (logical inter-

pretant) of a sentence such as "Rabbits are cute" calls for an untold series of supporting sentences qualifying it. A well-intentioned logician confidently setting out to analyze the sentence would soon drown in a deluge of sentences generating other sentences.

The upshot is that propositional knowing *that* endows humans with a remarkable capacity for understanding their understanding and for communicating it to others. Nevertheless, when put into words, this understanding inexorably remains to a greater or lesser degree fuzzy. Indeed, the highest achievements of humankind in the social sciences, the humanities, and the arts cannot but be vague due to their very nature; hence if a program were written to compute them, the product could not but be misleading. On the other hand, if a particular theory of the mind's workings were by happenstance correct, and if a computer were doggedly programmed like the mind—by a mind, of course—that program, if consistent, would demand at some point that a program from somewhere "outside" it be written in order that its consistency might be determined. Thus the program could not but be incomplete—i.e., Gödel's incompleteness theorem. It would be incapable of accounting for the mind's workings in its totality. In this vein, Lynn Baker (1987, 50) observes that

75

> it does not follow—and it is surely false—that views that cannot be realized in computational terms are incomplete or vague; nor does it follow that views that can be realized in computational terms are complete or precise. On the one hand, to characterize, say, Aristotle's views on virtue as incomplete or vague is to impose a standard of completeness or precision inappropriate to the subject matter, a standard that it would be impossible for any view on that subject matter to meet, and then to criticize the best views for not meeting it. The effect of such methodological imperialism is simply to stipulate that certain areas of deep human interest are intellectually suspect.

Our kingfisher, of course, knows precisely *how* to zero in on her prey and does so with neither hesitation nor a shadow of doubt. There is no vagueness here, no uncertainty. In Peirce's words: "The instincts of the lower animals answer to their purposes much more unerringly than a discursive [propositional, computational] understanding could do. But for man discourse of reason is requisite, because men are so intensely individualistic, and original that the instincts, which are racial ideas, become smothered in them" (CP, 1.178). In fact, so-called "lower" organisms who know little to no theory on any subject whatsoever seldom fall into serious errors—from their perspective, at least.[13] And they know enough animal psychology instinctively to find food and a mate, build a nest, hive, or lair of some sort, raise offspring, and occasionally commit mass suicide and engage in maniacal wars against other species. This is somewhat comparable in the human organism to the stomach's "knowing how" to digest food and the heart's "knowing how" to beat, while knowing *that* in a propositional and even computational sense is left to the physiologist and biophysicist.

More specifically, bees instinctively know *how* to construct the hexagonal wax enclosures that will house their young and best suits the purpose of their species in complete ignorance of the physicist's knowledge *that* the construction of their hive naturally follows certain geometrical principles. In other words, the organism knows *how* to do something, though this knowledge is by no stretch of the imagination theoretical. Knowing *how* is something at the most basic level akin to what Socrates dubbed the "right opinion" (*doxa*). Or, in the human animal, perhaps this knowing *how* at the most basic level is the product of a Peircean *abductive,* but equally instinctive, flight of fancy prior to the dialogical, dialectical agonistics leading to a general consensus *that* the *abduction* is correct.

Let us, then, dwell for a moment on *abduction,* which over the long haul may aid us in comprehending the import of our kingfisher's remarkable capacity to know.[14]

Is Reason, in Whatever Style, Enough?

Although the empiricist side of Peirce winces at the mention of innate ideas, according to his postulate of a continuity between nature and mind and between mind and body, he makes no categorical break between the well-reasoned and logical formulation of a concept and that *feel,* familiar to us all, for what is correct: *abduction* thus takes its rightful place beside induction and deduction. If there are no innate ideas, at least there is, Peirce argues, an innate tendency for the mind to hit upon the correct answer in the face of a bewildering array of possible answers. And if innate ideas there must be, an idea's innateness most certainly "admits of degree, for it consists of the tendency of the idea to present itself to the mind" (CP, 6.416).[15]

When the mind faces a problem, it begins searching for an answer, ignoring largely irrelevant data and homing in on more probable avenues, looking where it senses, feels, or intuits a solution must lie in wait. The process occurs at conscious and nonconscious levels, as reports from those who have had great insights testify. For example, Poincaré (1952, 39) writes of "the subliminal self" that is "in no way inferior to the conscious self; it is not purely automatic; it is capable of discernment; it has tact, delicacy; it knows how to choose, to divine." Poincaré's observation echoes Peirce's notion, interspersed throughout his texts, that it is quite reasonable—though unfalsifiable—to assume the mind has a "*natural light* or *light of nature,* or *instinctive insight,* or genius" that allows it to arrive at the correct answer. This is to be expected, for, Peirce tells us, the three categories of thought and the very existence of thought itself depend upon the fact that "human thought necessarily partakes of whatever character is diffused through the whole universe, and that its natural modes have some tendency to be the modes of action of the universe" (CP, 1.351). Why should the mind not be as much a part of nature as anything else? If it is, then there is no reason to believe that it must be reduced to computerlike trial-and-error guesses when striving to comprehend nature.

Of the three kinds of reasoning, corresponding to deduction, induction, and abduction, the first is necessary, "but it only professes to give us information concerning the matter of our own hypotheses and distinctly declares that, if we want to know anything else, we must go elsewhere." The second depends upon probabilities, which can give no guarantees but, "like an insurance company, an endless multitude of insignificant risks." And the third is that "which lit the foot-steps of Galileo. . . . It is really an appeal to instinct. Thus reason, for all the frills it customarily wards, in vital crises, comes down upon its marrow-bones to beg the succor of instinct" (CP, 1.630). From the rational mind to the instinctive mind, thought occurs by one style of reason or another along the continuum from consciousness to nonconsciousness, from explicitness to implicitness, and from knowing *that* to knowing *how*. In a manner of speaking, the rational mind is immature, while the instinctive mind is mature (Rochberg-Halton 1986, 10–11).

The abductive inferences of the instinctive mind, of concrete reasonableness, are "acritically indubitable," though "invariably vague," since at the outset they are usually plagued with inconsistencies, and they are radically fallible as long as they are not given deductive scaffolding and put to the inductive test (CP, 5.441–66). On the other hand, the rational mind is capable of progressing toward ever greater generality, but in spite of its Faustian, modernist desires for control and absolute knowledge, and given its finitude, the critical inferences that it generates are destined to remain incomplete.

Unfortunately, the modern tendency to consider Cartesian introspection, rational argumentation, logical proof, and direct, objective, empirical "facts" as the final arbiters of knowledge ignores "sentiment," a feel for what is right, and concrete reasonableness, which are the source of all new knowledge by way of abduction (CP, 1.615, 5.433). Suppression of (instinctive, habituated, embedded) knowing *how* by favoring (rational, propositional-computational) knowing *that* cannot but terminate in Whitehead's (1925) "fallacy of misplaced concreteness." It may well be that knowing *how,* by (1) the instinctive mind, and especially by (2) the sinking into nonconsciousness of explicit propositional and computational practices to become second nature, is a greater achievement of humankind than the conscious, intentional workings of the rational mind. Regarding (2), the capacity to view a Necker cube and other two-dimensional objects as three-dimensional, to encapsulate three-dimensional phenomena on a canvas with cubist techniques, to conceive of the earth as round and traveling around the sun, to take $\sqrt{-1}$ for granted in descriptions of "real-world" happenings, to accept infinity and the continuum as an intuitive matter of fact, are by no means negligible accomplishments when considering human cultures at large.

Of course, the rational mind can certainly not go unignored. It has been able to explain, say, why a stick in water is still straight rather than bent, as it appears to the senses; and, by means of Snell's law, it provides the computational power to determine the angle of the apparent "bend" of the stick with remarkable precision. The rational mind uses its own style of reason quite effectively as far as it can go. But it inevitably reaches a stalemate when two solutions to a problem appear equally plausible and equally verifiable. Then that other part of the mind, its instinctive, abductive, sensitive, nature—the poet in us, as Nietzsche would have it—takes over. Intuition defies control by reason and logic. The concept of a safe, indubitable, and infallible body of knowledge grounded in "reason" has been the dream of Western thought since the Greeks. But such sureties are apparently not of this world. Freely created mental constructs can appear to hold great promise, of course, but blindly to follow the lead of the rational mind, come what may, would surely end in sheer lunacy. No theory could be logically tighter than Zeno's paradoxes, Bradley's idealism, McTaggart's argument against time, or Einstein's relativity of time and curvature of space. However, a community's attempt literally to live its everyday life in accord with these purely mind-generated theoretical frameworks would surely end in despair. The intuitive mind tells us that such crystalline and apparently infallible logic and "reason" are not of the practical world of work and play.

In short, there must be an ongoing give-and-take, a dialogue, between the rational mind and the intuitive mind. Reason, whatever its countenance may be, frees one from instinct's demands, and instinct saves reason's skin when it obstinately reasons itself into blind alleys. The intellectual progress of a community quite content with its state of rational knowledge would virtually grind to a halt; and a community trusting instinct alone would be devoid of the dialogic interaction necessary for the growth and development of knowledge, which serves to decrease the viscosity of an otherwise molasses-flow of evolution. The biggest dividends are realized by the interaction between both minds. Such interaction renders instinct "capable of development and growth" occurring along lines "which are altogether parallel to those of reasoning" (CP, 1.648).

Regarding both minds, what is newly known as well as what is known anew is available to conscious awareness not immediately but mediately, and it arises out of a constant dialogic interaction between knowing *how* and knowing *that,* the topic to which I now turn.

Toward Melting the Oppositions

Psychologist J. J. Gibson (1950, 1966, 1979) argues that perception is direct and immediate, not mediated: a matter of relatively low-level psychophysiological mechanisms so constituted that they will automatically take in the information essential to an organism's survival. The relevant information is simply presented through photons of light bouncing off an object and received by the organism without the necessity of high-level inferences or cerebral schemata. The information is "out there" in the world and merely needs to be gathered. There is no need to operate on it or actively process it, no need for prior knowledge or expectations for proper recognition to occur. Simply put, what is *seen* is what there *is* (though it is a selection, since an organism cannot take in the totality of all possible information from its environment). In this sense, Galileo and Tycho Brahe actually *saw* the same sun, and the case is closed.

79

Gibson is clearly a champion of modernist representationalism. That is to say, if what is *seen* is what there *is,* then seeing *as* can be effectively described, the descriptive language potentially being a faithful mirror of the mind and of the world. Gibson is also quite removed from the tenets of cognitive psychology. In current cognitive practice, it is the processes associated with a problem that tend to determine its assignment to a psychological category. Sensation, perception, and conception are increasingly complex operations performed by an organism on stimuli as they travel from the peripheral receptors to the cortex. Eventually these stimuli will be transformed from mere seeing to seeing *as* and into a state either of knowing *how* or knowing *that.* In this sense, the term "cognition"

> refers to all the processes by which the sensory input is transformed, reduced, elaborated, stored, recovered and used. It is concerned with these processes even when they operate in the absence of relevant stimulation, as in images and hallucinations. Such terms as sensation, perception, imagery, retention, recall, problem-solving, and thinking, among others, refer to hypothetical stages or aspects of cognition. (Neisser 1967, 4)

The point is that immediate seeing never stands alone; it is part of the composite of sensations mediated and modified appropriately by seeing *as.* Psychologist Richard Gregory (1972, 707) concurs, adding that perceptions are not simply selections of reality "but are rather imaginative constructions. . . . On this view all perceptions are essentially fictions: fictions based on past experience selected by present sensory data." Neisser would in turn applaud Gregory's move. We have no "direct, immediate access to the world, nor to any of its properties." The venerable concept of direct copies of "real-world" things in the mind is rejected wholesale (Neisser 1967, 3).

The link between contemporary psychology and Peirce's thought receives yet another echo from Jerome Bruner. For Bruner, perception is an act of categorization. As a matter of course, we customarily go "beyond the information given" by inferring that a new object perceived belongs to a familiar cate-

gory, even though the new object differs from, in more respects than it resembles, other examples of the class of the same objects that we have previously encountered. We identify a speck on the horizon emitting a plume of smoke as a ship, just as we do a towering transatlantic liner at the docks, or a few schematic lines slashed onto a piece of paper. With no more than a few cues, we generally

> go beyond them to the inference of identity. Having done so, we infer that the instance so categorized or identified has the other properties characteristic of membership in a category. Given the presence of certain cues of shape, size, and texture, we infer that the thing before us is an apple; *ergo,* it can be eaten, cut with a knife, it relates by certain principles [*sic*] of classification to other kinds of fruits, and so on. (Bruner 1957, 42)

Bruner's "constructivist" view, it hardly needs saying, is radically nonrepresentational, and hence nonmodernist. The mind is no "mirror of nature"; there is no realism of the naive sort. The furniture of the world is not susceptible to a new perceptual grasp at each immediate present. Rather, perception and conception—both semiotic through and through—are mediated, the result of tacit to conscious inferential processes of seeing things *as* such-and-such, *that* they are so-and-so, and knowing *how* to do what is ordinarily done with them.

Gibson's radically simple orientation to perception has been contested further by, among others, Shimon Ullman (1979, 1980) and Jerry Fodor and Zenon Pylyshyn (1981). The latter, particularly, play cognitivism off against Gibson's somewhat behaviorist Skinnerian approach and conclude that Gibson's explanation of why objects are perceived the way they are is devoid of theoretical validity. It is not enough to posit that the first cave dweller directly perceiving a rock as a weapon was able to do so because it was "grabbable" and "hurlable." No account is provided concerning how such apprehension can occur without any sort of inferential process. If there is Gibsonian neutral information from the rock to the cave man, it cannot be relevant to weapon properties without inferential reasoning, and if the information is inferred by the perceiver to possess weapon properties, then it is no longer neutral.

This anti-Gibson view, which holds that perception simply cannot be accounted for with anything less than a cognitive approach, is somewhat like Peirce's inferential mediation by way of Thirdness. A rock-as-weapon is a mental construct, the creation of a semiotically real object in a somewhat altered world. It is a matter already of seeing something *as* such-and-such instead of what it would have been by conventional wisdom. This inferential process can then be made most adequately explicit and intelligible, in the human sense at least, in propositional or computational terms. But if we take Peirce at face value regarding visual perception, seeing *as* already involves, as for Kant, categories of space and time serving to filter and structure incoming stimuli. Such involvement is common to all species, not merely the human semiotic animal. How does the kingfisher know her prey is actually not where it appears to be due to the altered diffraction of light in the H_2O medium? How does a lioness pursuing an antelope know at what angle to run in order to intercept it at some further point? How is a two-dimensional photograph tacitly seen *as* a human face by a human being? Or a group of lines on a flat surface tacitly abstracted into a Necker cube?

81

Returning to the theme with which I opened this inquiry, postmodernism, in contrast to modernism, is a foregrounding of, and perhaps even a loose effort to come to grips with, *tacitly* known—though not neutral—happenings as a result of intuition, sentiment, gut reaction, spontaneity, process and participation, difference and divergence (Huyssen 1986, 53–54). Quite understandably, the celebration of difference, of *différance,* pervades postmodern work of the 1970s: *différance* as freedom, unbridled imagination, Kantian spontaneity of the will, where, in Nietzsche's vision, Dionysus replaces Apollo, creativity replaces hard-nosed reason.

Peirce was generally in sympathy with this view. However, he believed both tacit seeing *as* and computational-propositional seeing *that* to be inferential, whether by conscious or nonconscious pathways. Like Hanson, Peirce held that seeing is always and invariably interpreting. It is, in other words, hermeneutical: interpretation loaded with all the prejudices of which one may be aware or not. There is no modernist hierarchy at work valuing either observation language or theoretical language, seeing naively or seeing from an interpretative vantage, objectively collecting data or analyzing it. By the same token, knowing *that* entails some implicit mind processes (knowing *how*) that can be made at least partly explicit by inferential reasoning. In the evolution of a novel conception of one's world, for instance, initial stimuli as quality or feeling are ordinarily converted into action and reaction as one comes into contact with one's physical "reality." If at some point a change occurs in the expected stimuli, one's action and reaction also invariably undergo a change, even though perhaps to a barely perceptible degree. Then, as actions pile onto actions, and after sufficient time, these actions and reactions tend to become embedded and automatized, to sink into nonconsciousness. Eventually evolving into habit, they become part of one's corpus of knowing *how* and nonconscious seeing *as*. Finally, one acquires an altered belief in terms of what one perceives and conceives to be "actually real"—the world as it is and could not be otherwise—until one is confronted by a new "shock" of surprise, at which point one may be forced to reevaluate one's seeing *as* and knowing *how*.[16] In this sense at least, Peirce is neither modern nor postmodern but somewhere in between; his general theory of signs encompasses both the instinctive mind and the rational mind, both knowing *how* and knowing *that*, as well as the emergence of novel knowing.

Further specification of the ongoing interaction between knowing *how* and knowing *that* confirms the relevance of Peirce's thought. Certain AI researchers have noted (e.g., Marr 1979, 1982) that visual computation entails preprocessing at the retinal level that groups lines, points, junctures, chunks, and blobs together in diverse ways to separate figures from grounds. Such computations are thus constructive, interpretive processes carried out by a symbol-manipulating system that complements incoming stimuli from a physical receptor. Margaret Boden (1984, 159), after discussing this general theory of computational interpretive processes, observes that it "is plausible that many species have evolved . . . implicit computational constraints. That is, the animal's mind may implicitly embody knowledge about its external environment, which knowledge is used by it in its perceptual interpretations."

For instance, our kingfisher may have some sort of operational grasp of the refractive properties of water. The same is true of, say, migratory birds' possessing an innate sense of the earth's magnetic field or constellations. What I am speaking of here is, of course, *inborn* tacit knowing *how* rather than knowing *that*. In contrast, *noninnate* tacit—yet inferential—*knowledge* of the human variety entails, at its more explicit levels, learning in large part by instruction that later becomes embedded and automatized. That is to say, as I argued above, the relatively explicit aspects of learning to play a piano, for example, can submerge into nonconsciousness to become knowing *how*. And as the piano player continues to exercise her talent, she tacitly takes on new skills and strategies, some of which tend to gravitate beyond her conscious computational and propositional knowledge: she increasingly comes to know more than she can tell.

Our kingfisher, an expert mathematician, or an accomplished pianist all know *how* to exercise their craft. However, in contrast to the mathematician and the pianist, part of whose knowledge was once explicit but has gradually become embedded, the bird's ability to home in on its target remains quite independent of propositional or computational skills. Yet she is in possession of a mechanism, the equivalent of such skills, that enables her to know the position of the fish at varying depths in the water. Boden (1984, 161) suggests that these are "low-level processes," physical skills or visual computations rather than cerebral computations. But our accomplished pianist has over the years also embedded skills and strategies that now are beyond her ability to put them explicitly into propositional form. So where, precisely, is the distinction between human and bird?

The kingfisher's perceptual mechanism innately endows her with the ability to "compute" the depth and position of fish in water, and she always does so with hardly any deviation from her accustomed behavioral pathways. In fact, only rarely is she able to change the ways of her seeing *as* and knowing *how*. In contrast, her human counterparts, many of whose skills are in part learned by verbal instruction, can with relative ease alter their perception. We even learn to "see" and "know" things about what is not really there. Ernst Gombrich's (1960) fascinating work demonstrates how art perception has constantly shifted, occasionally to become radically transformed throughout history. Psychologists and phenomenologists such as Richard Gregory (1966, 1970, 1981), Don Ihde (1977), and Irwin Rock (1983) argue that our acquired modes of perception force us to see visual anomalies where none exist and to see diagrams as logically constructed, though they are actually out of kilter. Witness, for example, M. C. Escher's (1971) work, which plays havoc with our preconceived expectations regarding spatial order. And certain writers, chief among whom is Borges, create the same cognitive perturbations through literature (see Merrell 1991c).

Since the eyes of other more developed mammalian species are not very different from the human eye, one would expect them to obtain virtually the same optical information from a painting or a photograph as a human. Yet apparently no animal recognizes a painting as a model of reality, no matter how naturalistic it might appear to us. The chief reason for this deficiency is that animals cannot voluntarily disregard the sensory input informing them that the picture is merely an indifferent piece of cloth—one merely need recall the legendary grapes of Zeuxis, icons that were taken as real rather than replicas. The intentional disregard for certain channels of information, this willing suspension of disbelief, is most characteristically a human ability necessary for the processing of such symbolic information as paintings, literature, the stage, film, and, one must suppose, in the ability to lie or deceive with remarkable ease and to catch others in their acts of subterfuge.

Unlike such human learning and alteration of perceptual modes, then, the tacit knowledge instinctively built into nonhuman organisms is relatively fixed. If the kingfisher were to encounter fish adapted to life in a liquid with a

83

different index of refraction, like the frog in the presence of immobile flies, she would most likely starve to death. "This assumes," Boden (1984, 162) writes,

> that the kingfisher utilizes an inborn visuometer coordination, linking the perceptual active aspects of its *Umwelt,* a coordination that is not only innate but unalterable. Psychological experiments on human beings, and comparable studies of chimps, show that these species by contrast can learn to adjust to some stylistic distortions of the physics of the visual field.

The upshot is that humans, kingfishers, and for that matter all organisms, are to a greater or lesser degree lay physicists: we all possess implicit knowledge, innately or by learning, of the workings of physical objects and signs in the world. Of course, humans have Copernicus, Newton, and Einstein; Gauguin, Picasso, and Duchamp; Goethe, Shakespeare, and Beckett. Other species do not. Moreover, perception for the human semiotic animal, who has acquired a sophisticated level of language use, can hardly be divorced from propositional and even computational operations. This necessitates a break—most likely of degree rather than of kind—between the human *Umwelt* and animal *Umwelten.*

Once natural language enters the cognitive scene, however, there are no longer merely semantic primitives (*tones* and *tokens*) but, in addition, abstract concepts (*types*). Universals cannot be equated, nor are they compatible, with any aspect of the kingfisher's knowing *how* to catch a fish. When the attempt is made to articulate the kingfisher's semiotic world, linguistic window dressing invariably anthropomorphizes the whole affair. Primitive sensorimotor activity is hopelessly separated from language-bound inferential processes.

George Miller and P. N. Johnson-Laird (1976) make this separation in their pyscholinguistic study of the propositional-computational base of language ability. They describe how perceptual discriminatory procedures can function as semantic anchoring, giving words meaning in terms of relations. Such propositions as "x is in y," "x is to the left of y," "x is behind y," "x is larger than y," and "x is moving faster than y" can be procedurally defined as visible spatial relationships. This is no simple matter. Relations such as "in," "behind," "faster than," and "larger than" are exceedingly complex. Apes who learn to put bananas inside and take them out of boxes, to stack boxes on top of one another in order to reach bananas, and to use sticks to draw bananas toward them from outside their cage have internalized such complex perceptual computations, which would remain entirely outside the capacity of other animals. Moreover, apes purportedly learning the rudiments of a language vaguely comparable to natural language, it has been claimed, do so analytically rather than propositionally or computationally.[17]

When we provisionally relate this notion to Peircean semiotics—the topic will be taken up in detail in Chapter Six—*iconic* relations entail some significant correspondence by similarity, or more abstractly by homology or isomorphism, between the structure of the sign (representamen) and the structure of the semiotic object. *Indexical* relations call for relations by extension—such as cause-effect, part-whole, and container-contained—between the sign and that of which it is a sign. On the other hand, more complex propositional or computational (*symbolic*) relations need not enjoy direct linkage; they can be arbitrary. Thus the symbolic representamen does not always reflect the structure of the semiotic object itself. Rather, it reflects the operation or procedure (inferential or other cognitive process) by means of which the object is signified. Iconic and indexical relations are understood at conscious, embedded, and chiefly—though not necessarily—implicit levels, which can then be made at least partly available to discursive thought. In contrast, to understand a symbolic relation is explicitly to *interpret* it (generate an interpretant) so as to establish a link between a representamen and its object. The symbolic mode, then, *is* discursive thought *par excellence*.

85

This is not to imply that upon our opening our innocent eyes and looking at the big wide world "out there" we can finally get things right once and for all, and that tough-minded discursive thought can save the day by describing what we see and making explicit what was implicit. In contrast to the modernist obsession with representation by correspondence and the elucidation and interpretation of structures, structures should be more appropriately—and from the postmodernist vantage point—looked upon as invariably embodied and embedded (Hawles 1974). That is to say, interrelationships between structures are customarily automatically seen *as* (interpreted), and they are always part of knowing *how*. Consequently, instead of direct reference of the positivist (modern) variety, there is multivalued (postmodern) semiotic interlinkage; instead of correspondence, there is fit or complementarity; instead of finality (truth), there is ongoing *semiosis*.

Knowing Vaguely

I now return to Hanson, who navigated against the current of logical empiricism in championing a Peirce-inspired "logic of discovery."[18] Upon developing his postmodernist "non-picture-picture" theory of discovery, Hanson (1971, 358–74) tells the tale of the perennial human desire to fly, from mythical times onward (see also Merrell 1992, chap. 8). He warns the reader at the outset that the story he presents cannot be considered final. A scientific theory—or any other explanation-interpretation—cannot be determinate, for theories are context-dependent instruments of conceptualization.

As Hanson's story goes, during ancient times birds' wings were the object of concrete iconic representations of flying machines. But nature is deceptive. It was long assumed that since all birds flap their wings, flapping wings must be essential for any flying machine. To the question, What do birds do in flight to remain aloft? Leonardo da Vinci responded that they bring their wings down so swiftly that the air is compressed, offering increased resistance, and thus they are buoyed upward. After various experimental disasters by da Vinci, years later, Newton's laws of force relegated the project of human flight to the trash heap.

But not for long. With Daniel Bernouilli's study of hydrodynamics and the conception of a winglike object in a fluid—air being analogous *to* the fluid—the possibility of flight took on new meaning. It was conjectured that wings must be curved so that the air could move faster across the top than the bottom, which serves to increase the pressure below and decrease the pressure above, thus causing a partial vacuum and providing lift. The wing, it was concluded, need not flap at all but can remain stationary. By further analogy between wing-flapping birds and soaring birds, it was eventually discovered that the secret of flight lies in the physical relation between the airfoil section and its camber and the relative wind: the principle is the same, whether considering a flapping wing, a stationary wing, or the variable wings of rotating helicopter blades.

Hanson's theory concentrates on patterns and relations: the essence of Peirce's "diagrammatic thinking" (see M. Gardner 1968). The upshot is that just as the recognition of *perceptual* patterns at once gives significance to elements perceived and yet differs from any perception of dots, shapes, and lines, so also the recognition of *conceptual* patterns gives significance to the empirical elements within a theory and yet differs from any awareness of those elements vis-à-vis their primary relationship to things and events. Hanson argues, like the above comments on Wittgenstein, that the *Tractatus'* "picture theory" dwells inordinately on links between linguistic tokens and physical objects at the expense of structural or relational connections.

During this process, the ensuing resemblances are not visually substantive but formal, even at times ornamental, in terms of surface patterns. Significantly enough, Hanson brings his theory in line with the later Wittgenstein, who discarded the "picture theory," with its ambitious dream of formalizability, for his notion of language games, which entail vague and partly inarticulable "family resemblances." In this manner, Hanson's account provides for a natural development from relatively imprecise *shapes* and *images* to *algebraic formula-clusters* following natural lines of formalization within a particular framework. Each step in the process is in varying degrees explicit, though, like language games, the development is context-dependent, and the final outcome is available only in retrospect.

Hanson thus concludes that: (1) the visual shapes (icons) and the graphs and diagrams (indices) developed from them are informative as structural representations of the aerodynamics of a wing section; (2) there is no real structural difference between images, graphed lines, and diagrammatic forms on the one hand, and algebraic formulations on the other; and (3) the algebra "is *eo ipso* informative as a structural representation of the original subject matter" (Hanson 1971, 24).[19] At the same time, the inexorable tacit component of all context-dependent culturally and conventionally embedded language games serves to limit explication of the implicit. In this sense, there is, and there will always be, an important component of knowing *how*, for seeing is always in large part seeing *as*, and what is known and said is always more or less embedded and embodied in the semiotic activity of the knower and sign user.

Snell's equation in the kingfisher cartoon is symbolic in this regard, while a line drawn from the bird's eye to the water at an angle $\varnothing$ with respect to a perpendicular line is an iconic re-presentation of an indexical relation, or more specifically, a type of diagram—which, with images and metaphors, makes up Peirce's *hypoicons* (CP, 2.276–77, 2.320). Symbolic form qualifies chiefly as propositional or computational thinking; iconic form, chiefly as implicit or tacit thinking. The first is digital; the second is chiefly analogue and synthetic. The first entails knowing *that* in addition to knowing *how;* the second largely entails knowing *how.*

There is, very broadly speaking, a conjunction of modern and postmodern attitudes here. Both are ultimately necessary. And significantly, Peirce's thought is a combination of the two. Peirce was a scientist, logician, and mathematician—an explicator, a propositional-computational thinker. But he was also an analogical (iconic) and diagrammatic thinker, keen on schemata, patterns, relations, and wholes, all of which entail and imply quality, feeling, and tacit knowing—the concreteness of everyday life. Peirce's conscious self-control, guided by deliberate or intellectual conduct, is related to what I have called propositional-computational thought, while immediate, nonconscious, tacit or implicit, and spontaneous conduct is qualitative, the product of feeling (CP, 2.277, 3.418–20, 4.74–77). The former is chiefly knowing *that;* the latter is chiefly knowing *how.* The former highlights Thirdness and deduction, following from induction; Firstness and abduction, which leads to induction, are foregrounded in the latter. Peirce never forgot either feeling or intellection, instinct or self-control, concreteness or abstraction—all remained neatly tied in his notion of concrete reasonableness.

To be sure, the leading principle—i.e., the law determining the relation of the sign to its object and its interpretant—of proper thinking must involve conscious, critical, and controlled conduct: "It is not essential that the observer should have a distinct apprehension of the leading principle of the habit which governs his reasoning; it is sufficient that he should be conscious of proceeding according to a general method and that he should hold that the method is generally apt to lead to the truth" (CP, 2.589). Indeed, in 1902 Peirce set out the two functions of pragmatism: (1) the elimination of nonintellectual concepts, primarily from mathematics, logic, philosophy, and science; and (2) the development of the meaning of intellectual concepts. Pragmatism, in Peirce's view, is above all a method for becoming conscious of one's conduct, for achieving clarity of thought. But this becoming of consciousness is itself a further development of concrete reasonableness (CP, 5.4; also 5.423, 433). Hence it is doubly necessary to be mindful that there is a difference, and perpetual interaction, between immediate consciousness (feeling, knowing *how*) and intellectual consciousness (knowledge in the objective sense, knowing *that*), between the intuitive mind and the rational mind, between involuntary conduct and well-reasoned conduct, nonconscious inference and conscious inference—even though a line of demarcation between these modes can hardly be established once and for all (CP, 5.442, 4.531).[20] Interaction between these two tendencies constitutes an incessant push from the indeterminate toward the relatively determined.

On this note, let us turn more directly to Peirce with an eye on the relationship between knowing *how* and knowing *that*.

PART

Two

Up and down the Semiotic Staircase

An overriding problem regarding posited relations between Peirce and
postmodernism is that, *prima facie,* modernism's obsessive focus on intellection, abstraction, objectivity, and control, belying an unwavering faith in
episteme, also appears to characterize Peirce's thought. Postmodernism's often
implicit admonishment, "Stop trying to make sense of things and simply go
along with the flow," seems in large part alien to Peirce's *modus operandi:* he
always tried to make sense of things by systematically carving out a method
and following it to the letter. On the other hand, his antifoundationalist posture,
developed through reliance on indeterminism, feeling, sentiment, and tacit or
nonconscious inference, are quite "unmodern." In good Peircean spirit, the way
of abstraction need not necessarily culminate, in the fashion of modernism, with
lifeless taxonomies, rigid hierarchies, and static, synchronic slices out of the
flow of things. The chief watchwords are *process, evolution,* and *generation.*

From Whitehead's teachings we learn that, though we are condemned
to abstractions—that felicitous paradise of unmediated objects having been long
lost—we can at least maintain a posture of vigilant suspicion toward them,
focusing on how they fit into the big picture. Likewise, Peirce's emphasis rests
not on content, essence, or substance, but, more properly, on dynamic relations.
Events, not *things,* are highlighted. Things are what they are only fleetingly, as
they pass on and into their own alterity; hence to say what a thing *is* is invariably to say what it *is not.* Events, in contrast, *happen.* They are fluid rather than
corpuscular-kinetic; they defy specification rather than make a plea for it; they
slip through one's fingers without further ado rather than give one the illusory
promise that they are *there* and waiting. This processual view, as opposed to
modernism's fetishism of the abstract, is the general drift motivating a Peirce-
inspired "formalism," which, the reader will note—perhaps with a tinge of surprise, bewilderment, or even alarm—is characteristic of the present and
especially succeeding chapters.

In this spirit, I would suggest that whatever formalist trappings may
be found in these pages are not abstractive in the modernist sense but
interrelational, portraying generativity rather than taxonomization, process rather
than stasis, perpetual disequilibria and destabilization rather than balance and
harmony. The formalisms are not a determination merely of what *there is* but

what *might be* or *would be,* or at most, of *how* things *can be.* In other words, I attempt to give a rough account of the ongoing sign process—I say rough, since in any attempt to rope and hog-tie it, the wily sign always takes a turn down unexpected pathways. In this sense, by using Peirce's classification of signs, I hope to offer an illustration of signs incessantly becoming other signs. Let us begin, then, with . . .

The Triads

92 At the outset, one might wish, however, to protest: "Classifications are never innocent but streaked with arbitrariness and motivated by preconceptions and prejudices. Besides, they are constantly shifting, whether by design or in spite of our efforts to capture them."

And I agree. This problem is made jocularly—though perhaps all too painfully—evident with Borges's (1964, 103) Chinese encyclopaedia, mentioned in passing in Chapter Two and the focus of Michel Foucault's (1970, xv) notorious commentary, that divides animals into a bizarre set of categories:

> (a) belonging to the Emperor, (b) embalmed, (c) tame, (d) sucking pigs, (e) sirens, (f) fabulous, (g) stray dogs, (h) included in the present classification, (i) frenzied, (j) innumerable, (k) drawn with a very fine camelhair brush, (l) *et cetera,* (m) having just broken the water-pitcher, (n) that from a very long way off look like flies.

There is, of course, something disturbing here. Not only does the monstrous catalogue not allow recourse to any ordering principle outside itself—a characteristic of taxonomies the world over—but, when considering all possible systems of classification as a whole, one realizes that there is neither an anchor with which to stabilize a given classificatory scheme nor a determinate fulcrum with which to dislodge it. "What is impossible," Foucault (1970, xvi) writes of Borges's passage, "is not the propinquity of the things listed, but the very site on which their propinquity would be possible." Foucault terms this radical incommensurability between taxonomies "heterotopia," and in so doing, he quite properly qualifies the centerless universe of postmodernism. On a brighter side, a taxonomy can at least serve as a preliminary stage on the arduous road of inquiry—indeed, is thought even possible without taxonomies?—leading toward a model of generation rather than stultification. With this in mind, I turn to Peirce's sign triads.

While signs of Firstness are immediate experience, the fountainhead of *abductive* insights; and taxonomies themselves are the product of Secondness, a specification of the unstable items of *induction;* the generation of signness in the full sense, the potentiality of what *would be,* Thirdness, charts the way toward generals by convention—*deduction*. In this sense, taxonomies, which emerge from Firstness and offer the hope of a peek into Thirdness, are potentially a springboard to bigger and better things. Peirce's categories are not mere semiological distinctions; neither do they allow for a poststructuralist promiscuity of signifiers. Rather, they are the vehicles of ongoing sign processing. Thus the fundamental Peircean semiotic entity consists of a representamen (sign),[1] a semiotically real (not actually real) object, and an interpretant, each of which is further divided into triads—such as qualisigns, sinsigns, and legisigns; icons, indices, and symbols; and terms, propositions, and arguments (or words, sentences, and texts in current parlance)—corresponding to the categories of Firstness, Secondness and Thirdness (see figure 1).[2]

Ø	Representamen (R)	Object (O)	Interpretant (I)
	FIRST	SECOND	THIRD
	The sign of itself stands as:	The relation of sign to its object is dependent upon:	The sign's representation is:
1st	Qualisign An appearance of quality before there is consciousness of it	Icon Some property shared by its object	Rheme (term) Of quality of feeling
2nd	Sinsign An individual object, act, or event	Index Some actual or imagined relation with its object	Dicisign (proposition) Of statement of presumed fact
3rd	Legisign A general type, law, habit, convention	Symbol Relation to its interpretant (by convention)	Argument Of reason (by law)

Figure One

Briefly, *quale* is tone, feeling, vagueness, that which is as yet devoid of specificity. *Sin* is derived from singularity; it is a *haecceity,* a once-occurring token. *Legi* implies repeated use or replication, which becomes, by habit, a general *type*. An *icon* is any sign that signifies something by way of resemblance

(CP, 3.362) and "refers to the Object that it denotes merely by virtue of characters of its own, and which it possesses, just the same whether any such Object actually exists or not. . . . Anything whatever, be it a quality [Firstness], existent individual [Secondness], or law [Thirdness], is an icon of anything, in so far as it is like that thing and is used as a sign of it" (CP, 2.247). Examples of icons are paintings and caricatures (CP, 2.92), diagrams (CP, 4.418), metaphors (CP, 2.227), and all other exemplifications of objects that they resemble, even if the objects do not actually exist.

94

An *index* "is a representamen which fulfills the function of a representamen by virtue of a character which it could not have if its object did not exist, but which it will continue to have just the same whether it be interpreted as a representamen or not" (CP, 5.37). The index directs the attention of its interpreter to the object because of some semiotically real or contrived connection between it and the object. For example, a weathervane is an index of the wind's direction, and a falling barometer is an index of rain (CP, 2.286). Since there is an actual or semiotically real connection between the index and its object—unlike an icon—the index must provide information regarding its object, though without necessarily describing it.

A *symbol* "is the general name of a description which signifies its object by means of an association of ideas or habitual connection between the

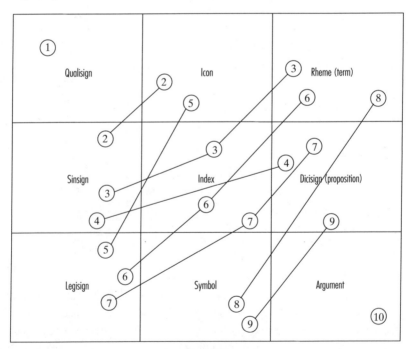

Figure Two

1-1-1	(1) Qualisign	A Sensation of "Blue"
2-1-1	(2) Iconic Sinsign	A Self-contained Diagram
2-2-1	(3) Rhematic Indexical Sinsign	A Spontaneous Cry
2-2-2	(4) Dicent Sinsign	A Weathervane
3-1-1	(5) Iconic Legisign	A Diagram, Apart from its Self-containment
3-2-1	(6) Rhematic Indexical Legisign	A Demonstrative Pronoun
3-2-2	(7) Dicent Indexical Legisign	A Commonplace Evocation or Expression
3-3-1	(8) Rhematic Symbol	A Term
3-3-2	(9) Dicent Symbol	A Proposition
3-3-3	(10) Argument	A Syllogism

Figure Three

name and the character signified" (CP, 1.369). Unlike icons and indices, symbols require no semiotically real or presumed natural connection with their material quality to be signs of the objects they represent. The connection can be purely mental, and in the beginning it is usually at least in part arbitrary. Natural language, quite obviously, is the prime example of symbols. The entire utterance "Quarks are the building blocks of the universe" is a compound symbol made up of various types of symbols relating to a semiotic object. The utterance is invested with the symbolic function by the mind's acquired propensity to associate "quarks," "building blocks," and "universe" with what the mind construes to be the object—an imagined or semiotically real rather than a "real" entity—of the utterance. Every symbol is in this sense an *ens rationis* (CP, 4.464). Its function is that of representing (re-presenting) its object as a result of some mental habit of association between the two.

From the categories of icon-index-symbol, qualisign-sinsign-legisign, and *rheme* (term)-*dicisign* (proposition)-argument, as illustrated in figure 1, Peirce developed his ten fundamental classes of signs (see figures 2 and 3), the interrelationships among which will be the focus of closer attention in Chapter Six. Figure 2 demonstrates how the nine categories from figure 1 combine to make up Peirce's ten basic classes of signs, which are shown in figure 3. The central column of figure 3 provides the nomenclature for the ten signs, the column to the right gives an example of each, and the left-hand column illustrates the composition of the signs, from three categories of Firstness (qualisign) to three of Thirdness (argument).

Admittedly, thus far I have accomplished hardly more than set out a classificatory scheme of debatable value. So on to a consideration of the becoming of the beingness of signs and the beingness of their becoming—which is perhaps the only legitimate way of saying "being" and at the same time not entirely misconstruing *semiosis*.

96

Signs of the Mind

The two questions, What kinds of ideas (i.e., signs) are possible? and How are they engendered in the first place? dogged Peirce to the end. The spectrum of his thought, from loose speculation to rigorous theory-building, can be grouped into two general lines of inquiry, both of which are intimately tied to the categories in figures 1, 2, and 3:

1. *Phaneroscopy,* the study of *phanerons*—signs of inner or mental experience ranging in duration from a fleeting fraction of a second to a lifetime or from generation to generation (in the case of relatively timeless myths, rituals, and archetypes),[3] and

2. *Semiotics,* the more general study of *semiosis* (the process of signs incessantly passing away and coming into existence as other signs).

Though Peirce did not always take pains to make an explicit distinction between phaneroscopy and semiotics, the former focuses on *thought-signs*, while the latter focuses on *sign-events* (sign instantiations "out there") in general (which include, to be sure, thought-signs). That is, the former deals chiefly with inwardly experienced thought-signs; the latter, with sign-thoughts as a result of experienced sign-events in the semiotically real world. But the mind is not to be divorced from the whole of nature, and in the mind, Peirce believed, we can find clues to the nature of the world, hence the internally real should not be categorically separated from either the externally real or the semiotically real.[4] In some respects, phaneroscopy and semiotics constitute the same theory described in complementary languages.

Richard Tursman (1987, 26) calls phaneroscopy a "chemistry of the mind" that "examines the *elements* and *compounds* of thought." While phaneroscopy does not take phanerons to be the equivalent of chemical elements and compounds, they do resemble the elements and compounds in important respects. Moreover, Peirce's use of chemistry is reasonable, since he was, after all, a chemist. He attributed a form of valence to phanerons whereby

Firsts, Seconds, and Thirds have a valence of 1, 2, or 3 (see figure 3). This trinary valence is sufficient for Peirce: a Third, capable of combining with two other elements, can, by repetition, combine with any number of them. "Nothing," Peirce (CP, 1.289) remarks, "could be simpler; nothing in philosophy is more important."

With respect to the combination of Firsts, Seconds, and Thirds by valence, David Savan (1987–88, 14) formulates what he calls the qualification rule: a First is qualified only by a First, a Second by a First or Second, and a Third by all three. Each compound sign can now be identified by a compound number, a First by 1-1, a Second by 2-1 or 2-2, and a Third by 3-1, 3-2, or 3-3. A further sequence of qualifications then yields the ten classes of signs as illustrated in figure 3. Thus signs "grow" by the recursive application of the sign categories to themselves.

Phaneroscopy bears a certain similarity with the contemporary use of the term "phenomenology" insofar as it appeals, by direct experience, to that which is originally given as a basis for derivation of subsequent mental constructs (see Savan 1952). But we must be careful when establishing this parallel. Peirce tirelessly argued against the possibility of experience immediately available to consciousness in favor of mediate, deferred consciousness of phenomena, which places him more in line with Derrida and deconstruction than with most phenomenologists (see Merrell 1985a). Peirce, however, does assert: "There is nothing quite so directly open to observation as phanerons. . . . [E]very reader . . . must actually repeat my observations and experiences for himself" (CP, 1.286). But phaneroscopy has little to do with the question of how far the phanerons it studies correspond to any "reality out there," for "it simply scrutinizes the direct appearances" as they pop into the mind (CP, 1.287).

However, no phaneron can stand alone; they are not mere atoms of experience. In a manner of speaking it can be said that signs in general (sign-thoughts plus sign-events composing *semiosis*) are to semiotics what phanerons (thought-signs) are to phaneroscopy. Just as, given the mediary function of Thirdness (the interpretant), signs meld into other signs in the process ultimately of generating a continuum, so also phanerons are not mere discrete items of experience in the sense of Hume or Ernst Mach but rather tend to make up a continuous whole. Each phaneron is continuous with a particular universe of thought-signs and is ultimately continuous with the whole of the universe itself. No single phaneron or set of phanerons can be isolated as the ultimate "building blocks" of the semiotically real world or of "reality." Consequently, we cannot determine precisely where one sign begins and where its predecessor ends, for signs are not *things* but *processes*.

Yet Peirce remains in this regard an enigma. He apparently avails himself of a psychological method of inspection—if not to say introspection—

when assuring us that "those features of the phaneron that I have found in my mind are present at all times and to all minds" (CP, 1.284). This assumption, one might retort, must rest on some presumed act of discovery from *within* the phaneron and by means of some sort of reputed immediacy, therefore it appears that Peirce falls victim to logocentrism, and the myth of presence. Otherwise, how could generality be made known by means of experiencing individual phanerons? Peirce must be presupposing that phaneroscopy can lead to knowledge of *this* phaneron *here-now* (Secondness) as well as knowledge of *any* phaneron, *wherever-whenever*—as possibility (First) or probability (Third). Hence whatever is known of one phaneron is potentially generalizable for all phanerons. Final validation of such a rebuttal to Peirce must remain uncertain, however, for Peirce's phaneroscopic self-observation is unassailable by appeal to immediate intuition or introspection. Self-observation is never immediate but mediate, in spite of our wishes to the contrary.

Isabel Stearns (1952, 198) notes that if Peirce's categories of Firstness, Secondness, and Thirdness are discovered from within the phaneron, the problem is that they "present themselves in a tangled, disorderly, and far from explicit way." It is the somewhat unenviable task of mind to free these categories from their fusion in experience, thus hopefully setting them over against each other in order that they "may be recognized as contrasting forms." This surely places us in a double bind: the categories are the product of mind, but to know them, mind must liberate itself from them, yet it cannot do so, for it has produced them. I shall argue in chapters Nine and Ten that the mind nonetheless somehow brings this impossible dream to fruition. Mind is both observer and participant: phanerons appear to and exist for it, yet it remains bound to, and inexorably trapped within, phanerons.[5]

Actually, this state of affairs is not so claustrophobic as it might seem. Regarding Thirdness or the interpretant, ongoing mediation—that is, process— is in effect: indeed, both phanerons and *semiosis* are conceivable solely through Thirdness. When Thirdness is properly plugged into the equation, we cannot but be perpetually moving on, perpetually catching up with ourselves in our pursuit of that elusive ultimate interpretant of each and every sign we confront and that confronts us. But as Peirce contends, and as I shall illustrate below, there can be no Absolute Thirdness, no ultimate or final interpretant, for us mortals at least. Any unattainable and virtually inconceivable notion of finality must include the entire universe as sign, as some sort of Grand Cosmic Joke. If we could somehow ever get to the punch line, the paradox would slap us in the jowls. The joke was on us: we were at the center of things, of our semiotically real world, all along; we were always already there, as participatory observers collaborating with the universe in its grand self-organizing, bootstrapping operation.

The beauty of our pathetically infinitesimal existence is that our feeble and fallible (semiotically real) universe of signs in a manner of speaking *is* us: we get out of it what we put into it in the first place. At the same time we are, albeit artificially, somehow set apart from—we *set ourselves apart from*—this domain of signs: its cosmic drama is always already in the process of being unfolded. From within, we appear free to play the *semiosic* game as we please. At the same time, we ordinarily remain blissfully ignorant of our paramount limitation: since there can be no finality for us, we actually never stand a chance of reaching—let alone understanding—the punch line. Our semiotically real world is, and will always be, an unfinished joke.

    99

In other words, if an individual sign, mind, or phaneron could be construed as a token of some most general type, as a sample and hopefully a *representation*—a presenting anew, but with a difference, as I shall hereafter use the term[6]—of the universe, it could not but be itself perpetually caught up in a process of development. It follows that what appears as the most insignificant sign, mind, or phaneron can have no determinable and self-ordained closure. In this sense, Peirce's categories might well be considered in terms of tendencies rather than forms, conditions of becoming rather than static categories (Stearns 1952, 198–99). Or in Heisenberg's (1958) conception, regarding quantum "reality," the categories-as-tendencies are potentia rather than essence.

However, I must reemphasize that though the categories conveniently—albeit somewhat artificially—lend themselves to lists, tables, taxonomies, and matrices to be regarded as "applicable to being" (CP, 1.300), in the final analysis all they pretend to do is "suggest a way of thinking" (CP, 1.351). They imply transient possibilities rather than immutabilities. Moreover, since the categories possess "only a limited or approximate validity" (CP, 1.301), any "absolutely pure conception of a Category is out of the question" (CP, 2.86). This is most fitting, given Peirce's thesis that there can be no absolute, fixed being for the finite mind. It is also appropriate in light of the above observations on the limitations of any and all taxonomies.

Yet, if we take Peirce at his word, that selfsame finite mind must be in theory capable somehow of mysteriously patterning the Cosmic Mind. Thus mind is potentially infinite in extension—a potential rather than actual infinity, which salvages Peirce's conception from the aura of rampant modernist thinking by a mere hair. That is to say, if Firstness is possibility and Secondness actuality, then Thirdness, as a future conditional, is potentiality, whether regarding sign, mind, phaneron, or the universe. This potentiality is slowly being played out with the appearance of actualities, an ongoing process. Even the whole of the universe as a self-referential Third—as we shall note further in chapters Nine and Ten—is incapable of standing still.

The Well-springs of Sign Production

The sign of Thirdness—the symbol—is the only sign in the full sense of the term; indices and icons are what Peirce called *de-generate* forms. I must hasten to add that Peirce by no stretch of the imagination meant to disparage indices and icons. His use of the term is from mathematics and divorced from its pejorative meaning in ordinary language use. De-generate signs are actually more fundamental, more essential to communication, than their more developed cousins. They are "of the greatest utility and serve purposes that genuine signs could not" (NE, 2:241; MS 517).[7]

Briefly put, de-generate signs are inauthentic. Consummate symbols, true and perfect in every aspect—an ideal to be achieved solely in the theoretical long run of things—are the only authentic signs. Indices and icons are not mere weakened and diluted Secondness and Firstness, however; they contain the potential to bloom into full-blown Thirdness, like the potential within an acorn to become an oak. But this Aristotelian simile is somewhat insufficient, for Peirce's concept is mathematical more than it is organic or ontological, metaphysical before it is essential or existential. A simple and more appropriate illustration is the map paradox: an absolutely complete map must contain itself ad infinitum (recall note 5 of this chapter). Since each map of the series will be contained within the preceding map,

> [t]here will be a point contained in all of them, and this will be the map of itself. Each map which directly or indirectly represents the country is itself mapped in the next; . . . We may therefore say that each is a representation of the country *to* the next map; and that point that is in all the maps is in itself the representation of nothing but itself and to nothing but itself. (CP, 5.71)

This point that Peirce refers to is self-sufficient, though not all-sufficient, since it is not a complete representation but only a point on the continuous, infinitely regressive map: it is a map of itself. Like Firstness or what Peirce calls a monad, the point is related to nothing outside itself. If it were related to another point by a straight line drawn between them, we would have Secondness: the point-map would "point to" another point on a map containing the point-map, that point-map in turn containing the point to which it was "pointing." And by considering from a higher dimension the entire, all-encompassing map as a two-dimensional sheet, we have the dyadic relation of Secondness mediated by Thirdness. In this manner, point, line, and rectangular sheet are counterparts to icon, index, and symbol, or First, Second, and Third. The map, like the symbol, is a relatively full, or *genuine,* sign, while the line and point are *de-generate* signs. But rather than being in any way inferior, these de-generate signs contain, within themselves, the virtuality of becoming complete signs. Just as de-generate signs are destined perpetually to remain incomplete, so also the interpretants of genuine signs must remain incomplete for their finite interpreters, since the absolute fullness of the sign is no more than an ideal: it cannot hope for a place in the starting lineup of the "real" but must continue to play its substitute role on the field of the semiotically real.

Sign de-generacy, which corresponds to phaneronic production, occurs in two degrees:

> A sign degenerate in the lesser degree, is an Obstinate Sign, or *Index*, which is a Sign whose significance of its object is due to its having a genuine Relation to that Object, irrespective of the Interpretant. A Sign degenerate in the greater degree is an Origination Sign or *Icon*, which is a Sign whose significant virtue is due simply to its Quality. (CP, 2.92)[8]

In other words, a symbol, the most complex of the basic sign types, can be degenerate either in the first degree, which involves what I shall term *indexicalization*, or in the second degree, by way of *iconization*.

A genuine symbol is in a "conjoint relation to the thing denoted and to the mind" (CP, 3.360). It is related to its object in terms of a mental association and depends upon habit. Such signs are abstract, general, conventional, and arbitrary. They include the general items of language use and any other mode of conveying judgments. A symbol de-generate to the first degree has a genuine relation to its object, irrespective of its interpretant (the mind): a sign-object relation. That is, the sign's relation to its object does not lie in a mental association that is governed by habit but rather in a direct two-way physical relation independent of the mind's (Third's) use of the sign. Such an index does not necessarily assert anything, but rather, "it only says 'there!' It takes hold of our eyes, as it were, and forcibly directs them to a particular object, and there it stops" (CP, 3.361). It solicits a line of sight between the eye and the object—between one point and another—without any interpretation existing (yet), by the mind, of the object. Isolated demonstrative and relative pronouns are linguistic examples of de-generate symbols, since they denote things without fully qualifying them. The letters designating the points on a graph before they are connected by a line are also such indices to the extent that there is no dyadic relation in the full sense but merely an object calling attention to itself. Similarly, algebraic symbols distinguish one value from another without specifying those values (CP, 3.361).

Peirce (CP, 1.365) writes elsewhere that de-generate Seconds may be conveniently termed "internal, in contrast to external seconds, which are

constituted by external fact, and are true actions of one thing upon another."
For instance, a thermometer reacts physically with its environment, and independently of minds, as the mercury column rises and falls with temperature
variations. This would occur just the same even if the instrument were entirely
forgotten and ceased to convey information to some interpreter (CP, 5.73). As a
de-generate sign, however, the thermometer's function can also be conjured up
in the mind whether or not the instrument is present, even though the interpreter might have learned of its use by verbal instruction or from a written text
in the absence of the physical object.

102

A symbol de-generate to the second degree is an icon that fulfills its
function "by virtue of a character which it possesses in itself, and would possess just the same though its object did not exist" (CP, 5.73). A statue of a centaur is not an authentic representamen, since there is no such thing as a centaur.
Yet it represents a centaur by virtue of its shape, which it would have whether
centaurs exist or not. In this sense, the centaur statue as a sign is self-contained
(see Merrell 1983 on Meinong in this regard). Unlike the point-sign (map) "pointing to" another point on the two-dimensional sheet, the centaur-sign is analogous to a point merely *as it is*. Like an unrelated point-map or point on a
graph, it involves a sign-mind relation without regard to any semiotically real
connection.[9]

The function of icons with respect to the "real" world, as perceived
and conceived from a given perspective and within a given context, entails resemblance of the sign to something "out there" to which it *might* be related (i.e.,
its possible semiotic object). Since pure icons (or second-degree de-generate
symbols) have not (yet) established a definite link between themselves and that
which they resemble, on occasion they can become

> so completely substituted for their objects as hardly to be distin-
> guished from them. Such are the diagrams of geometry. A diagram,
> indeed, so far as it has a general signification, is not a pure icon;
> but in the middle part of our reasonings we forget that abstractness
> in great measure, and the diagram is for us the very thing. So in
> contemplating a painting, there is a moment when we lose the con-
> sciousness that it is not the thing, the distinction of the real and the
> copy disappears, and it is for the moment a pure dream—not any
> particular existence, and yet not general. At that moment we are
> contemplating [a pure] *icon*. (CP, 3.362; see also 2.92)

In this process, when construed as self-sufficient, de-generate signs
(iconized symbols or indices) become self-sufficiently semiotically real rather
than re-presentations of something "out there." This qualifies them as icons,
whether or not they are the equivalent of Hans Vaihinger's (1935) operational

"as-if" hypostats, dreams, hallucinations, figments, fantasies, and fictional "objects," and whether or not in books, on a canvas or screen, or in the playhouse. It is as if the infinitesimal point common to each map in Peirce's infinite set of maps were taken to be coterminous with the whole of the territory. The point as such neither points to another point by way of a line between them, nor is there any mediation through their contextualization within the entire map. Rather, the two-dimensional map as Third has vanished, as has all reference to any other point. Put otherwise, when indexicalization threatens to produce a symptom[10]—a syndrome in a patient such that what he takes to be "real" is not so perceived by other members of the patient's community—then iconization becomes imminent. Signs consequently become simply that which *is;* they are self-sufficient and self-contained.

103

Second-degree de-generacy is like the sensation of a swatch of cloth, A, which is sensed to be the same as (undifferentiated from) another swatch, B, though they are actually slightly different; and that second swatch is reported to be "the same as" C, which is in its turn "the same as" D. However, if A were placed alongside D, a marked difference—first degree de-generacy, relation to something else—would now be noticed by a neutral bystander. In the first case, we have a continuum of sorts where everything simply *is as it is,* in good monadic fashion, without a significant other existing—this and comparable mind-benders have been called the *sorites paradox.* In the second case, there is a distinction between A and D, whose dyadic otherness is made manifest as is the potential line connecting two different points in Peirce's map. Regarding the continuum, there is no significant other, only quality; regarding the distinction, Secondness is made evident.

In contrast, if an observer, X, notes that A is distinct from C and D, that D is distinct from A and B, and that there is a discontinuous spectrum before her, the relation becomes triadic. It involves an agent (mind) for whom the distinction between A and D is made manifest. The triad entails a sign's signifying something to some interpreter in some respect or capacity, hence the sign is "real" for someone (CP, 1.516–20). The dyad and monad, as de-generate (i.e., unfulfilled or incomplete) signs, are not any less "real" than the triad as a potentially genuine sign, though the third party of the trio has not (yet) effectively incorporated them into some semiotically real domain (this topic will be taken up in more detail in Chapter Eight).

Everyday examples of second-degree de-generacy are the evocation "Hi!" or a knock on the front door. The interpretant of a symbol qua symbol is bypassed, as if the word or gesture were an entire evocation, such as "Hello, nice to see you, and how are you today?" "Here I am, at the agreed-upon time for our date," or some such thing. This first-degree de-generacy is also present in, for example, my imagining how I would act under certain circumstances as if to illustrate how another person (the Peircean social Other, or the other self) would be likely to act. On the other hand, if you see a portrait and form an idea of the person it is a portrait of, even though you have never been acquainted with that person, you are bypassing two stages—the proper interpretant and the index—in the full development of a sign. Your idea of the person in the portrait is merely an icon.

However, it is not a pure icon, Peirce would say. You are influenced not only by the icon qua icon but also by knowing *that* it is an effect, through an artist, caused by the original person's appearance, hence there is an indexical relation of Secondness to the original. A purer form of second-degree degeneracy is Peirce's example of one's contemplating a painting—or better, viewing a film—and for a fleeting moment losing consciousness that it is not the "real" thing. One spontaneously reacts to it as if it were actually a "real" object, as when, for example, a young boy screams when a monster suddenly appears on the screen (see Merrell 1983). In such cases, the sign's indexicality (direct relation to its semiotic object) and symbolicity (mediation, through an interpretant, of the sign and its semiotic object) have been suppressed. That is to say, awareness of the sign in terms of its fullness as a Third was either never realized, or the sign's Thirdness waned such that it became only tacitly acknowledged. What *was* or *could have been* explicit remains implicit; response to the sign has become automatized.

Figure 4 provides a diagram of de-generacy. In first-degree degeneracy, one of the relations is suppressed, and the other two engage in a two-way connection. If two relations are suppressed (second-degree de-generacy), the sign functions as if it were a self-contained, self-sufficient icon. Suppressing c highlights a, since the ordinary relation between R and O becomes indexicalized (hypertrophied), by "pointing," evoking, or calling attention to something in place of the absent O-I relation. In other words, the interpretant-object relation wanes, and the object-sign relation is consequently intensified. If, in addition, a wanes, the R-I relation is iconized (by taking the sign as the "real" thing) in order to compensate for the backgrounded R-O relation. This erasure of the sign-object relation brings about a fusion of the subject and the sign such that, in Peirce's example, the latter may become construed by the former to be "real." Hence:

First-Degree De-generacy: Sign ➤ Object (indexicalization).

Second-Degree De-generacy: Object ≈ Sign (iconization).

where "➤" signifies "defers to" and at the same time "differs from," and where "≈" signifies "is made tantamount to" (see CP, 3.359–62)

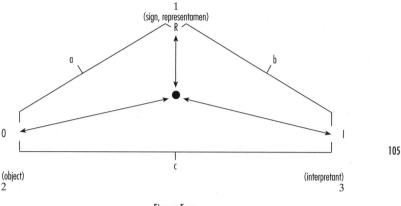

Figure Four

Within another context, the first-degree de-generate sign may be considered a hypoicon of the *diagram* sort, the second-degree degenerate sign a hypoicon of the *image* sort (see CP, 2.276–77). One encounters a more complex type of de-generacy—though as far as I know Peirce does not make this connection—in *metaphor*. Metaphors involve indexicalization (evocation of image as metaphor) plus iconization (virtual identity between image and metaphor).[11] But consciously and intentionally constructed metaphorical relations can, with time, submerge into nonconsciousness. When this occurs, the metaphor's indexical function becomes atrophied, and its iconic function hypertrophied. It is now a "dead" metaphor; its quality as metaphor qua metaphor has passed into oblivion.

The View from Down Under

As stated in the previous section, de-generacy of a sign can entail gravitation from explicit knowing *that* to tacit knowing *how* (albeit in desultory fashion), while sign generacy is capable of the reverse (see Merrell and Anderson 1989).

Thus the demise of a once-proud metaphor involves a transition from awareness of the metaphor as metaphor to mindlessness with respect to the sign's metaphoricity—that is, its relation to the object it resembles. It is a move from symbolicity to iconicity, legisign to qualisign, Thirdness to Firstness. A prime example of this evolutionary process is found in the Cartesian-Newtonian machine metaphor-model of the universe (to be placed in the spotlight in the next section), which, as generations piled upon generations, came to pervade the knowing *how/that* and seeing *as/that* of scientific activity to the extent that the final aim became a game of resolving everything into mechanics. The universe, nature, and all organisms, from the imperiously proud human semiotic animal to the humble cell, came to be construed tacitly as literal machines: the minds of Plato, Thomas Aquinas, Bach, and Michelangelo differed from a printing press only in complexity.

The abstract nature of modernity's machine metaphor-model as the product of an objective stance vis-à-vis the universe is fundamental to the modern mind-set, yet it illuminates the very notion of metaphoricity, of creativity. Romanticist tirades against modernity were accompanied by a search for spontaneity, feeling, sentiment, emotion, and immediate unity by plumbing the depths of subjectivity. Modernity, however, remained linked to inescapable dualities: an uncollapsible space between subject and world, subject and signs, thinker and the immediate surface aspects of intellection and sentiment. Modernity, in other words, generally focused on the function of metaphor, romanticism on the feeling it evokes. The irony of it all is that a metaphor, once having been slain, was taken by modernist and romantic alike as simply *that which is;* its function and the feeling it evoked were no longer considered either by the intuiting or the cogitating mind.

This is not to say that upon a metaphor's demise the sign becomes concrete and immediate, the source of raw experience. Nor is it that the degenerate metaphor now constitutes the fullness of the lived world, in contrast to the goal of abstract thought, which is tempered by disinterested conceptualization. Rather, the "dead" metaphor evokes a habituated response to a highly structured world of preconceived order as if it were directly and immediately *the way things are.* A deceased metaphor is the vehicle of mediation for the signs surrounding it and becomes part of defunct and etiolated, embedded and automatized, experience. It has, in a word, *de-generated* into the equivalent of a diagram (Second) and finally an image (First). All language, the poets have been telling us for centuries, begins with images, and from images metaphors bloom forth. Unfortunately, with use they become routinized and finally hardly noticed: nonconscious images. To combat this tendency, poetry is charged with the task of resisting this process of stultification by constantly refreshing language and thus recreating lost images and creating new ones. This process reverses the tendency toward de-generacy by bringing about de-embedment, de-automatizion and regenerates language itself.[12] But I am getting ahead of myself. Back to de-generacy (de-embedment and de-automatization will become the direct focus of the next section).

Tursman (1987, 26) suggests that Peirce's classification of signs is similar to group theory and set theory insofar as phanerons undergo an ordering operation that Peirce dubbed *prescission.*[13] In a nutshell, prescission is the act of abstracting one element (phaneron) from others in such a way that the relations between them can be variously determined and a certain order perceived. A red car can enter consciousness as (1) the sensation of some color, then (2) this red patch here, and (3) a car that happens to be red. Proposition (3) is more substantive than (2), which is in turn more substantive than (1). And (1) represents a greater degree of abstraction than (2), and (2) greater abstraction than (3). Tursman (1987, 37) suggests that Peirce used prescission to determine the most natural class of general ideas, Thirds, from which its parts, Seconds and Firsts, are abstracted, "thus doing for ideas what Mendeleyev's periodic table of the elements did for the chemical elements." Tursman's conjecture is admittedly rather euphoric.[14] However, his provocative examples of sign generacy and de-generacy illuminate an important aspect of *semiosis:* the idea that signs can cluster around one another, as we saw using Savan's qualification rule, to form a conglomerate, a *compound sign.*

Before proceeding, an example of compound signs is in order. The poet Ezra Pound's theory of ideograms involves relations between form and experience; it takes account of the tension among concrete experience (Firstness), the particulars cut (i.e., prescinded) from that experience (Secondness), and abstract general terms (symbols, Thirdness). Pound believed that Chinese ideograms are superior to Western linear, phonocentric script because they contain, embedded within themselves, the transition from particulars to universals. For a character depicting the quality of red, the ideogram can be a diagrammatic form signifying the image of a rose, iron rust, cherry, or flamingo, all particulars from which the images are abstracted (see Schwartz 1985, 87–88). The rose aspect of the ideogram can then become a metaphor of something else—the transitoriness of life, love, or some such thing—as a sign mediating another experience or sensation. Pound hoped that the embedment of original images, which deadens language, could thus be minimized, and language would be restored to its original immediacy and organic vitality.

The project, it hardly needs saying, did not bear much fruit. Yet the important point remains: according to Pound, when we contemplate an ideogram or a cluster of words, not only is the general *semiosic* process condensed to a space-time singularity, but in addition, there is a constellation of sign types—icons, indices, symbols, and their various admixtures—creating a reverberation in the mind. Hugh Kenner (1972, 154–55) calls this effect "electricity" or "radio-activity," a "force transfusing, welding, and unifying" signs. The sign cluster is an abstraction indicating (indexing) some particular or set of particulars, which, in turn, evokes concrete images, sensations, and feelings (icons). Peirce does not entirely dismiss this modernist ideal of a totalizing, abstract sign somewhere out there in Platonic heaven, nor does he exactly abandon romanticism's—or, by extension, postmodernism's—helpless and hopeless dream of immediacy. Once again, he attempts to incorporate the essentials of both camps in his admirably broad purview.

Extrapolating from Savan's qualification rule, and in light of Tursman's interpretation of phaneroscopy, we can say that every compound sign—an utterance, a poem, a text, in fact, the discourse of an entire community—is a natural class. It constitutes a set of phanerons, in each of which a sign (idea) is an extension of the sign (idea) that preceded it. Since the de-generative ordering principle is "top down," from 3 to 2 to 1, the "higher" classes are natural classes. The *semiosic*-phaneronic column in figure 5 illustrates how every natural class is a Third or a de-generate Third, hence the system must be arranged to follow an ordering principle consisting of the recursive application of binaries and unaries generated from the original 3 (Tursman 1987, 40). A series of 3s, 2s, and 1s produced from the originary symbol yields other symbols by repeated de-generation or subdivision "downward" and by their *semiosic* generation "upward."[15] In Peirce's (CP, 5.72) words:

> Taking any class in whose essential idea the predominant element is Thirdness, or Representation, the self-development of that essential idea . . . results in a *trichotomy* giving rise to three subclasses, or genera, involving respectively a relatively genuine thirdness, a relatively reactional thirdness or thirdness of the lesser degree of degeneracy, and a relatively qualitative thirdness or thirdness of the last degeneracy. . . . The genus corresponding to the lesser degree of degeneracy, the reactionally degenerate genus, will subdivide after the manner of the Second category, forming a catena; while the genus of relatively genuine Thirdness will subdivide by Trichotomy just like that from which it resulted. Only as the division proceeds, the subdivisions become harder and harder to discern.[16]

SEMIOTICS
the study of

Semiosic-phaneronic subdivision, de-generacy		Semiosic generacy	
(10)	333	(1)	111
(9)	332	(2)	211
(8)	331	(3)	221
(7)	322	(4)	222
(6)	321	(5)	311
(5)	311	(6)	321
(4)	222	(7)	322
(3)	221	(8)	331
(2)	211	(9)	332
(1)	111	(10)	333

Figure Five

For example, a representamen, as the empty category of 3, can divide by trichotomy into a symbol, an index, or an icon. An icon as representamen fulfills its function "by virtue of a character which it possesses in itself, and would possess just the same though its object did not exist" (CP, 5.73). As mentioned above, a statue of a centaur is not a genuine representation since centaurs do not exist; nonetheless, its iconic properties designate it as a centaur by the fact that it *is* what it *is,* whether there are any "real" centaurs "out there" or not. In contrast, an index as representamen could not function properly if its semiotically real object did not exist, though it could function even when uninterpreted as a representamen. A thermometer is an index in the sense that it is contrived to possess a certain relationship with hot, mild, or cold weather. But the mind's perception of temperature as causing either discomfort or pleasure can continue as such even though the function of mercury in a column constituting the thermometer is virtually ignored.

That is, a relation of causality or contiguity will endure "out there" even though there is no mind to interpret the sign in terms of a specific semiotically real world. But, as I shall argue in chapters Nine and Ten, if never endowed with an initial interpretation, the sign would never become part of a semiotically real world for some community of semiotic agents, though it would undoubtedly maintain a claim to the "real." On the other hand, a symbol is a representamen "regardless of any similarity or analogy with its object and simply because it will be interpreted to be a representamen. Such, for example, is any general word, sentence, or book" (CP, 5.73). Of these three genera of *representamina* (plural for representamen), the icon is *qualitatively de-generate* and the index is *reactionally de-generate,* while the symbol is a *relatively genuine genus.*

Regarding natural language—which is comprised of symbols, the most genuine forms of representamina—the original category 3 is capable of a three-fold subdivision into an argument, a proposition, and a term. A *term* is a de-generate index (i.e., the predicate of a proposition), but as such it does not conjure up an icon in the mind; it is merely a subjectless proposition. A *proposition* conveys information, since it is a type of genuine index, consisting of a de-generate index (the subject indicates the object) and an icon (the predicate reveals the properties of the object through the subject). An *argument* goes further, since it is—or at least can potentially be—the consummate symbol, a sign cluster or compound sign. It is a representamen "which does not leave the interpretant to be determined as it may by the person to whom the symbol is addressed, but separately represents what is the interpreting representation that it is intended to determine. This interpreting representation is, of course, the conclusion" (CP, 5.76). In this sense, an argument is capable of standing alone, though development of its interpretant is contingent upon an interpreter, which I shall discuss in chapters Nine and Ten.

Symbols, in this manner, grow by repeated de-generative subdivision "downward" in addition to their *semiosic* generation "upward." After mapping the third generation of natural signs—from arguments (3-3-3) to rhematic iconic qualisigns or rhematic symbols (3-3-1)—other mappings can follow to produce ever more complex signs that compose an intricately interwoven symbol, a semiotic web. In fact, Peirce would have us believe that "[s]o prolific is the triad in forms that one may easily conceive that all the variety and multiplicity of the universe springs from it" (CP, 4.310; see also 1.291). To this Tursman (1987, 44) enthusiastically adds that, had Peirce been around a half century later, "he most emphatically would have incorporated the messenger RNA codons within his system of triples."

Is all this merely a modernist-formalist pursuit? Is Peirce, as Herbert Schneider (1952) charges, guilty of converting his thesis into triadophilia, analyzing anything and everything into threes for the sheer fun or aesthetic pleasure of it all? Is Peirce's system a game of forms, the modernist enterprise exemplifying the will to power? Does the elegance of Peirce's architectonic, its Pythagorean beauty, its crystalline precision, take precedence over other, less formal concerns, as Paul A. C. Dirac (1963) and Eugene Wigner (1969) write of the use of mathematics in contemporary physics? Such questions, though relevant to this inquiry, must nevertheless be held in abeyance pending further development of the interrelationships and processual nature of Peirce's sign types.

A Generative Spiral of Complexification

In contrast to phaneronic progression, *semiosic* generation proceeds from relative simplicity at the "greatest lower bound" state to relative complexity at the "least upper bound" (figure 5). In other words, from the "least upper bound," arguments (3-3-3)—the most complex form of natural signs—can evolve by first-degree de-generacy into dicent symbols or propositions (3-3-2), and by second-degree de-generacy into rhematic symbols or terms (3-3-1). From the "greatest lower bound," qualisigns (1-1-1), by the *semiosic* process, can eventually generate the first-level symbolic sign, a term (3-3-1), from which a proposition (3-3-2) and an argument (3-3-3) can be generated.

Peirce further characterized arguments as deductive (what *would be*), while propositions are inductive (what *is*), and terms are abductive (what *might be*) (CP, 2.267–70). This formulation evinces more than a modicum of elegance. With generacy, in contrast to de-generacy, we begin with Firstness, abduction. For example, a thought-sign presents itself. According to the initial stage of Peirce's "logic of discovery," this thought-sign often surfaces unexpectedly, appearing with pristine clarity and stark simplicity. It seems to be a paragon of harmony, balance, and elegance. Nonetheless, since this initial thought-sign is

110

tentative at best, there is as yet little to no certainty, though things might initially appear otherwise. At this stage, the thought-sign is mere possibility. It can then become a conjecture to be subjected to the pragmatic give-and-take of everyday activity—which Peirce, from his scientific perspective, refers to as the testing process, induction. Finally, symbolicity, which involves deduction, the only genuine form of *semiosis,* gives final—though yet fallible—confirmation to the concept. Then, as supporting signs are heaped upon signs, and arguments accumulate to form a web of compound signs, a general perspective and conceptual scheme comes to pervade the entire community. But at this higher level, problems inevitably arise. As the web of compound signs takes on increasing complexity, ambiguities, inconsistencies, and paradoxes eventually surface. What once appeared to be clarity becomes muddled; the system at times even threatens to self-destruct. Then, at some stage, there is a breakthrough with the emergence of another thought-sign of apparent clarity and simplicity, and the process begins anew. At broad social levels, such is often the history of a relatively fruitful intuition, idea, theory, or even a paradigm—for example, classical physics, which became problematic and finally ceded to Einstein's relativity, then a cosmic can of worms (the quantum quandary) popped open, eventually alienating even the master himself.

In spite of its propensity to evolve toward ever more complex, and hence perplexing, levels, symbolicity stands out among the other two sign modes in that it represents the most effective avenue of inquiry, understanding, and knowledge, in regard to both the universe of the mind (the semiotically real) and the universe "out there" (the actually real). By its very nature, the symbol is not necessarily any more determinate than the index or icon, but, since it is characterized by relations of thought (in contrast to actual facts or relations of action, and possibilities or relations of similarity), it is capable of indefinite and ongoing determination. That is to say, every thought-sign as Third is a further determination of previous thought-signs, and it gives way to future determination by means of upcoming thought-signs.[17]

By and large, Peirce's theory of signs, and especially the idea of *semiosis,* evince the image of generality, evolution, the creative advance of the universe, to paraphrase Whitehead (1925). But, as contemporary theories of physical nature demonstrate, this process becomes a two-way street: for each step forward, a return to the previous square threatens; each negentropic development risks entropic retrogression. A proclivity toward maximum novelty exists through Firstness (generacy, *semiosis*), yet novelty is restricted by the opposing drift toward repetition, sameness, habit, and confirmation through Thirdness (and the promise—or threat—of phaneronic de-generacy) (see CP, 6.23–25). While Thirdness is the arena of cognition, of the mind's intimate workings—indeed, of the very *semiosic* process—on the other hand, what is once known and can be made relatively explicit (knowing *that*) invariably manifests a tendency to sink into nonconsciousness, becoming embedded, automatized, and thus constituting part of one's *tacit* knowing (knowing *how,* passive, unthinking seeing). Nevertheless, both novelty and repetition, emergence and confirmation, surprise and expectations, are absolutely fundamental to life's essential processes.[18]

However, as Peirce reiterated time and again, all organisms, and especially human beings, are capable of altering their expectations—and at a higher level, their expectations of expectations—in light of surprising phenomena that go against the grain of their embedded habits and belief patterns. Humans in particular are remarkably pliable. In contrast, computers are unmovable, the most stubborn brutes imaginable, for whom there is absolutely zero uncertainty when they flash, for example, "Cannot diskcopy to or from network drive" on the screen. This is why, given human resilience, Peirce's notions of habit, belief, and disposition have no definite or predetermined beginning, middle, or end. They are *would be*s along a vague continuum stretching out into the infinitely receding horizon.

Interpretants come in three flavors: immediate, or emotional; energetic, or dynamic; and logical, or final. An immediate interpretant, corresponding to Firstness, is what is or can be made explicit regarding the sign itself, apart from its context and the circumstances of its coming into existence. An energetic interpretant is the actual *semiosic* effect of the sign, a process requiring acknowledgment of the sign's relation to its object within the signifying context, such acknowledgment occurring over a certain length of time. And a logical, or final, interpretant is the *semiosic* effect that would inhere if the sign could be endowed with the totality of its possible *semiosic* effects with respect to its object and other signs.[19] Thus the meaning of a concept can be studied only by way of interpretants, or the proper significate effects of the sign. The effect corresponding to Firstness is feeling or emotion, which affords initial evidence to the interpreter that he has comprehended the sign in question. Full comprehension of the sign, however, requires that this emotional effect be acted upon energetically, in the sense of muscular or mental operations whereby the outer or inner world of the interpretant is subject to some change. And finally, the nature of this effect must be ascertained, which calls up the possibility of a corresponding logical or final interpretant of the sign.

George Gentry (1952) alludes to a contradiction between Peirce's earlier writings concerning the infinite series of interpretants along a continuum and his later account of habit as the ultimate interpretant. The first implies the impossibility of finality, the second some sort of arrival at the finish line. The first is infinitist, the second finitist. The two simply cannot logically be mixed. However, Gentry points out, habit as a logical interpretant is on a different level from the signs that it mediates. In order to derive meaning at the level of the habit or logical interpretant, another level is necessary, and then another, and so on. Here we have a regress no less exasperating than that of the most notorious of asymptotes, Zeno's paradoxes. If Peirce is on the right track concerning his logical interpretant, there is no reason for modernity's faith in either ultimate foundations or absolute finality. Neither is there any warrant for crystallized habit, law, regularity, or knowledge as timeless "truth" barring any and all forms of change. Just as sign systems are inevitably susceptible to degeneracy, embedment, and automatization, so, by thwarted expectations, awareness of error, and self-criticism, they are sooner or later subject to alteration by way of generacy, de-embedment, and de-automatization.

113

What You Don't Know Can Hurt You

Let us reconsider the Cartesian-Newtonian corpuscular-kinetic "universe ≈ machine" model with an example combining some fact and a bit of fiction.

The model is notoriously grandiose—the culmination of modernity's most august project. Descartes and Newton were, after all is said and done, in tune with their times. Leibniz sought an ultimate account of "reality" in the order of *mathesis universalis.* Spinoza viewed human desires and actions as though they were lines, planes, and solids. Hume, with his sort of attraction between sensations and ideas having the same extraordinary effects as the mysterious attraction across distances between physical bodies, attempted for the mind what Newton accomplished for the physical world. Later, we have Pierre-Simon de Laplace's superobserver, who is capable of knowing at an instant all past configurations of the universe and of predicting all future ones; Julien Offroy de La Mettrie's "man the machine"; and Thomas Huxley, for whom humans are "conscious automata" whose vital actions are the mere result of the molecular forces in protoplasm. This was approximately the time of Darwinism and social Darwinism, which culminated in Spencer's Grand Unified Theory of human societies, the early Freud's contradictory view of the mind as a sort of romanticized machine, and the early behaviorism of John Watson, who envisioned the control of human reactions in the same manner that physicists controlled and manipulated natural phenomena; a person thus became little more than a social atom in a statistical aggregate.[20]

After dominating scientific thought for three centuries, the machine model became so embedded in the mind, discourse, and activity of Westerners that it functioned like a "psychoanalytical symptom," in Milic Capek's (1961, 264) words, an indication of "the reluctance of our Newtonian subconscious to depart from traditional habits of thought." Whitehead (1925, 110) observed a radical inconsistency here between what he termed "scientific realism based on mechanism" and "an unwavering belief in the world of men and of the higher animals as being composed of self-determining organisms." And James Jeans

(1930, 30) remarked that our "modern minds have, I think, a bias towards mechanical interpretations. Part may be due to our early scientific training, and part perhaps to our continually seeing everyday objects behaving in a mechanical way, so that a mechanical explanation looks natural and is easily comprehended." It is quite plausible that Descartes and Newton were not the first great figures of the Age of Reason but the last of the magicians before the ghost became conveniently concealed in the machine. It is well known that Newton's "Hypothesis non fingo" was subverted, for his method was actually a long shot from innocent Baconian inductivism (Holton 1973, 49–53). Newton was actually a hypotheticist-deductivist of the first order. And Descartes himself also resorted to a conjectural a posteriori hypothetical method in spite of his propagating the idea that analysis must precede synthesis (Turbayne 1962, 28–53). So much for preliminary words on the machine model.

For the sake of illustration, let us assume that Peirce's triangulation of the "logic of discovery" and its aftermath into abduction, induction, and deduction is descriptive rather than prescriptive, and that, whether they knew it or not, Descartes and Newton availed themselves of that "logic" of the most general sort, abduction, when doing their thing. In this light, Descartes's declaration in the fourth part of his *Principles* (1983, 4:188) that "I have described the Earth and the whole visible universe *as if it were* a machine, having regard only to the shape and movement of its parts," is revealing.

From the Peircean framework, Descartes's machine model, which was, in its inception, the product of an abductive act, led to an inferential process somewhat in the order of the following:

    1a. The unexpected connection C (universe + machine) is brought to mind.

    2a. If A (the universe is like a machine) were the case, then C would follow as a matter of course.

    3a. There is reason to believe that A is the case, therefore it is worthy of further investigation. (CP, 5.189)[21]

In view of these steps, Descartes's words can be reformulated thus:

    1b. C: The shape and movement of a machine's parts appear analogous to (homologous with) the shape and movement of the empirically available—and, by extrapolation, the nonempirically available—parts of the universe.

    2b. If A (the universe is like a machine) were the case, then C would follow as a matter of course.

    3b. There is reason to believe that A is the case, therefore it is worthy of further investigation.

And these steps can in turn be reformulated as a syllogism of sorts:

1c. Machines are such-and-such in regard to the shape and movement of their parts.

2c. The universe is analogous to a machine (a conjecture or assumption).

3c. Therefore, the universe is such-and-such in regard to the shape and movement of its parts.

The syllogism is an argument (3-3-3), the final sign in Peirce's ten classes. The two premises and the conclusion are propositions (dicent symbols, 3-3-2). And "universe" and "machine" are terms (rhematic symbols, 3-3-1). 115 The argument is relatively explicit and demands that its author and readers maintain cognizance of the conclusion, the premises, the underlying assumptions, and the possibility of their being false. Significantly, in this respect, Descartes wrote in the *Principles* (1983, 3:120): "I will put forward everything that I am going to write just as a hypothesis, even if this be thought to be false," and "I shall also assume some propositions which are agreed to be false."

At the outset, we must suppose that Descartes maintained awareness of his model qua model. With the passage of time, however, as generations of scientists were heaped upon generations, such cognizance gradually slipped into the interstices of each scientist's mind as well as the scientific discourse of the day, and the original "as if" character of the model came to be tacitly assumed. In other words, de-generacy exercised its malignant force (through embedment and automatization). First-degree de-generacy (➤ 3-3-2) yielded a complete proposition juxtaposing "universe" and "machine" with the implication of their conjectured analogy or homology. At this stage, though the entire argument was no longer in effect, the metaphor-model remained highlighted, and the indexical relation connecting the subject to the predicate was still intact. This indexicalization entailed the machine-universe connections' becoming dynamic (in the mind) and as if they were immediate rather than mediated signs of Secondness relating to the world "out there." In a sense, the machine-universe metaphor (as hypoicon) was transformed into the equivalent of a diagram (as algebraic or geometrical), the original reference to the object of metaphoricity having been suppressed.

A further step along the path toward de-generacy (➤ 3-3-1) limited focus to the term "universe," which now contained the potential for becoming semiotically overloaded. At this stage, "universe" implicitly carried with it an image of itself as a sign that could become, by effacement of the qualifier "analogous to," coterminous with what would ordinarily be its semiotic object, "machine." When this occurred, "universe" was no longer considered merely analogous to "machine." Rather, the attributes ordinarily attached to "machine" became tantamount to the whole of the "universe's" attributes, and the terms took on relations of sameness, and even identity, rather than resemblance and difference. This is comparable to taking the point-map for the entire map—or, what is worse, for the territory (the index for the object indicated)—or sensing cloth swatches *A* and *B* to be the same color (a replica or repetition of the sign of itself). In other words, iconization of the sign reduced it to a mere image (the most basic hypoicon). As such, there was no explicit connection, no "line of sight." The image was self-contained and self-sufficient (see CP, 6.148).

To paraphrase a previous citation from Peirce, the "universe" became "so completely substituted" by its object (the metaphor) as "hardly to be distinguished" from it. As in contemplating a painting or watching a captivating movie or play, there came a time when investigators of the Cartesian-Newtonian universe gradually freed their minds of conscious awareness that the model they were using was not the thing modeled. Finally, the distinction between the real and the copy (metaphor-model) waned, and machine and universe entered into an intimate embrace as if they were a dream. When this occurred, the investigators were contemplating a pure icon (CP, 1.362). At this stage of de-generacy, explicitness became implicitness; sign processing became stabilized by habit; and interpretation became an embedded, automatized, and largely mindless enterprise—Capek's "Newtonian subconscious." This train of events was, as usual, both a bane and a boon. The mind was now unfettered by the demand to be constantly attuned to the model qua model and all the implications thereof, on the one hand, but on the other, the impending danger of taking the model (metaphor, sign, semiotically real) for "reality" eventually loomed large.

We can thus assume that of the three parts of the above syllogism, (1c) refers chiefly to empirical phenomena, the "shape and movement" of a machine's parts observable by the eye's gaze. These semiotic objects are "sign-events," *semiosic* entities "out there." Premise (2c), in contrast, refers to the "whole visible universe," though in its entirety it lies chiefly beyond what the eye can gaze upon. Therefore, the invisible and hence unknown aspects of the universe are to a large degree phaneronic thought-signs, accessible solely to the eye of the mind. The conclusion (3c), then, is a sign of mixed properties, partly *semiosic* (a sign-event) in the broad sense but also in part exclusively phaneronic (a thought-sign).

Further analysis of Descartes's statement regarding the universe as machine, in light of the above abductive inferences, yields: (a) the shape of a machine is visible, (b) the movements of the parts of a machine are visible, (c) the shape of a machine is describable, (d) the movements of the parts of a machine are describable, (e) only part of the universe (including the earth) is visible, (f) the shape of the universe (including the earth) is indescribable, (g) the movements of the parts of the universe (including the earth) are indescribable, and (h) the shape of the universe (including the earth) is describable insofar as it is like a machine, therefore (i) the movements of the parts of the universe (including the earth) are describable insofar as they are like a machine (see Merrell 1985b, 154–56). In this sense, and following Hesse (1966), the machine model, like all models, appropriates the known and establishes an analogy between it and the partly unknown in order to render the unknown a bit more intelligible. This is at one and the same time baleful and beautiful for science—and for all thought, for that matter. Use of metaphor-models and analogies implies acknowledgment of both the mind's and the eye's limitations. Yet, if successful, metaphor-models tend to breed unwarranted confidence in their authors, who, drunk with their new delusions of intellectual grandeur, may presume the capacity to exercise control over themselves, nature, and their fellow citizens in general.

117

This, of course, is also part and parcel of the modernist attitude toward science. The scientistic assumption has had it that what is not susceptible to the eye's gaze is not verifiable (i.e., falsifiable), and that what is known subjectively (i.e., aesthetically and ethically), by the mind's eye, is invalid. Kant knew the story well. He believed in the transcendental, though he conceded that it could not be grasped by sense or pure reason. Yet Kant's *Critique of Pure Reason* (1929) is a masterful analysis of what the structure of the human mind should be to account for the existence of a Cartesian-Newtonian conception of the world. So what can be known of nature is all that needs to be known, and the circle appears self-sufficient. As a consequence of this posture, all of classical knowledge collapsed on a physical world open to the scientist's gaze, once the Cartesian bedrock of intuition was set firmly in place. Adam named the celestial spheres, Pythagoras made music of them, Kepler set them in geometrical forms, Newton described them in terms of number, and Descartes supposedly validated the whole mess metaphysically.

The Cartesian-Newtonian legacy reigned supreme until well into the present century, from Mach to the empirical positivists and Willard Van Orman Quine, for whom the only things that exist are physical objects and the only valid knowledge is that of physical science. Most observers take modern science, with its fetishism of the abstract and its quantified nature, to constitute a monopoly of objectivism at the expense of subjectivity. Actually it was a matter of objectivist imperialism's appropriating and coopting matters of mind—thought-signs—and disguising them as "real-world" objects—sign-events. This Cartesian-Newtonian world order was not a matter of the facts of the matter but of fictions becoming embedded and automatized as if they were facts of the matter.

But where facts were thought to be, fictions will ultimately be found. Mechanism finally entered old age and is now well on its way toward extinction. This fall from the grace of the knowing gaze is nowhere more graphically illustrated than in the fate of the chimerical ether, that logical end-product of classical mechanics which epitomized a worldview and underwrote its demise. The invisible, indescribable ether was the deus ex machina designed to put things in their proper place once and for all. Yet it ushered in a proliferation of unanswered questions. No more than a hypothesis, it was

> introduced into science by physicists who, taking it for granted that everything must admit of a mechanical explanation, argued that there must be a mechanical medium to transmit waves of light, and all other electrical and magnetic phenomena of nature through space and deliver them up at the far end exactly as they are observed—much as a system of bell wires transmits mechanical force from a bell-pull to a bell. (Jeans 1930, 112)[22]

In accounting for the ether model, for example, Hesse (1966, 60) constructs a diagrammatic set of relations whereby the analogy between sound and light is established first by a set of similar empirical properties and then by the similarity between air and the nonempirical ether, such similarity being no more than a hypostat at the outset. Thus the "causal" (metonymical) relations accounting for the properties of sound (echo, loudness, pitch, propagated in air, etc.) are related by similarity (metaphor) to the "causal" relations accounting for the properties of light (reflection, brightness, color, propagated in ether, etc.) (see also Merrell 1991c; 1992, chap. 7). The important point is that, regarding the propagation of light, the medium—ether—is strictly hypothetical. Hesse's account thus pits the presumably describable and empirical against what remains in its totality nonempirical, the analogy or continuum between the two systems of propagation resting in the function of sound and light in their respective media. And significantly, "propagated in air" and "propagated in ether" entail relations, both internal and between *modelans* and *modelandum*.

That of which classical physicists were unaware is portrayed by Duhem (1954, 171–72), who wrote at the beginning of the classical paradigm's demise that "we can make an infinity of different formulas or distinct physical laws correspond to the same group of facts. . . . [A]ny other law representing the same experiments with the same approximation may lay as just a claim as the first to the title of a true law or, to speak more precisely, of an acceptable law." According to Duhem's "holism," hypotheses can become worldviews that subsequently are gradually embedded, thus bringing an entire community to overlook, or relegate to forgetfulness, the "essential abyss between experience and logically structured theory" (Holton 1973, 287).[23] And, as a consequence, the map is taken for the territory, the theory for what it was supposed to be about, *modelans* becomes *modelandum,* and signs become tantamount to, or replace, the things signified.

William James's "psychologist's fallacy" could well be generalized as the "theorist's fallacy" in this regard: that "inveterate habit" which the psychologist or theorist has of confusing "his own standpoint with that of the mental fact about which he is making his report" (James 1950, 1:278). In order to come to grips with experience, there is no choice but to fabricate a theory about it. But the theory then threatens to force itself upon the theorist as if it were direct experience, as Secondness, the clash of the "real," and finally it becomes for its maker identical with the "reality" originally serving to make it a bit more intelligible in the first place.

119

No Sign Is an Island

Recursion, but with a Difference

The way of the ether is not an isolated story. Indeed, throughout history the West's diverse scientific "cosmologies"—and all other belief systems, for that matter—have failed to withstand the test of time, and in all probability none will ever do so. Even though they eventually become embedded in the consciousness of the community of knowers, sooner or later there will be a dawning awareness that they do not correspond to the "real," after all. Nor have arguments for any cosmology ever been finalized. After the partisans of conflicting "cosmologies," ideologies, or whatever, have talked themselves into exhaustion, the arguments themselves invariably remain open, and the game goes on. Habits are generally subject to the same story of perpetually flowing variability: they are never an end in themselves but rather the means toward a receding end in a perpetual process of becoming.

Habits, like symbols, *grow.* They do so from within, immanently, along epigenetic trajectories, rather than as a result of some mystical or mysterious outside force. All habits evolve through their simply being exercised, and this exercise is necessarily a recursive activity whereby the habit brings about a not quite exact repetition of what transpired previously. This self-referentiality is perhaps most evident regarding thought-signs—phanerons—which entail, according to Peirce, "experimentation in the inner world" (CP, 5.491; see also Boler 1964). Peirce, in this context, makes the apparently bizarre claim that a problem in mathematics—that most cerebral of inner activities—can have no "real and living logical conclusion" unless it is forthcoming by way of habit. In other words, the verbal or written formulation of a mathematical proof is merely an expression of a habit, which constitutes the true logical or final interpretant. Peirce does not deny that a nonmathematical concept, proposition, or argument can be a logical interpretant. He only insists that it cannot be the *final* logical interpretant. He concludes with the observation that though a habit by itself

> may be a sign in some other way, [it] is not a sign in the way in which that sign of which it is the logical interpretant is the sign. The habit conjoined with the motive and the conditions has the

action for its energetic interpretant; but action [spoken or written words] cannot be a logical interpretant, because it lacks generality [hence it is always incomplete]. The concept which is a logical interpretant is only imperfectly so. It somewhat partakes of the nature of a verbal definition, and is as inferior to the habit, and much in the same way, as a verbal definition is inferior to the real definition. The deliberately formed, self-analyzing habit—self-analyzing because formed by the aid of analysis of the exercises that nourished it—is the living definition, the veritable and final logical interpretant. (CP, 5.491)

121

This passage cries out for commentary, even though it must of necessity be brief. Habit, or the logical interpretant, which is most adequately characterized as generality, is invariably incomplete, and as such it is outside strict application of the excluded-middle principle. It is never static, however, but perpetually on the move; it engages, by way of its agent, in self-analysis. Self-analysis and self-enrichment are not alien to other apparently different concerns. Witness, for instance, Julia Kristeva's (1969) semiotics, which must repeatedly question its own presuppositions, Feyerabend's (1987) "science in a free society," Agassi's (1975) "science in flux," Foucault's (1970) *epistemes,* and Derrida's (1974) deconstructive acts turning back on themselves, to say nothing of the self-organizing domains of general system theory (Jantsch 1980), the physics of complexity (Prigogine 1980), and self-perpetuating organisms and societies (Jantsch 1975; Laszlo 1987). Postmodernism itself is transient, constantly subject to critique and eventual displacement. In other words, styles of reasoning have proliferated in the past, and there is no indication that the process will not continue into the foreseeable future.

But just as the logical interpretant, in spite of habit, can neither stand alone nor stand still, so self-analysis cannot be carried out in the ideal Cartesian sense of the corpus being subjected to scrutiny with the assumption that subject and object undergo no change as long as the game proceeds. The notion of a discrete, timeless set of thoughts and events is, by the same token, a reduction alien to Peirce (CP, 5.450; 4.457). The nominalist typically holds that there can be no "General without Instances embodying it" or "thought without signs" (CP, 4.551). However, one errs, Peirce believed, in concluding that a general is nothing unless incorporated in its particular instantiations (CP, 5.312).

For Peirce, thinking simply cannot be reduced to a conglomerate of isolated signs (CP, 4.6). Although all thoughts are signs, they are neither divisible nor absolutely separable from other thoughts. Thoughts—like habits, logical interpretants, beliefs, and dispositions in general—are an extension of the general process of signs. Moreover, thoughts are interdependent, for to say that "thought cannot happen in an instant, but requires time, is but another way of saying that every thought must be interpreted in another" (CP, 5.253, 284), which implies, once again, an infinite series. This interconnectedness is further emphasized in Peirce's assertion that no thought or cognition "has an intellectual significance for what it is in itself, but only for what it is in its effect upon other thoughts. And the existence of a cognition is not something actual, but consists in the fact that under certain circumstances some other cognitions will arise" (CP, 7.357).

122   That is to say, each thought, as a *would be,* is the effect of the action of other signs on it and its own effect on other potential signs whose own *would be* lies in the future. The futurity revealed in this statement is Peircean through and through. And it bears on the self-correcting nature of logical interpretants, whose authentic definition, as Peirce puts it, is the "living definition" evinced by their very existence, by the dance they do on the world's stage. This "living definition," it appears, is extra- or translinguistic; it lies beyond mere utterances or marks on a page. Such signs define themselves by what they do rather than what they say. And since their dance is continuous and processual, their futurity holds no promise of finality or totalization. For

> as what anything really is, is what it may finally come to be known
> to be in the ideal state of complete information, so that reality de-
> pends on the ultimate decision of the community; so thought is
> what it is only by virtue of its addressing a future thought which is
> in its value as thought identical with it, though more developed. In
> this way, the existence of thought now depends on what is to be
> hereafter; so that it has only a potential existence, dependent on the
> future thought of the community. (CP, 5.316)

The perpetually virtual existence of this ideal state of complete information bears witness to the impossibility of there being a final state, an Ultimate Interpretant. It is also commensurate with Peirce's emphasis on the continuity of habit, belief, disposition, and the process of thinking, in contrast to events, acts, objects, and individual thoughts. This perpetual virtuality is directly relevant to the distinction between a given semiotically real world and the actually real, the topic to which I now turn.

An Uncertain Cloud of Unknowing

According to high modernist philosophy, the mind is a remarkable instrument capable of mirroring the world; and language is, potentially at least, a "picture" of "reality"—here, admittedly, Peirce's mind as "glassy essence" puts him dangerously close to classical thought. According to the venerable tradition, there is an object "out there"—say, a tree—and its image "in here," the product of some sort of *camera obscura* inside the skull. We have the material thing and its mental replica, and consciousness plays its role as author of pictorial reproduction as if it consisted of lenses, receptive surfaces, and mechanisms for carving out traces on these surfaces.

That tradition's days are numbered.[1] If we lend an ear to the teachings of recent quantum physicists, especially Wheeler's—to be discussed in chapters Nine and Ten—and suppose that without mind and its recordings we can have no universe, the message begins to ring loud and clear. The world "out there" may not be directly dependent on the mind, and much less on consciousness, but the world as semiotically real recorded phenomena put to use by someone for some reason or purpose clearly is. And semiotically real worlds are not mirror images, replicas, or simulacra but rather constructs, in the manner of re-presentations, each with an inevitable tinge of difference. In this sense, all re-presentations are something other than what they were and other than what the world *is*. Yet they never cease to entice us to believe that they are "real," clearly and simply. But actually, they are Nietzschean fictions, more or less invariably false to themselves.

Rather than mirror images, such signs are, more appropriately, re-presentations re-presenting not what *was* but what *is* insofar as it has become something that could always have been otherwise. In other words, a sign is not an exact replica of its predecessor but something else, something it *was not,* something new: one can never enter the same *semiosic* flow twice—indeed, one cannot even enter the *same* flow once. Consequently, human perception of images in the iconic or de-generate sense demands a paradoxical leap. Something must be perceived as what in part it *is,* but also as what in part it *is not.* The person whom Peirce's example in Chapter Four of a portrait re-presents is not two dimensional, she does not consist of variously colored smears of paint, she is not twenty-three or so inches tall, and so on. When the *is not* is not available to consciousness, problems threaten to arise. If the portrait is not seen at least in part as what it *is not,* then, in Peirce's words, "the distinction of the real and the copy disappears, and it is for the moment a pure dream" (CP, 3.362; see also Ransdell 1979).

When birds peck at the grapes in Zeuxis's paintings, when a coyote responds to a whistle approximating a rabbit in distress, when ducks land among a flock of decoys, they are not simply perceiving simulacra. As far as they are concerned, it is the "real" article. Their behavior is geared to what *is,* without their knowing that it is in part what it would not otherwise be. The *is not* alters their actions nary a bit—that is, until in one way or another they sense the deception. Upon becoming so sensitive, they somehow—and at some dreamlike level of consciousness, we must suppose—reach an awareness *that* what was "there" was not "really there."

123

Knowledge in the Peircean sense is thus possible solely when one becomes aware of that which *is not,* or in another manner of speaking, aware that one has erred. In order that one's sign perception might progress from the dim consciousness of, say, a fuzzy green patch (First), to *that* green *there-now* (Second), to the concept *tree* (Third), one must be capable of knowing the percept is *this* percept and *not* something else. This negative aspect of the sign at its most primitive level is of the utmost importance to semiotics. A replica or image can be part of—or, regarding compound signs, potentially the whole of—a mental model, a cognitive map, an agenda for living. With an inevitable degree of vagueness, it is capable of showing its bearer what the semiotically real world *is* for a particular human community. But what that world *is* cannot be said precisely, for any and all acts of saying will always be incomplete.

In other words, there can be no legitimate "metamap," no metalanguage. Any chimerical metamap would necessarily contain the map plus the world it maps, and therefore it would contain itself—the paradox of which Peirce was quite aware. Lacking in precision—that is, faithfulness to the world—any given image cannot but be a blemished icon. But it is an icon indicated (indexed) by the semiotic object to which it corresponds. Relations between parts of a partial or whole image that are analogous to relations between the parts of something else without there (yet) existing any reference to anything "out there" constitute a diagram, which, when coupled with the internal image, makes up the second of Peirce's three types of *hypoicons.* The third hypoicon, a metaphor, is the re-presentation of a primitive cognitive map as mere possibility, as Firstness (CP, 2.276–78).

A hypoicon or "dead" metaphor—the product of de-generation—re-presents "the representative character of a representamen by representing a parallelism in something else" (CP, 2.277). Notice that the re-presentation is that of a parallelism rather than of "something," and that the parallelism implies the sign's being what something else in part *is* but also in part what it *is not.* This negativity is a common feature of all metaphors (Hausman 1975; Merrell 1983). Metaphorical language has a sort of built-in self-destructive quality. It is playful, not to be taken in dead seriousness. Yet it allows its contemplator to see something *as* something else, and it thus refuses to be understood in terms of the logician's either-or (it transcends the logic of identity, noncontradiction, and excluded-middle). The metaphor sets up an undecidable oscillation between the *either* and the *or.* It neither means what it says nor cancels what it means. It merely offers itself up as a sign. It is displaced, a *difference* and a *deferral,* as Derrida (1973) puts it, with a tinge of arbitrariness and a dose of necessity by way of habit and convention.[2]

Peirce questioned whether icons, hypo- or otherwise, are necessarily likenesses. For example, "if a drunken man is exhibited in order to show, by contrast, the excellence of temperance, this is certainly an icon, but whether it is a likeness or not may be doubted" (CP, 2.282). Peirce quickly brushed this problem aside as a "somewhat trivial" question. Nevertheless, it effectively illustrates the point being made: where there is likeness, difference lurks in the shadows. The alcoholic is both like and unlike the person of temperance, in which case the onlookers are asked to attend to what the drunk *is not* but poten-tially—one would hope—*could be.* Particular differences between the two people can become likeness, given enough time, for the potential relation between them is of the nature of an image, not a metaphor.

125

If, on the other hand, someone were to say, "He's a sponge" with reference to his imbibition of spirits, then we must focus on the likeness be-tween the man and the object with which he is compared. He *is* a sponge re-garding his capacity to soak up and metabolize a particular sort of beverage, but a sponge is also that which he categorically *is not.* With metaphors, there must always be differences, for the relation is that of resemblance in certain respects and difference in others. Yet, although the first "drunkard" icon de-mands certain negative relations and the second certain positive ones, neither icon could operate properly without negativity: there is no absolute identity here, nor are there simulacra in the sense of re-productions so faithful that no difference is or can be acknowledged.

But an abatement of difference, coupled with an intensification of sameness—the product of de-generacy—can and does exist. I can point to a painting and remark, "That is a remarkable tree," to which a bystander might respond, "Are you referring to that two-dimensional painted surface or to that 'tree'?" (bring to mind, for example, René Magritte's nonpipe pipe painting). I have maintained a distinction between the image and the "real" article, if only tacitly. On the other hand, if I gaze at what I believe to be a tree and say, "What an unusual tree," I may be met with the response, "That image you refer to is actually not a tree but a lifelike 'tree' projection on the wall before you." What I took to be genuine was merely an image; I was taken in by the painting-as-simulacrum.

Whether in the first case I am referring to a painted surface or to a real tree, I think I am referring to something. The sign is charged with indexical properties, so it is not merely imagistic but also diagrammatic insofar as I have foregrounded relations of analogy between an image, be it simply the painted surface or what I labeled "tree," and what I consider to be an authentic tree as type, by habit or convention (CP, 2.277). In the second case, I viewed the paint-ing as if I were contemplating an actual tree, a token. I did not establish the necessary relations between the image and something else. As far as I was con-cerned, the sign *was* a tree, clearly and simply, without my being at the moment consciously aware of what it *was not.* The sign did not launch itself from the sphere of "treeness" as a semiotically real quality to take on diagrammatic characteristics in terms of what the tree-as-image *was not.* In other words, the painted image was for me a de-generate, iconized sign. It was as if the image were "real."

This distinction between image and diagram is in essence that between self-reference and reference to something else that the sign both *is* and *is not,* between autology and heterology. For example, the mind pictured as a mirror consists of the mind's conjuring up an analogy focusing on that self-same mind. The mind is its own image without legend or label (CP, 2.276). It merely looks at itself; it reenters its own space; there is nothing "out there" as a constant reminder and indication of what it *is not*—a *sine qua non* for indexical (diagrammatic) relations of analogy. In contrast, with Magritte's nonpipe pipe painting, the mind contemplates an image "out there" of a pipe along with the caption (index) "This is not a pipe." *Thisness,* as distinct from *otherness,* is established between the eye of the beholder and something "out there" and between that which the image *is not* and what it *is.*

If, with Peirce's first-degree de-generacy, a necessary relation between sign and object is retained, then indexicality is preserved, and the mind is capable of effectively distinguishing between something and something else. Possibilities and parameters of choice still exist: questions can be asked of the world "out there," and what *is* can be selected and distinguished from what *is not.* That is, what *is* can be set apart from what ordinarily *might have been* but *is not.* As such, the semiotically real depends upon its being set apart from what it might or could have been but *is not,* from its otherness.

In contrast, when second-degree de-generacy (iconization) is in effect, distinguishability can become well-nigh impossible. For the birds duped by Zeuxis's artistry, the two-dimensional paint smears *are* grapes; an ultrapatriotic North American (still) views the hammer and sickle icon as the adversary; for a Christian fanatic the number 666 *is* evil; a late nineteenth-century scientist views the universe literally in terms of machines; for an early sixteenth-century Aztec warrior, the sun *is* a god. In the case of animals following innate response mechanisms, simulacra rather than "real" things can elicit automatic behavior, as do Zeuxis's grapes. In the case of the human semiotic animal—and perhaps primates and other more intelligent species—there has been a declension "downward," from what was in its inception a symbol to an index and finally to an icon, such that the simulacrum, model, or logo becomes simply *the world that is.*

In figure 6, an extrapolation of Peirce's triad of signs, "image" and "concept" are a rough counterpart to Saussure's *signifier/signified* pair—albeit without semiology's trappings of modernism, its endemic binarism, its slaughtering of process, its myth of presence and logocentrism. According to Peirce's conception of the sign, *SO* relates to ("determines," in Peirce's terms) *R*, and *R* relates to *I*, which mediately re-presents *SO* as a result of *R*'s having been related to it. The sign is never immediately present to the mind but mediated, the *I*'s role being that of bringing *SO* and *R* together in such a way that the relations depicted by the sign triad are two-way. The sign components in this manner make up a democratic trio. The "real" object, *RO*, on the other hand, is not a full-fledged partner in the semiotic dance but teasingly lends an open hand here, does a do-si-do there, and sashays a bit somewhere else, remaining all the while in its totality beyond the semiotic considerations of a finite community of sign users. The "real," in other words, affects semiotic activity, but it cannot be absolutely known and remains as it is in spite of what its would-be knowers think about it (thus the arrows leading to *SO* are broken rather than solid).

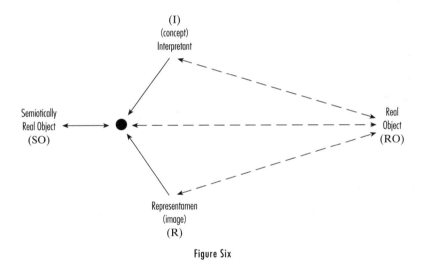

Figure Six

If a chemistry student dips a piece of looped wire into an NaCl solution and places it in a Bunsen burner flame, the "sodium ions" (*SO*) will produce (relate to, "determine") a "yellow-orange hue" (*R*), which serves to conjure up (relate to) in the mind of the analyst an interpretant (*I*) inferred (by mediation of the *SO-R* relations) from her semiotically real-world knowledge of halogens, spectral properties of the elements, valences, atomic structure, and so on. This interpretation is the result of the fabric of knowledge (signs) that she has internalized representing for her, by convention—e.g., learning in the classroom, reading her textbooks, previous experience in the laboratory, imitating her mentors, and so on—the presence of "sodium ions" in the solution. Of course, this entire process is not directly related to *RO*, which is "a dull affair, soundless, scentless, colourless; merely the hurring of material, endlessly, meaninglessly" (Whitehead 1925, 54). *RO* simply *is what it is,* in spite of our perception and conception of it. It is Peirce's "real," which remains independent of community opinions.

If, say, a phlogistonist had witnessed the characteristic sodium flame, he might have exclaimed: "Why, a veritable miracle! That water appears to be combining with phlogiston from the air, which, being of negative weight, would cause it to diminish in volume and density, but our better judgment dictates that this should not be so, for water cannot burn." Thus our student's interpretation was only one of a host of possibilities that might have presented themselves, some valid and some not. In fact, given Peirce's pragmatic maxim, there is potentially an infinity of ramifications to the analyst's apparently simple test, which bears on the entire *semiosic* fabric of interpretants (e.g., chemical composition, salts in solution, oxidation, spectroscopic theory, the relation of elements of valence +1 to others, and so on).

It is worthy of mention that the student's conclusion, "This solution contains sodium ions," bears the stamp of ordinary language's delusive simplicity, which tends to mask the wealth of her implicit knowledge about chemistry. The words she utters are a mere drop in the river—the ongoing stream of what she very vaguely knows, often without being consciously aware that she knows it: understanding lies beyond the mere use of individual words. Many assumptions, filtered up from habit, belief, and expectations, are put to the test without one's being consciously aware of testing them. Consequently, much of the act of understanding keeps the door to consciousness under lock and key, and explicit knowledge must wait patiently outside in the corridor for the result. The pragmatic maxim implies so much.

In this fashion, progression from the immediate interpretant (the range of possibilities allowing for polysemy) to the dynamical interpretant opens the pathway toward the unattainable final interpretant. In order that the sign be wholly understood, its potential infinity of relations to all other signs in the *semiosic* flow must be actualized, which remains beyond reach in a finite world. Thus *semiosis* perpetually subjects signs to change, and semiotic reality is, to a greater or lesser degree, perpetually altered. For this reason, when a particular interpretant has been actualized, there has been partial acknowledgment of the object's properties and effects as a mind-dependent, semiotically real entity. But at a particular time and place, there always remains an indeterminate range of unactualized possibilities re-presented by the immediate object as opposed to the dynamical or actualized object. The gap between *SO* and *RO* in figure 6 will apparently never be absolutely closed for us.[3]

Due to this unbreachable gap, connecting lines between the representamen, the object—whether semiotically real or "real"—and the interpretant

128

are of two sorts. The continuous lines in figure 6 represent *direct intensional linkage* "in here" (phanerons), and the broken lines represent *indirect extensional linkage* "out there" (the mind as set apart—albeit artificially—from the *semiosic* process). Unlike C. K. Ogden and I. A. Richards's (1923) empirical positivist triadic model of signification, I establish no direct connections between concept-image and what Ogden and Richards would dub the external referent.[4] Direct linkage between representamen and "real" object, which corresponds to second-degree de-generate signs, would be roughly equated with what Ogden and Richards term "word magic": the sign would be construed as if it were not a sign at all but the "real" article. In fact, sign and thing can, by successive embedment, become perceived and conceived as coterminous. Such a de-generate sign, however, is actually re-presentative not of the "real" object but of an imagined content, which, like any semiotically real object, can be no more than a selective abstraction from the "real."

129

Since the intensional object stands some outside chance of approximating the extensional object in Peircean asymptotic fashion, the broken lines can depict convergent series. Intensional linkage, like its extensional counterpart, is thus two-way: the signs in the triad are self-referential and can be constantly subject to self-critique and self-correction. In this process, they are incessantly becoming transmuted. Such linkage can appear to be freewheeling, gratuitous, and relatively autonomous of the world "out there." On the other hand, it can be the product of de-generate (embedded, automatized) signs mistakenly construed as if they were actually "real" (i.e., symptomatic of "word magic"). In this latter case, the broken lines have become *as if* solid lines—such as the iconization of the machine model-metaphor, or the result of hallucination (e.g., Macbeth's "dagger"). The sign relation "universe ≈ machine" became de-generate to the extent that "universe" as a sign passed into oblivion and "machine" took over its function, acting out "universe's" erstwhile role on the stage of *semiosis* with full confidence that it was coterminous with the "real." The scientific community, and Western civilization at large, was gradually taken in by this sign-universe, and as a consequence, the citizens of this community eventually came to conduct their lives accordingly.

But, of course, the machine metaphor is a monumental leap of abstraction. We also have the relatively simple yet dramatic example of a de-generate sign responded to automatically as if "real" in the viewers of those 3-D movies, who, behind their ridiculous bitinted glasses, involuntarily shrank back at the sight of a train appearing to project out of the screen at them. The sign became for them the "real" thing, and fiction suddenly engulfed the world as our previously rather neutral spectators gave a direct, automatized response to what should have been properly mediated by the signs' fictive interpretants. Linkage between *R-SO-I* and *RO* became, for a fleeting moment, direct.

Regarding this "real"/semiotically real distinction, let us consider Magritte's nonpipe pipe further.

A Pipe Is a Pipe Is a Pipe

According to one's ordinary "dictionary knowledge," a "pipe" is "a slender tube flattened at one end so that it fits comfortably between the lips and teeth and with a small bowl at the other end to be filled with tobacco for the purpose of smoking." The utterance "This is a pipe" seems simple enough. It is a proposition (compound symbol) consisting of an index ("This") and an icon ("pipe") whose proper meaning entails at least tacit awareness of our "dictionary" understanding of the word. This tacit awareness also comes into play in the use of "pipe" as a de-generate sign.

Suppose, for example, upon overhearing the comment on the evening news, "The senator's proposal is a pipe dream," one mindlessly reaches for one's pipe, places it in one's mouth, and lights it. This would appear to be first-degree de-generacy. The pipe is rather nonconsciously foregrounded as the semiotically real object of an index (dicent sinsign), after perception of the sign "pipe," without any necessarily explicit awareness of the relation between "pipe" overheard as a metaphor and the actual pipe as an instrument for a specific set of activities.

On the other hand, the evocation "This is not a pipe" underneath Magritte's lifelike painting can force awareness of second-degree de-generacy at the same time that it plays havoc with our comfortable ways with words. The caption forcibly brings to our attention the fact that the lifelike painting, if masquerading as "real," is actually false to itself; it commits the sin of a second-degree de-generate sign passing itself off as a genuine article. The ordinary function of a label is to say what something *is*. However, in Magritte's painting, it says what the thing *is not,* and in addition what the painting itself, as an *image* of something, *is not,* thus apparently negating even the caption's right to proper signhood.

Indeed, Magritte's work seems to suggest what Hegel might have written about negation, the most misjudged, misunderstood, and maligned function of *semiosis,* had he been less stodgy (Wilden 1987, 245). That is, Hegel's negation negates the other but not itself, in contrast to "This is not a pipe," the inherent negativity of which it carries within itself. The entirety of Magritte's painting *is* (as icon) and *is not* (as symbol) that which it signifies; it *is* and *is not* an indicator (index) of something else, and it *is* and *is not* a re-presentation for someone in some respect or capacity. That someone, presumably the onlooker experiencing Magritte's work, is, at the juncture when the painting begins to oscillate between the *is* and the *is not,* himself a sign. As merely a sign in the presence of, and before interacting with, the sign, he is no more than an unful-filled possibility. And until he determines what the sign *is* (at least for him) and interprets it, he, like the sign, is marked by negation. That is to say, insofar as he is set apart from the sign, he *is not* a genuine sign, and if he interacts with the de-generate sign, merging into it while it merges into him, neither he nor the sign bears genuineness: both are hardly more than negation. They are actually *no*-signs, but they *may become*—or better, *will have become*—somewhere along the *semiosic* stream, full-blown signs. In Peirce's words, the individual, "so far as he is anything apart from his fellows, and from what he and they are to be, is only a negation" (CP, 5.317).

131

The same applies to an individual's relation to other individuals (them-selves signs as well) in his community. He cannot pass from mere possibility to assume the role of an interpreter (interpretant) except by acknowledging the *is* and *is not* regarding himself, the signs around him, and his entire community of interlocutors. Only then is he in a position to mediate between the *is* and the *is not* and thus engender what he, his signs, and his community *will have become,* given the inception of certain *semiosic* moves. The real mind-bender stems from Magritte's revealing the paradoxical core of this very interpretive process itself. Demands are exacted on the interpreter-interpretant to set himself *apart from* the painting's signs he contemplates, but at the same time, he is himself an interpretant-interpreter inextricably caught up in the *semiosic* flow as part of the entire process. Suspended within the flow, he has no recourse but to con-tinue treading water, his immanence within *semiosis* having discounted the possibility of his reaching the shore, from which vantage point he could survey the whole scene before him. In other words, though he makes a valiant effort, he will not be able totally to escape his own immanence as signness. And it all has to do with the sign's (and the interpreter-interpretant's) element of nega-tion. It is as if he were to say, "I *am not* that which I *am,* and I *am* that which I *am not,"* revealing that he is nothing until he has exercised another move in the becomingness of his being in relation to the signs around him, while during that same act his being is that very becomingness.

The same is to be said of all signs. For example, Anthony Wilden (1987, 245) observes that if we ask ourselves precisely what it *is* about Magritte's work that *is not* a pipe, various responses are possible:

1. This "pipe" (icon) *is not* a pipe.
2. This image (icon) *of* a pipe *is not* a pipe.
3. This painting (icon) *is not* a pipe.
4. This sentence (symbol) *is not* a pipe.
5. This "this" (index) *is not* a pipe.
6. "This" (index) *is not* a pipe.

And I must add yet another, Gödelian-Quinean sort of possibility (see Quine 1966):

7. *"Is not* a pipe" *is not* a pipe.

The predicate (icon) of (7) mirrors the subject (index), and the subject mirrors the predicate, in an infinite regress of mutually negating Borgesian images illustrating the power of the sign's negativity. The latter half of the sentence is preceded by a quotation of itself that negates or falsifies it. Consequently, just as neither "pipe" nor image nor painting nor sentence nor "This" nor "this" is a pipe, so also the sentence *"Is not* a pipe" *is not* a pipe, either. In other words, the qualification *"is not* a pipe" attached to "pipe," image, etc., which denies their membership to the class of all pipes, is equally denied by its own mirror image. And that mirror image is in turn denied by its mirror image, and so on, ad infinitum. So if the signs in Magritte's work are signs only insofar as there is acknowledgment that they *are* signs of that which they *are not,* then the sign *"is not* a pipe," which qualifies them as potentially genuine signs, must be self-referentially subjected to its own qualification, which is precisely what it *is:* it *is not* a pipe.

There is a major difference, however, between sentences (1)–(6) and sentence (7). The former *are* what they *are not* with respect to their semiotic object; the latter's semiotic object is more severely restricted to words qua words. It remains suspended in language. In this manner, it more directly says what semiotics is all about: the study of *semiosis,* the process of signs of their respective semiotic objects for particular semiotic agents in some respect or capacity, and, at the same time, the process of signs denying that they *are* what they signify. That is, just as our semiotic agent, at the inception of the process of interpreting a sign, is such that it is as if he were to say "I *am not* that which I *am,* and I *am* that which I *am not,*" so also the symbolic sign, suspended within its own linguistic medium, says what it *is not* and it *is not* what it says. The sign's becoming a sign renders it a sign only in the sense that it is an ongoing act of becoming, therefore a perpetual denial of what it *is.*

In order to illustrate my point further, consider the following reciprocal forms, given as a variation of Alfred Tarski's (1956) "'Snow is white' is true if and only if snow is white":

8. "This 'pipe' (icon) *is not* a pipe" *is* true if and only if this "pipe" *is* a pipe.

And:

9. "This 'pipe' (icon) *is not* a pipe" *is not* true if and only if this "pipe" *is not* a pipe.

132

At the outset, we must observe that "truth" has been shoved onto center stage: what *is* or *is not* is subject to decidability. If assertions (8) and (9) are "true," then the *is* reigns supreme, and if they are "false," then what is questioned *is not* the case. But things are not as clear and simple as we might wish. We must now contend with "truth" and with those conditions that provide the props for the scaffolding upon which "truth" is to rest. Sentence (8) stipulates that the "pipe" must first be regarded as a pipe before it can properly be a nonpipe, and (9) stipulates that the "pipe" must be considered a nonpipe before it can properly be regarded as a pipe. This places us in a now familiar quandary. Like the two phrases in sentence (7), (8) and (9) appear to cancel each other out. The problem is that categories are confused in both instances, which, of course, goes against the tide of Bertrand Russell's interdiction in his theory of Logical Types.

133

But this is not so tragic. In fact, this confusion of categories is absolutely necessary for all perception and conception of things that are not "real" as if they were "real": models, metaphors, and fictions (see Merrell 1983).[5] The moral of this story, in brief, is that what for us is real is such only insofar as it may be gauged by a semiotically real (i.e., unreal) standard, and what is unreal or fictitious is such only insofar as it may be gauged by the standard of what is for us real, which is itself inevitably blemished with a streak of unreality. What *is* is nothing unless it entails an implicit background containing what *is not,* and what *is not* is mere "nothingness" unless it is noticed absence, the absence of what *could have been* or *will have been,* given other conditions.

It might appear that I am attempting to collapse "reality" into mere fiction, pure mind stuff, without a solid leg to stand on. However, I have no doubt that when a tree falls, it "really" falls, and with a crash, independently of any observer: the falling tree *is,* of course, what it *is.* If no observer is present, then the tree as a Peircean sign, as something re-presenting something to someone in some respect or capacity, has not been properly actualized (put to use). The physical event was "real" nonetheless, and the potential of a semiotic event for an agent, human or otherwise, was there; the potential for the sign's becoming authentic simply remained dormant. So pipes are "real"—"brute reality," Peirce calls it—whether or not they or their re-presentations are actually put to use as signs. Magritte's painting is in this sense also "real," as are the pipe image it contains and the word "pipe," though they *are not* pipes. Yet they are "real" pipe-signs. That is to say, they *are not* pipes, for, quite simply, they *are not* pipes. Neither are they *non*-pipes, for the pipe-signs could not have come into existence without there having been some set of prior conditions delineating "pipeness." The pipe-signs, like any and all signs for us, never emerge ex nihilo; rather, they are engendered from previous signs, and they engender future signs:

there is no first or last Peircean sign. In this sense, our pipe-signs are signs only insofar as there is some sort of noticed absence of what *could have been* or *will have been* under other circumstances but *is not.* As we shall note in the next chapter, there is no *non* or *not* in the sense of nothingness for signs that have been engendered and processed in some form or other. Rather, *non* and *not,* as far as any semiotic agent is concerned, are comparable to the empty set, ∅: the noticed absence of some-thing, some-thing that *could have been* or *will be* but *is not.*

134   It is definitely a sign's world. But we are not along merely for the ride. Rather, the semiotic agent collaborates actively with signs, and she is absolutely necessary for the becomingness of *semiosis.* (Please bear this crucial aspect of the sign in mind, for in Chapter Eleven we shall note that, in contrast to Jean Baudrillard's simulacra—autonomous signs that have become more "real" than the "real"—a sign is not a sign, perceived and conceived as such, without some tacit or explicit acknowledgment on the part of the active semiotic agent regarding what it *is not.*)

Semiotic Complementarity

Signs at the Time

Peirce's ten basic signs can be graphically illustrated by the connectors from figure 2 integrated into figure 7 and represented in more geometrical form in figure 8. The notations *R, O,* and *I,* and their respective subscripts in figure 7 correspond to representamina, objects, and interpretants, and the Peircean categories of Firstness, Secondness, and Thirdness, respectively (see the left-hand column of figure 3).[1] The three sign components designated by their corresponding subscripts are successively generated upon progressing from the "lower" to the "upper" portion of the schema, or they can be transmuted by degeneracy from the top "downward."[2] The subscripts indicate the signs' respective "mode of signification": Firstness (possibility, what *might be*), Secondness (actuality, what *is*), or Thirdness (necessity, what *would be,* given a specified set of conditions).[3] Firstness is the mode of signification "of that which is such as it is, positively and without references to anything else"—a sign of itself. Secondness is "that which is such as it is, with respect to a second but regardless of any third." And Thirdness is "that which is such as it is, in bringing a second and a third into relation with each other" (CP, 8.328).

Writing specifically on phaneroscopy, Robert Marty (1982, 170) wisely observes that there are no foolproof instructions regarding the classification of phanerons, nor is there any guarantee that a particular analysis of phanerons into their atomic forms is such that they cannot be split up further. He goes on to argue, contrary to many critics who believe Peirce's triadicity is a matter of chance and choice rather than compulsion and constraint, that triadicity involves necessity and follows what Peirce calls the "logic of relations." As Peirce frequently observed (CP, 1.298, 347, 363), and as Marty (1980) argues elsewhere, in elementary recursive formulations, any relation between *n* entities, where *n* is greater than three, can be reduced to, and described as, a combination of triadic relations.

The same, I would suggest, can be said of *semiosis.* In the case of either phanerons or signs in the most general sense, the three modes of signification—*R, O,* and *I*—are the basic signifying instantiations. As figure 7 demonstrates, the *I*'s mediary function is carried out by virtue of some resemblance (subscript 1, a First), semiotically contrived connection (subscript 2, a Second), and/or conventional link (subscript 3, a Third), between an *R* and certain mind-dependent characteristics inherent in an *O*. Realization of this mediation entails the creation of a semiotically real domain, which, while never absolutely coterminous with the actually "real," might asymptotically approach it.

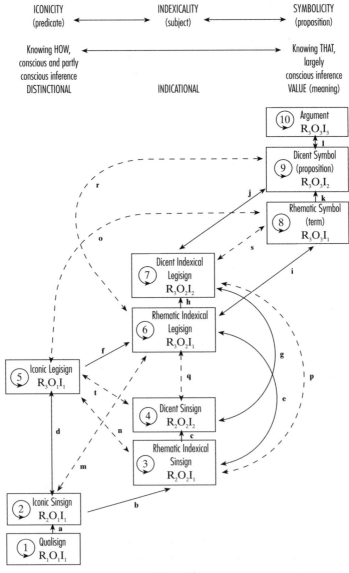

Figure Seven

As mental or phaneronic entities, R, O, and I are interrelated in the sense that, according to Marty,

or:

R determines I to refer to O

I maps R onto O.

Marty continues, with reference to Peirce's letter to Lady Welby of 23 December 1908 (Hardwick 1977, 73–86), that subdividing R, O, and I into R, O_i (immediate object), O_d (dynamical object), I_i (immediate interpretant), I_d (dynamical interpretant), and I_f (final interpretant), combined with the original ten triads, ultimately yields sixty-six sign classes.[4] Rather than attempt expatiation on this rather overwhelming mélange of signs, I will limit myself to Peirce's fundamental decalogue.

137

The lowercase letters in figure 7 can be regarded as *operators* taking signs from one type to another.[5] Solid arrows represent "normal" pathways of sign transmutation within the network of relations, while broken arrows represent "anormal" paths. "Anormal" transmutation entails either (1) a leap across two steps in the evolution of R, O, or I, (2) a single step taken by two of the three elements (denoted by the subscripts) making up a sign, or (3) a step downward, from a higher to a lower subscript. Unidirectional arrows, either solid or broken, signify sign *generation,* or evolution (*semiosis*), from relatively underdeveloped to developed and from relatively simple to complex signs. Two-way arrows signify, in addition to evolution "upward," possible pathways of degeneracy "downward"—or in the terms of this inquiry, what can under certain circumstances be qualified as sign embedment. Sign embedment, as we have noted, is a sinking into nonconsciousness of the effect of a sign such that an action or interpretation becomes tacit knowing *how.* As a consequence, relatively complex signs tend to be perceived and conceived as if they were of a "lower" sign type. Finally, one-way solid arrows encircling each of the sign types indicate reiterative instantiations of the same sign, each recursion of which serves as an alteration, though ever so slight, of the sign and of the possible range of its future signification. The sign is thus a haecceity, a singularity.[6]

In Search of the Main Channel

Let us now attend more closely to the classes of signs in figures 1–3, 5, and 7–8.

At the ground level, sign 1 is a *qualisign,* a mere possibility or feeling, such as the sensation "blue," without there (yet) existing any consciousness of the blue sensation as such. This *icon,* by operation a—the addition of a Second to the representamen, as shown in figure 7—becomes an *iconic sinsign,*

2, which consists of any object of experience whose quality is determined by the idea of it. Sign 2 is a "sign of essence," which is also an icon, without any definite linkage to an object to which it can potentially refer.

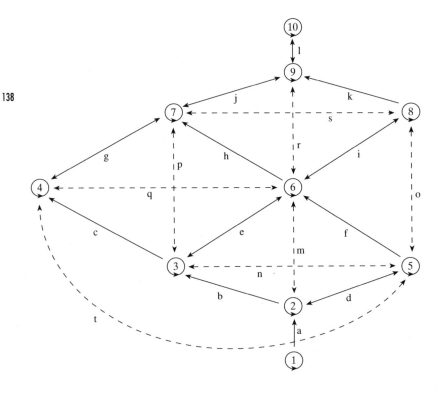

Figure Eight

At this most basic level, as I have argued elsewhere (Merrell 1991a), there is no *thingness* (semiotic object) of a specific thing, nor is there any interpretant specifying a thing's place in a semiotically real world or any definite sensation of something (sign 2) embodying the mere possibility of that sensation (sign 1). There is only the semiotic equivalent of a *mark of distinction,* according to G. Spencer-Brown's (1979) elegant calculus accounting for the original severance of the universe into something that "is" and something that it "is not"—i.e., a separation of *this* from *that, I* from the *world.* This mark (written ⌐), is tantamount to what Peirce (CP, 6.189–204) calls a *cut* in the "nothingness" of pure possibility, pure space, or a sort of "pre-First" (Baer 1988). Space, in the ideal Peircean sense, is continuous. The rudiments of an individual sign, like Spencer-Brown's mark of distinction, are first marked off in this space of "nothingness" and made discontinuous or "grainy." Then as signs—and, by extension, minds—proliferate, they begin to merge into one another; and the entire collection, in theory, eventually becomes continuous and, once again, spacelike. In fact, the universe of signs and space ultimately meet; signs create each other, as well as time, in their comings and goings in/through space.

However, there is a fundamental difference between Spencer-Brown's mark of distinction and Peirce's initial semiotic steps. An operator of the most primitive sort, Spencer-Brown's mark potentially indicates (indexes, points to), in space, the crossing of a partly to wholly arbitrary boundary, in order to sepa-rate something from something else. The lowercase letters in figure 7, in con-trast, are a more advanced semiotic form of the mark insofar as they take signs across boundaries as the signs become transmuted into something more than or less than, but always distinct from what they were—which now places them in a new signifying space. Hence the chief difference between Spencer-Brown's primitive operator and the operators in figure 7 rests in the latter's character as potential authors of *signification,* while the former is merely *distinctive* and at best indicational (binary), signifying no substantive function whatsoever (see Kauffman and Varela 1980).[7] The Spencer-Brownian mark, however, in estab-lishing a distinction and an indication, possesses the rudiments of icons and indices insofar as it *is* what something else—that which is potentially indicated by it—*is not.*

Operation *b* introduces the object of sign experience of the most basic form, such as the evocation "Look!" a flash of lightning, or a loud crash, which serve to draw attention to something by which its presence is caused. This *rhematic indexical sinsign* uses an iconic sinsign of a particular sort in order to attract the attention of the addressee without there yet existing something to be meant for her as such-and-such. The product of *b,* which generates the first *rheme,* is the signifying counterpart to the more primitive Spencer-Brownian *indication* ("index," following from the originary mark). At this stage, the sign re-presents some possible quality that might be embodied in a future object.

The *rheme* also approximates what Bertrand Russell called a *proposi-tional function* (see Savan 1987–88, 41). For example, the incomplete proposi-tion "——— is blue" leaves the blank as a possibility to be filled with an indefinite number of future sign-objects. This recalls the Peircean proposition (sign 9, a dicent symbol), in its most skeletal form. A proposition of this most simple sort, according to Peirce, consists of an index (subject) and an icon (predicate) (CP, 2.438). In the case of "——— is blue," the predicate is specified, though it remains indefinitely vague, while the subject is merely an empty set, therefore a general sign in the broadest sense. As *pure* Firstness, the sign, "———," is com-plete, since it merely indicates the possibility of all signs that can fill the hole. But as an authentic sign, it is indefinitely incomplete, for it specifies nothing. It

139

is a simple indication, not yet dressed in any signifying garment. In other words, icons and indices by themselves assert nothing. An assertion or proposition demands that there be a combination of both subject (index) and predicate (icon) (CP, 2.291).

Just as Spencer-Brown's distinction remains unfulfilled without its corresponding indication, so operator c, which yields a Second to the interpretant—though not filling the hole left by operator b's subjectless proposition—generates sign 4, a *dicent sinsign*, such as a weather vane "pointing" the direction of the wind to the interpreter. It is the initial sign that provides for direct experience of, and information concerning, the semiotic object. The representamen as such is now virtually intact. Here also we encounter the first authentic stage of semiotic duality: the weather vane is a sign of both wind and the wind's direction, both the thing and the product of one of its properties. Hence it incorporates the most primitive essentials of a proposition: a subject (the thing, index) and a predicate (its property, icon). In a comparable dyadic sense, a portrait (icon) with the artist's signature (index) informs the onlooker of the sign regarding its subject as well as its author (Savan 1987–88, 52). Hence it also contains the bare rudiments of a proposition (CP, 2.320).

Operation d breeds sign 5, an *iconic legisign*, which is the first sign of the nature of a general, a universal, or *type*. Each instantiation of this sign embodies a definite quality, or iconicity, which serves to call up in the mind a general idea—though at this point it remains quite vague—of the object. It is an icon, but of a special sort. It governs a series of singular instantiations of an object, each of which is an *iconic sinsign*, toward some general concept. This operation is relevant to Spencer-Brown's *iteration* and *condensation* by his Axiom 1 to yield ⌐⌐ = ⌐, which, to rephrase Spencer-Brown, would read: "A *distinction* (icon-sign) made again is the same as the first *distinction* (icon-sign), and the *value* (symbol-interpretant) *indicated* (indexed) two times in succession is the same as its having been *indicated* (indexed) once" (Spencer-Brown 1979, 1). That is, as an incessantly differentiating token, the sign is on its way toward becoming, by way of the mind, a full-blown type. This, for better or for worse, is how generalities are built up, as if accumulated haecceities were capable somehow of yielding legitimate quiddities, as if by accelerating staccato, legato would somehow result: differences tend to be ignored, while sameness is highlighted.

Yet, as I pointed out above and argue elsewhere (Merrell 1985a, 1991a), there is never absolute identity after each reiteration in the semiotically real world. For example, Brian Rotman (1987) illustrates how iteration of a mark generates enumeration—I, II, III, . . . n—like tally sticks, which, at a more abstract semiotic level, would be represented as natural numbers. While this general rule applies in the strict mathematical sense, regarding the relatively loose use of signs in everyday affairs, the doubling back of a less rigorously precise sign into itself is an inexorably incomplete recursion. The reinstantiation of a sign is never exactly what it was. There is always and invariably a slight difference from one sign to its successor sign.

This is not to imply that Spencer-Brown's calculus of distinctions and indications is inapplicable to the semiotic framework. It is, however, based on a more primitive act of distinguishing, indicating, and attributing value (by way of a name) to that which has been distinguished, rather than on Peirce's logical (that is, semiotic) value or form. At this more primitive level, all acts of distinction and indication are identical: qualitative differences are smoothed out, and focus is reduced to the mere act of creating boundaries separating *this* from *that*. All distinctions, indications, and values are thus treated alike.

In order for each Spencer-Brownian distinction and indication to be foregrounded as such, it must be named, and subsequently it takes on a particular value. "There can be no distinction without motive, and there can be no motive unless contents are seen to differ in value" (Spencer-Brown 1979, 1). In fact, a distinction, as will become evident as this and the following three chapters unfold, cannot exist as such without its concomitant value. If a distinction is named X, and X is sensed as something to someone, "I," then "I" has set herself apart from X ("I" X), in order that X ultimately may become something standing for something to "I" in some respect or capacity. That is, X inherently contains the potential to become a triadic sign in the full Peircean sense.[8]

In sign generativity, *value* is introduced with operators e and f, which collapse 3 and 5 into 6. Sign 6, a *rhematic indexical legisign*, "is any general type or law, however established, that requires each instance of it to be really affected by its Object in such a manner as merely to draw attention to that Object" (CP, 2.259). Each replica of this sign will be at the same time a rhematic indexical sinsign (serving merely to draw attention), a dicent sinsign (offering the object of direct experience), and an iconic legisign (contributing its character of generality). A demonstrative or relative pronoun is the prototypical case of a rhematic indexical legisign, the radical incompleteness of which is evidenced by a loss, via operation q from 4 to 6, of the second-level interpretant.

Generation of sign 6 by operator e adds a Third to the representamen, while the indication of *this* rather than *that* is not yet a definite object of specification. In contrast, f transforms 5—which necessarily involves both a *rheme* and a *legisign* (CP, 2.258)—into 6 by integration of a Second to the object (e.g., a weathercock), in order to specify what the *this*, now having been distinguished, *is*. Sign 6, which is both distinctive and indicational and has been assigned the rudiments of value, sets something apart in contrast to something else, as *this* instead of *that*, which involves the primitive expression of a binary relationship at the second level of the semiotic object.

141

In addition, sign 6 forms a *quasi-proposition.* That is, further development of the indexicality of the sign brings it closer to its role as the authentic subject of an embryonic *proposition,* toward which the sign is developing. As a result, 6 embodies information in the form of an assertion of some sort about some existent. This existent, as an object having now taken on a value—albeit still vague—develops toward a subject (index), which, combined with a predicate (icon), will eventually make up a proposition composing part of an argument—the ultimate goal of Peirce's decalogue of signs.

Operators *n, q,* and *s* involve reduction or partial cancellation, either of the semiotic object (by operation *n*) or of the interpretant (by operations *q* and *s*). This reduction is roughly the Peircean counterpart to Spencer-Brown's Axiom 2, the "law of crossing" ($\daleth = \blacksquare$), which, in semiotic terms—and once again rephrasing Spencer-Brown—would read: "If the boundary separating the *thisness* of a sign from the *thatness* which it *is not* is *crossed,* and then it is *crossed* again, the *value* indicated by the two *crosses* taken together is the same as the *value* indicated by none of them" (Spencer-Brown 1979, 2).[9] That is, there has been a cancellation—absolute in the Spencer-Brownian sense but no more than partial in the semiotic sense—of either the semiotic object or its interpretant, leaving the original unboundaried, $\blacksquare$.

Operation *n,* from 3 to 5, adds a Third to the representamen at the expense of the semiotic object. "—— is blue," for example, as the rudimentary structure of a proposition, reduces the status of the object of the sign, rendering it not the empty category, $\varnothing$, but an exceedingly vague entity, for "is blue" endows it with at least a potential quality. In contrast, *q* and *s*—from 4 to 6 and 7 to 8, respectively—create a loss of interpretive capacity.

Operation *p* entails a leap from the "lowest" to the "highest" level of indexicality in the absence of an interpretant in the full sense, hence the sign still remains radically unfulfilled. For example, the spontaneous evocation, "Go!" is a sign referring to the context of its emission and directed to someone for some purpose, though the task of its interpretation must be left to the interpreter, since very little has been specified by its emissary. On the other hand, operation *g,* taking 4 to 7—or vice versa—entails transition from a still-fuzzy general type to a more specific *dicent indexical legisign.* This sign "is any general type or law, however established, which requires each instance of it to be really affected by its Object in such a manner as to furnish definite information concerning that Object" (CP, 2.260). It involves both 4, in order to signify certain information, and 6, by way of operator *h,* to denote the subject of that information. Instantiations of 7 are typical of embedded, automatized (de-generate) forms of signification. Such is the case when signs sink from conscious, voluntary, and intellectual use to nonconscious, involuntary, and tacit use, whether for better or for worse. This is the transition from generality to vagueness, from knowing *that* to knowing *how,* from Michael Polanyi's (1958) *focal* to *subsidiary* awareness, and from symbolicity to iconicity.

These signs can be de-generate forms of sign 9 (a proposition), such as holophrastic expressions ("Hi!" "Ye gads!" "Wow!"), or certain nonlinguistic indexical signs that evoke a general contextualized response without there yet existing a definite object of the implicit proposition indicated (e.g., a knock on the door, the ring of a telephone). Such embedded or automatized and/or degenerate sign use, the result of a relatively advanced degree of habit, is also evidenced by Wittgenstein's (1953, 1958) evocations from language games, the prototypical case of which is "Slab!" In its fully embodied form as sign 9, this expression is the equivalent of "Bring me a slab," "Put the slab here," or some such thing. These condensed forms of sign use, for proper intelligibility, must be accompanied, within the appropriate communicative (pragmatic) context, by necessary and conventional nonlinguistic cues.[10]

While sign 7 at least implies the essentials of the predicate (icon) of a proposition, it nonetheless remains an unfulfilled form, not having been endowed with the *who, what, where,* or *when* of the subject. L. S. Vygotsky (1962) cites examples of this sign from literature, most specifically the works of Tolstoy, to illustrate how interlocutors who have known each other for years reduce many sentences to their skeletal (holophrastic) form, the meaning of the fully fleshed-out utterance being tacitly acknowledged by all parties concerned. In this manner, sign 7 is implicitly, and by nonconscious inferential reasoning, given corporeal dress through operators *j* (7 to 9) or *s* (7 to 8).

Operation *i* transforms sign 6 (*this* rather than *that*) into a *rhematic symbol,* 8, which serves explicitly to specify the subject or term of a proposition. This sign is "connected with its Object by an association of general ideas in such a way that its Replica calls up an image in the mind which image, owing to certain habits or dispositions of that mind, tends to produce a general concept, and the Replica is interpreted as a Sign of an Object that is an instance of the concept" (CP, 2.261). This sign is a symbol of a general type and thus a legitimate legisign rather than a sinsign (index) or qualisign (icon). Its particular instantiation as a replica qualifies it as a rhematic indexical sinsign as well as a rhematic indexical legisign, since the image (icon) that it suggests can be (indexically) called to mind, giving rise to a general concept (symbol).

In addition to the rhematic symbol's being merely *that* with respect to a particular sign instantiation referring to, say, a camel (as a rhematic indexical sinsign), it is the *general idea* "camel," which, in relatively limited semiological terms, is very roughly the Saussurean *signified.* Thus "camel," like the vast majority of all symbols, can be in the beginning arbitrary, though by habit it becomes conventional and therefore necessary. And thus this symbol, its aloofness regarding the *thisness* of any and all particular camels having been established,

143

can, with successive habituation, become many steps removed from the concrete experiences of everyday life, as we shall observe below. All words are legisigns, and they are either directly or indirectly related to their respective semiotic objects. Nonetheless, indexicality is more prominent in words (i.e., Roman Jakobson's shifters) such as "this," "here," and "I," and iconicity is hypertrophied by use of adjectives, such as "radiant," "short," "rapid," and "gloomy." Symbolicity, on the other hand, is most adequately embodied in concept words and abstract terms, which generally make up propositions and arguments.

Operation j takes the dicent indexical legisign to the dicent symbol (dicisign, or proposition), which contains a term or terms generated by $i, s,$ or o. Along with k, j links the noun or subject to the predicate. "Hi!" a knock on the door, or a telephone signal, as third-degree objects without any corresponding interpretants, can now be fully embodied. A proposition is a compound sign consisting of a subject connected to its semiotic object through its predicate by an association of general ideas. It functions much as a term, except that its intended interpretant signifies it as being actually affected by its semiotic object. Such signification requires that a semiotic connection exist between the proposition and an event. Thus the interpretant tends initially to interact with a term most properly as a dicent indexical legisign by way of operator j, since the *thisness* of the sign instantiation, rather than its general use as a term, is the more immediate focus of the interpretant.

But this is not the whole story. A proposition, like a term, is also necessarily a legisign. Like the dicent sinsign (which includes both a rhematic indexical sinsign and the iconic sinsign), it is a composite sign insofar as it involves a rhematic symbol. Hence it is for its interpretant in a certain sense also an iconic legisign—the bare rudiments of a predicate—in that it conveys its information, and a rhematic indexical legisign—the essentials of a subject— for the purpose of indicating the subject of the information. An isolated proposition, however, does not enjoy an authentic interpretant. A fully embodied interpretant is potentially—though never actually, given Peirce's asymptote— available through the generation of an argument from a set of propositions. An argument is the sign of law. What Peirce means by law is "the passage from all . . . premisses to . . . conclusions [which] tends to the truth. Manifestly, then, its object must be general; that is, the Argument must be a Symbol. As a Symbol it must, further, be a Legisign. Its Replica is a Dicent Sinsign" (CP, 2.263).

Consequently, the iconic legisign takes on axial importance due to its initial fulfillment as the embodiment of the third-level representamen, while the object and interpretant remain at the initial stage, to be filled out in the argument. It is for this reason that o, which takes sign 5 to sign 8, is the first operator capable of transmuting a sign directly to the symbol column in figure 7. Thus a weather vane as sign becomes the semiotic object of the general term "weather vane," which is capable potentially of referring to the class of all weather vanes.

It is noteworthy that c, h, k, l, p, and r magnify the interpretant. These are the principle stages toward the development of *habit, habit change,* and *habit-breaking.* As we observed briefly in Chapter Five, habit breaking is the "modification of a person's tendencies toward action, resulting from previous experiences or from previous exertions of his will or acts, or from a complexus of both kinds of cause" (CP, 5.476). Just as the valued can be devalued, and just as the embedded can be de-embedded, so habit incessantly undergoes succes- sive degrees of modification—whether willingly or unwillingly, consciously or tacitly—on the part of the signifying agent.

145

Symbolicity: *Semiosis* at Its Best or Tyrant?

The question may then arise, How is it that *I* brings about the union (mediation) of *R* and *O?* Peirce coined the term "interpretant" in *On a New List of Catego- ries* (1867) and never abandoned the concept, though he later added signifi- cantly to its meaning. *I* is itself a transformer. It is like an interpreter lying within a particular domain of signs, Peirce writes, because it is like saying in one language the same as has been said in another language. This immanence of *I* is fundamental. The notion of an interpreter traditionally implies a tran- scendental subject operating on the domain of signs. In contrast, Peirce's interpretant highlights the fact that the interpreter is inseparable from the sign: she is a sign among signs—i.e., Peirce's notorious "Man ≈ Sign" equation (Burks 1980; Fairbanks 1976; see also Merrell 1991a).

In a strict linguistic context, Savan (1987–88, 41) points out that the term "translatant" seems somewhat more adequate than "interpretant," though the latter is more generally applicable to the entire universe of signs. The interpretant translates signs into other signs and signs into their semiotic ob- jects. For example, if you are not familiar with the Spanish word "ciudad" and look it up in a Spanish-English dictionary, you will find "city," a replica of the general term "city," to the right of "ciudad." Now you know that (1) any semiotic object called "city" can also be called "ciudad"; (2) a grouping of *Homo sapi- ens* plus an assortment of other domestic and nondomestic organisms, of struc- tures of diverse sorts, of bureaucratic machinery, of trucks, garbage cans, skateboards, and so on, is a "city"; and (3) "city" is a sign of mediation between "ciudad" and the class of semiotic objects that can be assigned to the general term "city."

Savan (1987–88, 41–44) observes that the combination of (1), (2), and (3) makes up a syllogism, which, in Peirce's conception, makes up an *argu- ment.* This is not insignificant. Although Peirce later expanded his definition of the interpretant, at heart it is the prime motivating force taking signs potentially to their completion. Very appropriately, operators *c, h, k, l, p,* and *r* are crucial to sign development in the sense that they entail leaps from "lower" to "higher" interpretants. For example, the general image (sign 2) corresponding to the term "city" becomes a general yet vague idea (sign 5), the basis of a predicate. Then specification of *this* rather than *that* (sign 6) becomes a more developed indicator (pointer) for the semiotic object corresponding to *that,* or "ciudad" (sign 7). "Ciudad," in turn, leads to the term "city" (sign 8), which, when coupled with the predicate "is 'ciudad,'" which makes up a proposition (sign 9), potentially relates "city-ciudad" to a general class of semiotic objects. And subsequently, an argument (sign 10) can be generated.

Signs 8, 9, and 10, which fall within the category of symbolicity, reveal, at this outer edge of *semiosis,* the centrality of the speaker/writer engaged in dialogue with others and with his other self—as we shall note in the next section. The symbol, which is at least partly arbitrary, permits disengagement of the sign from its semiotic object such that it can veer away from customary pathways and begin referring to itself, which in turn frees it up to communicate *about* communication and actions. Hence it can lead the interpreter toward knowing *that*—explicit inferential processes—and communication about those processes. It also presents a relatively vast, even well-nigh unlimited, set of possibilities of signification. This characteristic of the symbol reveals, at the outer reaches of *semiosis,* a trend toward successive abstraction. However, abstraction need not become a fetish, as it generally has with modernity. Whitehead (1925), we will recall, counsels, in line with Peirce's concrete reasonableness, that the scientist—indeed, all of us, for that matter—must enter the game of abstracting, but always with a suspicious eye toward the product of her endeavors.

Successive abstraction, for better or for worse, marks the history of Western societies in general. Paper money is more abstract than gold, and gold is more abstract than bartering. Computers are more abstract than adding machines, which are more abstract than the abacus. From pictographs to hieroglyphs to cryptographs to phonocentric writing, or from tally sticks to arithmetic to algebra to group theory and quaternions, abstraction is on the rise. As signs evolve, they tend to be stripped of their referential clothing. They become universally and conceptually naked signs of absence, virtually connected to nothing (e.g., the gold standard, abstract bureaucratic procedures, the manipulation of signs in group theory, the arbitrary phoneme, Boolean computer logic, Rothko's art objects, Beckett's hyper-selfreferential narrative, Robbe-Grillet's detached prose, Cage's silence, Mallarmé's blank page). In other words, an emergent sign is capable of begetting other signs, which in turn engender enclosures of themselves. They become recursively self-referential, generating interpretants of a central, and hitherto implicit, feature of those very signs that gave rise to them.

Thus the connection—presupposed by modernist thought and radically highlighted during the glory days of logical positivism—between anterior "real objects" and posterior signs is illusory, the age-old dream of the sign's power of representation. "Objects" conjured up for a given interpreter cannot be any more than semiotically real. The signs of symbolic discourse refer directly neither to "things" nor to their absence but merely to the absence of their ancestors, which have long since become memory "traces," at worst unfaithful echoes, and at best vague. These signs are deferred, for they are not immediately present to their interpreters, and they necessarily differ from their predecessors. Nevertheless, symbols promise virtually unlimited capacity for knowing—and, unfortunately, for power and control, the obsessions of modernity—but, on the other hand, they can beguile and bewitch, once habit and belief (embedment, automatization) take their toll.

Sign 7 is the principle break-off point that opens the path to explicit knowing *that* and to the power of abstraction. On the other hand, 6 and 7 can be the product of de-generation from 8 and 9, respectively, in a transmutation from symbolicity to indexicality. The ensuing embedment is comparable to Spencer-Brown's (1979, 7) successive "depths" of marked and distinguished spaces. Like the rings of an onion, they can be recrossed ultimately to get at the "lowest" points, which, through actions sinking into consciousness, have become tacit knowledge, knowing *how*.

For a scheme representing the inverse of de-generacy, embedment, and habit, contemplate figure 9, where the uppercase letters in parentheses represent a booting up of *R, O,* and *I* to higher levels of complexity. This process most properly entails generacy, which can take on the form of de-embedment, a surfacing or resurfacing into consciousness of that which previously remained tacit. Iconicity is foregrounded in *A: I* booted up to 4. In contrast, *B* is primarily indexicality: *I* booted up to 7. And *C* highlights symbolicity: *I* booted up twice within the scheme. The signs of 4 and 7 are especially significant, since they are transitory: in their development toward "higher" forms they can either remain basically at the same level of *I* or move "down" by embedment.

If a sign is destined to remain at the same level, it undergoes iteration in self-referential recursive loops, which are represented by the self-returning arrows in figures 7, 8, and 9. Exclusively within this self-returning sphere, as an icon of itself, the sign also indicates (indexes) itself. It is, in a manner of speaking, both its own interpreter and its own interpretant. But there is no absolute identity here, as pointed out above. Each loop does not return exactly into itself. Rather, there is always a difference from one reentry to the next, like an aperiodic crystal, DNA, or life itself.[11] However, by habit, identity is imposed onto difference. Self-identity is not simply *there* for the seeing. It is in the eye of its habit-taking beholder.

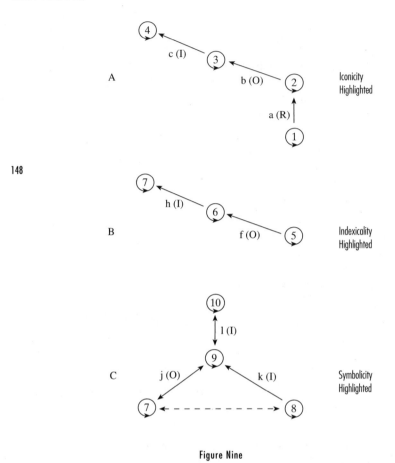

Figure Nine

The lingering question resurfaces: In spite of the above caveats, do the schemata in figures 7, 8, and 9 not blatantly commit the modernist sin of abstraction? This would certainly seem to be the case from one particular perspective. By virtue of their *ars combinatoria*—each of Peirce's ten signs possessing, as it were, its own triads—they are capable of generating 3^{10}, or 59,049, signs, which Peirce (CP, 8.343–47) reduces to his 66 fundamental classes. This indeed appears to be a Herculean feat of abstraction! However, one must be mindful that for Peirce there is a continuum between chance and law, feeling and form, quality and category, particulars and generals, semiotic objects and "real" objects, thought-signs and event-signs. He never intended to divorce pliable, concrete existence from hard-core abstractions.

One must also bear in mind that, in reference to his 59,049 signs, Peirce was writing about a long-range project entitled "Logic, Considered as Semiotic," which would include a disquisition on the three "modalities of Being" (that is, of signification).[12] The first modality is the *possible,* which is at all points "incapable of perfect actualization on account of its essential vagueness if for no other reason. For that which is not subject to the principle of contradiction is essentially vague" (Hardwick 1977, 81). The second is the *existent,* an object or "fact." And the third is the *necessitant,* a habit, or something expressible in a general proposition. It "includes whatever we can know by logically valid reasoning" (Hardwick 1977, 82). Peirce then goes on to call these three modalities *tone, token,* and *type,* corresponding to qualisigns, sinsigns, and legisigns. The watchword regarding the first modality is vagueness, which, coupled with generality, is responsible for the imperfect (i.e., incomplete) actualization of signs—and which is in part due to the imperfect return of a sign's self-recursive loop.[13] This vagueness by way of successive differentiation with each sign actualization, however closely it may approximate perfection, highlights the concreteness or near-concreteness of signs within their respective contexts. And the task of sign interpretation within these contexts lies with the interpreter.

149

A brief digression is in order, then, in order to qualify Peirce's concept of interaction between sign emissaries and addressees regarding interpretation. Peirce tells us that a sign which is indeterminate in any respect is vague insofar as "it reserves further determination to be made in some other conceivable sign" (CP, 5.447). The coy utterance "I could make a flattering remark about your looks this evening" suggests but does not specify, nor does the utterer necessarily authorize, any particular interpretation of his statement. Further determination of the sentence as a sign is left to other signs potentially generated at a future time, most generally as they depend on the discretion of their utterer. In this sense, every utterance to a greater or lesser extent "leaves the right of further exposition in the utterer; and therefore, in so far as a sign is indeterminate, it is vague, unless it is expressly or by a well-understood convention rendered general" (CP, 5.447).

It would appear that Peirce's vagueness principle makes for a strange sort of "logic" indeed. The meaning of a sentence as given either by future signs or by their respective emissaries can be subject to change from one spatiotemporal point to another: as the world turns, so also signs and their meanings. It thus cannot be said that the law of noncontradiction must invariably exercise its force. Nevertheless, the vagueness principle clearly falls in step with Peirce's general conception of signs. When one considers that a sign includes "every kind of thought and not alone external signs," one realizes that a sign must be not only subjectively indeterminate (vague) but also objectively indeterminate (i.e., its object is undetermined by the sign itself), and hence it is "objectively general" insofar as it "extends to the interpreter the privilege of carrying its determination further" (CP, 5.447).

So a generality principle complements the vagueness principle. The statement "Man is mortal"—a general proposition, or dicisign—is of the order of genuine Thirdness, in contrast to the possible or implicit note of flattery suggested in the above utterance, which most appropriately pertains to Firstness. Unlike the vague sign, whose further specification depends upon its creator, an interpretation of the general sign "Man is mortal," which evokes the question "What man?" is left chiefly to the interpreter. She can decide which man, how many men, all men, or all humans, as she will. However, if she wishes to verify the proposition absolutely, she cannot do so until she has witnessed the life and death of every living human, past, present, and future. Hence the excluded-middle principle does not necessarily apply to Peirce's conception of generality. With good reason, Peirce defines the final interpretant as the "full" semiotic effect of a sign if its purpose or intention were to be achieved. The "were to be" is destined to remain in the indefinite future, the theoretical long run of things. In this spirit, Peirce later writes that "[p]erhaps a more scientific pair of definitions would be that anything is *general* in so far as the principle of excluded middle does not apply to it and is *vague* in so far as the principle of contradiction does not apply to it" (CP, 5.448).

Thus, if a statement remains indeterminate, which is the case for all statements forthcoming from a finite community of speakers, there is no absolute guarantee that it will be identical with itself. So it is not necessarily either true or false, and it may be both true and false. At one extreme, we have the vagueness and indeterminacy of Firstness and, at the other, the generality and indeterminacy of Thirdness. In between is the world of actualized semiotic "facts" (the Secondness of signs), any given one of which, after being picked up by the mind, is relatively definite, though in the next moment it will have meandered on down the *semiosic* stream (CP, 5.449).

To shed more intelligible light on the issue let us, along the lines of Comfort (1984), engage in a play of "demonics." To do so, we must try to think how thinking could occur with modes ("styles") of thinking radically distinct from our own. Suppose we are playing a hide-and-seek game with a flatlander, who inhabits a two-dimensional universe. We move a pyramid of manageable size so that its peak touches our friend's impoverished planar universe. All he sees is a point, a Firstness of bare possibility. Then we slowly push the pyramid through his world, as if through the water's surface in a swimming pool. If one face of the pyramid is situated on an orthogonal plane with respect to the flatlander's line of sight, all he will see is the point extending itself in two opposite directions to form a growing line that threatens to cut him off from a large part of his world. The line disappears altogether when we finish pulling the base of the pyramid across the plane.

Of course, we find this exercise quite simple. From our imperious three-dimensional view, we can easily see that the initial point (Firstness) created the possibility for the generation of an infinity of triangles (Seconds) on the flatlander's planar universe by our slowly pushing the pyramid through it, and further, that this infinity of triangles actually makes up a solid pyramidal object. We can see the particular triangles *as* triangles and *that* they are isosceles or equilateral and of a certain size. We can see *that* the infinity of triangles actually makes up a pyramid, and we believe *that* all those triangles combine and collude to make up the general idea of a pyramid. The beginning dot was virtually infinitely vague, and the shapes of the infinite triangles generated from it depended entirely on the angle at which we, the creators of these geometrical objects, pushed the pyramid through the flatlander's plane; further determination of the triangle-signs was left to our whims and fancies. And as interpreters, we believed we could bring about further determination of this set of triangle-signs as a generality, for we could see it all quite clearly and distinctly. However, just as the lowly flatlander is limited by existence in a three-dimensional space-time manifold (two-dimensional space plus one-dimensional time), we are limited by existence in a four-dimensional space-time manifold (three-dimensional space plus one-dimensional time). It would be equally difficult for us to create the image of a hyperpyramid in our four-dimensional manifold as it is for him to imagine a hypertriangle—something like our pyramid—from his limited perspective.

151

The point on the flatlander's plane is like a vague seeing *as,* there as yet being no consciousness of anything definite. Any one of the given infinity of triangles is a generation from that point by a geometrical operator. This is the sensible world, which is "but a fragment of the ideal world" (CP, 3.527). Given other moments, an infinity of slightly to radically different triangles might have been actualized along the flatlander's plane. That infinity of triangles composes what we can consider in our hypothetical *Gedanken* experiment an ideal realm—for the flatlander at least. So if further determination of the vague sign (point) is left to the manipulator of the pyramid, and if further determination of the general sign (pyramid) is left to the interpreter viewing the triangles as they successively pop up on the planar surface, then there must be an intermediary stage between vagueness and generality and between total indetermination and total determination (CP, 5.450).

In fact, there is potentially an endless series of intermediacies consisting of the range of all possible triangles that can be actualized between the point and the base of the pyramid. This endless series consists of actuals in the sensible world, whether sign-events "out there" or thought-signs (phanerons) in the mind. The ideal, or general (Thirdness), is such that, with sufficient time, and given an infinite community, everything will be determinately either true or false. The ideal sign invariably remaining incomplete in our world of finite communities, however, its truth or falsity cannot be absolutely determined. And the possible, or vague, sign (Firstness) is such that one cannot absolutely determine whether it is not both true and false, for "two propositions contradictory of one another may both be severally possible, though their combination is not possible" (CP, 3.527). That is to say, each of the possibilities is vaguely, not distinctly, possible.

152   This constitutes the essence of what Peirce envisioned for his logic in the broadest possible sense. According to the tenets of classical logic, any property, once its identity has been discerned and determined, is either true or false. But for Peirce's more general logic, as long as it remains indeterminate—which will always be the case to a greater or lesser degree, given Peirce's fallibilist doctrine and his convergence theory of truth—it is not necessarily true that it is either true or false, and it is not necessarily false that it is not both true and false.

In view of Peirce's indeterminacy of signification, which renders his modality of signification semiotically rather than actually real, one is forced to conclude that Marty's (1982) postulate, "*I* maps *R* onto *O*," even though by and large correct, must be itself to an extent either vague or general, either inconsistent or incomplete—or, what is most commonly the case, it may be a mixture of both. Consequently, a given mapping must always remain to a greater or lesser degree indeterminate. Rather than following Marty's call for an "unambiguous axiomatics," and in light of Peirce's plea for "concrete reasonableness," perhaps we should make an effort to eschew the high-tech jargon of positivist discourse and modernist rationalism and gravitate toward the semiotics that Peirce envisioned in the first place: a sort of postmodern semiotics.

Semiotics is not a technical, methodological, theoretical panacea capable of melting down all phenomena into form and facts into formulas. Instead of the long-cherished dichotomies of instinct and reason, sentiment and logic, passion and objectivity, imagination and hard facts, Peirce conceived the world to be a fusion of nature and culture. Nature is not wholly unintelligible. Like mind, its operations are the result of an intermixing of chance, necessity, and cunning. The same can be said of culture. Both nature and culture are vibrant, not inert codes; they are flow, not a series of synchronic slices; they are dance, not still portraits.

This fusion coincides, quite aptly, with many of the tenets of the postmodern mind-set. Knowing *that* is never determinate, and knowing *how* is—especially regarding human signs and most particularly language—in constant flux. What is more, when knowing *how* is de-embedded and raised to a level of awareness, in most cases it can then be changed intentionally and at conscious levels. Such is, for instance, Bateson's (1972) *deutero-learning* and Popper's (1972) *argumentation* as a fourth Bühlerian mode of language use (see Merrell 1982). All signs are, over the long haul, *differences*. They are, as Bateson (1972) often put it, *differences that make a difference.*

A Matter of Context-dependent Signs

Regarding the triad of progressions—$R_1 \to R_3$, $O_1 \to O_3$, and $I_1 \to I_3$—consider the lattice in figure 10. (Those stalwart spirits who have successfully navigated the storm thus far but are made queasy by the abstraction of this section might consider skipping to the next section, where the waters are less turbulent.)

A lattice of this type can be defined as a set of interdependent signs—S_i (i = subscripts 1, 2, 3; S = categories R, O, I)—that are *partially ordered* and *nondistributive* (hence non-Boolean). For example, R_i is a representamen of the particular order i (First, Second, Third); O_i is the semiotically real object, therefore a sign of R_i; and I_i is the interpretant, a sign that passes on to become another representamen, either of generate or de-generate order. The empty set, $\varnothing$, represents what in lattice theory is called the *greatest lower bound domain,* and I_{f-1} is the *least upper bound domain.*

In other words, the sign $S_\varnothing$ is the null or empty set, the absence of combinations. And S_{f-1} is the sum of all possible sets—in a finite world of finite beings according to the assumptions underlying this inquiry. It is the practical limit with regard to a given individual or an entire community of knowers. On the other hand, the ultimate or final interpretant, I_f, the *sign of plenum,* is the Peircean ideal, that which would be the case in the theoretical long run. It is the totality of all possible universes of discourse. And the domain of nothingness, 0, is that which precedes the originary act of signification and even the empty set. The empty set is noticed absence rather than mere "nothingness," while "nothingness" is the total absence of absence (see Merrell 1991a, chap. 8).

The solid arrows in figure 10 represent *transitive, nonsymmetrical* relations, called *nondistributive* and *partially ordered,* and are comparable to *logical implication.* For instance, R_2, O_2, and I_2 are not cumulative but rather a nonlinear, partially ordered evolution of R_1, O_1, and I_1, their *complements.* They are in large part what their respective complements are not: the pairs R_2-R_1, O_2-O_1, and I_2-I_1 are linked (orthocomplemented) only insofar as the presence of one marks the absence—though a potential presence in some future space-time singularity—of the other (much like the ambiguous Bohr electron, which appears now as wave, now as particle). This sets the partially ordered lattice off as *context-dependent* as well as non-Boolean and nondistributive.[14] It is roughly comparable to what in microphysics has been called "quantum logic" (Heelan 1970, 1971, 1983; see also Merrell 1985a).[15]

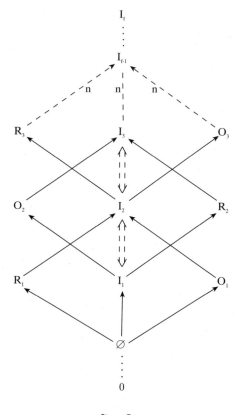

I_f

I_{f-1}

n   n   n

R_3 I_3 O_3

O_2 I_2 R_2

R_1 I_1 O_1

$\varnothing$

0

Figure Ten

The quantum logical characteristics of the *R-O-I* relations in the lattice are defined as follows:

1. If two units of the lattice, say, I_1 and R_2, are in relation "$I_1 \rightarrow R_2$," it can be said that I_1 implies R_2. The conditions for R_2 include those of I_1, hence whatever signification is possible within the narrower context of I_1 is also possible within the broader context of R_2. In other words, I_1 implies R_2, and R_2 ordinarily (though not necessarily) presupposes I_1. And both R_1 and O_1 imply I_2, which is to say that the broader context of I_2 is capable of encompassing both R_1 and O_1.

Regarding *semiosis,* what at the outset might appear to be an inchoate set of signs is actually partially ordered, beginning with the originary mark of distinction, or cut, which opens the door to an increasingly more complex, more complete, and less determinate corpus of signification. This occurs by way of those signs taking on, as a result of their interpretation by an individual interpreter or an entire community of interpreters, habit: they become increasingly regular, general, and lawlike.[16]

2. In the event that two units—say, I_2 and O_2—lie within incompatible contexts such that neither $O_2 \twoheadrightarrow R_2$ nor $R_2 \twoheadrightarrow O_2$, there may be a contextual domain common to both O_2 and R_2, which can be written: $I_1 = O_2 \times R_2$ (where "$\times$" is the logical product [or Boolean disjunction, $\cap$] of the two units). That is, a certain domain of context I_1 is in context O_2 and context R_2 such that $I_1 \twoheadrightarrow O_2$ and $I_1 \twoheadrightarrow R_2$. The logical product, then, calls for a move "down" to the "lowest" point of the lattice, represented by the symbols that the product is a product of. 155

3. A broader, more general, more complete, and less indeterminate context, I_3, may exist—the "lowest" inclusive context in the matrix as outlined in figure 10—that encompasses, for example, either the entirety of context O_2 or context R_2, or both. That is, O_2 and R_2 are at certain points incompatible but conjoined by a more encompassing context. This union can be written: $I_3 = O_2 + R_2$ (where "$+$" is the logical sum [or Boolean conjunction, $\cup$] of the two units). The logical sum, in contrast to the product, entails a move "up" to the highest point of the lattice, represented by the symbols that the sum is a sum of.

4. Since the impure and mixed contents of R, O, and I with subscripts greater than 1 imply that they contain within themselves vestiges of the other sign characteristics at their "lower" levels, the ordering relation "$\twoheadrightarrow$" indicates inclusion relative to the signifying (or pragmatic) resources of other sign types.

5. Logical negation (i.e., not-O_1) is coterminous with contexts O_2 and O_3. The field of signification appropriate to these contexts is $O_1 \text{-}/\!\!\twoheadrightarrow O_2$ and $O_1 \text{-}/\!\!\twoheadrightarrow O_3$ (where "$\text{-}/\!\!\twoheadrightarrow$" signifies "does not imply").

6. The "quantum logical" connectives "and," "or," and "not"—which effect the partial ordering of complementary, context-dependent fields of signification—require, for their paraphrase, more than the classical logical connectives "and," "or," and "not." In other words, for each unit and its respective context (e.g., R_1, O_1, and I_1), there are complements (R_2, O_2, I_2 and R_3, O_3, I_3) with the properties:

$$\varnothing \twoheadrightarrow R_1 \twoheadrightarrow I_2 \twoheadrightarrow R_3 \twoheadrightarrow I_{f\text{-}1}$$
$$\varnothing \twoheadrightarrow O_1 \twoheadrightarrow I_2 \twoheadrightarrow O_3 \twoheadrightarrow I_{f\text{-}1}$$
$$\varnothing \twoheadrightarrow I_1 \twoheadrightarrow O_2 \twoheadrightarrow I_3 \twoheadrightarrow I_{f\text{-}1}$$

etc.

7. According to classical Boolean distributive logic, $A + (B \times C) = (A + B) \times (A + C)$. In contrast, the non-Boolean character of the lattice gives, for example:

$$R_1 + (I_1 \times O_1) = R_1 + \varnothing = R_1$$
$$(R_1 + I_1) \times (R_1 + O_1) = I_2 \times I_2 = I_2$$

But:

$$R_1 =//= I_2!$$

Another non-Boolean feature of the lattice is its nonsimultaneity. In contrast to the units of classical logic, which are coexistent, the units of the non-Boolean lattice, like quantum entities, are complementary.[17] Only a part of the non-Boolean lattice lies open to view and can be made explicit (knowing *that*) at a given moment, the remainder lying implicit (knowing *how*)—much like the absent premise of Peirce's *enthymeme* or like the hidden relationships of quantum entities, which distinguish them from classical Newtonian objects. In Nick Herbert's (1985, 181) words:

> All quantum lattices consist of a union of Boolean sublattices (which some call "isles of Boole") adrift in a wave-logical ocean of non-Boolean relations. Within each isle of Boole, normal logical relations prevail, corresponding to the surface ordinariness (Cinderella effect) of compatible quantum attributes. However, relations between the Boolean isles do not satisfy the distributive law, which suggests that for quantum entities something is fishy about the connection between the whole and its parts.[18]

8. The notion of complementarily signifying entities implied by the matrix, according to which broader contexts include narrower contexts, might also suggest the idea of cumulative history, growth, process (i.e., self-correction). Of course, the relationships of complementarity are logical, and as such they do not require historical ordering, though their context dependency demands a temporal logic. Yet the principle of nonsimultaneity suggests that temporal though nonlinear relationships may parallel logical ones such that the sign of implication, "→," coincides with some sort of developmental process. In this sense, the passage from two otherwise disjoint entities to synthesis and mediation via *I* can pattern the general evolution of natural signs toward successive abstraction (i.e., symbolization), whereby the sign becomes increasingly divorced from its semiotic object for some interpreter.

The logic of complementarity would then be tantamount to a logic of interconnectedness, of *semiosis,* rather than of individual signs (see Finkelstein 1979 on quantum logic in this respect). It would relate signifying texts (sign textures, intertextuality) within their respective contexts. Such contexts would include not only the *this-hereness* (Secondness) of signs but also the *possibility* (Firstness) for signification and the *virtuality* (Thirdness) that, given certain conditions, the sign texture would take on such-and-such characteristics. Texture, in this sense, includes not merely the *explicate* but that which remains *implicate* (or enfolded) and can at a future moment become *explicate* (or unfolded).[19]

Put otherwise, what is absent (knowing *how*) can surface (into knowing *that*), and what is present can fade into virtual oblivion. Consequently, the ineffable stands a chance, at some future time and place, of becoming effable. (In his anti-Cartesian arguments, Peirce reiterated his faith in the ultimate intelligibility of the universe, though this can come to fruition solely over the theoretical—and therefore infinite—long haul of things [i.e., the asymptote].)

9. The paths $\varnothing \rightarrow R_1$, $\varnothing \rightarrow O_1$, and $\varnothing \rightarrow I_1$ and the equations $R_1 \times O_1 = \varnothing$, $R_1 \times I_1 = \varnothing$, and $O_1 \times I_1 = \varnothing$ denote alternate explications of implicates, or the unfolding of the enfolded, and vice versa. At "higher" levels, the same process applies, most dramatically in quantum shifts culminating in broader I contexts, $I_i \rightarrow I_{i+1}$. This occurs, for example, in the transitions in figure 7 from sign 3 to sign 4, or from 4 to 7, 6 to 7, 8 to 9, and 9 to 10. Such quantum shifts are, nonetheless, a process in time for the sentient observer.

157

10. $\varnothing$ is in essence no-thing, unless one of its alternatives is explicated such that its "no-thingness," a noticed or implied absence, is consciously or tacitly acknowledged (i.e., $a \times b$: a = not-b, b = not-a, with each iteration). In contrast, 0 is the "absolute nothingness" of what Peirce (CP, 6.512) calls the empty "sheet of assertion," which is ready for the inscription, by way of cuts, of that which can eventually make up a universe of discourse. This is the "nothingness" preceding all Firsts, Seconds, and Thirds (CP, 6.203–4). In this realm of pure chance, of myriad—and, for practical purposes, infinite—possibilities, no-thing *is;* yet everything is *superposed* (see CP, 6.352).

For example, if our Necker cube is viewed merely as a maze of lines on a flat plane, neither of the two cubes has (yet) been actualized. It can be said that the two possible cubes are superposed, and that the maze is the product of such superposition. Yet as nothing more than a set of lines, it is still something, though regarding the two possible cubes that can be generated from it, it is only an empty set. Familiar with the Necker cube, we can conceive of the two-dimensional maze as the noticed absence of either a three-dimensional face-up cube or a three-dimensional face-down cube.[20] Pure superposition as nothingness, in contrast, precedes any and all noticed absences. Consequently, given our finite capacities, it cannot be said that $a \times b = 0$. Rather, $a \times b = \varnothing$. In other words, superposition is the ultimate or ideal limit of Peirce's "higher logic" of pure vagueness, where everything is diffused continuously and merged with everything else, the classical principle of noncontradiction having become inoperative.[21]

11. On the other hand, $a \times b = I_{f-1}$, the result of the I's mediary role, invariably generates a by-product of indeterminacy and uncertainty, in addition to perpetual incompleteness, such that a and b are not simply mutually exclusive in the classical sense. Rather, both tend to be included within the I's domain, but not in simultaneity. For example, there is no single context within which the crystalline structure of ice as well as the viscosity of water can be

measured at 95° centigrade. The two experiments call for mutually exclusive contexts. In contrast, the relations inherent in the nondistributive lattice exist on a plane capable alternately of combining a context with b context. Regarding the electron, for instance, the inclusive context allows for measurement of its position or its momentum but not both in simultaneity.

This implies that: (1) though within the context of either a or b classical principles inhere, their combination into a manifold of contexts does not; (2) the manifold $a + b$, a nonlinear, nondistributive, partially ordered set, can be described as mediary, a conjoint between *this* and *that;* and (3) however, each of the subdomains a and b of the broader domain $a + b$ cannot properly exist without the implication of the other (its other). Returning to our example of water, in the classical sense, the investigator is limited either to an ice context—in order to observe crystalline structure—or to a liquid H_2O context—in order to observe viscosity. According to the nondistributive lattice, in contrast, there is nothing that is absolutely either a or b. Hence $a \times b =//= 0$. And the conjoint of a and b into an all-encompassing domain or context reveals that a and b are interdependent: if a is explicit, b remains implicit, but its implicitness must be tacitly acknowledged for the proper determination of a. Such is the yin/yang concept—which most likely influenced Bohr's development of the complementary principle. Nothing is exclusively either yin or yang, but each contains the seeds of the other.

Moreover, regarding the entire matrix, for instance, the subdomain $O_1 \to I_2 \to R_3 \to I_{f-1}$ is linearly distributed, as is $R_1 \to I_2 \to O_3 \to I_{f-1}$, but their conjoint into a larger domain is not a simple distribution. It is a mediary, synthetic context embracing otherwise mutually exclusive domains (see Heelan 1983, 182–84). Hence each of the interactive subdomains are never static but constantly changing, given the ongoing push of I_{f-1} toward its finality, I_f. This supports Peirce's contention that interpretation by an individual interpreter or an entire community of interpreters is not completable in a finite world (therefore, $a + b =//= I_f$ in any given semiotically real domain). There is an incessant tendency toward generality, without the possibility of arriving at the finish line (see Heelan 1970, 95–96).[22]

12. Hence any finite set of signs in the lattice is suspended between I_f and 0, two extremes beyond the horizon of conceivability for the interpreter, who is inextricably—as Bohr once said of the quantum physicist attempting to describe the phenomena under analysis—"suspended in language." 0, the domain of nothingness, must nonetheless appear inconsistent to this interpreter, who, in spite of herself, eventually resorts to classical principles. On the other hand, I_f which is equally inconceivable, is absolute generality (continuity), a model of which the community of interpreters can do no more than erect incomplete (hence discontinuous) castles in the air.[23]

158

In fact, we, as signs ourselves, as immanent knowers, are always already suspended within the diagrammatic matrix. It is as if you were caught within the map of a map of a map, ad infinitum, to which I referred in Chapter Three, trying to find your way about. If the map were complete in all its details, you must be able to locate yourself within the map you have spread out before you, and that self within the map must find itself in yet another map it has spread out before it, and so on. Such also is the case with Borges's narrator of "The Library of Babel" (1962, 51–58), who writes his text about the library while within that selfsame library, where the reader can also be found reading it. Incapacity or refusal to acknowledge this ultimate limitation and ultimate freedom, this source of Pascalian anguish and Derridean-Dionysian freewheeling play, has been a grave error of erstwhile semiologists, structuralists, and poststructuralists, some hedgehog semioticians, and, unfortunately, even a few of those who call themselves postmodernists. David Sless (1986) trenchantly makes this point about the early Roland Barthes of *Mythologies* (1972). By what right does Barthes presume the ability to stand above and beyond all "bourgeois practices" and pen rhetorically loaded and frequently witty, bombastic, and even condescending proclamations on the imperialistic tendencies, hypocrisies, peculiarities, and contradictions of French culture? "What special position does he speak from which enables him to indulge in such grand gestures? At stake is not whether his view is plausible or indeed whether he is right or wrong, but whether his position enables him to hold such a view without challenge. Clearly he does not" (Sless 1986, 46). This case is, I believe, somewhat overstated (and it must be conceded that Barthes had altered his stance radically by the 1970s).[24] Yet the point is well taken. As signs ourselves, we cannot hope to escape the diagrammatic matrix.

13. "Real" entities represented by a world of semiotically real objects between $\emptyset$ and I_{f-1} constitute the domain of Secondness, indexicality, the clash of "real-world" furniture on the mind. These are the ephemeral singularities, the nuts and bolts of our world, that render it "grainy" and somewhat accessible to our limited understanding. They are all we have to go on, since, if we follow Peirce, sensations—of either mental things or "real" things—lie at the roots of all knowledge.

14. The two-way broken double arrows in figure 10 stand out in apparent contradiction to much of what I have asserted thus far: they seem to take a giant step toward linearizing and ordering the otherwise partially ordered lattice. In the first place, the arrows do not depict logical implication but oscillation, from one state of affairs to another and from alternate frameworks, when an *I* mediates between an *R* and an *O*. If vertical lines are drawn between the *R*s and *O*s, figure 10 resembles two Necker cubes placed end-on-end and sharing one of their six faces. The cubes can be reconstructed by means of the subscripted

*I*s oscillating back and forth such that the squares alternately face outward. Thus the two superposed cubes constantly hold their alternating and complementary possibilities open.

Figure 11, which is abstracted from figure 10, is such a superposition of states, each with its own "eigenvalue"—in quantum-theoretical terminology. The drawing can be viewed as a two-dimensional set of interconnected lines without either of the two possible three-dimensional objects (yet) being actualized, and whose actualization cannot occur simultaneously but rather alternately. If *a* is the uppermost corner of the face-up, *b* fades back as the lowermost corner of the face-down, and vice versa. The resultant oscillation can be written as a binary Boolean wave train:

$$C = \begin{array}{|c|c|c|c|c|c|} \hline a & b & a & b & a & b \\ \hline \end{array}$$

which, in terms of figure 10's nomenclature, becomes:

$$O_i \times R_i = \begin{array}{|c|c|c|c|c|c|} \hline I_a & I_b & I_a & I_b & I_a & I_b^{25} \\ \hline \end{array}$$

In the context of Spencer-Brown's calculus, figure 11 is strictly two-dimensional. In order to account for the superposition and the intermittent actualization of the two possible three-dimensional imaginary states, which Spencer-Brown accomplishes with the imaginary number (value) $\sqrt{-1}$—to be discussed further in Chapter Eight—one must either "burrow under" or "jump over" the plane into a "higher dimension." This is tantamount to introducing a curvature on a two-dimensional plane that reenters its own space, in inverted fashion, much like the Möbius strip: twisted in three-dimensional space and connected at its two extremities, it oscillates, as one travels along its linear space, from "inside" to "outside" and back again.

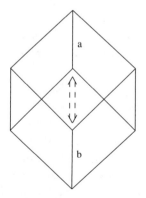

Figure Eleven

15. The centrality of *I*, I trust, has now become apparent. This centrality stems from sign interaction at the quantum, *microsemiosic* level (of Spencer-Brown's mark of distinction, or the originary cut in Peirce's imaginary "book of assertions" [CP, 6.512]). This is interaction of the most primitive sort between interpreter (observer-sign) and interpreted (observed-object), giving rise by way of a mediator (interpretant) to an interpretation.

Similarly, quantum complementarity stipulates that the instrumental setup or physical context lies between the observer and the observed, acting as a mediator to elicit, in the mind (sign), an interpretation (via an interpretant) not of what *is* but of what *has become* in the act of interpretation. Bohr (1934, 10) writes that quantum conditions force the scientist "to adopt a new mode of description designated as *complementary* in the sense that any given application of classical concepts precludes the simultaneous use of the classical concepts which in a different connection are equally necessary for the elucidation of the phenomena." To place Bohr's comments within the semiotic ballpark, the observed object of the sign can be given what may be presumed a natural-language description. This is the Secondness of the sign, that which apparently *is* in a *here-now* space-time singularity. But any corresponding interpretation (via an interpretant) inexorably remains to a degree tacit (implicit, entailing unmediated seeing and knowing *how*). Hence it is in part inarticulable, which renders the object not actually "real" per se but merely semiotically real. Much in Bohr's sense, then, the function of the entire context is semiotic; it is the leavening giving rise to the semiotically real, which stands between the observer and the actually real.

It bears mentioning that Bohr believed the only available descriptive language is the language of classical physics, which spells out the fundamental limitation of language itself. This idea is contested by Patrick Heelan (1970), among others (e.g., Feyerabend [1958]; Finkelstein [1979]). Heelan claims, contrary to Bohr, that the principle of complementarity actually entails the possible existence of a nonclassical language within a more encompassing context ($[a + b] \succ I_{f\text{-}1} \succ I_f$) capable in the theoretical long run of accounting for the more complex framework. This assumption, however, seems to go against the grain of Peirce's asymptotic model of knowledge as capable of no more than successive approximation—with fits and jerks and progressions and retrogressions—toward the "real." Under either interpretation, the central importance of the *I* is highlighted.[26]

16. The relationship between the elements in figure 10 can be further illustrated by an (admittedly quirky) Venn diagram (figure 12). R_1, O_1, R_2, O_2, R_3, and O_3 are two-dimensional non-overlapping, intersecting planes in a three-dimensional domain, their subscripts signifying their indefinite projection toward $I_{f\text{-}1}$ by way of the *I*s' mediary function. This function is made possible by

the fact that I_1, I_2, and I_3 are three-dimensional "bulbs," or "tunnels" in the Spencer-Brownian sense, capable of rotation and thus allowing access, through mediation, from R_1 to O_3, O_1 to R_3, and so on.

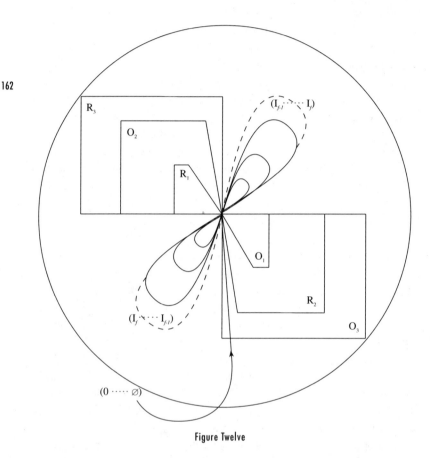

Figure Twelve

Each of these "bulbs" is the equivalent of a three-dimensional Möbius strip—comparable to a Klein bottle—allowing, at the juncture of its twist, a transition from the lower-dimensional habitat of the Rs and Os into the higher, mediating domain of the Is, potentially to open a pathway leading to I_{f-1}, and in the ideal long run, I_f, whose dwelling place is spherical, encompassing the entire "universe of signs." And $0.....\varnothing$ represents emanation from the center of the sphere, the "zero degree," the nothingness (*sunyata*), to the empty set of all possibilities from which the entire universe of signs is generated (Merrell 1991a, chap. 8).

17. At $\varnothing$, the values of R_1, O_1, and I_1 are radically indeterminate until a particular sign is actualized. The entirety of figure 10 could be construed as

topological, an infinitely pliable rubber sheet yielding a continuum of possible values, any one of which might happen to pop up at a particular moment. In fact, a possible sign is not determinately either R_1, O_1, or I_1, but, given the context, what might have been I_1 is actually R_1 or O_1 or something else, which seems adequately to account for the quality of vagueness at the "greatest lower bound of the matrix."[27]

In sum, the lattice's nonlinearity is at least partly linearized and temporalized by mind, as depicted by the trembling, scintillating Is such that sign generation of all sorts becomes possible. The Spencer-Brownian, Boolean wave train phenomenon cannot but occur in time. Indeed, it is what makes time manifest. Only through mediation of the Is can signs become signs for some interpreting mind in some respect or capacity. Thus the distinction between mind and sign, mind and matter, vanishes. Mind is a sign by inference, a sign is an act of mind; and matter, the ground of mind, is mind-bound by habit (CP, 6.101, 173, 201, 613). In fact, just as the universe is now conceived to be more mindlike than machinelike, so also Peirce, before the age of the new physics, argued that "[t]he one intelligible theory of the universe is that of objective idealism, that matter is effete mind, inveterate habits becoming physical laws" (CP, 6.25).

163

Thus the range of Is, the interpretants, holds a privileged position in the scheme of things. For example, R_2 and O_2 can be properly interpreted only through their disjunction within I_1 (or intermittently, I_2), while I_2 (or intermittently I_1) can be generated by means of the conjunction of R_1 or O_1. In other words, in figure 7, signs 4, 7, 9, and 10, generated especially by way of operators c, h, k, and l, which take I_1 to I_2 and I_2 to I_3, are of paramount importance. Sign 4 entails construction of the ground of a proposition in terms of generality or law, while 7 involves 4—which serves a signifying role—and 6, which is a pronoun containing the makings of the subject. Sign 9, a proposition, takes in 7 and 8—the term or subject of the proposition—and in concert with other propositions, an argument, 10, is generated.

I therefore enjoys its rightful position at the "least upper bound" in the matrix, given that:

1. Interpretants, representamina, and objects compose triads whose definitions are circular; they specify themselves by themselves.

2. Since every interpretant is also a sign, its relation to its object is the same as that of an antecedent sign; it replaces another sign of that same object.

3. Since every sign becomes an interpretant, it is related to its object by way of the sign of which it is itself a sign; that is, by way of the sign it interprets. For every interpretant there is an antecedent sign of which it is an interpretant and a consequent sign that becomes its interpretant; all interpretants follow on the heels of their antecedent signs.

4. For the finite individual or community of interpreters, there is no absolute first or last interpretant; all have predecessors and successors.

5. All interpretants mediate between their predecessors and successors to form the ongoing stream of *semiosis,* which is definable solely in terms of process, of temporality (see Savan 1987–88, 40–72).

Back to Concrete Reasonableness

A protest will surely be heard at this point: "Your formalist scaffolding is motivated by a modernist compulsion for control, power, omniscience, and totalization with a vengeance!"

And the point is well taken. I do not wish to apologize for the obvious obsession for abstraction that reveals itself throughout Peirce's writings. Yet I hope it has become apparent in this chapter that the cumulative, evolutionary, historical, processual character of *semiosis* coupled with the nonlinear, nondistributive, non-Boolean nature of the complementarity matrix; the indeterminacy, vagueness, and generality, and alternate (oscillatory) and superpositional elements inherent in the Peircean sign; and above all, the nondualistic, immanent nature of the universe of signs are quite in line with the postmodern mind-set. All possibilities can be embraced in the domain of *semiosis,* though not in simultaneity. In general accord with both postmodernism and the particular aspect of Peirce's doctrine of signs highlighted here, each and every interpretation is incomplete, and if this appears not to be the case of a particular interpretation, then it is inconsistent at some point. And, given an indefinite number of interpretations over unlimited time, finality can ideally, though not in practice, be reached.

Awareness of this limitation—which nonetheless makes us free—must be accompanied by a loss of any pretensions of imperial control over the world "out there," since the subject/object dichotomy is effectively dissolved. As Toulmin (1982b, 255) puts it:

> Within our . . . "postmodern" world, the pure scientists' traditional posture as *theoros,* or spectator, can no longer be maintained: we are *always*—and inescapably—participants or agents as well. Meanwhile, the expansion of scientific inquiry into the human realm is compelling us to abandon the Cartesian dichotomies and look for ways of "reinserting" humanity into the world of nature.

Natural science—as well as all other areas of intellectual endeavor, for that matter—is no longer modern, whether its custodians know it or not, and whether they like it or not. In good postmodern fashion, it is engaged with a world of incessant becoming. It has not been able to define this world a priori in terms of what is, but only in terms of what was, what just now ceased being. It follows, from the mediate, deferred, and differential *becomingness* of things, of knowledge, of signs, that the classical notion of cosmology (cosmos, order, stasis) and the Cartesian-Newtonian corpuscular-kinetic world picture of predetermined design, balance, and harmony are stepping aside to make way for a holistic view of pluralities, organized complexity, ordered chaos—call it a "cosmology" if you wish, as does Toulmin—capable of incorporating change, change of change, and constant adaptation to change.

My assertion that the formalistic tenor of this chapter is by and large 165 compatible with the postmodern perspective must in all probability still fall on incredulous ears. The claim is not so outlandish as it appears at the outset, however. If one contemplates the above pages sufficiently, I submit, one will conclude that it does not evince the image of static categories and stubborn dichotomies of reason. It represents, as a whole, a mediation of Hassan's own intransigent modernism/postmodernism dualisms. The evolutionary, developmental, generative model of self-organizing, "self-excited" signs that I have presented mediates between—and therefore includes—play and purpose, chance and design, indeterminacy and determinacy, process and product, participation and distance, pluralism and monism, and the impossibility of univocal interpretation. The universe of signs will work itself out as it may. Perhaps the most we can do is go along with it, doing the best we can whenever and wherever.

On this note, let us return to the concept of discourse (dialogue), which is contingent upon the evolution of signs, of interpreters, and of the world.

CHAPTER SEVEN

To Become or Not to Become

When Seeing Is Belial

From at least the time of Aristotle, a relational concept has been inherent in the distinction between creation or construction (*poiesis*) and social interaction (*praxis*). Marx applied this insight to the relation between economic production and praxis, Freud pitted the individual against society, and Dewey conceived the distinction to be that between communication and interaction. Peirce took a giant step in combining these two activities into the thought process in general insofar as thought, both social and individual, consists of a self-corrective operation on itself. The watchword is dialogic interaction between the self and its social and "real" *others* "out there" and between the self and its own *other* "in here."[1] In fact, for Peirce all thinking in and of itself is dialogic. It is

> an appeal from the momentary self to the better considered self of the immediate and of the general future. Now as every thinking requires a mind, so every sign even if external to all minds must be a determination of a quasi-mind. This quasi-mind is itself a sign, a determinable sign. (MS 195)

Elsewhere Peirce states:

> It is first of all needful, or at least highly desirable, that the reader should have thoroughly assimilated, in all its parts, the truth that thinking always proceeds in the form of a dialogue—a dialogue between the different phases of the ego—so that, being dialogical, it is essentially composed of signs, as its matter, in the sense in which a game of chess has the chessmen for its matter. (CP, 4.6)[2]

In this respect, Max Fisch (1986, 442) remarks that one of the most pervasive themes in Peirce's work is the idea that all thought is in signs and is dialogic in nature. Even at its most private and silent, it is nonetheless dialogue, between the self of one moment—which is, properly speaking, a sign—and the self of the next moment, a sign coming into being. The Peircean self entails ongoing process, unlike the Cartesian ego, which presumably stands outside the gush of signs. The self is a fabricator, by way of *poiesis,* and at the same time it interacts with itself (its own other), engages in praxis (with its social other), and interacts with its world (the "real" other), all of these processes making up *semiosis.* Dialogue, in the sense of Peirce—and Bakhtin (Ponzio 1985)—includes many voices rather than a mere contest between a winner and a loser.

Regarding the subject of dialogic interaction, Peirce uses the word "sign" in the widest sense as a medium of extending form. As medium, the sign is determined by its object and determines its interpretant. For this form to be extended, it must have been embodied in a subject before the communication of the form (which is the object of the sign). This being the case, the form remains independent of the sign, yet the sign, by way of its object, re-presents the form in the way the sign re-presents it to be. Hence re-presentation, though self-corrective, is never exactly identical with the "real."

The very existence of dialogue depends upon some sort of identity between a pair of interlocutors, yet there must also be some difference from one interlocutor to another. After all, interlocutors are themselves signs, and a sign passes away into another sign, whose interpretant may be taken as identical to or different from its predecessor. Identification of a sign, S, for us, is a process: $S_1 \rightarrow S_2 \rightarrow S_3 \ldots n$. In order to establish identities of signs, which is no mere relation of equality but a matter of abductive, inductive, and deductive inferences culminating in interpretations, a sign's *might be* becomes *this-hereness,* which is construed to be the same as what it would be at some future time, given certain sets of conditions.

This is by no means to say that the sign is fixed de facto. On the contrary, perception and conception of sign sameness is made possible by its very indeterminate and fluctuating nature, which renders it always not yet other later to emerge as *this* sign *here.* Identity is not possible through a totally isolated sign, a self-contained icon—which is simply and timelessly *that which is.* For a sign to evince identity with itself, it must catch itself up in a reiteration of itself that is *it* yet is other. The arrow of the equation $S_a \rightarrow S_b$ thus becomes over the long haul two-way—we, in our effort to establish identity, render it two-way—though time is not halted altogether, since the linear series $1 \ldots n$ remains intact: the equation implies the notion of mechanical, chronometric time rather than subjective time, as we shall observe in Chapter Eight.

For an illustration of the dialogical process in action, let us consult Shakespeare's Macbeth, who asks: "Is this a dagger which I see before me?"[3] Macbeth's second self, the other ("me"), questions what the more immediate self ("I") apparently perceives. Since we have it on high authority that Macbeth is hallucinating, we might want to answer him with a resounding no. In other words, if "the question of whether Hamlet was insane is the question whether

167

Shakespeare conceived him to be insane" (CP, 8.153), then, according to Shakespeare, neither does Macbeth see anything, nor was there any "real" existent thing to see. This would be the argument of Russell (1905) and Quine (1953, 1–19), for whom speaking about some-*thing* implicates the speaker: there must be some-*thing* about which her predicate is made. But the fact is that Macbeth is considering the possibility that he actually sees a dagger; that is, for a moment "dagger" neurons are firing inside his skull, producing the effect of a dagger "out there" in the *here-now,* in spite of whether or not a "real" dagger actually exists in his world. If indeed the dagger is not there, we might say that Macbeth is the victim of "naive hallucination." He merely *imagines* he saw the object in question. Yet he does not remain a victim of "naive hallucination" for long, for he soon entertains doubt about what seemed to appear before him. Let us call such a state of mind "vacillating hallucination," a dialogue between the naive self and the doubting self (see Dozoretz 1979).

An additional but no less important facet of the dagger scene is that Macbeth attempts empirically to confront the unexplained appearance before him:

> Come, let me clutch thee!
> I have thee not, and yet I see thee still.
> Art thou not fatal vision, sensible
> To feeling as to sight? or art thou but
> A dagger of the mind, a false creation?
>
> (Shakespeare 1939, 2.1;
> see also CP, 5.117).

A dagger of the mind? A false creation? It appears that Macbeth wants something akin to positivist verification—or better, one might conjecture, Popperian falsification. It all seems quite elementary, a pragmatic question-and-answer matter. The other self questions the more immediate self, who must then put the dagger appearance to the test. If Macbeth's hand reaches out and clutches thin air, then the other's suspicions will have been confirmed. The figment of Macbeth's mind will presumably dissolve, his dagger hypothesis having been falsified, and he can go about his daily affairs. His previous "vacillating hallucination" has now become "enlightened hallucination" (D. Smith 1983).[4] It is still a form of hallucination, nonetheless, for the fact remains that he previously (thought he) saw a dagger; the doubting self ultimately "wins" all arguments regarding the semiotically real.[5]

But things are more tangled than we would perhaps like. Popper (1963, 215–50) tells us that since confirmation is failed refutation, we must go on being wrong until we finally get things right. We can only discover positive evidence by looking for negative evidence, and if we are lucky, we may eventually stumble onto the truth. But in that case we will never know it, for no evidence available to us can be used to falsify an absolutely true theory, so it must have been ipso facto unscientific, therefore unacceptable. The problem is that a naive immediate self might categorically believe that such-and-such *is* true, come what may, and hence nothing can falsify it. Eventually the dialogue would cease, and computerlike certainty would follow. This radically anti-Popperian one-dimensional self would be incapable of knowing anything new, for he could no longer become aware of any error in his ways. If Macbeth were reduced to such a pathetic mental state, he would lose his capacity to prove the existence or nonexistence of any dagger, and the whole of his world would become tantamount to "naive hallucination." Given his ongoing dialogic self, he will probably not suffer this lonely fate. If he does not suffer it, then he is destined to push along in ignorant bliss, at each step being generally more wrong than right.

169

Quite understandably, Mary Warnock (1978) is able to relate Nietzsche, for whom all truths are no more than irrefutable errors (lies), to Popper. Nietzsche speaks of the periphery of science, that boundary where the scientist, having become poet, begins an endless push toward the unknown. But since any truth he can uncover is less than the totality, it can be nothing other than a falsity. Given Nietzsche's own form of "falsification principle," then, we are always and inexorably led—we lead ourselves—astray. That is to say, we tend toward a constant transition from "naive" to "vacillating" to "enlightened" realism or, in another way of putting it, hallucination.

The becoming aware of hallucination *as* hallucination bears on the phenomenon of dreaming—and on the concepts of de-embedment and de-automatization. Norman Malcolm (1959) points out that for a sleeping person to say "I'm asleep" is absurd, since in his sleeping state he cannot be conscious of his waking state, and thus he is incapable consciously of making a statement about his status in the sleeping state. Moreover, unlike Macbeth, he cannot, while asleep, be consciously aware that there is a boundary between his being asleep and being awake. Hence he can neither be lying nor be telling the truth: he is simply spouting out an absurdity. His utterance, "I'm asleep," is that of his more immediate one-dimensional self, who, denied the benefit of the other, is not in control of any means by which to become aware that he is either dreaming or awake.

Moreover, if this more immediate self, the only one in existence for our helplessly slumbering subject, were to say "*This* is a dream (or hallucination)," his utterance would be equally absurd, for he remains totally "inside" his dream (hallucination) frame. Consequently, there is no way for him to discriminate between this dream frame and any "outside" frame. He could not be aware of, nor would he be able to judge or assert, anything concerning the ontological status of his state as other than "real." He would have no other to place his perceptions, conceptions, and actions in question.[6]

If someone simply declares "I am conscious," her utterance might be meaningful if she is awakening from anesthesia and responding to her doctor, or some such thing. It is generally granted that she possesses—like Macbeth, we must suppose—the faculties necessary to distinguish among her perceptions, conceptions, and actions of one moment and relate them to herself—by way of the other self—in the next moment. That is to say, through her dialogic selves, she possesses self-awareness. Her assertion that she is conscious comes as no surprise, then. We tend tacitly to assume that a person is conscious if she merely demonstrates awareness of particulars in the world when speaking. And if she says "I am conscious of such-and-such," it is generally construed that she is not referring directly to the fact of her being conscious but to the object of her consciousness. Consciousness *of* plays a crucial role not only in the other self's doubting, and thus correcting, the more immediate self but also in the self's potentially becoming aware of her having been the victim of error.

This becoming aware of is germane to perception—and perception inevitably forces itself onto the scene in any serious discussion of Macbeth's plight. Peirce distinguished sharply between *percepts* and *perceptual judgments.* A percept is a single whole, an undivided event occurring here and now; a quality forced upon the subject by the "clash" of the "real," leaving him little or no freedom of choice; and fleeting and transitory, the product of the flow of immediately present moments; a percept is not, however, an instant of conscious and intentional knowing *that,* for the subject is not (yet) set apart from the object of perception (CP, 1.145, 253, 2.146, 5.568, 7.625). The intellect serves to *prescind* (abstract) from the flow of percepts a distillation, a "sort of stenographic report" (CP, 2.141), of the totality of the flow. A raw percept of a compelling nature imposing itself upon the perceiver is nonetheless a sign because it is itself a prescission, a tacit conclusion (interpretation), the result of an uncontrollable and unconscious (hallucinatory) inferential process. It is either instinctual, like the inferential processes in nonhuman organisms, or the product of embedment—symbolization and conscious inference having become indexical and iconic processes. That is, the iconic elements inevitably contained within all indices and symbols are highlighted, while the more developed sign counterparts are backgrounded such that perceptual judgments, once conscious, are now virtually uncontrollable. Such judgments are "absolutely forced upon my acceptance, and . . . by a process which I am utterly unable to control and consequently unable to criticize" (CP, 5.157).[7]

Though Peirce vacillates about the control or lack thereof of perceptual judgments of various sorts, he does distinguish between those that are voluntary, falling within the province of logic, and those that are not, pertaining to psychology (CP, 2.146, 5.157; Goudge 1952, 124). Perceptual judgments are the product of what I referred to in Chapter Four as hypostatic abstractions whose function is the construction of universals (CP, 4.235, 332). For example, from a perceptual quality of "redness," the second stage is a specification in the mind, the equivalent of "This is red." The third stage entails prescission of the proposition, transforming it into the equivalent of "This possesses redness," in the process converting an adjective into a noun and the specific "This is red" into the general term "redness." Generalizing the term sets it on the road toward a more or less well defined class of communally shared categories. The subject, "this" (index), can be separated from its quality or attribute, "red" (icon); and when linked to some item in the world—say, a "chair"—the completed proposition, "This chair is red," can be generated.

171

Peirce alludes to his inability to resist having particular percepts forced upon him and concludes that the only way to resist them is to close his eyes, for if one "*sees,* one cannot avoid the percept" (CP, 7.627). The percept as quality automatically, and against his will, becomes a *thisness,* a Second. And then, "if one *looks* [sees *as-that*], one cannot avoid the perceptual judgment" (CP, 7.627). Involuntary perceptual judgments, I would submit, are the product either of instinctive and *Umwelt*-generated worlds or of signifying activity having become embedded. They are no longer logical but psychological judgments. However, perceptual judgments, according to Peirce, should ideally involve, at least in regards to human semiotic, consciousness of the presentation of something to consciousness. They should be subject to a certain degree of control by the subject. This is ordinarily more easily said than done, however. If the mode of presentation—the content of the percept—is what something is presented as to consciousness, and if the object of presentation is that which is perceived—the semiotically real, not the actually "real" object—then, as Peirce was wont to concede, some aspect of our daily affairs, and our individual and collective aesthetic, ethical, and various intellectual practices, will remain elusive and beyond our capacity for doubt, critique, and rejection—that is, beyond our control.[8]

Total doubt is a pipe dream; the paradoxical core of the injunction to doubt everything goes without mentioning. And if one harbors no doubt whatsoever concerning what one perceives, then one's belief is judged infallible—albeit erroneously—for the simple reason that there is no doubt. In contrast, if there is at least some doubt regarding what is apparently perceived "out there," then one's perceptual judgment must be considered as fallible as any other judgment.

We Are Always behind Ourselves

Prompted by his other self concerning the "reality" of the "dagger" floating in the air before him, Macbeth's doubt allows for a number of semiotic operations that he could perform on the "dagger" in order to confirm its existence either "out there" or in the mind. He could grasp at it. He could try to cut something with it. He could ask someone else if she also saw it. And so on.

In other words, from the statement "This is a dagger" or the query "Is this a dagger?" the hypostatic abstraction, "This possesses daggerness," is derived. From the generality, "daggerness," a set of propositions can then be set up, each of which calls for a test. For example, according to the pragmatic maxim, Macbeth might propose for himself a set of hypotheticals: "If this 'dagger' is 'real,' and if I were to clutch it, I would feel a resistance on the palm of my hand"; "If I were to take a snapshot of it, the developed film would be proof of its existence"; or something of the sort. There is theoretically no upper limit, in view of the maxim and the ongoingness of inductivity, to the number of operations Macbeth could apply to his apparition (D. Smith 1983). By the same token, given the problem of induction, there is no absolutely infallible method for determining the "real" existence of any perceived object, hence the range of operations does not constitute a logically sufficient criterion for "real" existence. Peirce intended his maxim generally to render pragmatically workable, though not infallible, results (Hookway 1985, 172–73).

Semiosically speaking, Macbeth's perception of what appeared to be a "dagger" could follow a number of generative paths, as indicated in figure 7, by proceeding "up" the figure 10 matrix, depending upon his particular mindset and by means of various modes of signification. For the purpose of illustration, I will choose one possible pathway, which I will label in terms of the signs' operators and their concomitant transformations through the oscillating mediation of interpretants:

a: An oblong patch of variegated colors is sensed (felt), and there is an initial dim consciousness of it, though its existence cannot yet be explicitly acknowledged. A mere quality has been prescribed, leaving Macbeth, at this stage, no freedom of choice:

$$R_1 + O_1 = I_2 <=> I_1 \twoheadrightarrow R_2 : R_2 O_1 I_1{}^9$$

b: Macbeth's attention is called toward it, as if it were to say "Look!" A "boundaried space" containing the colored patch is subsequently marked out and distinguished:[10]

$$R_2 + O_1 = I_3 <=> I_1 \twoheadrightarrow O_2 : R_2 O_2 I_1$$

c: The patch is indicated and set off in relation to Macbeth's hand, and by extension, his body:

$$R_2 + O_2 = I_3 <=> I_2 = I_2 : R_2 O_2 I_2$$

d: In virtual simultaneity with operation *c,* the patch becomes an explicit whole, an undivided percept, and is roughly demarcated as to shade, hue, shape, and size. This is the rudiment of generality, the first legisign, which can eventually lead toward an interpretant:

$$R_2 + O_1 = I_3 \Longleftrightarrow I_2: R_3 O_1 I_1$$

e: The percept becomes *this* rather than *that*. It is singled out from other possible percepts that could have been perceived but are not and is given a primitive sort of value:

$$R_2 + O_2 = I_3 \Longleftrightarrow I_1 \twoheadrightarrow R_3: R_3 O_2 I_1$$

f: At the same time, a body-object connection is established, and a "dagger"-value—though it is not yet named—is explicitly set apart from the self:

$$O_1 + I_1 = I_2 \Longleftrightarrow I_1 \twoheadrightarrow O_2: R_3 O_2 I_1$$

g: The percept, now sensed (by unconscious inference) as a universal ("This possesses daggerness"), is potentially coupled with its function via its value:

$$R_2 + O_2 = I_3 \Longleftrightarrow I_2 \twoheadrightarrow R_3: R_3 O_2 I_2$$

h: The percept's function as a dagger comes into consciousness. There is awareness of *this* rather than *that* or something else. Macbeth's expectations are now met with a conscious shock of surprise:

$$O_2 + I_1 = I_3 \Longleftrightarrow I_2 = I_2: R_3 O_2 I_2$$

i: *This* rather than *that* is named, and the term, "dagger" (the subject or index of a possible proposition), is generated in the mind, which presupposes the dagger's value in connection with its functions. "Dagger," insofar as it is something possessing "daggerness," is a token of a general type. It represents the percept and raises it to the level of a class of intersubjectively shared categories containing a specific quality:

$$O_2 + I_1 = I_3 \Longleftrightarrow I_2 \twoheadrightarrow O_3: R_3 O_3 I_1$$

j: The dagger function implies the predicate (icon) of a possible proposition:

$$O_2 + I_2 = I_3 \Longleftrightarrow I_2 \twoheadrightarrow O_3: R_3 O_3 I_2$$

k: This, in conjunction with the subject, generates a proposition: "This is a dagger." A choice has been exercised between a range of possible symbols representing semiotically real objects:

$$I_1 \Longleftrightarrow I_2 = I_2: R_3 O_3 I_2$$

l: The proposition, and its accompanying doubt ("Is this a dagger?"), if put to the test according to the pragmatic maxim, potentially establish the conditions for the generation of an argument:

$$I_2 \Longleftrightarrow I_3 = I_3: R_3 O_3 I_3$$

Quite remarkably, this entire *semiosic* process constructed by Macbeth's conscious and nonconscious experience as a continuum of signification occurs, for practical purposes and given our limitations, in the blink of an instant! At each major step, there is oscillation between I_1 and I_2 and between I_2 and I_3, which creates the possibility for the construction of a dialogic give-and-take, thus creating in turn the possibility of movement within the complementarity matrix (figure 10). This apparently flies in the face of traditional empiricism and naive notions of "reality." If Macbeth was prompted by what appeared to be sensory stimuli to utter the observation "dagger," the general implication has it that he assented to "the presence of dagger stimuli 'out there.'" But assenting to "dagger" is not necessarily tantamount to assenting to the presence "out there" of something daggerlike, regardless of whether the dagger actually existed or not. The universe is most likely a perfusion of signs, Peirce once mused, and if this is indeed the case, then the signs of the universe include not only physical objects "out there," waiting to impinge upon our sensory organs, but the range of all possibles, actuals, and potentials, whether "in here" or "out there." Moreover, for a given individual—Macbeth in this particular case— what is necessary and what is not, and what is actual and what is not, are continually subject to change. Thus there is no way of absolutely demarcating between thought-signs "in here" and sign-events "out there." What at a given space-time singularity is one person's fantasy might be another person's fact, and vice verse.

As for Macbeth's enigmatic percept, there was either a sign-event consisting of something oblong "out there" that reflected wave frequencies producing the effect of steel gray and brown colors as a particular sign in his semiotically real world, or there was a thought-sign "in here" conjured up by his compulsive mind. The sign could have been determined by the "real," or it could have been the product of his mental condition and thus a de-generate sign initially assented to in near-immediacy without explicit awareness that it was not what it appeared to be. In either case, on the spur of the moment, Macbeth assented appropriately in the sense that he was seeing—or thought he was seeing—a daggerlike patch before him.

To conclude, whether or not that patch was "real" as a sign-event or merely mind-stuff must remain somewhat of a moot question. Yet, according to Peirce, a hallucination or dream is "real," if by hallucination or dream we mean a certain psychic experience. And in the event that a hallucination or dream happens to become construed as "true," then it was not necessarily a mere figment of the imagination. In this sense, there is a certain middle ground between supposedly "irreal" figments and the "real out there" (Dozoretz 1979). This middle ground, I would suggest, is populated by the furniture of one's semiotically real world. Semiotically real items of experience can certainly be "real" "in here"— for instance, mathematical constructs—and they can be semiotically real "out there." Regarding interaction at the dovetailing middle ground between the semiotically real and the actually "real," there is perpetual dialogic interaction between the self and its other, rendering the semiotically real infinitely pliable. But, I must reiterate, there can be no absolute certainty that what is at a given time and place considered to be "real" by a given individual or a community of knowers is actually "real," for the actually "real" is independent of whatever it may be perceived and conceived to be.

In the periodic transmutations of semiotically real worlds through dialogic interaction, explicit knowing slides along the slope toward implicit or tacit knowing through embedment, and when awareness dawns that a particular aspect of one's implicit knowing does not conform to the world as expected, it may be subject to alteration, through de-embedment, and subsequently raised to the level of explicit knowing, which is then once again threatened by embedment. The ongoing dialogue—which is no game at all but rather the play of the world—shows no signs of abating, which is perhaps fortunate for us all. It represents postmodern plurality in contrast to monolithic dogma, reverie within scintillating flux in contrast to a mania for permanence, asymmetry in contrast to balance and harmony, and disequilibrium in contrast to symmetry.

175

More than Two Must Play the Game

A Triangular Tryst?

Savan (1987–88, 40) observes that the concept of the interpretant is exceedingly problematic, often ambiguous, and at times even contradictory. Nonetheless, it "is the most extensive and important part of Peirce's theory of signs." In fact, the interpretant is absolutely essential to the notion of signs, for meaning, particularly regarding intellectual concepts, "can only be solved by the study of the interpretants" (CP, 5.475).

The chief function of the interpretant is mediation, for a sign "mediates between the interpretant sign and its object" (Hardwick 1977, 31). And mediation is made possible by a determined effect, since a sign is "anything which is so determined by something else, called its Object, and so determines an effect upon a person, which effect I call its interpretant, that the latter is thereby mediately determined by the former" (Hardwick 1977, 81). Meaning, then, is given by the interpretant, not by its object or referent (Buchler 1952, 26)—and traditional theories of meaning are thrown into a tailspin.

Insofar as it embodies the sign's meaning, the interpretant is the effect that a sign produces on the mind, hence the sign takes on—becomes—an interpretant only if it is understood as such. The initial sign (representamen) at the lowest level determines its interpretant and object; in turn, the interpretant mediates between the initial sign and its object, such mediation being strictly mental. In this manner, the interpretant *is* a sign for mind, and, since sign processing is the name of the game, it is the dream of every sign to become an interpretant. In a paper written in 1868, Peirce asked: "In what does the reality of the mind consist?" to which he responded: "We have seen that the content of consciousness, the entire phenomenal manifestation of mind, is a sign resulting from inference. . . . [W]e must conclude that the mind is a sign developing according to the laws of inference" (i.e., in human semiotic chiefly by signs 9 and 10, via operators *j, k,* and *l*) (CP, 4.393). And in his later writings, Peirce reiterated his early conviction that "[a]ny set of signs which are so connected that a complex of two of them can have one Interpretant, must be determinations of one sign which is a Quasi-mind" (CP, 4.550).

This admittedly circular definition of sign, object, interpretant, and mind strikes a discordant note for modern and postmodern observers alike. However, it must be pointed out in Peirce's defense that sign and interpretant are distinguishable by virtue of the interpretant's following from, or being effected by, the sign, while the sign does not usually follow from the interpretant in the same fashion—thus the irreversibility, the temporality, of *semiosis*. Moreover, the interpretant stands for its antecedent sign, and at the same time it is itself a sign for some further interpretant; it is in a sense the "moment" that, for Whitehead, is tinged with memories (traces) of the past and anticipations (Peirce would call them expectations) of the future.

Given the disconcerting irretrievability of a first sign and the impossibility of reaching a final sign, there can be no interpretant without a predecessor and a successor. Hence the triadic character of the sign implies an infinite progression as well as an infinite regression—which immediately prompts the analytical mind to take out a metaphysical hunting license. Perhaps, following Humberto Maturana and Francisco Varela's (1980, 1987) concept of *autopoietic,* we could describe the indefinite and potentially infinite Peircean production of signs as *autosemiopoiesis.* The term implies a sign's (organism's, mind's) relative autonomy, while it remains coupled with, and intimately tied to, all other signs (organisms, minds). The watchword, once again, is *process;* there is never a finished product (Gentry 1952).[1]

Imagine a physicist who, after gazing at a photographic plate of the condensation track from her bubble chamber for a moment, remarks: "This is a Feynman diagram of X sort." She observed the tracks and inferred the presence of certain particles, then she put forth the claim that the tracks were an indication of particles of such-and-such a type. The tracks are the sign, or representamen (First); the particles are the object (Second); and the interpretant consists of our physicist's inferred thought-sign (Third), which is derived from the inference that since the particles would be there, given a certain set of conditions, and since these conditions have been met, the particles were there.

She thus arrived at a thought about the particles, but her cognitive interaction with them was at the same time mediated by the sign. In fact, we might wish to assume that the particles were the object of her indirect inferential reasoning by way of the sign. After much formal training—faithfully serving her apprenticeship under master physicists, casual shoptalk, reading the literature of her chosen profession, and conducting her own investigations—she has come to believe, as a habit of thought, that subatomic particles actually exist. They are for her, we must suppose, "real" rather than merely semiotically real. She believes they have determined the observable tracks, which serve further to determine and fortify her belief. In other words, the nonempirical determines

177

her belief in the empirical, and she automatically generates "particle" interpretants, for they have become embedded in her form of life.

This example demonstrates Peirce's three types of sign relations, but it leaves the notions of mediation and determination fuzzy, for at this point it might appear that we have no warrant for considering sign relations to be triadic rather than dyadic. Concerning dyadic *relata,* Peirce wrote:

178

> An event A, may, by brute force, produce an event, B; and then the event, B, may in its turn produce a third event, C. The fact that the event, C, is about to be produced by B has no influence at all upon the production of B by A. It is impossible that it should, since the action of B in producing C is a contingent future event at the time B is produced. Such is dyadic action, which is so called because each step of it concerns a pair of objects. (CP, 5.472)

And sure enough, in good dyadic fashion, the subatomic particles produced the marks on the photographic plate, and the marks subsequently evoked a belief, and that's that. It might appear that there is no call for triadophilia at all.

However, Peirce goes on to remark that triadic action is evident inasmuch as "an event A, produces a second event, B *as a means* to the production of a third event C," which implies that "B will be produced if it will produce or is likely to produce C in its turn, but it will not be produced if it will not produce C in its turn nor is likely to do so" (CP, 5.473). Peirce cites the example of the officer of a company of infantry giving the command "Ground Arms!" The order is a sign, and that which determines it is the object represented by the sign, which is

> the will of the officer that the butts of the muskets be brought down to the ground. Nevertheless, the action of his will upon the sign is not simply dyadic; for if he thought the soldiers were deaf mutes, or did not know a word of English, or were raw recruits utterly undrilled, or were indisposed to obedience, his will probably would not produce the word of command. (CP, 5.473)

Triadic action in this sense implies something that one could easily take as *purpose.* But the notion of purpose is as deceptive as it is subtle, if not at times thoroughly muddled—and it is Peirce's lack of clarity here that has led to confusion regarding his putative "teleological" thrust. It is not that (1) subatomic particles left vapor trails in order that the physicist would know their whereabouts. On the contrary, (2) the physicist inferred from the tracks that subatomic particles had made their appearance at a particular space-time juncture, which implies intercession, or better, mediation, of the mind—after all, the mind itself is an interpretant, a sign within the fabric of all signs. In this sense, understanding, along with one's entire set of prejudices and preconceptions, is inherent in the pragmatics of (2), while it is not in (1), which forces something onto the physicist whether she likes it or not, and whether she knows it or not.

Sentence (2), then, indicates the result of the physicist's involvement in what is tantamount to Kuhnian "normal" or "problem solving" science from within a given "paradigm." Since the physicist is actively involved in determining the interpretants of the signs-as-natural-phenomena, and since those interpretants are generated in constantly changing contexts, there is perpetual alteration of the meanings of such terms as "particles," "tracks," and "Feynman diagrams" from one year to the next, one generation to the next, one paradigm to the next. In this manner, the possibility exists that she will at some point in her activity become aware (by tacit inference—or abduction) that her paradigm is flawed, and thus the ground may be tilled for the seeds of a new paradigm.

The distinction in question here is between the traditional notion of *sign generation through received cultural codes* and *purposive sign generation*. The first follows embedment; the second is the living force behind growth, development, novelty. The first involves—though not exclusively—de-generacy; the second is guided by generacy. Most observers expounding on conventional "codes" and their categorical imperatives do not seem to realize that codes themselves are part of the vastly broader *semiosic* force of perpetual becoming, which lends itself to the idea of purpose—though its consequences are, and must remain, largely unforeseeable.

To assume that human *semiosic* activity operates solely on the basis of coded behavior would be virtually to place credence in sentence (1), as if the particles themselves caused the physicist to respond as she did. On the other hand, (2) always leaves the door slightly ajar, allowing for the possibility of alternatives that, when the entire community is included in the picture, can potentially be realized as novel interpretants of signs for someone in some respect or capacity. The mind does not necessarily enjoy any imperious posture over any other sign.

Or Merely a Tangled Triangle?

Given the mind's capacity, by means of Peirce's triadic sign process, to become aware of the errors of its ways, the notion that mind is itself an interpretant lends support to the hypothesis concerning all thought as interior dialogue. One self emits signs, and they are almost immediately transmuted into interpretants for the other self, which in turn counters the first self's signs with its own signs. The full meaning of a sign can emerge only as the dialogue expands, and as it expands, it takes on other minds and signs, virtually the entire community of minds and the entire flow of *semiosis*. But since the expansion is destined to continue indefinitely, this process toward an ever receding horizon is itself patterned in the interpreter by what I have christened *autosemiopoiesis*.

A modicum of security might be had, however, in the belief that Peirce's *habit* is potentially capable of judiciously directing sign activity. The conditional *would be* of the interpretant is the governor that guides signs toward their destiny. But habits themselves are not signs in the proper sense; they are virtual interpretants or sign correlates that, by their very nature, do not require or presuppose any interpretant. They are both conditional and exceedingly general, which is another way of saying they are, and will always be, incomplete. Hence to the question "What is the final logical interpretant?" Peirce suggests that the only answer is "A change of habit of conduct," a "modification of a person's tendencies toward action resulting from previous experiences or from previous exertions of his will or acts, or from a complexus of both kinds of cause" (CP, 5.476). In other words, one can potentially understand the ultimate meaning of a sign if one knows how one would modify one's conduct if one came to accept it as true. But since one cannot a priori be aware of all the myriad ramifications of one's modified conduct, one cannot at any point grasp the ultimate meaning of a sign.

This entails process, not static product. And it is a long shot from the idea that if only computers—and by extension humans—could be properly programmed, utopia would be just around the next bend in the road. Such a project would be the stultifying end product of embedment. In contrast, Peirce's notions of habit taking and habit breaking takes into account changes of mind and their pragmatic consequences—intermittent de-embedment and hence generacy—whether speaking of the individual or of the community, of psychologists or ethnographers, or of "paradigmatic" shifts in the arts, humanities, and sciences. Habit-taking and -breaking is the grease that enables intuitions, ideas, conceptual schemes, and broad worldviews to slide up and down the uncertain slope of history, suffering mild to traumatic catastrophes when thresholds are surpassed. It is the way of novel conjunctions through abductive leaps, whereby what *is not* but yet *might be,* as boneless, fleshless *possibilia,* is actualized into the *this-hereness* of things.

But taking a particular sign to be "true" by the force of habit and belief and its actually being "true" are horses of a different color. According to Peirce's convergence theory, whatever is considered "true" at a given point will invariably be subject to revision at some stopping place along the protracted journey. "Truth," *our* "truth," like habit, will never cease to change. One cannot, then, infallibly know how one will modify one's conduct when one comes to accept a sign as "true," for it is not possible to know when one's conception of that sign's "truth" may come to be considered incorrigible. Even if it were in no uncertain terms "true," one could not know it without the aid of the virtually infinite stream of knowers. For one is always *within* the stream, changing oneself as the current changes, altering one's signs and being altered by them, as one navigates, perhaps driven by some unknown purpose, toward that receding safe haven. Any final interpretant, in Savan's (1987–88, 62) words, "must include some principle beyond the endless mechanical repetition of identical patterns of behaviour." Indeed, the final interpretant is beyond such repetition, for it is a mathematical rather than a physical idea, metaphysical rather than actualizable, conceptual rather than empirical, a think-sign rather than a thing-sign.   181

Take, for example, the evolution of the term "atoms." "Atoms" may originally have denoted some solid and impenetrable empirical object. The term was beaten into an entirely new shape by Leucippus and Democritus, for whom "atoms" were still solid and impenetrable but now nonempirical. "Atoms" suffered minor to major alterations through the monolithic era of classical physics. Then, shortly after the birth of the present century, the apple cart was completely upset. "Atoms" became something like a plum pudding according to J. J. Thomson, a miniature solar system in the early Bohr conception, vaguely cloudlike in Schrödinger's wave mechanics, an unvisualizable matrix represented by abstract symbols in Heisenberg's interpretation, and it was finally conceded that they could be most adequately conceived as either particles or waves or both or neither, take your pick.

The layperson might intuitively sense that some kind of control and purpose lie behind the various changes in the term, though he remains fuzzy on this issue and even more fuzzy with respect to his comprehension of the present-day notion of "atoms." His idea of "atoms," in other words, is *acritical*. However, if, in addition to Peirce's notion of belief (CP, 5.538–48), we heed the later Wittgenstein (1953, 1956), Polanyi's (1958) *postcritical* philosophy, and most other radical meaning variance philosophers of science, especially Feyerabend (1975), we will be likely to concede that even the mathematician and scientist, locked within their particular cultural horizon and scientific paradigm, generally embrace their group's tacit presuppositions and prejudices *acritically*.

This conservative strain, which is most likely endemic within our hearts and minds, by no means cancels the possibility of our taking a look at conventions with a critical, skeptical, cynical, and even jaundiced eye, which hopefully will be in the long run more beneficial than not. Peirce himself was a champion of self-criticism. For some observers, this characteristic would qualify him as a helpless child of modernity. But it does not in the sense of the critical brand of postmodernism adopted in this inquiry. Critique and self-critique are implied in the fact that each interpretant's (and interpreter's) very existence depends upon its transience. Its coming into the world announces its passing away into other signs; its propagation of other signs demands reinterpretation from the critical posture of its interpreter, and its interpreter is eventually forced into self-criticism. According to Savan (1987–88, 63),

> The most important turning point in the history of a sign or a set of signs is the point at which deliberate critical appraisal of the norms themselves begins. It is at this point that thought comes of age and that mature science is born. What is characteristic of this final scientific stage in the evolution of interpretants is that the guiding principles are themselves subject to deliberate critical evaluation, and that the principles governing the *methods* of evaluation are also subject to deliberate critical appraisal.

While Savan's remarks pinpoint the destiny of the interpretant, they do not fully account for the tacit strain inherent in Peirce's philosophy: that something will always remain beyond critical scrutiny, and that what is in one context open to review in another context might remain outside censorial control. As Peirce himself reiterated, one cannot entertain doubts about the entirety of one's beliefs. Something invariably remains absent, beyond the captious eye, like the *enthymeme's* "hole." Though the final interpretant would be the total semiotic effect of a sign, there can be no absolutely total semiotic effect of a given sign in our semiotically real world. We can do no more than swim, Peirce tells us, in a continuum of *semiosis,* a remark that foreshadows Bohr's observation that we are suspended in language, incapable of knowing which way is up and which down.

Hence the representamen (R) and the object (O), given the context dependency of the nondistributive, orthocomplemented, non-Boolean scheme in figure 10, and even though belonging to distinct and nonintersecting domains, are conjoined through mediation by the interpretant (I). Every sign must have an interpretant to function as such, and in turn every interpretant is itself a sign. There is no "myth of presence" here, for both a sign and its complement cannot be contextually realized in unison. This nonsimultaneity of sign processing necessarily renders distinct domains at certain points contextually incompatible, that is, complementary. Assuming the simultaneous coexistence of incompatible signs within incompatible contexts would be tantamount to Saussurean poststructuralist signifiers and their signifieds coexisting like the two sides of a sheet of paper. Such a notion implies signs strung out along a sequential chain ruled by linear, transitive relations.[2] Semiological generativity is not, however, the way of *semiosis,* which is by its very nature nonlinear.[3]

Obviously, the nonsimultaneity of R, O, and I raises the question of time. Sign engenderment is unavoidably a time-dependent process, the transition from quality to actuality to potentiality occurring solely through a temporal increment. This time binding unquestionably lends support to the partially ordered, nonlinear R-O-I system, where some of the pairs are ordered by transitive and nonsymmetrical relations. I_2 and O_3, for instance, compose an ordered pair that can be combined into a sequence $(R_3O_3I_2)$ in the form of a hypothetical conditional. According to the pragmatic maxim, the final outcome of the consequences—whether physical or mental—brought about by I_2 can potentially be the final outcome of the implications of O_3, but not necessarily vice versa. In terms of Peircean pragmatics, this situation can be augmented to include the dialogical self: I_2, generated by the self of one moment, can be extended to O_3 or R_3 by the self of the next moment—the second sign including the first as a subset—but not necessarily vice versa. Yet the fact remains that R_3 and O_3 are only complementarily linked, which partly accounts for the matrix's nondistributivity. Regarding the I_2-O_3 and I_2-R_3 systems, it can be said that the outcome of O_3 for the self of one moment can be countered by the self of the next moment whose outcome followed the path through R_3. This dialogue may remain internalized, but if at some point one of the two components happens to be represented by another mind, the dialogue may become externalized, made social. In this sense, the paths $I_2 \twoheadrightarrow O_3$ and $I_2 \twoheadrightarrow R_3$ represent distinct time-bound complementary grasps, thus implying Peirce's dialogic at its fullest.

183

Given these implicit complementarities, there can exist two or more paths to the same end, which, in good Peircean fashion, cannot be realized short of an infinity of space-time contexts. For such to be realized would be equivalent to a vision, *sub specie aeternitatis,* capable of embracing any and all complementarities in simultaneity. Finite beings that we are, we must be content with partial visions that include direct focus on, and consciousness of, either $I_2 \twoheadrightarrow O_3$ or $I_2 \twoheadrightarrow R_3$ but not both at the same instant. There is, of course, a largest contextual domain, the "least upper bound," common to both O_3 and R_3. The meaning of the particular sequence $(R_3O_3I_2)$, even when connected to other propositions within its universe of discourse, however, is to be found in a "lower bound" (I_2), hence the categorical distinction between R_3 and O_3 endures.

Such categorical distinctions can be found in the most rudimentary forms of sign activity. Take, for example, the case of the mating of herring gulls (Count 1969; Merrell 1982). When a nestling pecks at a red spot on the parent's bill, it expects food to be regurgitated into its gaping beak. The meaning of this sign is something like "Please feed me." Interestingly enough, the female gull also solicits sexual attention from the male by the same sign—the equivalent of which would be roughly "A little sex, please."

A cry of protest will undoubtedly be raised: "Your anthropomorphism is unpalatable, and you should be properly aware of this, given your arguments in chapters Two and Three. Dumb brutes instinctively respond to signals, clearly and simply. There is no intention here, no purpose." However, T. L. Short (1982) argues convincingly that, according to Peirce's sign categories, rituals such as bird mating and bee dances are best described as intentional and purposeful, though the purpose remains implicit, instinctive, and/or nonconscious (i.e., automatized). In Peirce's own words, "[t]hought is not necessarily connected with a brain. It appears in the work of bees, of crystals, and throughout the purely physical world" (CP, 4.551). In this sense, nonhuman forms of communication involve legisign characteristics usually attributed exclusively to the symbols of human language by many semioticians.

"But," a voice again surfaces, "these signs do what they do only because the lower organisms are programmed to interpret them in the way they do. Humans, in contrast, generate and interpret signs whose intentions and purposes are either explicit or can be made explicit, for we are endowed with self-consciousness. We engage in dialogue, by means of which we can be critical and self-critical, so our discourse is constantly open to modification."[4]

Short does not deny this. He does argue that

> animals and plants communicate in the way that humans do. Of course human speech is unique: it consists in the ability to replicate legisigns in ever new patterns, as well as in the ability to create new legisigns. . . . The point, rather, is that the distinctive power of human speech is not a supernatural gift but is a remarkable development of basic principles found elsewhere in nature. . . . There are signs throughout nature, but there are legisigns only where there is life, and legisigns always exist in order to serve the purposes of living things.

To return to our herring gulls, if we assume that $R_1 O_1 I_1$ is the immediate feeling of a peck by a nestling, potentially referring to the sensation of regurgitated substance O_1, then R_2, which is generated by means of $I_2 <=> I_1$, could signify nourishment as a result of two paths yielding sign 3 ($R_2 O_2 I_1$):

1. R_1 (a peck as standing for something) $\rightarrow I_2 <=> I_1 \rightarrow R_2$
2. O_1 (regurgitated substance brought about by the peck potentially for the purpose of consumption) $\rightarrow I_2 <=> I_1 \rightarrow O_2$ ("food").

In contrast, if R_1 for the female gull entails a release mechanism stimulating mating activity, then "sex" rather than "food" is implied by way of a distinct pair of paths:

1. R_1 (a peck as standing for something) $\rightarrow I_2 <=> I_1 \rightarrow R_2$
2. O_1 (a display of mating signs brought about by the peck for the purpose of eliciting sexual responses) $\rightarrow I_2 <=> I_1 \rightarrow O_2$ ("sex").

If we designate "food" by $R_2O_{2a}I_{1a}$ and "sex" by $R_2O_{2b}I_{1b}$, the element of "arbitrariness" in the two signs leaves them open to a primitive ambiguity of the sort inherent in Wittgenstein's rabbit-duck drawing. In light of Short's essay, it follows that there must be a continuum rather than a discontinuous break between animal communication and human language.

Now, if the female gull intends to say the equivalent of "I want sex" and gives him the proper signal, but he interprets the message as "Please feed me," she can consequently either accept the food or not. We would suppose that she is incapable of disambiguating the message by talking about it—such as, "No, you idiot, I want sex"—which human language renders a distinct possibility. Yet an incompatibility between the two potential interpretants exists at the break between two distinct representamina and their respective objects.

Putting this in the vocabulary of figure 10, if the female intended $R_2O_{2b}I_{1b}$ ("sex"), then for her, the male's message was the equivalent of $R_2O_{2b}I_{1b}$ ($= \emptyset$), for his response, $R_2O_{2a}I_{1a}$ ("food"), was incompatible with the response expected as a result of the message she intended. The representamina and objects from one incommensurable interpretation to another are disjointed—$R_2O_{2a}I_{1a} \times R_2O_{2b}I_{1b} = \emptyset$—since there is at this point no correlation between the male's generation of further signs and the female's expectations. Subsequent generation of the female's message to yield "sex" is for the male now apparently out of the question unless somehow there is a 180-degree turnabout on his part, and the same can be said of the male's interpretant, "food," regarding the female's subsequent reaction.

With reference to human communication, consider sign 3 further. Assume you are walking down the sidewalk in a congested neighborhood in New York City and overhear someone shout "Watch out!" This sign is as yet extremely vague and indeterminate. It could mean that a large flower pot is falling from the tenth floor of an apartment building toward some people on the street below, a sinister young man is sneaking up behind a gentle old lady carrying a handbag, or a car is bearing down on you as you step off the curb into the busy street. However, in spite of the myriad possible interpretants for this unqualified sign, the context at least serves to establish some set of expectations for the range of possible semiotic objects to which it refers—for example, one would ordinarily not imagine that a twelve-foot alligator is stealthily approaching an unwary bird-watcher.

In other words, given the extensive range of possible Rs and Os for the evocation "Watch out!" and given I's limitations to the category of Firstness, the interpretation rests on the interpreter's collaborating with the interpretant as a mere image, without there being at this point any indication or possibility of a description of the contextualized semiotic object indicated. Nor can there be at this stage any propositional or argumentative statements about the interpretant as image. Generation of an interpretant and the attendant action or reaction that it produces can at this stage be no more than a rather unthinking, automatized, relatively unmediated response. Yet, given the context, the range of possible interpretants that can be slapped on the signal "Watch out!" is immense.

Sign 6 in figure 7, representing a quantum jump toward generality of the sort of which natural language is capable—and which it shares at the most basic level with herring gull communication—presents even greater degrees of

freedom. Continuing up the hierarchy, operator f governs the generation of single replicas, but also sets the basis for the interpreter's developing a readiness for a set of possible future replicas, which is overwhelming in its vastness, given the range of all possible contexts. What, for example, is the meaning of a particular *token,* "lion," taken from the *type,* "lion," in the classroom, on the football field, during an African safari, at the zoo, with reference to *The Wizard of Oz,* or whatever? As we move up the scheme to signs 8, 9, and 10, which now include rules of language use and the formulation of propositions and arguments in the full sense, ever greater degrees of semiotic freedom and a myriad of possible interpretants are there for the taking. Even though semiotic constraints (rules of syntax, implied rules for language games, social conventions) become in a sense more restrictive, the subtlety of the range of possibilities increases by exponential leaps.

Throughout the general sign process I have briefly described, simple either-or ambiguity tends to become either an all-embracing *both-and* or a radically uncertain *either-or . . . or . . . or . . . n.* *Both-and* synthesis can in particular cases be made of incompatible semiotic foci. This occurs by means of movement "up" in the lattice through the logical sum, $R_1 + O_1$, to yield I_2, whose context includes both foci. R_1 and O_1 are, given the inherent ambiguity of the sign in question, partly incompatible but capable of interaction—with time, of course—in varying degrees because there are a few lines of comparability between them. An interactive mixing of an R_1 domain with an O_1 domain is mediated by I_2, whereby $R_1 \rightarrow I_2$ and $O_1 \rightarrow I_2$. And since mixing of portions of R_1 and O_1 is impossible within the exclusive context of either one or the other, I_2, as mediator, is necessarily richer than the sum of R_1 and O_1: the whole is greater than the sum of its individual parts. On the other hand, *either-or* disjunction in the order of $R_2 \times O_2 = I_1$ entails the possibility of oscillation between the one and the other, without their both being simultaneously present to the mind—much like Wittgenstein's rabbit-duck or the Necker cube.

Time and the Sign

The relations described in the previous section evince three significant characteristics:

1. Passage from one interpretant to another is generally, though not always, limited to one step at a time.

2. Translation from O_i to O_{i+1} or from R_i to R_{i+1} is possible solely by way of I_{i+1} (or I_i), which mediates between and connects the Os and Rs.

3. Only one path, whether "up" or "down," is available to R_i and O_i, while I_i has a choice of paths—movement "up" from I_i gives rise to either R_{i+1} or O_{i+1}—hence ambiguity is made possible.

Peirce's "nothingness," 0, it is becoming increasingly apparent, is an absolute realm logically preceding $\varnothing$ (CP, 6.217). It is pure symmetry, lack of differentiation, absence of information and meaning: there is no here or there, up or down, this or that.[5] 0 is absolute vagueness, just as I_f is absolute generality. We naturally tend to take flight from the first, and we cannot help being drawn toward the utopian horizon of the second. But, alas, we are inexorably limited to the nitty-gritty thingness of the things of our concrete existence. To establish distinctions and indicate them, set them off, and give them value depends on particular contexts sensitive to larger contexts, which are in turn embedded in larger ones, with no end in sight. In view of this indefinite range of all possible contexts, all signs, like the furniture of the world, are both related and unrelated, both similar and different in some respect or other, and our establishing such similarities and differences depends upon our particular styles of reasoning.

Indeed, given our overriding automatized behavior, we pigheadedly persist in extracting discrete bits and pieces from myriad differentiations, whether we are aware of it or not, and we persist in forcing identity onto them with every reiteration. So we discriminate indiscriminately, as it were, slicing signs from the flow and giving them preassigned value. Nevertheless, such activity cannot be divorced from contexts, either. Following Hanson's "nonpicture-picture" theory outlined in Chapter Two, once a *semiosic* beginning has begun for some semiotic agent, there is no structure or even discrimination without context. Thus all acknowledged distinctions are embodied, manifest distinctions. Just as there is no innocent eye, so also there is no absolutely isolated and abstract distinction, no perception and interpretation unencumbered by embedded or otherwise *Umwelt*-dependent dispositions. Musical notation of a fugue as black marks on paper, patterns on a CD, intermittent compact and diffuse areas in the air, and vibration of your eardrums are quite distinct. As embodied or contextualized discriminations, however, their structures can be conceived, by an act of mind, as fundamentally the same; they ultimately have the same value. But from within this sameness, differences are extracted in order to make a fugue a fugue for the heart and mind of the Bach enthusiast, to demonstrate the relevance of Fourier analysis of sounds for the physicist, to allow the engineer to design better electronic media, and to keep the bucks coming in for the eye, ear, nose, and throat specialist. They are all, in Gregory Bateson's words, *differences that make a difference.*

Our human penchant for recognizing differences is nothing short of phenomenal. Neisser (1967) once conducted a series of experiments consisting of people scanning newspaper clippings for particular words. He found that, in addition to their being able to cover the clippings at an incredibly rapid rate with about 80-percent accuracy, they could also scan for a number of words, once committing them to memory, as efficiently as one or two words. Such scanning, seeing everything but focusing on nothing in particular, is best suited for such pastimes as finding needles in haystacks. The visual array is experienced without any conscious construction of that experience. Neisser's scanners did not really see what they were looking at. They saw it, but did not see it directly *as* such-and-such. The vast majority of the words were "noise" making up the visual field, with occasional meaningful items of experience. In Polanyi's (1958) terms, their focal attention took in a large segment of the entire visual field—like the piano player attuned to her whole activity rather than the wiggling of each finger—such that, when the proper cue happened to pop up—a difference that made a difference—their focus was reduced to a particular item in the field.

It is actually not necessary that we become machines, automatized by habit, in order to carry out these and similar acts of recognizing differences. Quite simply, we do it. And as things turn out, it is usually the most effective way of doing it. Peircean habit, purpose, goals, dispositions, tacit inferences, and uncontrollable perception are an indelible part of living. They are what ties us intimately to all other organisms. This attests to the primacy of distinctions or differences. Through habit-taking, differences can become embedded ever more deeply, or they can evolve at biological rather than psychological levels to the extent that it becomes well-nigh impossible to (re)cognize what was once known or to know what has not yet been cognized.

(Re)cognition of differences, and even Spencer-Brownian distinctions at the most primitive of levels, are cardinal to the very nature of *semiosis*. (Re)cognition simply cannot be divorced from the notion of a first sign. Peirce battled long and hard against Cartesian indubitable impressions and atomic propositions that would purportedly establish some originary and hence privileged thought or sign. Thinking, Peirce repeated, cannot be reduced to individual thoughts, nor can *semiosis* be reduced to a static set of discrete signs in the nominalistic or semiological sense. The arrow moves, the horses run past the stadium full of anxious spectators, Achilles overtakes the tortoise and with a heave breaks the tape at the finish line, all in spite of Zeno's mighty logic. There is neither a static point in space from which Achilles lurches out of the starting block nor a first point where he touches the tape. It all happens in the space-time flow of things. By the same token, it is not that thought cannot begin; it simply begins, somewhere and somehow, in the process.

In order to account for such beginnings, recall figure 12 from Chapter Six. At the intersection of the three-dimensional Möbius bubbles, we can conceive of the Spencer-Brownian wave train intermittently playing one side off against the other in a vibrating play of *semiosic* minicatastrophes, creating movement, change, dynamic interaction, and ultimately the possibility of difference in terms of an entity being one thing at one instant and something else at the next instant. This oscillation can be conceived as occurring at the "inside-outside" switch on/in the Möbius bubbles, which can be illustrated by a variation on the so-called Penrose triangle in figure 13—a sort of collapsed counterpart to figure 12 but devoid of the implications of 0, I_f, $\varnothing$, and $I_{f\text{-}1}$. It depicts finite, fallible *semiosis* as it exists for us.

189

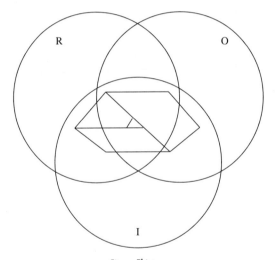

Figure Thirteen

The triangular figure consists of a flattened Möbius strip. Those portions of the strip within $R \times O$, $R \times I$, $O \times I$, or the R-O-I intersect, each of which is in isolation empty of Möbius strip properties, since they do not necessarily require a three-dimensional fold for their construction, are "noncontradictory." In other words, within their two-dimensional framework, they are ordinarily conceived as mere sets of straight lines meeting at various angles. The familiar Möbius contradiction becomes apparent solely with conjunctions $R + O$, $R + I$, and $O + I$, and exclusively within I, where the entire combination of folds in three-dimensional space manifests itself. The I, as mediator, holds R

and *O* together in a sort of sign-mind (particle-wave) embrace. It is an effect produced by a sign upon the mind, itself yet another *I*, for any set of signs "which are so connected that a complex of two of them can have one interpretant, must be determinations of one sign which is *Quasi-mind*" (CP, 4.550). The inevitable burden of circularity, the strange loop, the eternal tangle, falls squarely on Thirdness, on the *I*, since it can come into existence solely when the mind puts the sign to use, though Seconds and Firsts are equally necessary in order that the sign might fulfill its mission as such. Hence the meaning of the sign is found precisely in the space of a conjunction between the three sign components.

This is true especially of symbols. Only through a symbol's *I* can a word be the sign of a generality, rule, or habit—for which memory and time become imperative. Since this *I* must actualize a general habit from antecedent signs and, by signifying some object, must translate its meaning into a consequent sign, the *R-O* conjunction is by itself static—like the Saussurean salami slice—while the *I*'s role as mediator dynamizes and temporalizes the whole affair. Its mediation entails a general rule for relating and comparing members of two sets of signs, antecedent and consequent, both of which are indeterminate in extension. Hence, in the final analysis, the *I* is potentially general in the most general sense.

Any portion of the Möbius strip in figure 13 is by itself mere lines and angles on a plane. But when the whole comes into view, perception and conception from within three-dimensional space and one-dimensional time are necessary in order to appreciate the oscillation from "inside" to "outside" and back again. This perspective is made possible solely from an orthogonal view "outside" the page. A flatlander, trapped within his planar world, would be wellnigh incapable of comprehending the "higher" perspective. In this sense, the strip as three-dimensional construct lies "outside" both *R* and *O*, yet, through *I*, it takes on its "higher" dimension in the constant interaction between sign and object, sign and interpretant, sign and other signs. The strip possesses a property outside both *R* and *O*, and only in their conjunction, mediated by *I*, can this property become manifest.

The Möbius strip as three-dimensional construct, given the fold, is thus both *R*-less and *O*-less, for both *R* and *O* exist exclusively along the two-dimensional plane. Nevertheless, following one aspect of Peirce's "logic of continuity" as derived from his "logic of relatives" (CP, 6.402), the strip's *R*-lessness and *O*-lessness constitutes a certain commonality between *R* and *O: R-O*-lessness, which is neither *R* nor *O* but the equivalent of an imaginary yet invisible and indivisible line between them. A line on a graph separating one boundary from another is itself empty, a nothing. It is neither the one nor the other. Yet it serves to distinguish and mark off something from something else, hence it is something shared by the two boundaries; it is what both of them are not, and without it they would not be related to one another in the way they are.

In other words, R-O-lessness, like the line, necessarily lies "outside" both R and O. It evinces the negative characters' un-R-ness (which is possessed by everything except R) and un-O-ness (which is possessed by everything except O). The composite of these two negatives, R-O-lessness, is dependent upon both R and O and nothing else. Thus R-O-lessness, what R and O are not, nevertheless ties them together by its character as a negative commonality between them. However, unlike the line, R-O-lessness is also included within another domain, I—that is, within $R + I$ or $O + I$. Though the strip "contains" R-O-lessness, when intermittently viewed in time as oscillation between $R + I$ and $O + I$, R-O-lessness takes on its full meaning solely within the three-dimensional realm. Access from one of the two complementary domains to the other, then, is possible, if only by oscillation between $R + I$ and $O + I$, thanks to the mediation of I. Hence there is a commonality between the complementarities, R and O, even though their disjuncture is null; and access to the two distinct modes of organization is made possible by leaps from one domain to the other in a "higher" spatial dimension.[6]

In sum, complementary contexts can be conjoined when the signifying agent devises a means for incorporating, in near-simultaneity, two or more foci and their respective contexts. To return to a previous example, the physicist's vapor track as an icon, and also as an index pointing to the existence of a particle, represents the collaboration of a Peircean First with a Second to compose a Third, the particle, whose semiotic manifestation is strictly symbolic and conceptual, through mathematical or linguistic signs. In other words, the vapor track is a representamen, though its iconic properties bear no resemblance to its object; rather, it is the effect produced by the particle's having passed through that particular trajectory. The sign image, as qualisign ($R_1O_1I_1$), becomes an iconic sinsign ($R_2O_1I_1$), whose interpretant gives rise to a "pointer," a dicent sinsign ($R_3O_1I_1$). The dicent sinsign indicates a rhematic indexical legisign ($R_3O_2I_1$), whose object, the particle, cause of the original qualisign, is now a prime candidate for membership into the "higher" order of symbolicity insofar as it evokes a rhematic symbol ($R_3O_3I_1$) as a term, "particle," identifying the entity in question. This entire process is made possible by the Is' holding the complementary Rs and Os together while oscillating to and fro, thus generating the term from the most primitive semiotic beginnings: $R_1 + O_1 = I_2 <=> I_1 \rightarrow O_2 + R_2 = I_3 <=> I_2 \rightarrow R_3 \times O_3 = I_2 <=> I_1 : R_3O_3I_1$

And if our physicist is so disposed, a proposition and an argument can be engendered from this initiary sign—recall the Macbeth scene.

191

Flip-flops into Time

Attending more specifically to the *R-O-I* model, consider the translation example from Chapter Six of "city" into "ciudad." When we discovered that "ciudad" corresponds to "city," we then had a sign that could serve as a designator of its object, *ciudad-city,* the two being related complementarily. In addition, the sign-designation relationship is related complementarily to its meaning.

This genuine triadic relation, according to Peirce, cannot be reduced to dyadic or monadic relations. And it is exclusively mental; no set of physical relations can be on a par with it. For example, the sentence "John believes a 'ciudad' is a 'city'" is analyzable only into the form "'Ciudad' and 'city' are signs of the object *ciudad-city* to some interpretant sign, namely 'John'" (Savan 1987–88, 43). "John" as such is not merely the concrete flesh and blood John but a full-blown sign among signs, an interpreter-interpretant, a dialogic mind. His belief that "ciudad" corresponds to "city" has become the result of habit; the connection has become embedded. This belief entails perpetual translation of "ciudad-city" into further signs that can then serve to increase—or perhaps decrease—the depth of John's embedded interpretant or predisposed conception of the two terms. In this sense, the *I,* in translating signs into signs, brings about a constant push beyond, toward increased knowledge.

However, there is an apparent quandary inherent in figure 13. Given that the definitions of *R, O,* and *I* are circular, the tangled angles represented by the squashed Möbius strip appear as a severe limitation to those observers with positivist visions of clarity still dancing in their heads. In fact, the basic triad of signs—icons, indices, and symbols—appears equally circular: a term is chiefly iconic by nature, and a proposition is indexical, but a proposition in its most basic form contains an icon as predicate and an index as subject, both of which are terms. And an argument, the ultimate expression of symbolicity, contains both terms as icons and propositions as indices, the latter laying claim to their own icons and indices. All these signs come in varying degrees of complexity, so we are not speaking exclusively of one level of *semiosis* but many levels. They are Byzantinely intertwined to the extent that their disentanglement would appear virtually impossible when one is confronted with a complex, subtle, and profound body of discourse. Yet, with marvelous aplomb, the mind is generally able to wade through various and sundry discursive muddles, with a question here, a rebuttal there, bewilderment somewhere else, and somehow derive a conglomerate of meanings from the whole snarl.

In order better to illustrate this perplexity, let us construct a Grelling-type paradox by assembling a list of "autological" (self-referring, monadic) terms and sentences and another list of "heterological" (non-selfreferring, dyadic) terms and sentences (DeLong 1970, 246):

192

AUTOLOGICAL	HETEROLOGICAL
English	Green
Adjectival	Moody
Polysyllabic	Monosyllabic
Chicago has six letters.	Chicago is a large city.
This sentence is false.	All sentences of the liar type violate the law of logical types.

The autological strings evince certain iconic (monadic, self-referen- 193
tial) properties, while the heterological strings are indexical (dyadic; they cry
out for linkage to some other). Most words and sentences that we encounter in
everyday communication are heterological. But consider the word "heterological" itself as an adjective. In which column does it belong? Put it in the
"autological" column, and it is heterological because it refers to the right-hand
column. Leave it in the "heterological" column, and it cannot be heterological,
for it applies to itself, therefore it must be autological. It is heterological only if
it is autological, and vice versa. It acts intermittently as monadic or dyadic,
according to its context. As the context goes, so also the sign. To repeat, all
distinctions are embodied, contextualized distinctions.

I have stretched the use of terms from Grelling's paradox in order to
make a point: all such paradoxes, in one form or another, are at least indirectly
relevant to the limitative theorems, the most notorious of which is Gödel's. If
we are to accept these theorems, then we must concede that (1) no consistent
human—or community of human semiotic animals—is capable of formulating
a body of knowledge that, if described in all its details, would include all the
true and only true statements about the world (the first incompleteness theorem); and/or (2) no consistent human can prove the consistency of his/her own
knowledge (the second incompleteness theorem). This semiotic indeterminacy
is due to our systematic incapacity to generate enough or the right sort of premises to prove the truth of what we think and say, in part because of the hidden
iceberg of our embedded propensities, in part because of our inherent ignorance, and in the formal sense because of the implications of the limitative
theorems.

These theorems should serve to open our eyes and minds to the notion
that some set of abstract structures or distinctions exists beyond reach. Consequently, it is impossible to give complete and consistent account of them, since
our structures and distinctions are inextricably embodied, contextualized. For
example, in spite of our best intentions and whatever effort might be expended,
we cannot talk about a pure icon, index, or any other fundamental sign—not to
mention such ineffables as "nothingness"—without talking around them. Just

as our perception is limited by our physical capacities—some organisms can see better, some can smell better, and others can hear better—so also is our conception. In fact, there is no reason to believe that our conceptual faculties are any less limited than our perceptual faculties. The first have language, logic, mathematics, science, and the arts to help them out; the second have telescopes, thermometers, speedometers, television, computers, and other instruments to afford them greater acuity. Yet at a given juncture, there is no telling with absolute certainty how far we have come and how much lies beyond (DeLong 1970, 191–229). Hence if an *I* can be related to an *O* through the *R* it reinterprets, if an *I* can always follow an *R* but not vice versa in the same way, and if an *O* can determine an *R* that in turn determines an *I*, then, given this circularity, the best we can do is try to hold a few *I*s, *O*s, and *R*s in check with the awareness that we cannot expect to toss them down the cognitive gullet in a whole package.

194

A perplexing question still remains: How can *R*, *O*, and *I* as distinct foci separated by temporal increments be reconciled with Peirce's process philosophy and his synechistic doctrine, according to which we move along swimmingly in the continuum of existence? It would appear that we have the Zeno dilemma here: not merely a contradiction between continuity and discontinuity, but how to get from one sign to another and from one time increment to another within the ongoing flux and flow of things (see CP, 7.349–51). We have the equivalent of McTaggart's (1927, 10–13) conception of time as a "constant illusion of the mind." And time is now very definitely foregrounded.

McTaggart's notorious and often maligned argument distinguishes between what he calls the A-series and the B-series. The first consists of past, present, and future, the latter of "earlier than" and "later than." The B-series is static insofar as the statement "The Battle of Hastings occurred before the Battle of Waterloo" is permanently true: an event takes its place in a static series of events. This series, McTaggart contends, is the way in which the mind ordinarily construes a sequence of events—"as if" they occurred in time. It is analogous to numerical ordering and compatible with the concept of the "block" universe. In contrast, the A-series characterizes our concrete experience of events: an ever changing stream giving meaning to the idea (or illusion, as McTaggart puts it) of "becoming." The fact that the A-series is for us ongoing—what was future will pass through the "now" on its way to the past—leads us to make statements that are categorically false from within the B-series. From the standpoint of the continuity of the A-series, it can be said that "Achilles is overtaking the tortoise," but within Zeno's framework, this "becoming" cannot be actualized. The only reality, McTaggart contends, is limited to either "Achilles is behind the tortoise" or "Achilles is ahead of the tortoise." There is simply no middle ground.

The foundation of McTaggart's argument rests on the assumption that an event was always, is, and will never cease to be the same event. Take any happening—say, "Achilles is behind the tortoise"—and consider what changes can be wrought in its characteristics: that something is behind something else, that it is Achilles behind the tortoise, that the cause of this event was the decision to engage in an athletic encounter, and so on. No matter how the cookie is cut, a static set of pieces will be found on the platter. From the dawn of time, McTaggart tells us, the event in question was Achilles behind a tortoise, and it will continue to be so. Only in one respect is there any change. The event *was* in the "later than," but *now* it exists in the "earlier than." And while at some point "Achilles is behind the tortoise" was in the "earlier than," and "Achilles is ahead of the tortoise" was in the "later than," both are for us, in our experienced but artificial time, now in the "earlier than."

195

C. D. Broad's (1938, 318) response to McTaggart is based on the way we naturally use language. He points out that we do not generally say "The Battle of Hastings *precedes* the Battle of Waterloo" but that it *preceded* it. The copula in such propositions asserting temporal relations between events is not the timeless copula of classical logic or the "=" of mathematics; rather, it is tantamount to the temporal natural language connectives "is now," "was," and "will be." The sentence "The particle left a vapor trail" does not mean that in some mysterious nontemporal sense of "is," there *was* a particle that momentarily "passed through" the space in the bubble chamber with the property of *presentness,* which it immediately lost, and took on the property of *pastness.* What it means is that the phenomenon (or better, event) of particleness *has been,* but no longer *is being, manifested* in that particular vicinity of that bubble chamber. By the same token, the sentence "The vapor trail of a particle of such-and-such a type will appear somewhere in the bubble chamber" does not signify that there *is* an event in the physicist's apparatus that possesses some property of futurity, which will be transformed momentarily into presentness and then dissolve into pastness. Rather, it indicates that the trail in question paradoxically *will have become* but *has not become* and *is not yet becoming* an event.

Peirce, in his own way contrary to McTaggart's thesis, stresses the importance of lived experience, the dynamics of life's processes, which is not entirely separated from mind processes. Experience, the stream of consciousness, the ongoing flow of the mind as interpretant, is the means for interpreting our existence. We assume that Achilles can overcome the tortoise as a result of experience and experience alone. And, as illustrated by the figure 13 trope-topos, the mind mediates between and moderates relatively incompatible percepts and concepts such that, rather than resulting in a Zenoesque, indecisive oscillation between two static states of affairs, the discontinuity they present is smoothed over by the flow of experience.[7]

That is to say, one might tend to assume that the conjoint between a given part of the Möbius strip in two-dimensional space and the whole strip in three-dimensional space is null. *R* is *R* and *O* is *O,* and the twain shall never meet. Mind is process, however. *R-O*-lessness is itself null in regards to *R* and *O*. Nonetheless, it provides a bridge, or tunnel, through *I* that enables passage from one to the other. This passage functions to smooth out the distinction between two incompatible domains such that flip-flops in time from one to the other are melded into the flow of experience. When *R* is not yet present to consciousness and perceived as an *R* event, it is Firstness. If it is actualized in the *here-now,* as Secondness, *O* potentially can be, but is not yet, an actuality for consciousness. If it is so actualized, then *R* fades back into the *semiosic* soup to become, once again, a possibility, and *I* may already be emerging into conscious to be translated—to translate itself—into its consequent *R*.

Here we have, I believe, the essence of complementarity. A sign's *thisness* emerges out of another sign's having just passed on, and it depends upon yet another sign's *possibleness* of becoming. This is the bane and the boon of *semiosis,* insofar as it entails the generation of signs for some purpose to be interpreted as something by some agent, which is perhaps best epitomized in the human semiotic agent's feeble to fantastic, but always fallible, signifying acts.

But the equation must be taken a giant step further.

Timelessness and Signs Becoming

Lars Löfgren (1984) draws from McTaggart's conclusion and the Grelling paradox. He suggests that Grelling's "autological perspective" weds continuous theories of time with linguistic complementarity as a driving force, concluding that "time is a concept of such complexity that it (or an extended physical model of it) cannot be characterized completely in a formal language" (Löfgren 1984, 13).

Löfgren first points out that formal language descriptions and interpretations exist at distinct levels of discourse. But rather than being incompatible, they are complementary. If a metalanguage embracing both the description and the interpretation exists, the complementarity is transcendable, and if not, it is nontranscendable. Löfgren then distinguishes between descriptions of time and models (or interpretations) of time. The first are, like McTaggart's B-series, static strings: one damn thing after another. The second, like the A-series, must depict ever changing phenomena and hence set up severe barriers preventing their description. In this fashion, any formal theory of time must be incomplete. Static descriptions simply cannot consistently be linked with dynamic interpretations. The theorist must either refer to dynamic time (intuitive time), which is constantly engaged in a cat-and-mouse game with us, or to static time, which can be quite effectively captured with a formal theory. This is somewhat comparable to the Einsteinian space-time "block," the whole of which can be described in formal language, but when considered from a particular frame of reference, any account must be partial at best. In the first case, the hypothetical observer rests "outside" the system, which is heterological. In the second case, the observer is "within" an autological system, which can be observed, described, and interpreted solely by his simultaneously observing his own observation, describing his description, and interpreting his interpretation: an apparently impossible task, indeed, as arduous as the final or ultimate *R-O-I* embraced in an instant.

197

H. A. C. Dobbs (1972) writes on the structure of the phenomenological "sensible present," which is kindred in spirit with this nonsimultaneity of sign instantiation and sign interpretation. He first alludes to experiments demonstrating that when the time between successive items of experience falls below a certain minimum level—about fifty milliseconds—it becomes impossible, given the torpidity of our perceptual faculties, to place them in simple linear order.[8] He then proposes, in addition to the three dimensions of space, a spacelike temporal dimension, following Eddington's (1946) suggestion for relativity theory. This is imaginary time, so called after imaginary numbers. It is ordered like McTaggart's B-series in terms of *prior to* and *subsequent to:* static, mathematical time. Then a fifth dimension becomes necessary, a dynamic time accounting for the real time of everyday life and of intuition (much like McTaggart's A-series). Imaginary time is not directed; it is merely a line in Euclidean space, a reversible order without any indication of a moving *now.* It is a static series of simultaneities, while real time is a directed, irreversible line with an arrow (see CP, 6.111, 127–30).

These time dimensions are most adequately conceptualized when related to numbers. The rational numbers are the whole integers. Irrational numbers are expressed in terms of infinite decimal expansions—such as $\sqrt{2}$. Imaginary numbers, such as $\sqrt{-1}$, are those undecidables—amphibians between being and nonbeing, as Leibniz put it—that were stashed away in the closet for centuries because mathematicians were not sure what to do with them. Real numbers have no imaginary parts and comprise the rational and irrational numbers. And complex numbers are of the form $a + b\sqrt{-1}$, where a and b—called the modulus—consist of real numbers. Corresponding to these number categories, imaginary time—the fourth dimension—can be combined with real time to yield a complex time variable—the fifth dimension—whose order is partial rather than reversibly or irreversibly linear (compare to the nonlinear figure 10 matrix).

Imaginary time is "dead" time, much like the time in the storage system of a computer. But it contains "expectations," all of them simultaneously held in memory or a storage bank, to be retrieved at a propitious moment—like a computer printout. It is the equivalent of what I have called, following quantum states, a "superposition," such as the two possible Necker cube states, which are *there* in a sort of trembling or twinkling pulsation of readiness—comparable to the moiré effect, and, much like Kristeva's (1984, 26) *chora,* it is "not yet a position that represents something for someone (i.e., it is not a sign)."[9] In fact, Dobbs uses the Necker cube to illustrate his hypothesis that transformation from cube-up to cube-down and back again is possible only within a fourth dimension; no spatial degree is manifested in this transformation; and when combining the imaginary time dimension with the real time dimension to produce a complex time variable of partial order, near-simultaneity of distinct—complementary—events, such as the flip-flops of the Necker cube, can be perceived.

In other words, the symmetrical, reversible, intransitive, nonlinear domain (storage bank), when combined with the asymmetrical, irreversible, transitive, linear domain (printout), yields a dynamic, dyadic, pulsational *this-that* which is neither appropriately symmetrical nor asymmetrical, neither reversible nor irreversible, neither intransitive nor transitive, neither nonlinear nor linear. This *both-and,* or *either-or,* depending on the vantage point, could well constitute the roots of time, and of consciousness and self-consciousness (Kauffman 1986; Matte Blanco 1975; Varela 1975). It is, so to speak, Möbius strip vacillation between "inside" and "outside," continuity and discontinuity, identity and difference.

It was the geometer August Ferdinand Möbius who suggested in the nineteenth century that continuous transformations between incongruous three-dimensional counterparts—the Necker cube or Möbius strip—are mathematically impossible within the three-dimensional manifold. Such transformations require rotation of the entire plane, not merely a line within the plane, which calls for an extra dimension. For example, along a line, no rotation can occur; within a plane, rotation can occur about a point; and within a cube, rotation can occur about a line. A fourth dimension, then, is needed for rotation about a two-dimensional plane. As an example of Möbius's observation, a characteristic of complex numbers—the combination of imaginary and real numbers—is that they have no simple linear order, nor is there any meaning in saying of a complex number that it is either positive or negative, or that it is larger or smaller than any other complex number. They are all there all at once (superposed), and as such, if no value has (yet) been assigned to them, they are ipso facto valueless. Complex numbers are oscillational, an enchanted mathematical realm whose dancing back and forth as points along a real line or in a phase-space on

198

a two-dimensional plane can produce a dynamic wave form somewhat comparable to a rough two-dimensional image of a hypersphere (figure 14).

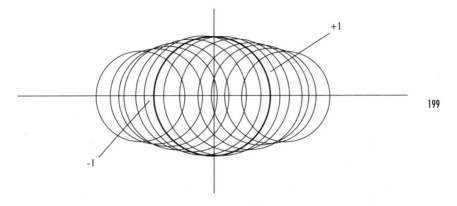

+1

-1

199

Figure Fourteen

Louis Kauffman and Francisco Varela (1980) demonstrate how figure 14 is the result of the complex numbers viewed in terms of wave forms by the oscillation of $a + b\sqrt{-1}$ between $a + b$ and $a - b$ represented on the Cartesian plane. Technically speaking, oscillation is displayed as the circular orbiting of a point determined by a variable radius—itself determined by b—and by associating the orbit of each point, a, along the horizontal axis with a unit circle in the complex plane. In this manner, each orbit corresponds to two complex numbers, $a \pm b\sqrt{-1}$, where +1 and -1 are de-generate circles and $\pm\sqrt{-1}$ is the large unit (generated) circle.[10] This geometrical display of the complex numbers expands the real number line (horizontal axis) not to the entire plane but to an oscillational to-and-fro line with an infinity of dancing, synchronized circular orbits associated with each point. What we have here is the one-dimensional representation of the real numbers, with the plane representing the complex numbers—the plane being necessary for the rotation of a real number (point, de-generate circle) to describe the authentic circles. The excluded-middle principle does not apply, so the scheme is general in the most general sense, and since all values and their opposites exist in a superposed state, the noncontradiction principle is inoperative, rendering the scheme at the same time vague. In short, Kauffman and Varela's equation depicts the ultimate in Peirce's sign generativity as well as the ultimate in de-generativity.

Moreover, the whole conglomerate, slapped onto a two-dimensional flatland, is such that, from our 90-degree orthogonal perspective, we can see the circles in the *here-now* all at once. This 90-degree orthogonal grasp would be as inaccessible to strictly linear, mnemonic thinking—such as a computer printout—as it would be to a flatlander dwelling within the flat surface. Linear thinking could do no more than follow the generation of circles along the line, one after another. Such a linear computing system is probably no more phenomenologically concrete than a real number series, and the direction of its arrow would reflect not real time as we experience it but linear ordering of the most rudimentary sort. In contrast, our nonlinear, 90-degree orthogonal view of figure 14 knows no definite serial order, for we are capable of seeing the two-dimensional scheme in one perceptual gulp. It is like viewing the juxtaposed grid of an op-art object displaying its moiré scintillation; we see it as if in simultaneity and nonlinearly (recall the status of *I* in figure 10).

200

And we must remember that a fourth dimension is necessary for rotation about the two-dimensional plane of figure 14 to generate a hypersphere, which stretches our capacity for imaginary constructs beyond the limit. Thus, lest we become unduly smug about our phenomenal cerebral powers, we must remind ourselves that, within our own three dimensions of space and one of time, we are able to react appropriately to no more than minuscule lumps from the whole of things, much like the hapless flatlander linearly assimilating, with excruciating torpidity from our point of view, the pattern in figure 14. We are, after all is said and done, helplessly constrained regarding our own world. Thought is chiefly sequential, successive, and one-dimensional, while our world presents itself as a multidimensional, nonsuccessive pattern of indescribable richness and variety, and the mind's every effort to grasp this world is like trying to appreciate a beautiful landscape by looking through a narrow slit in a fence. From a perspective beyond our own three dimensions of space and one of time, we would be only slightly more sophisticated than a pocket calculator programmed to spit out linear mathematical expansions. An imaginary demon from that "higher" perspective would look upon us much as we imagine the pathetic world of the flatlander.

Fortuitous Happenings

The two perspectival modes developed here pattern, on the one hand, a synchronic "block" model and, on the other, a model of becoming. In order further to illustrate these complementary perspectives, let us consider a game governed by probability factors—Mallarméan throws of dice—supported by a few images from Borges.[11]

A die thrown once affirms chance. If thrown many times, the throws in their composite affirm a certain necessity (based on a probability equation). Put 1,000 identical dice in 1,000 identical dice-throwing machines and throw all of them at once. Record the results. Then take one of the dice and throw it 1,000 times from one of the machines. The results will be very close, perhaps even identical. Call the first experiment an *ensemble* ("block"), and the second *history* (linear sequence).[12] The first is analogous to the universe as a totality, which is quite determinate. The second is analogous to the universe as pure linear succession, which, at any given point, is for all intents and purposes indeterminate with respect to future points. Combining the two perspectives produces a "complex system" that is neither continuous nor discontinuous, neither nonlinear nor linear. But questions arise. How can 1,000 apparently unconnected events combine to produce a predictable outcome? How can one die without memory give the same predictable pattern? Why is the ensemble average interchangeable with the time average? How can the accumulation of purely chance events culminate in necessity? Significantly, what Nietzsche calls necessity is not "the abolition but rather the combination of chance itself" (Deleuze 1983, 26).

201

These questions are far from irrelevant. The problem is that, as chiefly serial organisms, we are incapable of seeing, of knowing, the whole of things, the ideal to which we invariably aspire. Borges (1964, 128n) illustrates the contrast between ourselves and an imaginary infinite intelligence thus: "[T]he steps a man takes, from the day of his birth to the day of his death, trace an inconceivable figure in time. The Divine Intelligence preconceives that figure at once, as man's intellect perceives a triangle. That figure (perhaps) has its determined function in the economy of the universe." This image, which is comparable to a static, transcendent view of the "block" universe in contrast to the time line of an immanent, individual entity, is also related to the distinction between an ensemble of dice throws as opposed to a linear sequence of throws. A time-bound (historical) being, from the larger view, can appear to be the product of necessity, but as far as she is concerned, she exercises free will. Yet this being can never really know, for the larger view is inaccessible to her.

Another prime example of the "block" universe is Borges's "Library of Babel" (1962, 51–58), which exists *in aeternum.* The library's books are generated randomly until presumably the canonical works happen to show up, hence order should eventually prevail. But the library's inhabitants, victims of immanence, can perceive no order, since the books appear to be no more than the random juggling of letters, perhaps to infinity. This vision of the universe as a chaotic library, when viewed from within, complements the re-presentation of life as a cosmic lottery in "The Lottery of Babylon" (Borges 1962, 30–35). If what appears to be worldly chaos from within the library is actually the work of a divine being, in the lottery the game of chance determining one's destiny is the result of "sacred drawings," divine throws of cosmic dice. But if the lottery is "the basis of reality, an intensification of chance, a periodical infusion of chaos," and if in reality *"the number of drawings is infinite,"* then how can there be any order whatsoever—from a finite perspective, that is? And if by happenstance there is, how can it be known?

Peirce (CP, 2.661–68) also confronted these *ensemble/history* enigmas and the virtual impossibility of knowing whether the whole of things is ordered or not. A pioneer in probability before it became fashionable, Peirce began with the reasonable premise that if a die is thrown, there is a probability of one in three that in the long run a number divisible by three will turn up. Now, what is meant by "in the long run"? The only response can be infinity, for we cannot know if the probability is indeed one in three without exercising an endless series of trials. Since this is physically, if not logically, impossible, we must remain eternally uncertain. Yet the mind generally abhors chaos and strives to find order, even when there is none. The Greeks saw mythical figures in the random patterns of the stars. Tea leaves and the entrails of animals have been used to foretell the future. The gods have been consulted by casting bones, and a toss of sticks or coins is used in the I Ching. Yet, though apparent randomness strikes fear in the human psyche, it also fascinates; the success of Borges's stories bears witness to this human characteristic.

In an effort to draw order from randomness, the narrator of Borges's "Lottery" first tells us that the number of drawings is infinite. The implication is that if all these possibilities branch into one another, and if no decision can be final, then every possibility must eventually transpire, each one of them ideally forming an ordered system. As an embellishment on this idea, suppose we construct a lottery wheel with an infinity of divisions. If we spin it once and predict that the pointer will stop, say, on 5, our chances of winning are infinitesimally small. In order to win with a degree of certainty, we must construct an infinity of such lottery wheels. So let us do so. We now have both an ensemble and a history. Either by spinning one wheel an infinity of times or all the wheels at once, we are sure to win, no matter which number we select. This situation is like Borges's lottery, which has an infinity of possible drawings requiring only finite time, if time can indeed be infinitely subdivisible.

Assuming time is infinitely subdivisible, let us divide one fiftieth of a second into an infinity of increments and spin one lottery wheel once during each time duration. This is history. Spin all the wheels in simultaneity, and we have the ensemble. For practical purposes, however, one fiftieth of a second can be considered of null duration for us perceptual sluggards. In this event, history is packed into the same framework as the ensemble, which is to say that if a player plays the ensemble of wheels, her number, no matter what she chooses, is certain to turn up on at least one of the wheels, and if she plays the history wheel for one fiftieth of a second, she will still win during what she conceives to be a simultaneous drawing. Absolute uncertainty becomes absolute certainty, unadulterated chance becomes necessity!

Borges's Babylonians, caught within this type of dilemma, attempt to falsify the inevitability of infinitely contingent happenings that ultimately become necessity. Their historians invent a generally reliable, though devious, method for correcting chance. But ultimately, the attempt to subvert the infinite disorder, which is also tantamount to an infinite order from the opposite perspective, falls into the hands of the company in charge of the lottery, for in an apparently chaotic world in which all possibilities will eventually occur—either in the "now" (of the ensemble) or at some "point" (in history) in this infinite game—everything must be a decision of the company. In other words, we have the problem of the One and the Many, nonlinearity and linearity, symmetry and asymmetry (this problem is also found in the complex time frame discussed above). From the omniscient gaze of the Company, the One, the lottery is ensemble: all things must occur. In contrast, the Babylonians are helpless and hopeless gamblers inside history, the Many. Yet since the company introduced infinity into the game of chance, everything must occur in history as well, hence, given Babylonian collectivity, ultimately no losses are to be suffered. The problem is that they do not, and cannot, know this (compare to Peirce's community asymptotically reaching out toward absolute Truth).

Escher's (1971, 15) words create a similar image of history and ensemble from our own limited framework:

> Anyone who plunges into infinity, in both time and space, further and further without stopping, needs fixed points, mileposts, for otherwise his movement is indistinguishable from standing still. . . . Anyone who wishes to create a universe on a two-dimensional surface (he deludes himself, because our three-dimensional world does not permit a reality of two nor of four dimensions) notices that time passes while he is working on his creation. But when he has finished and looks at what he has done, he sees something that is static and timeless; in his picture no clock ticks and there is only a flat, unmoving surface.

Escher's work is successively and indeterminately elaborated. This is history. When completed, as a totality, it is a timeless, determinate entity. This is ensemble. The artist, of course, forges order from chaos, necessity from chance. But in its composite, the infinite randomness I have referred to regarding the lottery is tantamount to Escher's static, timeless order. In this respect, Borges's company is not the construct of a mischievous demon who buffets the lottery players about at will. It is the product of infinite chance, which in its composite paradoxically becomes the equivalent of necessity.

The two perspectives—ensemble and history—pattern, on the one hand, a "block" universe of synchronicity and, on the other, a universe of becoming. They also pattern the B-series and the A-series, Löfgren's description and interpretation, the *enfolded* (embedded) and the *unfolded* (de-embedded).

By associating imaginary time with real time, the complex time variable plays the role of history, the becoming of events—much like the linear generation of integers (real time)—in contrast to the static measure of already elapsed events, which represents synchronicity of past and future (imaginary time). The happenings of history have a distinct direction between past and future, thus allowing for a knife-edged race of the "now" for us. In this sense, time is a *virtual dimension,* not an object of knowledge but an experiential ordering operation.

Weizsäcker (1980) refers to the distinction between static time and dynamic time in terms of a tense logic built into conscious and self-conscious experience, in contrast to a logic of instinct (embedded behavior), which is devoid of tense and provided with operating instructions. The first is capable of critique and self-critique; the second is a computing system like a Turing machine. The first constructs linear time; the second knows no "now," it is a passive state of readiness. A combination of both yields a perpetually self-referential system, to which the focus now turns.

Unfoldment by Re-entering the Enfolded

In order to relate the above section to Peirce's categories, let us reconsider figure 13 as it is shown in figure 15. Like real time, the squashed Möbius strip can be continuously rotated 360 degrees on the same plane about a point by a group operation, and it thus reenters its own space—it remains the same as it was (though keep in mind that after each iteration, in the semiotic world of things, a difference inexorably ensues). Like imaginary time, by two 90-degree orthogonal flips outside the plane about a line on the plane, the strip can reenter its own space—compare to the oscillational flip-flops of I in the figure 10 matrix.

This double flip can represent the ushering in of a novel experience, an abduction, a First as "an instance of that sort of element of consciousness which is all that it is positively, in itself, regardless of anything else" (CP, 1.306)—an idea emerging from "somewhere" else, in imaginary time. Then, the mediacy of real time along the plane, which is represented by smooth, continuous transitions, follows Peirce's process by which all thoughts are of the nature of sign; they require time, real time, to enter the stage of signification. Dobbs takes pains to demonstrate, by the same mathematics, that the two superposed enantiomorphic Necker cubes can be transformed one into the other only by a mathematical spacelike dimension of imaginary time that is indefinitely ordered and that we sense much as we do a rapid staccato of sounds or blinking lights, without the ability properly to differentiate and order them. If Dobbs is correct—and I believe he is onto something, though experimental evidence must bear him out—the same could be said of the Möbius strip in figure 13.

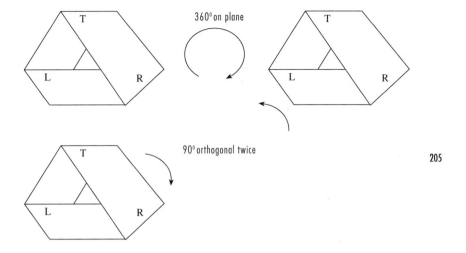

Figure Fifteen

"Fine and dandy," one protests, "but what do these cute twists and turns in space have to do with Peirce and signs?" Well, take one of Peirce's many triads: *feeling, experience* (of both "inner" thought-signs and "outer" sign-events), and *knowing* (*how* and *that,* and seeing *as-that*). With regard to feeling, consider the emergence of novelty, or *abduction*.[13] For Popper (1959), and most positivists, novel ideas are the product of irrational flights of fancy, purely random happenings. There is no absolute guarantee, Popper writes, that one idea popping into the head has any better chance than any other of leading to the truth. Knowledge is the result of blind guesses—Popper's Darwinian theory of "evolutionary epistemology."

Peirce, in contrast, believed that feeling has its own "reason," though it is inaccessible to reason. Fitting abduction into his general pragmatist philosophy, he once suggested that it is the instinctive capacity of the sufficiently prepared mind for informed guesses, for the mind has "a natural bent in accordance with nature" (CP, 6.478). As a consequence, the "elements of every concept enter into logical thought [imaginary time] at the gate of perception [real time] and make their exit at the gate of purposive action; and whatever cannot show its passports at both those two gates is to be arrested as unauthorized by reason" (CP, 5.212). This "gate of perception" can result from the outward clash of sign-events in the "real" world, but more likely it is the product of inwardly generated thought-signs. Perception, in either case, is of the mode of Secondness.

Since there is no wide-eyed, innocent percept, all percepts are accompanied by perceptual judgments. And since seeing *as-that* is interpreting, there is no hard and fast line of demarcation between perception and knowledge (CP, 5.184). There is, however, a distinction between abductive judgments and perceptual judgments: the former are usually subject to some degree of control, though they can also shade into the latter, which are by and large uncontrollable. Recalling observations in Chapter Four, controlled thoughts are the tip of the iceberg, "the mere blossom of a vast complexus, which we may call the instinctive mind" (CP, 5.212). What we have here is a tense logic (of consciousness and control, real time) and a nontense logic (of instinct, automata, imaginary time), to which I alluded in the previous section.

The reader who cavalierly takes Peirce's instinct (nontense logic) to be outmoded biological thinking has not read him closely. Instinct entails embedded tendencies as well as inborn propensities and proclivities. Although quite obviously it cannot be specified—and Peirce, as far as I am aware, never denied this—it serves as a tool offering a conceptual grasp of an exceedingly complex phenomenon, to wit, a nonconscious linking of the qualitative Firstness of sign, object, and interpretant by resemblance, which allows the sign to suggest a hypothesis (abduction) to its interpreter-interpretant. Such suggestion is *prima facie* beyond control, as are all instincts, though after the fact of its emergence, as Secondness and Thirdness, it can be subjected to increasing control. Thus a nonconscious linkage by Firstness can enable the interpreter-interpretant to interpret the sign in conjunction with the character of its object, such interpretation providing for the possibility of an alteration of feeling, action, and thought through self-control.

On the other hand, embedded signs that have become instinctive or quasi-instinctive lie in the mind all at once in readiness to emerge at the propitious moment—ensemble rather than history. Speaking of this "presence" of mind, Peirce (CP, 1.310) observes that

> all that is immediately present to a man is what is in his mind in the present instant. His whole life is in the present. But when he asks what is the content of the present instant, his question always comes too late. The present has gone by, and what remains of it is greatly metamorphosed. . . . Indeed, although a feeling is immediate consciousness, that is, is whatever of consciousness there may be that is immediately present, yet there is no consciousness in it because it is instantaneous. For . . . feeling is nothing but a quality, and a quality is not conscious: it is a mere possibility.

I must point out, however, that Peirce's concepts of the "immediate present" and "immediate consciousness" by no means suffer from the "myth of presence" or logocentrism. It is ensemble, granted. But the ensemble, having been thrown into real time, is never immediately available to the human agent. On the contrary, there can be no more than a display of bits and pieces of the ensemble through a traveling time-slit in the "now" of things, beginning with feeling and culminating in knowing.

Feeling, or the sign of Firstness, issues forth as a stream or not at all, though this stream may be vague. Although immediate, its specification can be made possible only after the fact and by way of mediating Thirdness. For example, an abduction emerging as feeling is at that point acritical, undoubting, and exceedingly vague, though on the spur of that particular moment it may seem to be a paragon of clarity (CP, 5.446). And it might bring with it, as Secondness enters the scene, the shock of surprise, for it is entirely different from what was expected; it contradicts habit. This applies, I would suggest, to the most insignificant of abductions to major overhauls in the ways of societies of organisms, of human knowledge, and of the universe.

By *evolution,* I mean continuous development (history) punctuated by *revolutionary* schisms (as if from an ensemble).[14] Such evolution and revolution are the macrolevel counterparts to microlevel events in the A-series and ruptures in the B-series, tense logic and nontense logic, real time and imaginary time, the self-consciously controllable and that which is at the outset uncontrollable, respectively. In spite of his concept of the general asymptotic push of the universe and human knowledge toward the ultimate interpretant, Peirce believed that abrupt (revolutionary) transformations occasionally punctuate smooth (evolutionary) transitions, though he remained somewhat ambivalent in this regard. Development, he wrote,

> does not take place chiefly by imperceptible changes but by revolutions. For some cause or other trade which had been taking one route suddenly begins to take another. In consequence merchants bring new goods; and new goods make new habits. Or some invention like that of writing, or printing, or gunpowder, or the mariner's compass or the steam engine, in a comparatively short time changes men profoundly. It seems strange that we who have seen such tremendous revolutions in all the habits of men during this century should put our faith in the influence of imperceptible variations to an extent that no other age ever did. . . . That habit alone can produce development I do not believe. It is catastrophe, accident, reaction which brings habit into an active condition and creates a habit of changing habits. (NE 4:142)

Regarding such catastrophes, let us begin at the most fundamental level of abduction, say, the flip of the Möbius strip in imaginary time as depicted in figure 15 as a model of Poincaré's discovery of the Fuchsian functions. Poincaré's (1913) lively account has him working on the problem for

207

fifteen days without success. One evening, after drinking black coffee, he spent a sleepless night experiencing jumbles of ideas colliding until they interlocked, convincing him that the tentative hypothesis he had constructed was incorrect. He then went on vacation, and, while boarding a bus, he suddenly realized that the Fuchsian functions were identical to a set of functions that already existed in mathematics, the transformations of non-Euclidean geometry, which he could then use to solve his problem.

Poincaré claims that the incidents of travel put his mathematical work in cerebral limbo, where it gestated and gelled on its own, to surface at an unexpected moment. This is the ensemble. His next, somewhat arduous task was that of patiently and in a more or less linear, continuous operation, taking up pen and ink and setting his discovery down on paper. This is history. In other words, Poincaré's discovery is patterned by a flip of the strip in terms of 90-degree orthogonals in figure 15, thus bringing a disarray of signs into a more benign collection—order from chaos. Then, by smooth transitions—360-degree rotation on the plane of figure 15—the signs could be manipulated to obtain the desired, and orderly, results. Similar experiences are legion: Kekulé's discovery of the benzene ring experienced as intertwined snakes after a coffee-drinking marathon; Coleridge's dream of Kubla Khan and his palace which, upon awakening from a drug-induced slumber, so we are told, he wrote as if the composition were all there and awaiting its realization on the page; Mozart's melodies coming to him in their entirety in one massive clash. In each case, the flip within the ensemble occurred at the level of Firstness, where myriad thought-signs and sign-events are possible but none actualized. Smooth rotations on the plane are a continuous generation of signs in the sphere of Secondness.

On a greater—though not necessarily grander—macro, social scale, scientific revolutions do not exactly sweep across the community and radically alter minds, means, and methods overnight. I have mentioned in passing that the Copernican view—initially dubbed "Copernicus's paradox"—required a few centuries to become commonly accepted. Closer to home base, the so-called Einsteinian revolution actually had its beginning before the special theory of relativity entered the scene in 1905 in the work of Maxwell, Boltzmann, Poincaré, and others, and the details of this grand flip are still being worked out, a process that will undoubtedly continue into the unforeseen future (Barrow 1990; Casti 1989). After their initial outburst, broad social revolutions also require from years to decades to blossom and come to fruition, if they will at all (Brinton 1965).

Though in a few short lines I have launched my story into the ethereal orbit of mass movements and virtually infinitely complex lines of discourse, what I have illustrated, I would submit, is that microlevel perturbations can have their effect on macrolevels. Such microlevel agitations in Prigogine's far-from-equilibrium states are capable of becoming magnified finally to throw the entire system into disarray. This is like a young lad who, from a bridge overlooking a flooding river, tosses his beer can into the water, which causes a slight perturbation, the ripples of which bring about a degree of turbulence some yards downstream, which gradually increases finally to reach a threshold that is crossed, then a dike gives slightly, disintegrates, and a town is devastated.[15]

In summary, at whatever level the triangle decides to flip within imaginary time (the ensemble), the ramifications of its act can have real (historical) time repercussions at all levels along the chain of command. Given the myriad possible flips altering semiotically real worlds, perceptual and conceptual modes, and styles of reasoning, there can be, for us, in view of the overwhelming depth, complexity, and magnitude of the realm of possibilities within the ensemble, no center, master pattern, or model, no privileged knowing subject, no neutral perspective but merely people talking and trying their best to cope. Modernism itself is thus thrown for a loop.

So to the question, How can the *R-O-I* model be reconciled with Peirce's process philosophy? we must respond that the "model" is no model at all in the traditional modernist sense. The classical "Universe ≈ Machine" image demands a transcendental perspective, a *modelans* of totalizing iconic (analogical) properties referring (indexically) to a presumably timeless, invariant *modelandum* (symbol). In contrast, the *R-O-I* scheme, rather than being imagistic or metaphorical, is more properly diagrammatic—to complete Peirce's hypoicon triad, which includes images, diagrams, and metaphors. As a diagram, it implies not essence but non-Platonic Spencer-Brownian form; not merely being (ensemble) but, in addition, the continuity of becoming (history, in the complex, multiply variegated, nonlinear sense); not the "real" but the semiotically real. It evinces a matrix of indeterminate possibilities rather than some granitic actuality, an interconnected fabric of interplay rather than merely disjointed atoms.

Most significantly, we are always already in the diagram, or in the matrix. The general assumption has it that images, metaphors, diagrams, language, and signs in general require pictures, logocentric mirrors of the world, and hence our obstinate penchant for essentialism, ontological security, the myth of presence, and the "really real." The trouble is that, since we are embedded within the matrix, there is not merely abstraction, as we would perhaps like, but concrete living, not simply things but events, not fleshless taxonomies and structures but living processes. This needs be the case, for from within there is no conceivable totality, no plenitude of all things.

Peirce's community-oriented naturalistic pragmatism is thus variously aligned with James (1877), John Dewey (1925, 1929), Whitehead (1925), and to a degree with Wittgenstein's (1953) language games, Rorty's (1979, 1991a,

209

1991b) "epistemological behaviorism," and the "new pragmatism" in general. These views are anthropological, historical, and ecological (postmodernist) in contrast to the views of objectivism, logical empiricism, and realism (modernist epistemologies that evaluate human knowledge according to absolute, transcendental, and timeless standards, as if from some outside vantage point). In a manner of speaking, focus is shifted from McTaggart's B-series to the A-series: the crystal sublimates into random fits and jerks of bits of gas, which, in their aggregate, bring about continuous change; the clock becomes a cloud; stasis becomes process; and at long last, there may exist the possibility of our returning "home" to the concrete world of nature-qua-culture and culture-qua-nature.

PART

Three

A Bootstrap Operation

Argument: The Pinnacle of *Semiosis,* and the Limits of Time

Let us speak further of sign 10 as an introduction to John Archibald Wheeler's semiotic universe.

The iteration of sign types coupled with an infiltration of time to create novel re-presentations such that they appear different from what they were tends to become for us an irresistible temptation. Indeed, perhaps we could hardly conceive of ourselves and our world otherwise. The flow of signification implied by Peirce's ten-fold sign system produces a sense of temporality, while the pattern itself, given its recursive nature, allows for what seems to be a timeless constancy of that which is signified (and therein lies the apparent non-postmodern flavor of Peirce's sign typology, mentioned in Chapter Four, which is, nonetheless, postmodern in spirit). In a manner of speaking, just as the quantitative progression of Peirce's decalogue is isomorphic with a linear time sequence, so also the qualitative facet of each authentic sign evinces an uncanny isomorphism with that timeless unity, the monad (see Merrell 1991a, chap. 2).

In this sense, the number 10, corresponding to a sign as argument, embodies the possibility of a reentry of the form of the sign into itself. And a cycle is thus completed. In fact, if we look upon the entirety of figure 7 as a Möbius strip, with the upper right-hand corner connected to the lower left-hand corner such that the sign of 10, as a self-contained whole, is contiguous with the sign of 1—though it is now a compounded, self-returning sign—perhaps we can begin to get the picture.

Lest I put the cart before the horse, however, and more adequately to grasp the ongoing, processual character of Peirce's *semiosis,* I will focus attention specifically on the argument, which Peirce once summarily defined as "any process of thought reasonably tending to produce a definite belief" (CP, 6.456; see also 2.266–68, 3.160). Arguments arise from a combination of the three now familiar sources, deduction, induction, and abduction (CP, 2.95–96). Since abduction merely suggests, there seems to be no basis on which to justify it, if by justification is meant undeniable proof according to positivist dictates. Peirce nevertheless contends that the abductive process is inferential, though he denies the existence of a precise algorithm for the logic of discovery. Abductive inference is, most properly speaking, tacit or nonconscious—in the sense of

Hermann Helmholtz's "unconscious inference," to which Peirce occasionally refers. This appears to throw the matter into a bed of conceptual quicksand—especially considering my remarks on Popper and abduction in Chapter Eight. Nevertheless, Peirce's position never wavered, from the 1860s through 1903, and he wrote that "among those opinions which I have constantly maintained is this, that while Abductive and Inductive reasoning are utterly irreducible, either to the other or to Deduction, . . . yet the only *rationale* of these methods is essentially deduction" (CP, 5.146). However, to suggest that abduction is justified because it can be validated ex post facto by deductive reasoning and explain certain phenomena "out there" is not, in these postpositivist, postmodern, times, saying much.

But there may be some saving grace, since abductive inference establishes not that a hypothesis is true but only that pursuit of the implications it holds is reasonable. The grounds for pursuing the hypothesis are *prima facie,* since other hypotheses, potentially an infinite number of them, could have been put forth but were not, and at least one of them is capable quite adequately of accounting for the phenomena in question. In other words, at the outset, there is no scientific certainty that the hypothesis is correct. Rather, it appears only to be plausible.

Peirce obviously places considerable stock in inferential reasoning processes. As I pointed out above, much, and at times even most, of this process remains tacit. That is to say, a reasoner "may be conscious of the premise, but he is not conscious that his acceptance of the conclusion is inferential" (CP, 8.67). We do not necessarily start from hypotheses but rather from what we take to be the data—which is inevitably theory-laden and never presuppositionless. After gathering this data, we lurch out of the starting block with a premise in hand and proceed to move toward a conclusion, though we also tend to lose our way and end up on the long-jump runway without knowing how we got there, for part of our reasoning is nonconscious. As a rule of thumb, during tacit reasoning, the first premise is conscientiously and consciously experiential; the rest tends to lie further down in the mind's workings, which accounts for "unconscious inference." The absent portion of inferential reasoning can be deemed, roughly speaking, *enthymemetic*—recall the remarks on the enthymeme in chapters Six and Eight. Peirce (CP, 2.466) once wrote that an argument whose leading principle contains nothing that can be eliminated is complete, in contrast to an incomplete, rhetorical, or enthymemetic argument. And, regarding Peirce's attack on Cartesian intuition, if all cognitions depend for their existence on other cognitions, then a first cognition cannot be directly available to the mind. Hence something will invariably be absent, unaccountable; the argument will have a hole in it, which under other circumstances could have been filled but is not.

An argument, as a self-contained universe of discourse—disregarding the tacit assumptions underlying it, which remain unarticulated—is at once finality and re-commencement. As finality, it patterns the incessant push of a sign and its interpreter toward a perpetually elusive final interpretant. And as re-commencement, once the semiotic peak has been scaled and the sign of 10 reached, either there is embedment and de-generacy "downward" toward more primitive sign processes, or the sign doubles back on itself to reinitiate, by way of some abductive leap, *semiosic* generation from 1 to 10. That is, as the apparent consummation of a universe of discourse, it can become the commencement of another, more complex universe of discourse.

Peirce distinguished between *argument* and *argumentation,* defining the former as "any process of thought reasonably tending to produce a definite belief" and the latter as "an Argument proceeding from definitely formulated premises" (*pace* Popper). He branded the idea that all reasoning is a form of argumentation as prejudicial (CP, 6.457). There are processes of thought directed solely toward the development of belief concerning matters of vital importance that, due to their general nature and necessary vagueness of concepts, cannot be constructed in precisely set foundations. Belief is somewhat at variance with pure science, which is the result not of belief or *episteme* but of opinion (*doxa*). Belief is relatively passive, relatively stable, while opinion can be, though it is not always, active, whether the community is complacent or caught up in a cultural maelstrom, a series of violent eddies in the otherwise meandering flow. Thus arguments, which are constantly threatening to congeal into belief regarding matters of vital importance (in logic, science, and religion, as well as ethics, values, and aesthetics), must be adequate to the task, for they are the last best hope we have. And since an ineradicable element of vagueness and generality will always remain, any attempt toward a rigorously determinate formulation or application of argumentation will ultimately be abortive.

Arguments can be further distinguished from argumentation by their relation to what Peirce terms *musement.* In order that the inquirer abductively hit upon an effective argument, she must enter into a state of readiness—indifference, Epicurean *ataraxia,* stoic *apatheia*—or in its extreme form, *adiaphora*—Zen thoughtlessness. The prime requirement for such readiness is theoretical detachment: the mind must be disengaged from well-reasoned thinking about the problem at hand and free to dabble undetachedly in a form of gratuitous, unadulterated mental play. Otherwise, an abduction might be prevented from surfacing. Musement is a state of mind that "involves no purpose save that of casting aside all serious purpose" (CP, 6.458). The mind must also be uncluttered by methodological imperatives. The only absolute injunction concerning musement is that it be unfettered and free to develop along any lines that may suggest themselves to the inquirer (CP, 6.461).

Musement bears on Peirce's suggestion that "there is something in nature to which the human mind is analogous" (CP, 1.316). It consists in wonderment regarding some characteristic of the universe or regarding the universe as a whole. It cuts through the tangled knot of conscious purposes to arrive at a state of mind akin to the wide-eyed curiosity of a child. If purpose is for one reason or another interjected into this state, the spell is broken, for one who consciously sets out to become convinced of the truth of a vitally important issue available solely to subjective, qualitative proclivities of the mind "is plainly not inquiring in scientific singleness of heart, and must always suspect himself of reasoning unfairly" (CP, 6.458). When this proper attitude is achieved, contemplation regarding the universe can commence, the end product of which is the entertainment of some nonempirically verifiable or refutable experience.

Musement is a self-reflexive, relatively autonomous, *autosemeiopoietic* activity. The mind as sign, instead of pushing "outward" toward other signs or the physical world, tunes in on its own wavelength. It listens to itself. This inner dialogue without an explicit knowing subject and without any definite object of knowledge is self-returning. Instead of the indexical sign, "$\rightarrow$," this sign reenters itself in the Spencer-Brownian sense: $\bigcirc$ (see Kauffman 1986). That is, as shown in figures 7 and 10, on a microscale each sign is self-returning, and on the macroscale, S_{f-1} returns to $S_{\varnothing}$ to begin the eternal spiral anew. Since there is always an expansion, a *difference,* with each re-entry as circles include circles, an interpretant grows until, if that final and ideal step could be taken, it would become monadic and ultimately coterminous with the entire universe.[1] In Peirce's (CP, 5.119) words:

> The universe is a vast representamen, . . . working out its conclusion in living realities. . . . [E]very symbol must have, organically attached to it, its Indices of Reactions and its Icons of Qualities; and such part as these reactions and qualities play in an argument that, they of course, play in the universe—that Universe being precisely an argument. . . . The Universe as an argument is necessarily a great work of art, a great poem—for every fine argument is a poem, and a symphony— just as every true poem is a sound argument.

However, elsewhere we read that

> every representamen must be capable of contributing to the determination of a representamen different from itself. Every conclusion from premises is an instant in point; and what would be a representamen that was not capable of contributing to any ulterior conclusion? I call a representamen which is determined by another representamen, an *interpretant* of the latter. Every representamen

is related or is capable of being related to a reacting thing, its object, and every representamen embodies, in some sense, some quality, which may be called its *signification*. (CP, 5.138)

These two quotes present the notion of the argument's interpretant reentering itself to become another representamen related to its own object, which then determines an interpretant to represent another of the self-organizing sign's cycles of signification: and the universe thus continues to lift itself up by its bootstraps. Therefore, to the question, How can this notion of the representamen be reconciled with the universe as argument, as a grand poem, or thought? the most plausible response must be that the universe itself is a self-reflexive, self-referential, relatively autonomous, *autosemeiopoietic* entity, a magnificently complex compounded sign constantly engaged in reentry.[2]

That is to say, in our mundane existence, where sign activity is governed by our paltry and fallible capacities, each argument, as a self-contained, self-organizing entity, is a representamen reentering itself as its own object. Without representation "out there," it can either happily gyrate about its own axis, or it can reenter the *semiosic* soup and begin another circuitous journey. One thing is for sure: it cannot realize completion in the absolute sense without embracing the entire universe. But even then, it would remain incomplete, since the universe itself ceaselessly pushes toward something else, thus with each reentry becoming different from what it was. Each argument is therefore general (incomplete: the excluded middle does not necessarily apply) and/or vague (inconsistent: the principle of noncontradiction does not necessarily apply). To evoke Nicholas Rescher and Robert Brandom (1979), expansive arguments as signs—paragraphs, chapters, a book, many books, an entire horizon of discourse—entail either underdetermined world-conjunction (generality, incompleteness) or overdetermined world-disjunction (vagueness, inconsistency) (see Merrell 1991a, 1994 for a more detailed discussion).

For instance, if we become aware that an argument is incomplete, we by nature wish to realize its completion. Gaps are therefore filled, rough edges are filed down, weak spots are buttressed. And a slightly different and more encompassing argument is thus constructed. Another argument, we notice, is vague or inconsistent: it becomes unstable, it vibrates uncontrollably, threatening to disintegrate. So back to the nonselective sphere in order to draw out a few replacement parts, or perhaps an entirely new conceptual vehicle of thought, and we reenter the main current. To give those who continue to search for a stable center another headache, as demonstrated in chapters Four and Five, a mediary universe of complementarity exists in sign generacy/de-generacy, but at the expense of losing Boolean certainty. Consequently, smooth borders inevitably become serrated, contours become fuzzy; crystalline precision evolves into clouds of unknowing. Any and all arguments short of The Argument (Universe) can be nothing other than signs testifying to their own inadequacy.

The same must be said of the self, or better, self-consciousness: the self returning into itself—which is a sign by inference. Peirce alludes to self-consciousness as all-sufficient, self-sufficient, and, with tongue slightly in cheek, in-sufficient (CP, 5.71). He compares it further with the map paradox. Faithfully reduplicating the province it re-presents, the map must contain itself, and the map that *it* contains must reenter its own self, ad infinitum. The last map, which is infinitesimal in proportion, will contain all the maps containing it. This image, Peirce concludes, is "the precise analogue of pure self-consciousness" (CP, 5.71).[3] Such an ideal state of pure self-consciousness, like a sign recursively reentering itself, is also the analogue of musement, of pure play. It is by and large—though not quite exactly—symmetrical, reversible, and two-way, in contrast to competitive games and symbols that grow, which are asymmetrical, irreversible, and one-way. Yet self-consciousness, as a living product of biological need, social demand, and individual desires, fantasies, and whims, is anything but passive. In the form of pure self-consciousness, it is ongoing change that nevertheless remains identical with itself. It consists of myriad interpretants becoming representamina, which in turn gather in their own interpretants; they sink, but only to rise again, Phoenixlike, with a slightly to radically different set of feathers. *Semiosis* is never static or dormant. It is ongoing change, Heraclitean fire.

A brief digression may aid us in getting a better handle on the self-reflexive, fluctuating character of signs becoming signs and on the interdependence of all signs: the interconnectedness of the *semiosic* fabric.

Merely an Illusion?

The question ultimately becomes, to put it in necessarily circular form, What is a composite sign such that it may be coterminous with each one of its parts, and what are its parts such that they may be, each and every one of them, capable of embracing it?

Consider in good metaphorical fashion, regarding Peirce's theme of sign indeterminacy, the three levels of signification, Thirdness (proposition), Secondness ("semiotic object," or subject of the proposition), and Firstness (sign, representamen, or predicate of the proposition), in light of three levels making up the physical world, *molar, molecular,* and *micro*. Boyle's law stipulating that the temperature and pressure of a gas are directly proportional constitutes a *molar* argument pertaining to aggregates. From the perspective of *molar* versus *molecular* domains, and disregarding life phenomena, if we ask any molecule whether or not he has his own free will, Wheeler (1980b, 145) remarks, "he will laugh at us. He does what he wants. In this sense each event is random." Nevertheless, by virtue of our dealing with very large numbers of molecular events at the molar level, we get a law "as accurate as any designer of steam engines could desire."[4]

That is to say, as far as each molecule is concerned, he is free to do his own thing. Yet a collection of gas molecules in an enclosed container rather faithfully follows a law of aggregates that is statistical and predicated on random rather than controlled molecular action. Established upon a foundation of apparently blind accidents, this law stipulates, however, that accident will ultimately prevail, and organization will be reduced to a minimum, with entropy at an all-time high.[5] Mass destruction awaits the entire community of molecules, whether as individuals they will it or not. In other words, the particulate *thisness* (Secondness) at the molecular level, as an aggregate, and after enough time has elapsed, brings about the fulfillment of the *would be* (Thirdness) as a potentiality, that which is destined to be realized in the theoretical long run, finally to become generality, regularity, the plenitude of law.

At the *microlevel* (Firstness, possibility), radical indeterminacy of another sort, Heisenberg's uncertainty principle, raises its ugly head. It is a fundamental tenet of the so-called Copenhagen interpretation that the available information concerning a wave function is theoretically the maximum information possible. Hence, as outlined in previous chapters, there is, from the classical point of view, an intrinsic uncertainty; and knowledge, which is limited to the mere statistical likelihood of events, must inexorably remain incomplete. Putting the problem in Heisenberg's terms, *"Knowledge of the 'actual' is . . . from the point of view of quantum theory, by its very nature always an incomplete knowledge"* (in Pauli 1955, 27–28). Knowledge of an actualized event as Secondness, as the wave function collapsed into a particle, is necessarily incomplete, for it was unpredictable before the fact. This before-the-fact, or Firstness, pure chance, is defined in terms of the probability of a collapse at one of a potentially infinite range of space-time coordinates.[6] Hence a before-the-fact event can be no more than exceedingly vague in Peirce's terms, for it holds in superposition a mutually exclusive set of potential events.

Nonetheless, though classical and quantum physics are radically distinct at their roots, empirical measurements must be eventually forthcoming, and for obvious reasons, since the physicist is limited to operations with macroscopic (molar) instruments and data that are describable in terms of classical observations. Yet the character of quantum phenomena places severe restrictions on classical measurements. This is profoundly portrayed by Bohr's (1934, 19) seminal complementarity principle, which specifies "relata of mutual exclusion characteristic of the quantum theory with regard to the application of the various classical concepts and ideas." Bohr, keenly aware that the conjunction of a wave property with what appeared to be a corpuscle played havoc with

219

the Newtonian space-time framework, suggested that physicists give up their futile attempt to obtain a point-by-point description in space and time of processes at the subatomic (micro) level. This abandonment was not to be construed as a defeat, however. The problem was that quantum phenomena were simply incompatible with classical modes of description. Observation could be arranged in such a way that space and time localization could be obtained for a particle, but in the act of such observation, the particle's momentum and the energy conditions defining the atomic event—a process rather than a static fact—

220   were disrupted. Thus the microscopic world (Firstness) is aggravatingly complex. Insofar as the quantum system goes unobserved, its wave function evolves continuously and in accord with Schrödinger's equations. But at the moment it interacts with an external observer, it collapses into a hitherto unpredictable state, which gave Schrödinger, Broglie, and Einstein fits. In a manner of speaking, the system changes in time in two ways, continuously and discontinuously—when nobody is "looking" and when somebody is "looking."

Bohr's complementarity revealed that nature does not define itself at the microlevel with the same conjunction of space-time localization that had been axiomatic in classical mechanics for centuries. Heisenberg added to Bohr's emphasis the suggestion that we have in quantum theory a parallel to the concept of possibility, the *potentia*. "If we want to describe what happens in an atomic event," he writes:

> we have to realize that the word "happens" can apply only to the observation, not to the state of affairs between two observations. It applies to the physical, not the psychical act of observation, and we may say that the transition from the "possible" to the "actual" takes place as soon as the interaction of the object with the measuring device, and thereby with the rest of the world, has come into play. (Heisenberg 1958, 54–55)

In Peirce's terms, Heisenberg's "possible" is Firstness, and the "actual" is Secondness—dyadic interaction, awaiting its proper mediation by Thirdness. With respect to the possibility of—though Maxwell's monster is able to distinguish at the molecular level (Secondness) between a hyperactive and a sluggish molecule—herding the one into one flask and the other in another so as to alter the push toward heat death at the molar level (Thirdness), he is helpless regarding quantum phenomena, the microlevel (Firstness). As soon as he inspects a given subatomic superposition, it collapses into an unforeseeable state from among an indefinite number of possible states. He can gather no definite information about how quantum reality was before he looked at it.

In other words, quantum uncertainty is no mere coin toss. While a coin is flip-flopping in the air, heads and tails alternately face upward. Maxwell's demon, given his lightning reflexes and acuity of vision, could easily record the number of flips and flops, one an even number and the other an odd one—a convenient dyadic computation—which accounts for its final resting state. Not so with the quantum domain, however. Here, the demon's hands are tied. He is confronted with a superposed wave state that is neither heads nor tails, and at the same time both heads and tails. It is not identifiable until after the monster takes a peek at it—a situation somewhat like the lottery wheel in Chapter Eight as ensemble or as history.

There is more than a tinge of paradox in this conception of things. The quantum domain can be meaningfully defined solely with respect to the macrodomain, for it is necessary that macroentities and concepts such as measuring apparatus and classical mechanics already exist in order that microentities and properties can have any meaning. However, the macrodomain is composed of entities constituting the microdomain: they are themselves made up of quantum events. Thus the macrodomain depends upon the microdomain for its existence, and the microdomain depends upon the macrodomain for its status as a domain about which descriptions can be formulated in the first place. The entire self-referential, self-reflexive system must somehow lift itself up by its own bootstraps.[7]

This apparently quasi-mystical conclusion is of the sort that led John von Neumann to attempt to respond to the questions of when and how the transition from the superposition of a pair of possibilities to a single classical state occurs. The very questions entail a distinction between continuous, causal, rationally describable processes in the quantum domain and the discontinuous change associated with observation. In his effort to resolve this problem, von Neumann took into consideration the quantum system plus the measuring apparatus, which was itself treated as a quantum system. The system as a whole was then mathematically described to ensure that the wave function representing it would behave deterministically. Von Neumann argued that the act of coupling the electron to the measuring device brings about a collapse of the part of the wave function pertaining to the observed electron, but the wave function representing the system as a whole does not collapse. This implies that electron, apparatus, and observer, as *potentia,* are always already (inter)connected as a composite wave function (compound sign) into a single whole, and when the observer interacts with the wave function through her apparatus, there is a collapse into a particular state. On the other hand, if no collapse occurs, then there is no definite (actual) world but a plurality of superposed (possible) worlds.

In essence, von Neumann's solution seems to imply that, in the double-slit *Gedanken* experiment, if a photon is diffracted at one opening and forms a dot on a photographic film, the physicist can conclude that *that* spot which appeared at *that* moment was left by an electron. However, her formulation of photon-plus-film entails a superposition of several possible states (spots where the dot might have appeared but did not) whose reduction to a single state occurs only with the act of observing the film. The theory seems to predict no single reality and even suggests that whatever reality may happen to pop into existence depends upon the observer. In other words, the observer plays a role in determining quantum events.

Peirce's semiotics assigns a similar role to the observer insofar as, regarding vagueness and generality, chance and conditionality, Firstness and Thirdness, determination of the sign is left to interpreter-interpretant interaction. That is to say, vagueness, for Peirce, is "the antithetical analogue of generality"—recall that the general sign "leaves to the interpreter the right of completing the determination for himself," and the vague sign leaves its interpretation "more or less indeterminate, it reserves for some other possible sign or experience the function of completing the determination" (CP, 5.505).

Let us pursue this question further.

Schrödinger's Schizophrenic Feline

While von Neumann did not himself draw the apparently bizarre inferences implicit in his treatment of quantum phenomena as macrolevel superpositions including observer-observed interaction, others have been considerably less timid.

Schrödinger's cat wins hands down as the most notorious treatment.[8] Schrödinger asks us to suppose there is a cat in a sealed chamber with a vial of lethal poison that will be released if a Geiger counter is triggered by the decay of some radioactive material. There is, after an hour, a 50-percent probability that the poison will have been released and the cat will be found dead, and a 50-percent probability that it will still be alive and well. As with von Neumann's experiment, the entire system—possibility of emitted particle, Geiger counter, flask, poison, cat—are at the outset a single state, hence the cat remains as a wave function until observed. After observation, the wave superposition collapses into either a live cat or a dead cat. This collapse is one-way, asymmetrical, and irreversible, in contrast to the two-way, symmetrical, and reversible wave superposition. The superposition can be given a classical description; the collapse cannot. The question to be asked is, Precisely *when* does the collapse occur? One story has it that it occurs at the instant the observer interacts with the system. In such case, before said observation, the cat was simply a superposition of the two states—recall the Necker cube.

This interpretation implies, for some physicists—the most noteworthy being Wigner—that consciousness plays the crucial role in actualizing quantum phenomena: without consciousness there is no "reality," which is Berkeley

222

in a new garment and, as Wigner (1967, 176) somewhat reluctantly concedes, logically consistent with solipsism.[9] Wigner's hypothesis apparently stipulates that *any* being with consciousness is capable of collapsing wave functions merely by observing them. But a problem immediately arises, since, if an observer is required to collapse the wave function, then who collapses the observer? Why, another observer, of course. And an infinite series is implied. In Peircean terms, one observer (interpreter-interpretant, himself a sign among signs) collapses (translates) a representamen into its interpretant, which becomes another representamen to be collapsed, but that very observer, as a sign, could not have become an interpreter-interpretant until collapsed by another interpretant-interpreter, and so on, all of which serves to pattern Peirce's dialogic character of the sign.

223

Actually, in light of Schrödinger's cat, Berkeley slightly missed the mark. It is not simply a matter of *esse est percipi*. The quantum quandary specifies not only a subject, or the subject's consciousness, but also the subject's instrument interlinked with the object. More adequately, Berkeley's axiom should state "To be is to be measured." In the final analysis, measurement is what condenses the wave cloud into an event. We might presumably say, then, that the value of a quantum quantity prior to measurement is different from the result of the measurement. But in so doing, we have extricated ourselves from the system, which includes wave packet, instrument, and subject. So our statement cannot be true with respect to the system, for it is not in the system. But neither is it false. It is simply undecidable, or indeterminate, like the vague domain of Firstness itself—which is also the Tarskian problem of metalanguages, mentioned in Chapter Eight (see also Merrell 1992, chap. 5). The upshot is that, as Schrödinger (1967, 176) puts it, "the observer is never entirely replaced by instruments; for if he were, he could obviously obtain no knowledge whatsoever. . . . The most careful record, when not inspected, tells us nothing." "Reality"—a given semiotically real domain, that is—is left to the physicist's inspecting (reading) the data (text of the world).[10]

This bizarre conclusion stemming from von Neumann's work was openly embraced by R. Landon and E. Bauer (1939), who claim to limit the infinite series of observers mentioned above by postulating that the key element in consciousness causing the collapse of wave functions is *introspection*.[11] In their view, the self-conscious observer, in contrast to inanimate objects, possesses a distinct point of view as a result of her recursive, self-referential awareness. For her, Schrödinger's dead cat or live cat and the experimental apparatus belong to the external world. In addition, she is in possession of a special faculty, *introspection,* by means of which she can give immediate account of her own state. This inner knowledge enables her to create for herself her own objectivity, her own world. In other words, she can cut the chain of statistical command expressed by the whole observer-observed superposed system by asserting either "I am in state 1" or "I am in state 2." She can reflect on past states and contemplate possible future states.

The problem, semiotically speaking, is with Cartesian *immediacy of consciousness,* which compelled Peirce indefatigably to lock horns with rationalist philosophy.[12] Admittedly, not a small number of physicists and scientists in general are skeptical of the quantum-theoretical formulation when it is extended to sentient organisms. Penrose (1986), for example, finds something deeply unsatisfactory about the two modes of transition incorporated in the current formulation of quantum theory: one deterministic—following Schrödinger's equation—and the other probabilistic; the first continuous, atemporal, and reversible, the second discontinuous, temporal, and irreversible. Moreover, it is not clear when one mode must make way for the other except for the fact that it occurs when there is observation or interaction with something. There seems to be, however, agreement on one important point: observation—measurement—has only occurred when some sort of record or trace is left in the form of a track in a bubble chamber, the click of a Geiger counter, the blackening of photographic emulsion, or a memory trace in a brain. These traces are definitely discontinuous, irreversible, and temporal. That is, they are always embedded in the world of experience, with which we are familiar.

The relevance of Peirce's categories to this discussion, I believe, has adequately surfaced. Firstness is a counterpart to the microlevel wave function, a possibility or *might be* (Heisenberg's *potentia* mathematically described as a continuous superposition). Secondness, what *happens to be* at the molecular level, accompanies the collapse of the wave function into some-*thing* that, if not exactly caused by consciousness, is mediately available to consciousness as that which is. But there is as yet no consciousness of it as such-and-such in relation to some-thing else; nor is there any *thatness* as opposed to the *thisness* of consciousness. *This-thatness,* as molar Thirdness, is not immediately but mediately available to consciousness (recall Macbeth's experience).

It bears mentioning that mediacy also prohibits simultaneity in the Laplacean sense. Some imaginary initial observer must set the stage for the community of observers. Just as that imaginary Adamic first consciousness peering out into the new quantum world is no solipsist but must at least conduct a dialogue with itself, if not with some community, in order to arrive at a more advanced stage of its inferential process, so the Peircean self must hold a dialogue with itself and its community in order to establish what is semiotically real and what is not. In this sense, the semiotically real is accounted for dialogically, whether by interaction with an individual self and its own other or with that self and its community.

Once again, the semiotically real is not "real" per se. Samuel Johnson once kicked a stone in his attempt to refute Berkeley's idealism, which was, we would ordinarily suppose, an interaction between an observer and the observed within the "reality" framework. This is Secondness. On the other hand, Johnson's kicking act (whether it actually occurred or not is irrelevant) as recorded history, as Thirdness—the derivation of an interpretant as a result of the physical event—has had a vastly greater impact than did the mere physical act of a swiftly moving foot once upon a time coming painfully in contact with a stone. By a similar token, Auschwitz was "real," but Auschwitz as semiotically real in terms of its symbolic import—how it was interpreted by the Third Reich, by Germany's citizenry, by Jews, and how it has been and continues to be recorded—is what became construed as the "really real."[13] Thus, to rephrase Derrida, we are always already within *semiosis,* yet our discourse need not—indeed, should not, cannot—be disengaged from our semiotically real world.

The semiotically real is constructed by way of Thirdness, that is, mediation. It consists in the composite superposition of *possibilia* (Firsts), a selected portion of which are collapsed (into Seconds) subsequently to become what *would have been* (Thirds), according to the specified set of conditions. Any "reality" that happens to be collapsed by a particular individual or by the entire community could always have been something other than what it is. So the semiotically real is neither exclusively what is seen nor what is cognized nor what is said nor what is measured but a combination of them all. It is not a matter of modernity's defining relations or interactions between things on the basis of substance; it is a matter of defining substance on the basis of relations or interactions—all of which is quite appropriate to Peirce's relational philosophy and his struggle against the Cartesian tradition, both of which he shares with postmodernism.

The World That Was/Is/Will Have Been

Wheeler tentatively explores the quantum notion of collapse in terms of intersubjective or community agreement. The most intriguing facet of his theory is the notion that the "joint product" of the members of a community collectively collapsing wave functions provides a means for bringing the entire universe into existence.[14] Wheeler's point of departure is found in the opinion of, among others, Bohr (1958), Heisenberg (1958), and Weizsäcker (1971)—of the Copenhagen interpretation of quantum mechanics—that particles manifest no particulate properties until they are observed (recorded). Up to that instant, they are "real" but not semiotically real. They are existent, but not in the full sense of existing *for* some observer *in* some respect or capacity.[15]

Wheeler elucidates on three features of this thesis: the term "elementary" refers to a single quantum; "observation" does not directly refer to a human being or any other organism purportedly with one form or another of consciousness (contra Wigner) but to an irreversible "act of amplification," such as the blackening of a grain of silver bromide emulsion or the triggering of a Geiger counter; and the "meaning" of an observation is denied until phenomena are brought to a close (collapsed) in an act of amplification, and put to use by an observer (interpreter) (Wheeler 1980b, 147).

226

What Wheeler calls a trace left by a quantum event as the blackening of silver bromide emulsion is no more than that: a trace, a self-contained iconic sinsign without there yet existing a full-blown index for someone pointing to a *this-ness* signified by it. At this juncture, it is indistinguishable from all other individual occurrences to which it might possibly be related. The trace is no more than a potential dicent sinsign (token) standing for a general semiotic object (iconic legisign, type) available to experience. If this potential is actualized and recorded by someone, it then becomes, as the prefix "sin" indicates, a singularity, a haecceity, a *happens to be*. In its particular context, it *is* only once. Before the quantum event was actualized, it was, in regards to its properties as a sinsign, no more than a vague, nebulous sort of existence. It had not yet taken on meaning in terms of its relations to other particles flying about in space or to the idea (rhematic symbols, thought-signs) of subnuclear particles and their collisions, radioactive decay, intergalactic activity, and so on. Only when the trace is duly recorded—by instruments, the mind, on paper, or at a computer terminal—and put to use does it become a sinsign and then a sign in the authentic sense.[16]

Savan (1987–88, 21) gives the example of a moon rock as a sinsign when it is analyzed by lunar scientists:

> Every singularity and peculiarity of the moon rock is recorded, analyzed, and used as a clue or sign of the structure and history of the moon, the earth, and the solar system. However some object or event is used as a clue to some other object or event, past, present, or spatially at some remove, this clue is a sinsign. A clue like the moon rock is in fact a collection of clues. Every peculiarity of the rock, every molecule of it, is significant as a possible clue to the past.

Applying Savan's terminology to Wheeler's example, the "trace" in Wheeler's blackened grain of silver bromide has become a "clue" providing a possible answer to a question that the scientist has asked of nature, the question itself being the result of her choice from a given set of complementary or alternative possibilities (Firstness). After the object in question has been analyzed and duly recorded, the clue takes on meaning, and it can now say something about the past. In collaboration with the scientist, it recreates the past. The semiotic object, by virtue of its function as a clue, has become an interpretant, an authentic sign. It can potentially become law, part of community opinion and belief (*doxa*), part of the semiotically real. The trace evidenced by the silver bromide emulsion is thus capable of telling its story "through the physical laws it instantiates" (Savan 1987–88, 23).

More specifically, let us reconsider the double-slit experiment. A stream of electrons rushes toward the barrier, which has one hole open. The electrons act, for practical purposes, as if they were particles; after all, they pass through the hole, and the screen behind the hole detects them as actualized entities. When both holes are open, something entirely different occurs. Rather than having two streams of electrons passing through the holes to be detected on the screen as individual particles, upon penetrating the barrier they set up wave patterns that interfere with each other and strike the screen to become actualized as if they were riding on a series of water waves setting up an interference pattern. Consequently, a combination of dark and light bands appears on the screen rather than two spots. 227

To say in one breath that the electrons passed through one slit in the first case and through both slits in the second is logically inconsistent, Einstein argued, for reality is not schizophrenic; the electrons must have some stable identity. Bohr responded that these statements involve two different experiments separated by time; thus the experiments are not contradictory, they are complementary. But the question remains: If the electrons passing through one hole behave like particles, and if passing through both holes they take on wave characteristics, then how could an individual electron at the point of penetrating the barrier know another electron was at the other hole in order to change itself into a wave? Quantum weirdness reaches a climax here. Is there faster-than-light travel (by way of tachyons) from one electron to the other conveying information about its status? Or is there some mysterious quantum interconnection between the particles approaching the metal sheet at different points? This perplexity stems from the fact that quantum theory marks the demise of classical objectivity: what happens to the electrons in the double-slit experiment is simply unobservable.

For example, I stated above that the electrons approaching the sheet behave as if they were particles, but upon entering and leaving the two holes they act like waves. Actually they were waves all along, that is, as long as they went undetected. Suppose we are reduced in size sufficiently so as to see individual electrons. Walking along in front of the barrier when both holes are open, we can see the swarm of particles obediently headed toward their destination. We reach the barrier and peer on the other side, expecting to see nothing—for we assume there is nothing but waves—but to our surprise an apparently chaotic array of particles heading for the screen meets our eye. What happened? Our observing (detecting) the "wave packets" collapsed them into particles. In other words, the "electrons" were never electrons in the sense of particles until striking the screen, which actualized them (i.e., collapsed the wave packets). What we thought were particles in front of the barrier were viewed as such only when we saw (interacted with) them. And when we assumed we would see nothing between barrier and screen, there was nothing to see, that is, until we saw the particles. Quantum physics demonstrates that there is no objective world "out there" as we thought we knew it.

228

Enter what Wheeler calls the delayed-choice experiment. Assume we use photons rather than subatomic particles, and instead of an unruly stream of them, we release only one at a time to do its thing. With the conventional double-slit apparatus, when photons pass through a single slit in the barrier, we can unambiguously identify their path to a solitary spot on the screen, since there is no interference pattern. When they pass through both slits, an interference pattern made up by the collection of individual photons is recorded on the screen. However, Wheeler tells us we do not have to decide in advance which feature of the photons to record, through both slits or through which slit. He asks that we alter the apparatus. Suppose we set up another lens and barrier between the first lens, with its double-slit barrier, and the screen. Let us equip this second barrier with a venetian blind-type shutter. If open, the blind lets an individual photon-as-particle through to be detected on the screen; and if closed, it acts like a screen and detects the interference pattern of the photon-as-wave.

Now we can make a last-instant choice, after a photon has already traversed the doubly slit screen, whether to open the blind or close it. If we close it, it records a photon-as-wave pattern on the blind. If we leave it open, an individual photon is diffracted through the second lens, reaches the second screen, and provides us the information that it went through either the first slit or the second one. It is we who decide, after the individual photon has passed through the first lens, whether it shall have gone through only one slit or both. A decision whether to leave the blind open or shut does not have to be made until the photon has already proceeded through the first lens. This is much like the case, in the above paragraph, of ourselves as electron-sized observers causing the waves to collapse into particles after they have already penetrated the barrier.

Wheeler concludes from his thought experiment:

> We make the decision whether to open or close the blind, whether to make the photon go through both holes or only one hole, *after* the photon has *already* gone through this piece of metal with the holes in it! One here and now makes a decision, which has an irre-

trievable effect on what one has the right to say about the past. There is an inescapable sense in which we in the here and now can decide what we have the right to say about what has already happened. And although here we are talking about a period of nanoseconds, there is nothing in principle that prevents the time from being billions of years. (Wheeler 1980b, 148)

If Wheeler is on the right track, his delayed-choice experiment radically alters our conception of the past. A particular photon in the cosmic fireball billions of years ago can only be said to have such-and-such polarization and such-and-such properties *after* it has been duly observed and recorded by an observer-participatory agent. This is not to say, Wheeler hastily remarks, that the unrecorded photon has no form of "reality." Rather, its "reality" is of a paler hue than that of the recorded photons—recall the unobserved trace above. It is more like a photon of pure mathematical theory than a photon making up the concrete world of sensory experience. It is "real," undoubtedly, though it hasn't *yet* taken its place in any observer-participatory agent's scheme of the semiotically real as such.

229

At this juncture, I must append a caveat. Wheeler (1980a, 358) rightly admits, as any conscientious contemporary scientist and philosopher must: "What we call 'reality,' that vision of the universe that is so vivid in our minds, we plaster in between a few iron posts of observation by an elaborate labor of imagination and theory." He even quotes art historian Ernst Gombrich (1960, 394), who argues that knowledge is inexorably colored by what one (believes one) sees, instead of what one actually sees. For Wheeler, phenomena as they are recorded depend upon our decision in terms of "what we will want to say about the past—a strange inversion of the normal order of time." The past is in this sense nonexistent as such until recorded in some present state by some agent. To use the paradoxical future anterior once again, a past phenomenon *will have happened* as soon as it is a recorded happening resulting from a particular choice exercised by the recording agent.[17] In this manner, actual "reality," semiotic reality, consists of an intricate imaginative-theoretical construct. A distinction between the semiotically real and the "actually real" is thus absolutely imperative.

Putting Wheeler's hypothesis in a Peircean framework, our decision in the *now* (Secondness) determines what the character of the electron *might have been* (Firstness) before it was anything—when it was a mere possibility—such that what it *would have been* (Thirdness), given the proper conditions, *will be* actualized for us in such-and-such a respect or capacity. In other words, a representamen, as First, is the mere skeleton of a fleshed-out sign, a possibility or promise of that which might come to pass. As such it coincides with a qualisign, which can be collapsed into a semiotic object to be mediated by its respective interpretant—product of the sign's being put to use—which is the equivalent of a legisign (type). Legisigns "only exist *in order* to be used—that is, to signify through replication—and that presupposes the existence of creatures prone to interpret those replicas according to the rules associated with the legisigns replicated" (Short 1982, 292). Theoretically, representamina need not be restricted to living, breathing, and cognizing beings; nor need their interpretants necessarily be mental in the human sense.

Were Peirce alive today, he might be inclined to term an RNA molecule a "representamen" and Manfred Eigen's (1971; Eigen and Schuster 1979) "hyper-cycles" *semiosis.* DNA, RNA, and representamina are the stuff life is made of by means of hypercycles-*semiosis,* and life is essential for the generation of legisigns.[18] Signs exist throughout the universe, no doubt, but "there are legisigns only where there is life, and legisigns always exist in order to serve the purpose of living things" (Short 1982, 298). Short writes that we often talk about "uses" of signs without necessarily implying any conscious or intentional purpose. A male fowl uses colors to attract a mate, beavers use branches to build dams, chimps use twigs to get at grubs, and the number of tools and naturally occurring items used by humans is legion. Such use can be embedded, or it can be instinctive. Conscious and intentional use is another story, but the fact remains that it is use just the same. With all such uses, business goes on as usual within semiotic worlds, though always with differences and frequent punctuations by surprise, revised intentions, and new uses to bring about variations in, and reconstructions of, semiotic worlds. When such changes take place, latent signs of the past that have not yet been put to use may be actualized as full-blown signs to take on the appearance of that which *would have become* actualized. By transposing the conditional to a before-the-fact setting, the sign can be expressed in terms of what *will have become.*

The future anterior, then, is a counterpart to Peirce's conditional Thirdness insofar as a decision in the present brings about a fulfillment of the conditional to dictate the state of affairs during a past present. In Wheeler's (1980a, 358) words:

> In the delayed-choice experiment we, by a decision in the here and now, have an irretrievable influence on what we will want to say about the past—strange inversion of the normal order of time. This strangeness reminds us more explicitly than ever that "The past has no existence except as it is recorded in the present."

Thus, no elementary phenomenon is a phenomenon until it is a recorded and put-to-use phenomenon. "Recorded" signifies an irreversible act of amplification of a wave packet such that it becomes at least partly communicable in some language, for "all our ordinary verbal expressions bear the stamp of our customary forms of expression" (Wheeler 1980a, 358). This tends to fuse the observer not only with her instruments but also with the observed, in contrast to the orthodox interpretation of quantum theory.

In other words, we are back to a Sapir-Whorf sort of idea that what is *said* is what there *is*—a current view in ethnography, especially that of Tyler (see the Introduction and Chapter One). This attests once again to the ultimate import of language. We see the world *as* we see it, we see *that* it is *this* way, and we know *how* to do things in it and with it. But in order explicitly to know *that* 231 it is the way it is, we need language. This language cannot be just ordinary language, however. Before Wheeler's act of amplification, a quantum entity is simply inexpressible in natural language or the language of classical physics— the language of the empirical world. Feeble efforts to account for the quantum realm by way of traditional linguistic modes could well end up contradictorily describing it as both a particle and a wave or neither a particle nor a wave. But this is no description at all; it tells us no-*thing* about any-*thing* "out there." Wheeler is quite cognizant of this problem. His conception of an irreversible act of amplification is equivalent in many respects to an observation. Yet it explicitly denies the notion that quantum theory rests in any way whatsoever on the consciousness of the observer or on the details of her observation— hence Wheeler's bone of contention with Wigner and others who argue that consciousness collapses the wave packet.[19] Rather, consciousness, or mind, *is itself just another a sign among signs* much in the Peircean sense, and as such it is brought into existence by way of sign interaction in much the same manner as any other sign: it enjoys no privileged position in the cosmos.

Wheeler further illustrates his delayed-choice experiment with a parlor game in which he once participated as a guinea pig. He was with a group playing the familiar game of questions asked by an outsider to a group about the identity of some specific item in the room decided upon by that group in the outsider's absence. When it was his turn to step outside the room, the group agreed that no word would be chosen, but that they could all respond as they pleased, the only requirement being that the respondent must have a particular word in mind compatible with all preceding responses made up to that point. In other words, the word was not "in the room"; it was gradually teased into existence by all participants concerned while the game was in progress. The minds of the participants and the word collaborated in bringing about the latter's semiotically real existence (recall vagueness—where further interpretation is left to some other sign—and generality—where further interpretation is left to the interpreter).[20]

Relating his parlor-game experience to the world of quanta, Wheeler writes that

I, entering, thought the room contained a definite word. In actuality the word was developed step by step through the questions I raised, as the information about the electron is brought into being by the experiment that the observer chooses to make. . . . Had I asked different questions or the same questions in a different order I would have ended up with a different word as the experimenter would have ended up with a different story for the doings of the electron. . . . A major part of the selection lay in the "yes" and "no" replies of the colleagues around the room. Similarly the experimenter has some substantial influence on what will happen to the electron by the choice of experiments he will do on it, "questions he will put to nature"; but he knows there is a certain unpredictability about what any given one of his measurements will disclose, about what "answers nature will give," about what will happen when "God plays dice." . . . In the game no word is a word until that word is promoted to reality by the choice of questions asked and answers given. (Wheeler 1980a, 356)

Like the language game in which a particular word is constructed by way of the interaction of a community of interlocutors, Wheeler's delayed-choice experiment allows the observer to wait until the electron *has already passed* through the screen before choosing whether it *shall have gone through* both slits or only one. By a decision *here-now,* he exercises an irreversible influence on what he wants to say *about the past.* That is, before an entity was recorded, it was part of the "real." It had been actualized from the vast realm of *possibilia,* but it still belonged to the nonselective domain; it had not (yet) been selected (recorded) as a semiotically real entity by some sign-processing entity for some purpose.

In other words, a semiotic agent in dialogue with a particular community (the social Other) and with its other self begins (from Firstness) by asking a question of (engaging in dialogue with) nature (the Other "out there"). Then a decision is reached regarding what would be "real" (Thirdness) under certain circumstances, and after the dialogic signs—whatever their nature—are put to use, they have become actualized (Secondness) as part of a particular semiotically real orb. The semiotically real sign, like Wheeler's word that was no word until "promoted to reality by the choice of questions asked and answers given," is thus teased into existence.

History: Bunk or Bedlam?

Still, an enigma remains: observation collapses a "wave" into a "particle," which is an irreversible act, but that collapse was determined, in the *here-now,* by what *would have happened,* hence a certain reversibility remains. Some omniscient future agent *will* determine the outcome of a past event, and a past event *will have been* determined by the future agent. Wheeler's model implies the apparently outlandish notion that choices in the present construct events that *will have already occurred* in the remote past, and that our present world is the result of choices that *will have been made* in the equally remote future!—quite reminiscent of the Einstein-Minkowski block universe.[21] This not only plays havoc with our customary intuition of time, but in spite of Wheeler's notions of choice and selection, when viewed from an all-encompassing perspective— that of the Future Agent—in a bizarre way it also threatens to divest us of that last coveted modicum of free will we might desperately try to hang onto— compare to Wheeler's molecule declaring itself to be "free."

233

Other discomforting questions now arise: Who is the Ultimate Future Agent, if there is indeed any? A Laplacean Superdemon? God? Is there some future community *always already* in existence, engaged in actualizing our own semiotically real world? Such questions, which are also relevant to Peirce's philosophy, defy any attempt at a response. The very necessity of an "outside" agent demands a bizarre inversion of the orthodox order of time. It recalls Einstein's observation that the theory decides what one *will have been* capable of observing. It is also reminiscent of postmodern historiographers, for whom the past takes on its existence through what is recorded in the present. Or of Borges's (1962, 3–18) prisoners on the chimerical planet Tlön, who, when told that they should unearth certain artifacts in order to earn their freedom, discovered, after a few abortive attempts, that they were capable of finding (inventing) precisely what had been mandated of them.[22]

Yet Wheeler makes no bones about it: the past depends on present choices, the present depends on future choices, and at the same time, the system for a given observer remains open. In order to illustrate this openness, Wheeler offers the example of a cosmic ray that once penetrated a mass of granite in the wilds of Brazil. A billion years or so later, a scientist chips off a piece of the granite, slices it, and treats it in such a way that it reveals its past. The streak in the rock served as a permanent trace eventually to be recorded as an elementary quantum phenomenon. Of course, we can quite safely assume that no sentient observer was there to witness the arrival of the cosmic ray, nor was it essential that one be there. The phenomenon was "real" before it was observed. Yet the cosmic ray did not become a consummated irreversible act of amplification until it was put to use by someone or something for some purpose—until it became semiotically real.[23]

If another billion or so years had transpired, during which time the granite mass shifted under the earth's crust, the potential phenomenon could never have been put to use for the purpose of determining the effect of a cosmic ray. Or if the scientist exploring the cosmic ray's trajectory had been demolished by a stray meteorite, the data being constructed could not have been used in that particular case. Wheeler (1984, 129) writes:

> The decisive distinction between the "might-have-been" or "never-never-land" phenomenon and the one that is "put to use" is evident; it is employed in the construction of meaning. What is a dream but something that can't be checked out with one's fellows? How do we tell whether an impression is a delusion or genuine except by checking it out with those with whom we communicate?

Wheeler's mention of dreams cuts to the core of the semiotically real/"actually real" issue. Peirce did not believe that dreams and hallucinations are in no sense "real." He sharply distinguished between the occurrence of a dream or hallucination and its particular sort of "reality" status. If you experience a hallucination, it will be "true" in the sense that it consists in your "seeing" something, though it was not actually at that particular time in the place where you saw it. And it would be "real," provided "we mean by the hallucination a certain psychical experience." But the "*substance* of the hallucination, . . . would be *unreal*," since everything that would be "true" of it would be "true" only in the sense that you *thought,* or imagined (a species of thinking), that you saw something at that time and place—recall Macbeth's dagger.

In contrast, the *substance* of a dream "is not real, because whatever is true of it is so in that so the dreamer dreamed; and dreaming is only a particular kind of thinking. But that fact of the dream, if it actually took place, is a real fact, because it will always remain true that so and so was dreamed, whether the dreamer remembers it or not" (MS 852, 11f., cited in Dozoretz 1979, 78). If some particular event occurs in your dream, that event will be what you dreamed and it will be a fact that you so dreamed it. But it "must be called a Figment, . . . unless, indeed, the dream 'came true' in part, in which case it was, in that part Real, however accidentally" (MS 683, 24f., cited in Dozoretz 1979, 78).

Peirce puts forth the caveat that one might be prone to suppose thought-signs—creations of reason, or *ens rationis*—are figments and thus not "real." But if this were the case, then the pragmatic maxim itself, which calls for the generation of hypothetical conditionals, would be relegated to the dump, to say nothing of *Gedanken* experiments, logic, mathematics, philosophy of science, indeed any cerebral activity regarding all disciplines. If, following the maxim, a community of knowers is able to strike out on the road to self-improvement, then some boundary or other must be established between mere figments or fictions (that which is arbitrarily imagined, idiosyncratic, or the product of crazy thinking) and the "real" (which remains independent of what any individual or the entire community thinks of it). Any such boundary will be to a certain degree arbitrary. It will grate or glide, skip or leap, according to the prevailing circumstances, as fictions become fact and vice versa along the *semiosic* fabric, which awaits, like a wilderness, any explorer wishing to wander around in it. At a given point in time and space, whatever set of signs is hewn out of this wilderness becomes for the individual, and in general for her community, the semiotically real, a selected array from the myriad possibilities that are always there for the taking.

Over the long haul, then, Wheeler's concept of phenomena that cannot be semiotically real until they have become useful for someone and their meaning has been constructed accords, I would submit, with the essence of the pragmatic maxim. The maxim—which implies that the meaning of a proposition is given in another proposition, and the meaning of that proposition in yet another one, and so on—is in its simplest form the result of all the conceivable tests, experiments, or perceptual grasps that can be made as mandated by the conditionality inherent in the initial proposition. In other words, the particular phenomenon that a proposition refers to must be put to use before it can be pragmatically meaningful. But this putting to use is ongoing, since there is no conceivable end to the series of propositions veering off along tangential paths from the initial proposition. If the existence of a private and idiosyncratic entity that one conjures up—such as Macbeth's dagger—cannot be verified by one's neighbors, then it cannot take its rightful place alongside the domain of community-generated semiotically real entities. "How do we tell whether an impression is a delusion or genuine," to repeat Wheeler's question, "except by checking it out with those with whom we communicate?"

In this respect, Wheeler's streak caused by a cosmic ray plunging into a mass of granite as "real," is a mere possibility for signifying something to someone as something in some respect. One of the myriad possibilities consists of the streak's being translated into a representamen, a "cosmic ray." If this translation is brought about by an enterprising young scientist hoping for tenure in the university of her choice, she can then generate an interpretant (representation) to which the sign refers. And if in her effort to communicate this interpretant with others of her community, it finds its way into a journal, it can potentially serve forever to alter the meaning of "cosmic ray" and all other terms intimately or remotely related to it in the entire discursive network, though only to a minuscule degree if the journal merely collects dust on library shelves. Such is the power of a lonely trace when properly put to use.

Our Immanent Domain

236 The Meaning Is in the Maelstrom

With regard to "meaning," Wheeler (1984) alludes to the "three great eras of physics": era 1, "which gave us the parabolas of Galileo and the ellipses of Kepler, motion with no explanation of motion"; era 2, which includes "the mechanics of Newton, the electrodynamics of Faraday and Maxwell, the geometrodynamics of Einstein and the chromodynamics of our day, law that explained change, but law with no explanation of law"; and era 3, which gives rise to the evolution, Wheeler predicts, of "meaning physics," which seeks not corroboration but collaboration of physical law itself (Wheeler 1984, 123).[1]

From the perspective of "meaning physics," the material world provides the machinery for generating meaning, while meaning contributes the machinery for constructing physics. Existence thus becomes a closed circle of meaning. By the addition of a Peircean qualifier, existence or "reality" is what *would be* (or, from the vantage point of the infinitistic Future Agent, *would have been*) known in the long run by the joint product of all the propositions generated by a community of communicators relevant to a set of phenomena in the process of their being put to use.

Meditations in chapters Two and Three led us to an awareness of the numbingly multifarious appearances manifested by the sum total of human cultures, past, present, and future—to say nothing of nonhuman semiotics.[2] Quite apparently, the idea of a joint product calls for an *n*-dimensional sliding manifold of countless possible differences. Of course, the "real" physical world provides the machinery for constructing meaning, but whatever meaning is constructed depends upon the semiotic thrust to which it is subjected. Wheeler's cosmic ray streak in a Brazilian mound of granite would have enjoyed hardly any semiotic import for the Tupi-Guaraní tribespeople of the eighteenth century. Some of the mound could conceivably have been quarried and used in the construction of a mansion for Dom Pedro I in the nineteenth century. It could have been material for an avant-garde sculpture during the 1930s. Or the area might have become as heavily populated during this century as the East Coast of the United States and the focus of a nuclear war in 1991 that completely wiped out the streak. In Wheeler's example, on the other hand, that portion of the mound containing the streak offers a more specific semiotic message for contemporary science. In each case, from a totalizing perspective, the circuit appears equally closed, yet it is obviously open, since there have been, over time, numerous joint products of intracommunity and intercommunity communication from a host of semiotic standpoints.

According to Wheeler's variation of the double-slit experiment, after the streak appeared in the granite, the Tupi-Guaraní, Dom Pedro's construction engineers, an angry young sculptor, Brazilian warmongers, and Wheeler's physicist were free to decide whether the mound containing the streak was worthy of semiotic consideration. Only the context—or experimental arrangement, in Bohrian-Wheelerian terms—changed in each case. An important point regarding human semiotics is that every account of the streak, in light of Chapter One's account of physics as talk about talk, is a story, a narrative. Altering the context alters the story at the same time that the story prefigures or shapes the future, even as the future depends on stories. What the phenomenon is or is not and what does or does not qualify it as a fact is dependent not upon its raw physical existence but upon the signs used to describe it. But ultimately, it is all a matter of stories, and stories about stories. Stories, of course, are mere stories. Yet they are capable of making the past, and at the same time they depend upon it. "Cosmic rays" did not exist prior to the twentieth century because there had been no need for any stories about them. Now, however, they are believed to exist, and as far as the contemporary physicist is concerned, they have existed since the big bang. This implies that "cosmic rays" do not exactly exist independently in the physical world, nor are they independent of the stories about postmodern science. Rather, they depend upon a particular semiotically real sphere of existence.[3]

Wheeler's "meaning physics" is intimately linked to knowledge as the result of putting natural phenomena to use and telling stories about them, of narrating human interaction with the world. In this regard, "meaning physics" dovetails with Wheeler's conception of a self-referential, self-excited circuit making up the entire universe (see figure 16). The first stage involves question asking, choice, and a selection from the nonselective domain of possibilities. This serves to establish the focus of inquiry as in part mandated by habit and expectations, though there is always room for novelty. For example, according to the double-slit experiment, an electron is capable of traveling along two routes, of acting as either a particle or a wave. According to Bohr's complementarity, it is impossible, given the experimental apparatus, for the electron to manifest both its selves at the same instant. So the physicist chooses her apparatus, subjects the electron to it—which is tantamount to asking it a particular question—solicits a response, and narrates the result.

237

Choice in this regard entails an act of distinction. Unlike Spencer-Brown's *mark of distinction,* however, Wheeler's *distinguishability* is not that of the initiatory or primordial sort. On the contrary, the syntax of Spencer-Brown's starkly primitive *this* distinguished from *that* is at Wheeler's elementary stage already taken for granted. What is up for grabs is the nature of *that,* given the universe's inherent ambiguities. Is the (semiotically real) electron a particle or a wave? *That*₁ or *that*₂? The inquirer's question is motivated by pragmatics, in addition to semantics and syntax. *That*₁ can potentially take on meaning for the physicist in interaction with, and in regards to, what it *is not, that*₂, and vice versa. "Meaning physics," in short, entails phenomena that, in order to become semiotically real, must stand for something to some semiotic agent in some respect in terms of what has and has not been selected.

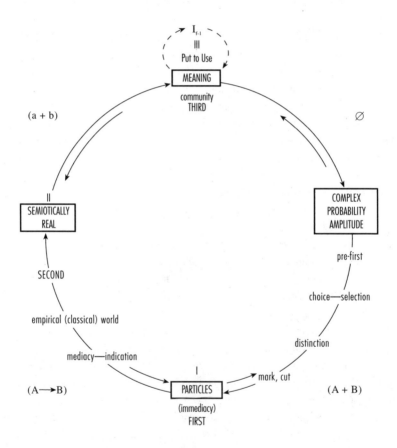

Figure Sixteen

Integrating Peircean terminology into the equation, it can be said that a distinction brings about a collapse of the range of *semiosic* possibilities in the space-time manifold into a sign (particle) or set of signs, which can then be indicated (indexed, by way of Secondness) in terms of their relations to other signs. Like the Necker cube with its face now up, now down, the nature of the question (angle of the gaze) determines the nature of the semiotic reality finally to be perceived and conceived. Interaction with the physical world, a matter of questioning its very nature, is in this manner a choice, and the choice has a definite bearing on whatever outcome is in store. "Meaning physics" (the semiotically real) thus becomes possible by means of empirical manifestations (light, pressure, sound, taste, odor, inorganic and organic entities, biological organisms) of molar or macrolevel collections, such meaning being the result of mediation (symbolicity, Thirdness) of that which was distinguished and indicated at the roots, the microlevel, of "reality." Ultimately, meaning, as joint product, is thus made possible. **239**

Hence, as shown in figure 16, the nature of the complex probability amplitude, $\varnothing$, as *possibilia,* already depends upon the meaning (world model) attributed to the universe by the community. It is a function of the range of possibilities, one of which can be actualized into the immediate or microlevel (I), which is then mediately accessible to observation in the molecular domain (II), to be put to use and thereby endowed with meaning (III) in the macrolevel, or molar domain.[4] Meaning determines the nature of the complex probability amplitude, from which meaning arose in the first place. In essence, the self-excited circuit, or, if you will, "hypercycle," $\varnothing \rightarrow I \rightarrow II \rightarrow III \rightarrow \varnothing$ is an interminable spiraloid, like Peirce's self-reentering sign decalogue depicted in figure 7 or like the "Endlessly Rising Canon" in Bach's *Musical Offering.*

To put this conception in the context of figure 10, $\varnothing$, $a \times b$, $a \rightarrow b$, $a + b$, and $I_{f\text{-}1}$ exist within the horizon of intelligibility concerning the semiotically real for a given community. In contrast, I_f and 0 do not. They are available solely to some demoniacal Future Agent whose timeless existence, from a finite perspective, remains virtually unintelligible. The timeless, extrafinite orbs I_f and 0 are both beginningless and endless: the beginning always already *will have become* the end, and the end always already *will have become* the beginning. This yields the equivalent of Wheeler's (1980a) cosmic equation, "0 = 0," much in the spirit of Russell's Great Mathematician, who, surveying the totality of mathematics, observes that at bottom the composite of all proofs makes up an empty tautology. It is, in a manner of speaking, a trivial equality, a trivial identity, a trivial tautology. It is the silent Tao, the "I am that I am" of Jehovah, Peirce's cosmic poem. It simply *is what it is.* In Wheeler's view, the universe began, devoid of law, with a big bang, and it will end destitute of law, with a great crunch; the stuff of the universe begins with a white hole gushing forth matter and ends with a black hole sucking it back up (see also Merrell 1991a, chap. 8).

It will have been noticed that the small reversed arrows in figure 16 appear to contradict Wheeler's irreversible act of amplification. We are speaking, however, of semiotic reality, not the "real" per se. A given semiotic reality excludes all that could have been selected but was not, just as Wheeler's notion of "reality" as joint product excludes everything that has not been put to use by a particular community. What remains unselected, though it could have been teased into one semiotically real world or another, may yet take its place among the actualized set of signs, while its competitors, having won the previous round, sink back into the *semiosic* soup. Hence, though the equation is by and large irreversible, certain facets can be reversed. If we correlate this aspect of Wheeler with Peirce, we have:

Generality

.

.

$\downarrow \uparrow$
Re-presentation — A + B (*Would-beness*)
$\downarrow \uparrow$
Relation — A ➤ B (*Isness*)
$\downarrow \uparrow$
Quality — A × B (*Might-beness*)
$\downarrow \uparrow$

.

.

Vagueness
(where $\uparrow$ = generacy and $\downarrow$ = de-generacy)

What could have been or might have been may yet become, and what is may be relegated to virtual oblivion, though it may once again have its day.

To place this notion of interrelatedness more squarely in a semiotic perspective, Savan observes that just as the moon rock reveals its story through the "regularities" or "laws" (*would bes*) it instantiates, so the (embedded) ritual and performative uses of language operate as signs by way of the regularities or laws governing them. These regularities and laws, from within the domain of the semiotically real, are part and parcel of the hegemony of legisigns, which, like qualisigns, do not exist directly and immediately in experience. They are always in the process of coming into being through their instantiations as replicas, sinsigns, and objects. If qualisigns are "nonstuff" in the sense that they are *as yet* merely *possibilia* (*might bes*), legisigns are "mind stuff" (*would bes*) insofar as they refer—if we dare use that word in this context—to the semiotically real (the *isness* of things), which is always moving on, becoming something other than what it was.

Wheeler also has a word or two regarding law, which, according to the premises of this inquiry, must be construed as semiotic rather than physical in the classical sense. He claims that if his approach is indeed correct, then one principle and one alone, that of observer-participancy (or interpreter-interpretant interpretation), suffices to construct "everything from 'nothingness'" (Wheeler 1980b, 154). This "nothingness" Wheeler speaks of is not mere vacuum physics loaded with geometry and field fluctuations. It is "pre-geometry," a "nothingness" devoid of structure, law, or plan. This primitive level is in line with Peirce's "nothingness" (or pre-Firstness), as pointed out above, and it is comparable to Spencer-Brown's state prior to the originary—and irretrievable—distinction. Out of "nothingness," physicist and photon interact somehow to transmute one of the multitudinous quantum possibilities into a dialogue that apparently pervades everything we can know, for we are *in* it: "Beyond particles, beyond fields of force, beyond geometry, beyond space and time themselves, is the ultimate constituent [of all there is], the still more ethereal act of observer-participancy" (cited in Zohar 1990, 45).

It is not that mere observation "creates reality," but rather, observation involves a dialogue between quantum wave function and observer (whether sentient, organic, or inorganic) that evokes, and thereby gives concrete form to, a semiotically real event. To be sure, a "dog" wave function cannot be collapsed into an actual cat, no matter how much an observer-participant might wish to bring it about. Yet, just as Schrödinger's cat is purportedly neither dead nor alive until *we* determine her fate, so also whatever event that becomes a meaningful part of our everyday affairs does so in that particular way because we make it so. This should come as no surprise to the modernist mentality for, in the words of cyberneticist Heinz von Foerster (1984, 46), "'out there' there is no light and no colour, there are only electromagnetic waves; 'out there' there is no sound and no music, there are only periodic variations of the air pressure; 'out there' there is no heat and no cold, there are only moving molecules with more or less mean kinetic energy, and so on." The postmodernist mind takes Foerster's remark a giant step further by demolishing additional landmarks of epistemological stability: "electromagnetic waves," "variations of the air pressure," "moving molecules," and "kinetic energy" become as semiotically real as "light," "color," "sound," "heat," and "cold." Territorial divisions are swept away by the whirlwinds of change. Distinctions between science and nonscience, art and nonart, are leveled. And we discover that we

241

are all—human and nonhuman, living and nonliving, organic and inorganic alike—in this thing together.

It is ultimately the mind that sees, hears, smells, tastes, and feels. It edits experience to conform to its preconceptions. It cogitates, bringing imagined, hypostatic objects, acts, and events into the world. It learns to ignore certain aspects of the world that are considered—according to particular conventions and *Umwelt*-dependent constructions—ridiculous, fictive, hallucinatory, false, or evil, in order properly to see geometrical forms, numbers, useful things, good things, and to conduct its life in a respectable, cultured, intelligent manner. And so it comes to participate with its world. What the mind senses is by no means separate from what is "out there." Rather, interaction between mind and the "real" involves a complex physiological and psychological process of construction. Just as Schrödinger's cat is neither dead nor alive until the participatory mind makes it so, a sign is not a sign in the full-blown sense until interpreted by an interpreter, who is him/herself just another sign.

Law Is Law?

Wheeler concedes that his picture of a participatory universe will collapse if it cannot account for the creation of law, space-time as the product of law, and out of law the physical universe. The problem is that there is nothing more than, nor can there be anything more than, a higgledy-piggledy method for constructing law: it is generated out of the statistical aggregate of billions upon billions of incidences of "observer participancy"—acts of amplification—each of which in isolation is to all appearances entirely random. An individual gas molecule is buffeted about at random; a collection of like molecules approximates, to a greater or lesser degree, Boyle's laws. Yet without the composite acts of every molecule in the jar, there is no law. Even the energy of our collection of molecules—indeed, their existence as substance—loses its meaning in a closed, tautologous system. On the one hand, the chicken-and-egg regress is in full force here. Did law precede the molecule, or the other way round? On the other hand, we have the one/many or holism/pluralism antagonisms. The many compose the one, but from an omniscient eye observing the whole, the parts do not even enter the picture. And from a finite view of a minuscule part of the parts, the whole lies beyond the imagination.

In the beginning, to repeat Wheeler's aphorism—which is much in the Peircean spirit—law, like the stuff of the universe, lifted itself up by its bootstraps;[5] in the end, with gravitational collapse, time, space, and law will collapse back into "nothingness." And the universe will be left "with no law except the law that there is no law" (Wheeler 1980b, 142), for law "cannot stand engraved on a tablet of stone for all eternity" (Wheeler 1980a, 350). We are led to conclude that mutability is the ultimate principle in the description of nature—a description which, since it is within the *semiosic* stream, is of nothing other than the semiotically real.

At the outset, it seems preposterous that a physicist, of all people, might propagate the apparent absurdity that law is at its roots lawless. How can one hope to push forward with no solid ground underneath? It leaves an empty feeling in the pit of one's stomach. Yet the ultimate extrapolation of Wheeler's hypothesis is generality of the most general sort, which is also the focus of Peirce's "logic of the universe," a logic in the broadest possible sense. Another watchword regarding this logic is vagueness, which is responsible for the imperfect (incomplete) actualization of all signs—in part due to the imperfect return of a sign's self-recursive loop with each reiteration. The vague sign determines itself by the utterer, who thereby defines and interprets him/herself by the sign's being defined and interpreted. And the general sign is determined by the interpreter—who thereby defines him/herself by the sign's being defined and interpreted. The hopeful—and perhaps utopian—train of events is from the unintelligible to the intelligible, from chaos to order, from the uncut to multiply variegated cuts—or vice versa whenever either embedment or dissipation occurs.

Actually, in true Peircean spirit, there can be exclusively neither the one nor the other pole of the opposition. Order dissipates either suddenly or in gradual steps by way of de-generacy; and the resultant chaos can then become order. The same can be said of the idea of multivaried differentiation and discontinuity found in Prigogine's work, which is in certain key respects strikingly compatible with Wheeler's (and Peirce's). I refer to dissipative structures emerging out of far-from-equilibrium conditions, which lead to bifurcations and renewed order.[6] A bifurcation in a far-from-equilibrium system constitutes a vital instant when a very slight perturbation—a match lit on the Indian ocean, a butterfly flapping its wings in Brazil, a wayward electron—rapidly grows by chain reaction into a cascade of bifurcation points, until a catastrophe of major proportions occurs (cf. note 1 of this chapter and the final paragraph of Chapter Eight). The important point is that "real-world" bifurcations are irreversible—though their being put to use can be reversed in mind-dependent, semiotically real worlds—in contrast to the reversible laws of classical mechanics. In such irreversible processes, small effects can become magnified due to feedback at all levels and in all directions.

Bifurcations, constituting maps of irreversibility, render time paramount. Yet they are part of the baggage that history must drag along its plodding path: regarding their status in the semiotically real, they are held in check, recycled, forgotten, and perhaps recalled, but never entirely out of the picture. They reveal reversible as well as recapitulant time. Yet time can never merely tread water; it is swept along by the current at the same time that it *is* the current. And just as each bifurcation is the result of an unpredictable act of amplification, so also there is no predicting where or when a major catastrophe will occur. That is to say, the system is always dynamically shifting, though as a whole, from the classical view, it appears to move along roughly predictable lines—i.e., the individual molecule and many molecules example. Hence a mixture of chance and necessity is built into the system, which accounts for its creativity.

Thus we have Prigogine's uncertainty principle from micro- to macro-levels as a counterpart to Heisenberg's exclusively microlevel uncertainty principle. The role of randomness and chaos in the creation of order and structure disallows a determinate future. There are no parts of the whole enjoying priority over any others. All are interconnected at all levels; all constantly transmute into something else—giving rise to Deleuze and Guattari's (1987) rhizome metaphor. Wheeler extrapolates this contingency of nature to the extreme, observing that since black holes are the mechanical accident of stellar collapse, and since the laws of nature as we know them are dependent upon the existence of black holes, those very laws themselves must be contingent. Ultimately, the universe is guided by "law without law"; in its composite form, it is tantamount to the cosmic equation $0 = 0$.[7] Wheeler (1979, 11, cited in Dyson 1980, 377) continues:

> It is difficult to see what else than that can be the plan of physics. It is preposterous to think of the laws of physics as installed by a Swiss watchmaker to endure from everlasting to everlasting when we know that the universe began with a big bang. The laws must have come into being. Therefore they could not have been always 100 percent accurate. That means that they are derivative, not primary.

Like the open-ended, self-organizing, expanding universe, law is not invariant but constantly evolving. And like the quantum observer (interpreter-interpretant), who, with the tools of her trade and by means of a given context that creates certain conditionals, interacts with a wave function (Firstness) to bring an event (Secondness) into the world, she also collaborates as a participator—along with her entire community—with law (Thirdness) in order that the future it has enfolded within it may be unfolded. The universe "is a self-excited circuit. As it expands, cools, and develops, it gives rise to observer-participancy. Observer-participancy in turn gives what we call tangible reality to the universe" (Wheeler 1979, 11, cited in Dyson 1980, 377).

According to Wheeler, nature cannot be understood without the concept of observer-participancy: it was built into the universe from the very beginning. Without observers, there is no universe as such; without interpreters there are no interpretants, and without interpretants no interpreters. The activity of observers (interpreters-interpretants) in the remote future is foreshadowed in the remote past and steers the development of the universe—of signs, the universe as sign—throughout its entire history. While Dyson (1980, 377) concedes that all this "sounds to a contemporary physicist vague and mystical," he counsels that "we should have learned by now that ideas that appear at first sight to be vague and mystical sometimes turn out to be true." Nevertheless, one retains a hankering to speculate that Wheeler's statements are completely off the wall. In so doing, one misses the point, however: embracing the evolution of the universe as a whole without any outside agent or mover affords no guarantee of immutable laws; on the contrary, the laws of the game must change as the game itself proceeds.

245

The universe is not given once and for all. The very idea of the big bang and an expanding universe—an idea first suggested by Einstein, which then he retracted, confessing that it was his biggest blunder—is the idea of a universe of constant creative change in all its aspects. Such is Prigogine's universe. It is also Peircean in flavor. From the premise that "the only possible way of accounting for the laws of nature . . . is to suppose them the results of evolution" (CP, 6.13), Peirce posited, like Wheeler, that the evolutionary process began from a state of "nothingness," an "initial condition in which the whole universe was non-existent" (CP, 6.215).[8] He qualified this initial state as "utter vagueness," a "dimensionless potentiality" (CP, 6.193) of pure "freedom, chance, or spontaneity" (CP, 6.200), which, we must presume, is timeless as well. From this undetermined potentiality there arose a state of determined potentiality with the emergence of the world of experience, during which time, space, substance, the laws of nature, and even logic itself arose (CP, 6.189, 200).

The laws of the universe emerged in the same manner as laws of mind and physical activity: they are the product of the universe's habit-taking tendency. Peirce tells us that "all things have a tendency to take habits, for atoms and their parts, molecules and groups of molecules, and in short every conceivable real object, there is a greater probability of acting as on a former like occasion than otherwise" (CP, 1.409). Moreover, if a habit-taking tendency applies not only to the universe but also to the very laws governing it, then it is the law of laws—or, as Wheeler puts it, the "law that there is no law"—for "if the laws of nature are results of evolution, this evolution must proceed according to some principle; and this principle will itself be the nature of a law" (CP, 7.515). In the process of developing other habits, this supreme law lifts itself up and "grows by its own action, by the habit of taking habits itself growing" (CP, 8.317). Evolution is not merely a static law defining change; it is itself change of change. It changes while governing change; the change it governs in turn changes it.[9]

In short, Peirce's cosmology essentially corroborates postmodernism's view that science is not the path to truth and nothing but the truth. Rather, it is conditioned by language, culture, the dominant worldview, and personal and group idiosyncrasies and interests. Science, and all of culture for that matter, is context-dependent: a linguistic system addressing itself to itself, incapable of hooking onto the "real" world in the grand one-to-one style of positivism-modernity's correspondence theory.

Meaning through Use: A Different Twist

Hardly anybody seems more ready to embrace paradox than Wheeler. That the observer must distinguish between phenomena put to use, which thereby become semiotically real, and phenomena that are not and hence are relegated to the pigeonhole labeled "that which might have been" involves the microlevel quantum world rather than our macroworld of sights, smells, noises, and such.

Yet Wheeler is undeniably speaking of macrolevel meaning. What is put to use is employed in the generation of meaning, the joint product of the accumulated evidence of the entire community. Wheeler favorably alludes to Parmenides' contention that what *is* is identical with the thought that thinks it, which is surprising, given his penchant for a Heraclitean eternally transmuting river, which suggests a one/many, holism/pluralism conflict. From another perspective, the association is quite clear: the participatory universe, insofar as it exists for us, is semiotically real, not "actually real," which is to say that it is as much think-signs as thing-signs. If we bear in mind Wheeler's impatience with Wigner and others of similar mind-set, who opt for a consciousness-created "reality," we are led to the conclusion that his "reality" is definitely "out there" at all times, though if it is not put to use, it remains devoid of meaning, which is, for us at least, the only meaningful meaning. Consequently, Wheeler's meaning is, when translated to the macrolevel, pragmatic through and through inasmuch as it is possible, in principle, to dissect all we hear, see, feel, taste, and smell at the macrolevel into quantum phenomena, which serve as the base from which meaning is generated.

Objections are sure to arise at this point: "Is Wheeler not guilty of the most positivistic sort of reductionism?" Not necessarily. His meaning is generated from quantum phenomena as part of a "meaning circuit" projecting out from the microphysical domain. This is the "bottom-up" aspect of meaning. On the other hand, there is a complementary "top-down" component (not to be confused with "bottom-up" *semiosic* generation and "top-down" phaneronic de-generacy implied in figures 7 and 10). This Peircean two-way "meaning circuit" entails the participatory mind generating meaning, as depicted in figure 16. Mind is dependent upon, and acts on, matter at all levels, and vice versa. In a Peircean way of putting it, matter is congealed mind, and mind is sublimated matter.

Wheeler concedes the apparent untenability of his "meaning physics" of era 3 with the disclaimer that his account makes no pretense of being a complete theory: at most it specifies guidelines. Nevertheless, what is most significant to our concerns is his "community of communicators" establishing meaning through dialogic interaction. Of course, a given communicator's activity within the community has little consequence regarding the whole. She makes a difference, undoubtedly, but it is well-nigh imperceptible, like an integer along the infinite stream computed in the name of π, from 3.14159... Each additional cipher brings the decimal expansion slightly closer to its plenitude, but that single bit of information is capable neither of bringing the forward march to a definite close nor of making much of a difference.

247

Yet Wheeler's abandonment of physics hardware "out there" and its replacement with "meaning" software could result in a revolution of paradigmatic proportions. It implies that mere information (software), by a "top-down" operation, is capable under certain conditions of modifying the physical state (hardware) of things (Davies 1988). The wave function, as software, is not a representation of what the system *is* but offers information in order that the physicist may know something about her relationship with the system. The wave function evolves with time, and depending upon the interaction with the physicist through her measuring instruments, it collapses into a particular hardware state, a particle, which forever alters the trend of future states. A change in software brings about a change in the hardware. Thus meaning is elevated to primary status, while the microlevel of particles—and by extension, the macrolevel furniture of the world—become secondary. In this manner, the wave/particle duality bears some commonality with the software/hardware duality. Just as a computer can be described as software containing a set of possibilities (information), part of which, in interaction with its hardware, can be actualized as printouts, so also the stuff of the world is subjected to two complementary descriptions: wave and particle. The wave interacts with the world's hardware—for example, the physicist (through her instruments) asking a question and eliciting a response, or the semiotic agent as interpreter-interpretant (through the semiotic object) soliciting an interpretation—and collapses into one of its possible states according to the information contained within it. And the resultant "electron-state," in conjunction with myriad contiguous states, makes up the macrolevel furniture of the world, including both physicist and instruments, semiotic agent and semiotically real object.

In Peircean language, Firstness—as an unmediated sign, like the wave function—contains information regarding the set of possibilities for signification. Secondness is the actualization—tantamount to a collapse—of one of the possibilities resulting from the interpreter's interaction with the information given. Such interaction draws Thirdness, an interpretant of the actualized semiotic object, into existence, which, in conjunction with the interpreter—herself an interpretant—creates yet another relation with the sign to produce another sign further down the stream. We might summarize this triadic interaction as "A is a sign of B to C" or "C interprets A as a sign of B." In either event, the sign, as a repository of information—a certain set of possibilities—exercises a power to evoke some interpretation from within a range of possible interpretations: the sign, in Peirce's terms, "determines" its interpretant and is "determined" by its object. That is, the particular semiotic object drawn from the set of possibilities determines the sign's nature, which in turn determines the range of possible interpretants of that sign, one of which, at a given moment, can come into existence for some interpreter. Thus the sign, which contains information evincing the possibilities of interpretation, can be endowed with meaning. But the interpreter is essential for this to occur, just as Wheeler's participant putting a natural phenomenon to use is necessary for it to take on meaning. Meaning is to the wave and the particle what it is to the sign and its object. For Wheeler, there is no world without meaning; and without meaning, there is no sign or its object in the semiotic sense.

One might assume that the brain/mind duality evinces characteristics similar to the hardware/software and particle/wave complementarities. Care must be exercised when using such metaphors. Yet it appears plausible that, by analogy, actualized artifacts in the form of books, artworks, ideas, physical constructs, technological innovations, and assorted gadgetry and time-saving gimmicks—Popper's World 3 items in semiotic reality—are thought-sign sublimates (printouts) from the mind (software) through the brain (hardware). The mind functions as the realm of *possibilia,* which give rise to physical re-presentations or sign-things, and the brain's memory storehouse consists of precipitates (traces) programmed into it by subjective experiences (thought-signs), including ideas, emotions, dreams, and hallucinations—Popper's World 2—as a result of its interaction with the "real"—Popper's World 1.

But there is a profound difference between brain/mind on the one hand and computer hardware/software on the other. A computer program stands nary a chance of changing the computer's hardware. There is no downward causation from software to hardware but rather a parallelism in the software and hardware descriptions of the same events in distinct symbol systems—for example, natural language in the first and Boolean algebra in the second. However, Paul Davies (1988, 173) asks us to imagine a computer equipped with a robotic mechanism capable of modifying its own circuitry. Now software and hardware become a logically entangled, recursive, self-organizing system: the robot engages in a bootstrap operation. Multiple nonlinear feedback can exist at all levels up and down the hierarchy. This system is more akin to the physicist's wave function (software) plus measuring apparatus (hardware), or the brain (hardware) plus mediating mind (software). When interaction occurs, mind (World 2) brings about a collapse of the microlevel software into hardware (World 1), which is then recorded on paper, tapes, or diskettes (carriers of World 3), and at the same time a trace is deposited in the brain (hardware, World 1) for future interaction by mind with the microlevel quantum world. All of this helps account for a change in the information, or software, that can bring about the actualization of one of a number of possible hardware states. In Peircean terms, the physicist's instrument causes a collapse of the wave (Firstness) into a particle-event (Secondness) to be recorded (Thirdness). The wave function containing the information that allows the physicist to compute the range of possible collapses can be associated with the mind's propensities to act in a certain fashion as a result of expectations, habits, and beliefs. The collapsed particle, on the other hand, is comparable to the brain's being programmed with traces of past events.

249

How is it possible, then, that information alone can come to modify conditions, not only at the microlevel but also at the macrolevel? Wheeler's answer seems to be that an irreversible act of amplification results in a recording or trace, which elevates meaning to the primary status, while the physical stuff of the world is relegated to secondary status. But there still seems to be a problem here. The normal course of "upward causation" is forward in time (a wave collapses, a particle is detected, and an observer reads the instrument and records the result). There is no turning back. "Downward causation," from meaning to the hardware of the world, on the other hand, might appear, according to Wheeler's strange formulation, to go "backward" in time. It is a sort of "retroactive causation," the observer-participant bringing about what *happened* or *will have happened.*

The very idea of "retroactive" or "downward causation" tends to breed a somewhat false impression. Perhaps, more adequately stated, the whole affair is merely "timeless." That is, as discussed in Chapter Eight, everything exists in imaginary time as if *en bloc* (the ensemble), with complex time as a Boolean printout consisting of imaginary time producing our perception of real time (or history). With imaginary time, a question is asked, the universe manifests itself in a certain way, and what *is* is there for the recording. It is what *would have been* under certain circumstances, the conditional resting in an atemporal framework. For the time-bound observer (or semiotic agent) getting along swimmingly in the stream of real time, what *is* is what *was* in the immediate past, before the observation was made and recorded. Then meaning was generated, and in that immediate past before the observer was mediately conscious of the event, there *is* what *will have been,* the future perfect revealing the all-encompassing present of Wheeler's primary, microscopic domain. This apparent contradiction, when viewed from our macroworld perspective, stems from the fact that our real time falters in the face of the microscopic scale, and it is of no account in the initial phase of the big bang, just as it is of no account in the final stage of the gravitational collapse. Moreover, with respect to the microlevel, Feynman diagrams demonstrate that there is no irreversible time: events can go either "forward" or "backward." Time, within this framework, is simply *that which is,* it is *no-time,* or *imaginary time.*[10]

250

Downward causation appears hopelessly enigmatic, if not well-nigh unintelligible. Nevertheless, Wheeler's delayed-choice *Gedanken* experiment, which involves a type of "retrocausation"—when viewed from our own perceptual world—has been subject to actual experimentation, with positive, though not absolutely conclusive, results.[11] Physics thus becomes, Wheeler (1984, 123) declares, "the child of meaning even as meaning is the child of physics." Or, to rephrase Wheeler, the mind (interpreter-interpretant) is the child of the physical world (filtered through the semiotically real) even as the physical world is the child of the mind. The one is the other sublimated; the other is a crystallization of the one.

Yet Wheeler remains somewhat uncommitted on the topic of time. He has remarked that

> we too easily view [time] as a pre-established umbrella, stretching over the scene of physics from big bang to gravitational collapse and beyond. . . . We once likewise thought of elasticity as a primordial concept. Today, we know that elasticity, however useful in describing the properties of a sheet of glass or a sheet of rubber, makes no sense in the space between the atomic electron and the nucleus. Out of the quantum theory of the motion of the electron, we construct elasticity as a secondary and derivative concept. Likewise, in time to come, we will surely understand "time" as a term that makes no sense at all under extreme conditions and that derives its meaning under everyday conditions from a line of reasoning that makes no reference at all to time in the first place. (Wheeler 1982, 22)

Wheeler is inspired by Leibniz's notion of time and space not as things but as orders of things and by Einstein's idea of space-time as a mode by which thinking is facilitated, not as conditions in which we live. But the ambiguity persists, and it reflects the general ambiguity, even conflict, regarding time in the history of Western thought. During the latter part of the nineteenth century, this conflict settled on reversible Newtonian mechanics and irreversible entropic decay, as specified by the second law of thermodynamics. In this century, we have various theories of time wrestling with one another: the "moving now" of continuous processual time (Bergson, Whitehead); a refutation of time according to which past and future have the same ontological status (McTaggart, Russell, Grünbaum); bizarre theories such as reversible time of the block universe within which time travel becomes theoretically possible, though unfeasible (Gödel); and branching time in the block, within which all possibilities are actualized in parallel universes—the "many-worlds interpretation" of quantum mechanics (which Wheeler once accepted). Quite understandably, Prigogine has called time the "forgotten dimension" because of the unimportance assigned to it by the Newtonian worldview—and doggedly perpetuated by Einstein to the end of his life.

251

Peirce, unfortunately—or perhaps quite understandably, given his historical setting—is unclear on this issue.[12] His conception of time and space is somewhat Kantian, though he would contend from the perspective of his "objective idealism" that space and time are constructs. But if they are true of all we can know, then they are "real" (i.e., semiotically real), even if postulated (CP, 1.489–513, 6.82). For Peirce, without change there can be no time; and without time, no change. Something is one thing before and something else later, but it cannot be both things at once. Although the mere succession of events in Secondness corresponds to timeless Newtonian laws—according to which all mechanical processes are reversible, without any uniquely defined causal direction—time, "real" time, is mind-stuff, psychic; hence it projects beyond mere physical action and reaction. And since all processes ultimately are, according to Peirce—and Wheeler—mindlike (whether the active mind of living matter or the congealed mind of the inorganic universe), all processes are psychic. Hence time must be *really real* (CP, 6.554, 6.68).

The pantheistic—and admittedly anthropocentric—notion that all processes are ultimately psychic bears on habit-taking, a product of "mind" the world over. Just as Peirce reduces the brain/mind dualism to rubble, so also, as a consequence of Peirce's definition of habit, material phenomena cannot be absolutely distinguished from mental phenomena. Peirce adopted the view that the only truly distinctive feature of mind is consciousness, or feeling, and while habits are the end product of consciousness, they have already dropped out of conscious awareness to become embedded. This process of habit-taking is indelibly time-bound: change by habit-taking is in time, and time is in it. And it is mind-bound, for mind not merely is tantamount to some ideal form of present consciousness but remains in a tight embrace with time (CP, 5.492, 7.364). If we extrapolate this equation to its limit, habit, having precipitated out of consciousness, becomes more and more entrenched, eventually passing from animate to inanimate matter, or *effete mind,* as Peirce was wont to put it.

At the "roots of time," the most elementary form of habit either did not yet exist or it had not yet become crystallized into inorganic matter. To speak of a sequence arising from this state of affairs, if sequence there be, one cannot appropriately speak of "past," "now," and "future," for there is no time as such—that is, experienced (real) time in the sense of McTaggart's A-series (CP, 6.214; Horwich 1987). Peirce ruminates on how time, from nothing but "nothingness," purely symmetrical, reflexive, and static, somehow shot out of the starting block and into the A-series.[13] In the beginning, out of the "womb of indeterminacy," he writes:

> There would have come something, by the principle of Firstness, which we may call a flash. Then by the principle of habit there would have been a second flash. Though time would not yet have been, this second flash was in the same sense after the first, because resulting from it. Then there would have come other successions ever more and more closely connected, the habits and the tendency to take them ever strengthening themselves, until the events would have been bound together into something like a continuous flow. (CP, 1.412)

In the context of Prigogine's universe, Peirce might rephrase this embarrassingly murky passage in terms of a spontaneous self-organizing system hard driven by far-from-equilibrium conditions that spawn broken symmetries and dissipative structures to create order by means of perpetual transition to more complex phases. And Peirce, it seems, *is* writing in the above passage of the beginning of time and of evolution in terms of an engenderment of broken symmetries.[14]

The very idea of broken symmetries at the deepest level of existence flies in the face of our gut intuitions. John Barrow and Joseph Silk open *The Left Hand of Creation* (1983, ix) with the observation that if "paradise is the state of ultimate and perfect symmetry, the history of the 'big bang' resembles that of paradise lost." Indeed, the mind seems to be naturally repelled by asymmetry, and few phenomena have fascinated thinkers more than symmetry. Symmetry gives assurance that humankind and its world are in some mysterious manner the duplication of an eternal model. It has traditionally been synonymous with the proportioned, balanced, and harmonious. This definition pertains not only to space but also to auditory and sensory qualities in poetry and music—that is, to time. Spatial symmetry and temporal symmetry—where $-t$ and t can be substituted in equations without changing the system—were the standard in classical science. Nature, it was believed, is symmetrical through and through. Common assumption had it that structure is symmetry and symmetry is structure.

The problem is that symmetry, simply put, is lacking in distinctive features, in markedness. A perfect sphere enjoys the ideal degree of symmetry. It can be rotated through any angle about its center and it remains the same. A blemished sphere has no such rotational symmetry, though another form of symmetry is retained, since after a degree of rotation, it will be symmetrical with respect to its mirror image, its enantiomorphic twin. The perfect sphere is the ideal monad, a First—Nicholas of Cusa knew the formula well—while the defective sphere evinces at least the trappings of Secondness, since it possesses something that marks it off as distinguishable from its previous form; it has become something other than what it was.

It is now becoming increasingly evident through the work of Prigogine and his associates that the emergence of structure usually marks previous symmetry-breaking. Something must give before a new order can arise. Order and structure emerge from chaos, not from existing order; that is the way of the creative advance of nature. So it appears that what Sebeok (1983, 4–5) calls the evolution (Thirdness) of "gravitation, the electroweak force, and the strong (Hadronic) force that binds the particles of the nucleus in the atom"—which would hopefully lead to the Grand Unified Theory (Peirce's "law")—is, as far as our fallible semiotic worlds are concerned, a rather hopeless and helpless dream: the asymptotic trek will never reach the end of the trail. What we can hope to grasp is the history of the universe as a succession of symmetry breaks gradually producing more structure and differentiation, regarding signification; and an increasingly bland cosmic dough, regarding the entropic push toward heat death. What I mean by "signification" is that, beginning with nothing at all, a Spencer-Brownian distinction or Peircean cut was established, and gradually the world as we know it evolved by a sequence of symmetry breaks. Each step involved further distinction, which generated increased entropy—the very dear price for a little development—which opened up new opportunities for further organization and increased complexity and at the same time closed off other potentialities. In this view, the notion of "creation" is no once-and-for-all event but an ongoing drama that is and will remain, according to all indications, incomplete.

Quite obviously, then, Wheeler's "physics as meaning" entails an asymmetrization of things, the creation ultimately of differences that make a difference. And it involves primarily the semiotically real, that which is made meaningful by being put to use by someone for some purpose or other. The semiotically real, as *Umwelt,* is mind-stuff more than matter-stuff. The mind is a participator, says Wheeler. As mind is, matter may become; and as matter is, mind once was, says Peirce. In this sense, mind does not mutilate "reality," as certain Hindu traditions would have it. Mind participates with, and in the process creates or invents, its semiotic reality by selecting and bringing about an unfolding of difference from the nonselective and unfolded. Thus the triad of *possibilia,* semiotically real, and knowledge (description-interpretation) is tantamount in this respect to Firstness (brain, feeling, seeing), Secondness (consciousness, seeing *as,* knowing *how,* action and reaction), and Thirdness (the product of mind, of consciousness of, of seeing *that,* and knowing *that*). Only at an obstinate snail's-pace have we come fully to realize the fundamental unity that this triad constitutes. United the three legs stand; divided, and the entire pyramid falls.

254

Kant, who was a constant inspiration to Peirce, with an equally incisive scalpel proposed that the structure of knowledge (and therefore of the semiotically real) must cohere with the categories of the mind, and not the other way around, as classical empiricism had it. Kant's Copernican revolution did not quite go to completion, however: he wedded his concept of mind to Newtonian mechanics with the intention of liberating science from the straitjacket of empiricism once and for all, but the marriage was never consummated, for he remained imprisoned within Newton's rigid conceptual universe. In spite of Kant's insights, this century has witnessed the heyday of logical empiricism and analytic philosophy—which have been perhaps more devastating than any of their predecessors. Materialist theories dictated that the mind is nothing but a kind of mirror reduplicating the objective stuff of the world as if it were a camera. And dreamy-eyed positivists offered elegant logical constructs that could purportedly coincide with "reality."

Now, finally, with the new attitude toward observer, mind, and matter, a paradigm appears to be emerging. The euphoria of empiricist innocence is over, and hard-nosed materialism is on the wane. In their place, we do not find yet another business-as-usual description of "reality" *as it is.* The new wave entails not an extension of the physical but a reconstruction of the imaginary (Charon 1987). This is another of those exciting periods when working out a new conception of the universe demands the ultimate in mind labors. When one finally loses one's clutch on the security blanket of the old classical paradigm, it is not as if one were now in a void; rather, one is no longer chained by certain fetters of the past.

In this vein, I now turn to a further link between Peirce and Wheeler with an illustration from the work of Borges.

Caught with(in) the *Semiosic* Fabric

Wheeler's distinguishability, which implies the freedom to ask, to choose a question, to decide, suggests Peirce's abduction. Peirce puts forth three rules for abductive inference, the implications of which are in line with Wheeler's physical world phenomena as "real" only when put to use: (1) the hypothesis should be put as a question before empirically testing and recording (observing, writing) it for its truth content; (2) there must be no a priori predicates regarding the hypothesis—that is, it must remain as a hypothetical conditional (i.e., if it were put to use in such-and-such a way, certain consequences would likely follow); and (3) failures as well as successes, refutations as well as validations, are important—putting the phenomena to the test (use) does not give infallible results, but, like the various uses of the cosmic ray phenomenon, what becomes part of the semiotically real at a given time and place *could always have been* otherwise (CP, 2.834).

Regarding the process of ratiocination and its consequences as embodied in Peirce's three rules, consider that supreme rational animal, detective Lönnrot in Borges's (1962, 76–87) "Death and the Compass." Lönnrot, the super-calculator, infers from his reading of Jewish texts, from number magic, and from geometry that after three enigmatic homicides a fourth murder is inevitable. By an elaborate process of inferential reasoning, he determines its exact location on a map and proceeds to that point at the precise time he calculates the murder is to be enacted. Scharlach, the murderer, appears with two accessories, who disarm and handcuff Lönnrot—the intended victim. Then there is a brief exchange between Lönnrot and Scharlach, during which the latter explains how Lönnrot's remarkable reasoning power had been the author of his own undoing. His purely formal construct did not correspond to his perceived world but to another world created by another mind, Scharlach's.

This short story, labeled an "extreme case of geometrization" by the Argentine writer Ernesto Sábato (1945, 104), evinces an imposing construction of bilateral symmetries, most important of which is an interaction between threes and fours. Not only does trinary space become quaternary, the same occurs to time also, but not as Lönnrot had calculated. The first three murders occurred on the third day of three successive months, and each murder was separated by thirty-one days from the others. A fourth murder, Lönnrot inferred, must occur on the sixth of March to separate it by thirty-one days from the third event. However, Scharlach, after apprehending Lönnrot, tells him: "You are very kind. You have saved us a night and a day" (Borges 1962, 84). Scharlach then explains that actually the deaths had occurred on the fourth days of the first three months, for the Hebrews compute days from sunset to sunset. Lönnrot had calculated with threes, which were fours in Scharlach's scheme, hence the fourth death was to occur on the seventh rather than the sixth day of the month. Lönnrot's scheme, developing linearly and through time, was grasped *in toto* by Scharlach's omniscient gaze. Time for Scharlach consists of another dimension of space. What according to Lönnrot's calculations would be the case was otherwise for Scharlach, for he had already decided what *was to have* happened—Wheeler's future anterior.

Classical physics depicted a linear concept of time, like that of Lönnrot's experiential world. Special relativity changed that picture entirely: an instant is identified with a single point in space, and the totality is to be conceived only as a block. This is comparable to Scharlach's view, which held Lönnrot's labyrinthine path in a timeless instant, as if in block. Time, or timelessness, in this relativist conception, is symmetrical: regressing is no different from proceeding forward. And space is entirely democratic: up, down, forward, backward, are all equal rather than hierarchically valued. Lönnrot was caught in a trap of his own making, but the trap was, from Scharlach's perspective *sub specie aeternitatis,* always already set for its prey. The decision was already made, the selection exercised, and the conditions established. That is to say, the logical sequence of steps that Lönnrot devised to determine what *had been* the case regarding past events and *would have been* the train of events in the future were contrary to Scharlach's sphere of existence, according to which the world existed as a simultaneous *now:* everything *had already happened;* all events were *faits accomplis.* From within his universe of signs, Lönnrot's abductions were predetermined by another's deductive machinations.

As in the Wheelerian scheme in figure 16, meaning, which is derived by the entire community of knowers in the theoretical long run, has already determined (hypothetically deduced) the nature of Firstness, which, if it were viewed in its totality—a practical impossibility, though theoretically a plausible hypostat—would preclude any spontaneous abductive acts or time-bound, inductive actualizations. There would be, from such an impossible totalizing gaze, no chance or choice, no freedom. On the other hand, absolute choice, chance, and freedom would be available from the immanent domain of a particular linear time-line within the whole. Once again, Wheeler's equation "$0 = 0$" applies. The absolute at one extreme meets the absolute at the other extreme. Scharlach's role is that of Laplace's Superobserver; his initial choice predetermined his universe. Lönnrot's role is that of Faust—the first choice determined his undoing. The universe offers either freedom or determinism, depending upon the mind of the interpreter-interpretant.

The question to ask is, Can it really be that such dilemmas lie at the heart of "reality"? As Wheeler (1980b, 133) once iconoclastically put it: "I am going to call upon the ancient principle of physics, 'no progress without paradox', where by 'paradox' we mean difficulty, apparent discrepancy, or discord between what we expect and what we find. If we have one paradox, we have some hope. However, we need two to make real progress. Then we can play off one against the other." Paradox, of course, is paramount in our postmodern age. Bohr, who was aware that classical principles were incapable of accounting for incompatible quantum phenomena, created complementarity, by way of which two domains could be neatly packaged, but not in simultaneity. Others rebelled. The Copenhagen interpretation, they countered, was incomplete. The task was to continue the search for an adequate theory capable consistently of accounting for everything. That debate has not subsided completely, nor has the search proved conclusive. Wheeler, in good postmodern spirit—and he is not alone here—openly and brazenly calls for paradox. This comes as no surprise these days. What provokes knee-jerks is the magnitude of the paradox: it takes on cosmological proportions.[15]

But actually, when either of the two great cosmologies of Western thought derived from the pre-Socratics—one a world of pure change, and the other of changelessness—are extrapolated to the extreme, paradox inextricably results. The celebrated Eleatic philosopher Parmenides—or Einstein-Scharlach—propagated the idea that mere nothing cannot be thought of, and so even less can it exist. In order to bring nothing into the discourse, something must be introduced, and thereby we contradict ourselves. Parmenides' antagonist Heraclitus—or Bohr, but not Lönnrot—openly embraced contradiction. In fact, he maintained that paradox exists at the heart of "reality."

The very idea of a contradictory world falls in step with the conflicts and alliances between experience and "reality." This should be adequate preparation for embracing a contradictory cosmology. But generally it is not. We tend obstinately to nurture, often in spite of ourselves, faith in the consistency of the world and hope, even expect, that ultimately the mind will be able to impose order upon its apparently chaotic surroundings. This faith could very well prove to be misplaced, Wheeler tells us. It is at best a Pollyannaish wish that a reconciliation of all discordant and conflicting entanglements will eventually be possible. But there is no reason, a priori, for thinking along these lines. While consistency may be an epistemological desideratum, there is no guarantee whatsoever that it will ever reign supreme. Indeed, the starting point of inquiry, of creativity itself, is conflict, tension, for

> the actual course of human inquiry undoubtedly exhibits the structure of a St. Simonian ebb and flow of alternation between synthetic eros of consolidation and analytic eros of conflict, of (relative) cognitive dissonance and cognitive harmony. Inconsistency plays no less important role on the stage of our cognitive affairs than does consistency. (Rescher and Brandom 1979, 43)

Semiosis, Symptom, Psyche

258 Speaking of tension and conflict, let us turn to Baudrillard's controversial work, which returns us directly to a discussion of postmodernism, thus completing the tired circle of Western discourse. Very generally, Baudrillard weds Marx's analysis of surplus value production in terms of exchanges of capital and goods to Saussure's description of language in terms of exchanges of signifiers and signifieds. Saussurean—and, by proxy, Baudrillardian—signs, whether in the form of sounds or of graphic images, engage in a frenzy of signifying activity, the upper level of which is buoyed by some mysterious underlying current that is neither the "real" nor the semiotically real as I have used the terms in this inquiry. That is to say, the signs do not necessarily refer to any objective "reality," whether preordained or fabricated, but rather, they act as their own referents, creating endless citations to themselves. They become the only "reality" worthy of the name, for, very simply, no other "reality" is to be had.

At the outset, this brief encapsulation of Baudrillard appears to fall in step with the postmodern bandwagon, which celebrates the local, the individual, the contextual, the fragmented. Postmodernism's consequent overriding tendency to prioritize aesthetics and debunk traditional rigorous intellectual concerns often brings with it the assumption that postmodern practices somehow speak their own sort of "truth," a "truth" that does not lug the nuts and bolts of formal constructions around in its bag of tricks but is merely narrated. No logic of identity and contradiction is employed here; rather, differences are merely verbalized, for, in Saussure's words, language consists of nothing but myriad differences.

The problem is that Baudrillard ignores the more radical posture, which discards both the meat-and-potatoes logic of identity and contradiction and the diet-food logic of difference. I refer to the implications, outlined above, of a "logic" of complementarity, of vagueness and generality, inconsistency and incompleteness that draws attention to the semiotically real rather than the "real," to what *might be, would be,* or *could be,* rather than unadulterated "truth." From this view, public enemy number one is not hard-nosed logic and reason, as is so often assumed. Nor is any answer to be found in any of the laid-back alternatives propounded in recent years. Both responses suffer from tunnel vision and incurable dyslexia. Life simply cannot be so simple, as evidenced by fractals, far-from-equilibrium systems, nonlinear development, and chaos physics, all of which point toward the possibility of meaning only after signs have been put to use.

Let this topic, with respect to Baudrillard's work, engage our attention in our final chapter.

Travails of Hyperreality

Arthur Kroker (1987, 183) laments that Baudrillard suffers from a host of blind spots, among them a theoretical blind spot: he fails "as a systematic (scientific) theorist because of his privileging of the poetic imagination." On the contrary, I would suggest. Baudrillard fails as a theorist because he scientizes the poetic imagination, therefore privileging the outmoded science of modernity, which is oblivious of its poetic roots.

Jameson (1979, 131) observes that contemporary Western culture is "the very element of consumer society itself, no society has ever been saturated with signs and images like this one." Jameson's announcement hardly comes as a surprise these days. Consumer culture and the mass media have generated an outpouring of images and signs, the consequence of which, in Baudrillard's terms, creates a "simulational world" erasing the age-old distinction between the "real" and the imaginary. Jameson (1979, 1983) calls this world the product of a depthless, schizophrenic posture capitalizing on a plurality of styles, idiosyncrasies, fads, and fashions, the end product of which is a "pastiche"—hollow imitation, "blank parody," empty masks. Baudrillard would not exactly disagree with this estimation.[1] Both he and Jameson allude to a progressive abstraction—the fetishism of the abstract—of cultural signs. However, he does Jameson one better: the logic of contemporary commodity capitalism is not merely depthless; it breeds a Nietzschean sort of nihilism. The privileged domains of modernity (Lyotard's metanarratives), science, philosophy, labor, private enterprise, social programs, and above all theory, are sucked up by a blaze of signifiers and into a black hole. The cherished illusions of the referential sign vanish; signs and their objects implode into mere disembodied signs (Baudrillard 1983a, 1–4).

Baudrillard sees the whole of society organized around conspicuous consumption and the unabashed display of commodities, by means of which one acquires prestige, identity, and status. The more renowned one's possessions, the higher one's standing. But these commodities have lost their value as material goods; they exist only in the realm of semiotic value. Like signs in Saussure's differential system of language, they take on value according to their relations with all other sign-commodities in the entire system. Everything is flattened to the same level, that of signifiers referring to other signifiers. Ultra-commercialized goods, having become signs, are homogenized and shoved onto

259

the public in the form of a pablum diet, the totality of which composes a vast tautological system whereby individual needs are created by the system responsible for satisfying those needs. Individuals are nothing more than socially invented agents of needs. Each individual becomes coterminous with any and all individuals, for a given sign-commodity is equal to all other sign-commodities of the same name and value.

The transformation of society that Baudrillard outlines is marked by the onslaught of *simulacra,* an inundation of infinitely reiterative signs ushering in the aftermath of individuals. Objects, and society at large, have been subjected to the effects of cybernetic codes, models, modulations, and the steering mechanisms aimed at perfecting the project of social control. This, Baudrillard writes, is the chief characteristic of neocapitalist, post-Marxist, postmodern society. The masses ("silent majority") passively consume whatever is dished out to them—television, sports, toys, movies, politics, processed food, cars—which renders any idea of class struggle obsolete. Boundaries and categories of social life and commodities dissolve. Dichotomies between appearance and reality, subject and object, everyday life and art, collapse into a delirious concoction of signs, a self-perpetuating system generated and controlled by simulation models and codes, the product of society's accelerated computerization.

Three "orders of simulacra," Baudrillard writes, have gradually come to dominate social life. They were introduced with the rise of modernity, when simulacra implied power and social relations; with the industrial revolution, when serial production, and finally automation, opened the door to infinite reproducibility, and machines begin to take their place alongside humans; and with cybernetic society, when models began to take precedence over things, and since models are signs, signs now begin to exercise their hegemony.[2]

This third order of simulacra is obsessively binary in nature—which is to be expected, for after all, Baudrillard's own model is linguicentric and Saussurean. Baudrillard's story has it that language, genetics, and social organization are analogous (in the order of structuralism, the DNA code, and semiology). All are governed by a binary (cybernetic, Boolean) logic that underlies social models and codes that control institutional and everyday life. Consequently, an individual's range of choices and responses is severely regulated by programmed and precoded messages. In contrast to classical theories of social control, Baudrillard's theory *prima facie* appears to be radically indeterministic: there is no grand omniscient administrator with a master plan in hand, but rather, everything resembles "a Brownian movement of particles or the calculation of probabilities." Such is, for example, voting in democratic cybersocieties, "as if everyone voted by chance, or monkeys voted." Party distinctions have been flattened. It really "makes no difference at all what the parties in power are expressing historically and socially. It is *necessary* even that they represent nothing: the fascination of the game, the polls, the formal and statistical compulsion of the game is all the greater" (Baudrillard 1983a, 132).

Power can be absolute in this system only if it is capable of diffracting into a spectrum of variants, each defined in terms of binaries: remove something here, put something else there; change this, and reciprocally alter that; and so on. This applies to brands of soap as well as to peaceful coexistence between superpowers. Two superpowers are necessary to maintain control; one superpower standing alone would soon crumble.[3] The macrolevel binary opposition between them is regulated by the manipulation of myriad series of binaries within the system to retain the image of equilibrium. Though at local levels a flurry of diversified activity appears to reign, the matrix, by its very nature, remains binary and does not change on the whole. It is "always the 0/1, the binary scansion that is affirmed as the metastable or homeostatic form of the current system" (Baudrillard 1983a, 135). Everything apparently comes in twos, whether giving the appearance of opposition or identity (simulacra). In either case, the sign purifies itself by duplicating itself, and on so doing, it destroys its meaning and its referent. Andy Warhol demonstrates this with his multiple replicas, which "show at the same time the death of the original and the end of representation" (Baudrillard 1983a, 136). Cybernetics triumphs by reducing everything to binaries that are not binaries at all but oppositions fused into differences that are ultimately destined to be canceled entirely.

Baudrillard's society of simulations is symptomatic of a cybernetic system that is composed of individuals, each soporifically doing his/her own thing (like monads or atoms), and that, viewed as a whole, has all individuals doing the same thing (like a statistical aggregate of atoms). Consequently, the imaginary world of simulacra becomes, from the perspective of each individual, more "real" than the "real" itself. It is as if imaginary time had absorbed "real" time, as if the ensemble had absorbed history, and as if the stream of events, ongoing process, were spatialized into a static series of "nows" (cf. Jameson's "hyperspace").[4] Disneyland, for example, is an imaginary space whose very existence is for the purpose of concealing the fact that

> it is the "real" country, all of "real" America, which is Disneyland (just as prisons are there to conceal the fact that it is the social in its entirety, in its banal omnipresence, which is carceral). Disneyland is presented as imaginary in order to make us believe that the rest is real, when in fact all of Los Angeles and the America surrounding it are no longer real, but of the order of the hyperreal and of simulation. It is no longer a question of reality (ideology), but of concealing the fact

that the real is no longer real, and thus of saving the reality principle. (Baudrillard 1983a, 25)

The time of Disneyland as "real" is thus reduced to space, to place (*topos, [u]topia, here-now*). What happens happens in the "now," with no legitimate reference to anything elsewhere or elsewhen. Signs brilliantly shine forth to signify themselves and nothing but themselves, without reference to their objects of signification and without mediation but rather as pure immediacy. If we heed Baudrillard's words—though with a certain grain of salt—we must entertain the idea that there has been a transition from signs that simulate (represent) something to signs that dissimulate that there is nothing at all, and that this nothing somehow becomes "real," or "hyperreal." Hyperreality is not the unreal; it is "superreality." What was originally the *modelans* becomes the *modelandum* raised to a higher exponential power. It takes precedence over the erstwhile "real," which has been banished to another space and another time.[5]

The ramifications of Baudrillard's digital, binary conception of the sign appears at the outset similar to J. David Bolter's (1984, 132–38) conclusion that we have entered the age of "computer thought"—which began during and shortly after World War II and was accompanied by the development of information theory and cybernetics. In the cybernetic world of computers, thoughts are flattened to the level of computer language, which consists of strings of absolutely arbitrary—discrete, conventional—symbols manipulated by the use of stringent Boolean rules.

This is a recent development. The ancient Greeks were mesmerized by the resonant qualities of the spoken word. Words and the ideas they incorporated were conceived to be as real as the chair I am sitting in. The Sophists continued to so use spoken words, but, rhetoricians that they were, they taught their disciples to regard language as something to be arbitrarily manipulated for the sheer purpose of suiting their fancy. Language, in their eyes, had lost much of its awesome power. Plato had no use for this radical new article of faith. He could not regard any facet of the world to be arbitrary. The written sign became the most obvious culprit, for he believed it to possess an abstract, distancing power that threatened to relegate language to the status of whimsical marks and scratches embodied with determinate meaning.

In spite of the birth of modern science and the predominance of writing, the Platonists had their way for generations. The sound of language was retained in ancient reading, for texts were to be read aloud in order that they be made adequately intelligible—in much the sense that most people must play a musical score in order to appreciate it properly. In the Middle Ages, the debate concerning the relationship between words and their referents became the realist-nominalist controversy. But the magic of the spoken word continued to reign supreme, at least until the age of the printed word, when the visual linguistic image gradually became the medium for assimilating knowledge. Mathematics followed the same route. The Pythagoreans equated the cosmos with number, and number with a mystical conception of geometry. Even down to the time of Galileo, mathematics remained tied to the spoken word. With the introduction of analytic geometry and calculus, arbitrary symbols became the order of the day. Mathematics was now transformed into a language in its own right, an artificial language. And significantly, Leibniz's binary system, which was based on the root two, paved the way for modern computer language. The result has been more astounding than the wildest of dreams. According to the Western tradition of realism, the mind discovers ideas, which have a power, necessity, and reality of their own; whereas modern thought, following the computer revolution, requires no necessary link between thought and the world. Computer thought, then, very effectively represents the triumph of nominalism, and William of Occam appears to be having his day (Bolter 1984, 77). Once this nominalist computer thought, which is clearly in line with the abstractions of Enlightenment ideals, had realized its hegemony in society, modernist manipulation and control of the populace was facilitated, and its efficacy multiplied manyfold.

263

At this juncture, Bolter and Baudrillard take divergent paths. Baudrillard writes that the so-called silent majorities are not simply tantamount to the poststructuralist "other," manipulated by the media through the use of signs in the classical sense; indeed, they control the media by their very apathy, which creates systemic inertia. Apparently accepting everything with stolid passivity, the masses, without resistance, redirect the media and the entire social system. Requiring no overt meaning or code, they induce everything into a slide along the indeterminate slope to generate not nonsense but merely a frivolous, ephemeral fascination, a momentary ecstatic grasp of whatever happens to have been produced and is now there for the having. While the media's manipulation of the masses had generally been the focus of semiological analysis, the tables are now overturned by Baudrillard, for semiology's "naive logic of communication" has overlooked the fact that "*the masses are a stronger medium than all the media,* that it is the former who envelop and absorb the latter—or at least there is no priority of one over the other. The mass and the media are one single process. Mass(age) is the message" (Baudrillard 1983b, 44).

The masses dominate the media by taking their cultural logic to the extreme, by engaging in "hyperlogic."[6] This demands "hyperconformity" and "hypersimulation," which hypertrophies the compulsion to consume. Commodities at work and at play, infatuation with sports, popular icons and celebrities, health and diet fads, exercise mania, blind faith in medicine, tinsel-town entertainment, commercialized religion, all are extrapolated to their extreme, hyperbolic form. Popular culture is amortized, its demise and extinguishment is hastened. It will become overloaded until the dike bursts, and everything will dissipate in the ensuing deluge. It is by their very inertia that the masses go beyond the cultural logic of capitalist consumerism and will finally destroy the whole edifice (Baudrillard 1983b, 47). Boolean binarism is taken to the absurd, without ceasing to exert the force of its binary imperative.

264   I believe, however, that with due consideration to Baudrillard's occasionally enticing conception of things, he is mistaken on an important point. Let me try to illustrate this with a tangential walk.

Dyadophilia Imploded

Baudrillard takes a few "topological" cues from Jorge Luis Borges in hopes of thus endowing his thesis with greater respectability. A juxtaposition of a Borges quote and a Baudrillard citing of Borges may prove helpful in further elucidating the problematics inherent in Baudrillard's proclamations. Borges begins his "Book of Sand" on an enigmatic note:

> The line is made up of an infinite number of points; the plane of an infinite number of lines; the volume of an infinite number of planes; the hypervolume of an infinite number of volumes. . . . No, unquestionably this is not—*more geometrico*—the best way of beginning my story. To claim that it is true is nowadays the convention of every made-up story. Mine, however, is true. (Borges 1978, 17)

And Baudrillard begins "The Precession of Simulacra" with these words:

> If we were able to take as the finest allegory of simulation the Borges tale where the cartographers of the Empire draw up a map so detailed that it ends up exactly covering the territory . . . then this fable has come full circle for us, and now has nothing but the discrete charm of second-order simulacra. . . .
>
> Abstraction today is no longer that of the map, the double, the mirror or the concept. Simulation is no longer that of a territory, a referential being or a substance. It is the generation by models of a real without origin or reality: a hyperreal. The territory no longer precedes the map, nor survives it. Henceforth, it is the map that precedes the territory—PRECESSION OF SIMULACRA—it is the map that engenders the territory and if we were to revive the fable today, it would be the territory whose shreds are slowly rotting across the map. It is the real, and not the

map, whose vestiges subsist here and there, in the deserts which
are no longer those of the Empire, but our own. *The desert of the
real itself.* (Baudrillard 1983a, 1–2)

First, an example of *precession* is the axis of a spinning body—a top,
or a gyroscope—slowly rotating about the line intersecting the body, thus describing a cone caused by the application of the torque tending to alter the
rotation axis. In another way of putting it, if we begin with a solitary point and
spiral outward, the point describes larger and larger not quite self-enclosing
circles whose summation is a cone. Recalling a previous thought experiment,
this is like our shoving our pyramid through a flatlander's world while rotating
it and gyrating its axis. The point becomes a line that describes a two-dimensional surface making up a three-dimensional conical form.

265

Borges affords us the image of a point that can *generate* a line, a
plane, a volume, and finally a hypervolume. Conversely, a hypervolume can
de-generate (implode) into a point—recall previous observations of Borges's
map. Baudrillard's and Borges's tropes necessarily draw infinity into the picture, which is quite appropriately Peircean as well. Moreover, if, as in Chapter
Five, we pattern de-generacy by transition (prescission) from a plane (Third) to
a line (Second) to a point (First)—or from a hypercube to a cube to a plane—
we have, by analogy, passage from symbolicity to indexicality, and then to
iconicity. In the discussion of the "universe ≈ machine" equation, by de-generacy
(embedment), Thirdness collapses (implodes) into Firstness. What is now there
is, for the true believer of the Cartesian-Newtonian corpuscular-kinetic model,
simply a machine, without acknowledgment of the original model or map as an
analogy or of the *as-if* construct generated by Thirdness. In Baudrillard's words,
in the age of third-order simulacra, the territory neither precedes nor survives
the map; it is the map that engenders what is taken to be in no uncertain terms
"real."

Baudrillard evokes the image of the Möbius strip to illustrate his concept of simulacra. The strip metaphorically illustrates how normal binary oppositions implode in the third order of simulacra, thus losing their differentiation
in the dough of sameness. For instance, the political polarization of right and
left is conflated into an endless and endlessly reversible whirligig. Dialectical
polarity no longer exists in this "field *unhinged by simulation*" (Baudrillard
1983a, 31). The system and its extreme alternate are conjoined, like the Möbius
strip folded back on itself, such that affirmation and negation intermingle in a
circular mishmash of discourse. By the same token, while not long ago "sex
and work were savagely opposed terms; today both are dissolved into the same
type of demand" (Baudrillard 1983a, 36). In this fashion, theater is substantiated by antitheater, art by antiart, pedagogy by antipedagogy, psychiatry by

antipsychiatry. Like lines, surfaces, and folds, like one-, two-, and three-dimensional topologies, the Möbius strip is generated from the *punctus,* and it de-generates (implodes) back into the *punctus.* But with a very crucial distinction. Along the surface, "inside" and "outside," one and the other, or the digital 0/1 do no more than oscillate interminably, as one navigates through conceptual space.

As to space, Renaissance painters employed the technique of linear perspective, the vanishing point, the convergent vision, as a window to the world, which aided in initiating the eye into the diaphanous zone of objectivity such that the observing subject was presumably a neutral spectator, removed from the clutter and helter-skelter of things (see Romanyshyn 1989; Rotman 1987). In fact, since the Renaissance, space has been prioritized, which ultimately served to spatialize time. This was quite a radical turnabout. Today, in the postmodern age, Bergsonian "deep time," the time of Marcel Proust and Thomas Mann, "seems radically irrelevant to our contemporary experience, which is one of a perpetual spatial present" (Stephanson 1988, 6). Jameson, one of the chief proponents of hyperspace—postmodern spatialization having replaced classical temporalization—argues that on the contemporary scene, categories tend to become spatial: structuralism and poststructuralism generally privilege space over time; the mathematical concept of mapping has been popularized; models—outside the hard sciences—are more picturable than formal or temporal; and conceptions of language, institutions, and power are defined in terms of hierarchies, constructs, and other spatial relations. Just as hyperspace enters the scene when discernible things are dissolved into simulacra, the relations between things vanish. Clear-cut body/mind, subject/object, inside/outside, "real"/"unreal," fact/fiction, science/nonscience distinctions have consequently become nebulous (Stephanson 1988, 7).

I would qualify both Baudrillard's implosion and Jameson's hyperspace as "time-space compression," following David Harvey's (1989, 284–307) provocative thesis. Acceleration of the pace of life in contemporary capitalist societies has revolutionized the objective and subjective qualities of space and time such that we are forced to alter radically how we re-present our semiotically real world to ourselves. This compression has inevitably produced a sense of the world collapsing in on us, as information is transmitted in near simultaneity, and spatial environments from diverse parts of the world and from other times are reconstructed wherever and whenever. The "global village" of telecommunications and the increasingly more diminutive "spaceship earth" tend to reduce temporal and spatial horizons to a space-time point where everything is there all at once. Jameson says, "Time has become a perpetual present and thus spatial. Our relationship to the past is now a spatial one" (cited in Stephanson 1988, 6).

In fact, Baudrillard (1988b) sees the United States as a society so infatuated with spatiality in the form of speed, motion, rapidly altered TV and cinematic images—a "logic of subliminity," as Jameson puts it—throw-away commodities, and technological gadgetry that it has created a crisis of explanatory adequacy. How can one account, we are asked, for disconnectedness and fragmentation, the triumph of effects over causes, the priority of surface over the depth of desire, the instantaneity of time? How can one describe a violent whirlpool of change that immediately writes off what is written, that muffles what is said into silence and disallows both security and certainty?

Jameson (1988, 351) views these spatial peculiarities, the hyperspace of postmodernism, as

> symptoms and expressions of a new and historically original dilemma, one that involves our insertion as individual subjects into a multidimensional set of radical discontinuous realities, whose frames range from the still surviving spaces of bourgeois private life all the way to the unimaginable decentering of global capitalism itself. Not even Einsteinian relativity, or the multiple subjective worlds of the older modernists is capable of giving any adequate figuration to this process, which in lived experience makes itself felt by the so-called death of the subject, or, more exactly, the fragmented and schizophrenic decentering and dispersion of this last.

It appears that the spatialization of time that Jameson addresses, this timeless symptom, this schizophrenic digital oscillation between the *either* and the *or,* is completely devoid of any assuring Sartrean-existentialist sense of history, of the comfort offered us by the philosophers of process, including Peirce, Bergson, James, and Whitehead. Becoming seems to be a vanished dream, and being is sucked into the unruly sea of Baudrillardian simulacra. The fluid legato of Newtonian motion is displaced by a staccato of quantum fits and jerks; homogeneous space has given ground to heterogeneous lumps, crevices, and jagged edges. The only possible responses are a reduction of knowledge and meaning to a digital sequence of disconnected signifiers, a delirious play in the text of the world, and either a denial of the whole complex mess altogether or an attempt to ride out the storm of time-space compression while engaging in a frivolous *ars combinatoria:* successive permutations of what is at hand (Harvey 1989, 350–52).

However, the forecast need not be so bleak. Our contemporary scene is perhaps the natural outcome of a collective effort to empathize—*pace* Comfort—with the world model emerging out of relativity, quantum theory, chaos physics, the physics of complexity, and the new biology. Take, for example, relativity—since it is most closely tied to the spatiality of time—though its astonishing implications were largely ignored until recently. In the first place, the space of general relativity to which Jameson refers is non-Euclidean; and in the second place, time is relative to a particular frame of reference, which dissolves when injected into the combination of all possible frames of reference. So, it might appear, time is either indefinitely variable, or it is nothing at all.

But to end things on this note would be premature—the space-time wedding has yet to be properly consummated, as evidenced by the efforts of Bohm, Prigogine, Wheeler, and others to bring about an alliance between relativity and quantum theory. As early as 1921, Weyl hinted at the possibilities presented by a non-Euclidean approach to a block universe. He was one of the first to reveal that in non-Euclidean topology it is possible "for the (light) cone of the active future to overlap with that of the passive past; so that, in principle, it is possible to experience events now that will in part be an effect of my future resolves and actions" (Weyl 1921, 274). Significantly, Weyl's speculation follows from his considering a topology with one-sided properties: the Möbius strip, where inside and outside, top and bottom, left and right, two-dimensional space and three-dimensional space, merge, as with Baudrillard's Möbius-spiraling precessional conic metaphor.

Equally significantly, the Möbius strip is a topological model of hyperspace. The strip contains no harmonious, homogeneous Euclidean spatiality. Any point on one "side" can be paired with a corresponding point on the other "side." Although the two points are insulated from one another in the purely topological space of two dimensions along the ring, from our three-dimensional gaze, we can match them. They twist or dissolve into each other in the "higher" dimension; they become as one in a particle-wave, yin-yang embrace. Our existential grasp of space converts discontinuities into continuities, distinctions into similarities and even identities, dissonances into compatibilities: the strip is an infinitely interconnected topology. And so it is a metaphor of time spatialized—recall the imaginary and complex time dimensions in Chapter Eight.

Thus the import of Baudrillard's Möbius metaphor becomes clear. It is a matter not so much of Jameson's insertion of the individual subject "into a multi-dimensional set of radical discontinuous realities" but rather, as demonstrated in previous chapters, of the radical interconnectedness of everything in what *appear to be* radically discontinuous "realities" (see Merrell 1991a). If hyperspatiality there be, it is a multiply related, infinitely pliable, tangled, knotted, diverging, converging, involuted, convoluted, jungle of signs now pressing forward, now backpedaling, now reentering their own spatiality. True to this image of Möbius hyperspatiality, Baudrillard's three stages of simulacra advance from analogy and reflection of the "real" to equivalence or indifference to the sign and nothing but the sign, from masking "reality" to masking the absence of "reality" to dissolving all relationship with "reality." The first stage is *replica,* a folding back, a close reproduction or facsimile; the second is an image or representation of "reality" that, over time, becomes perceived and conceived as tantamount to the "real"; and the third is pure simulation, mere sham, reflection, shadow, where all things are flattened to the same level.

In order to qualify these three stages more properly, let us take art as an example. From the time of Plato, naive aestheticists have assumed that the ultimate goal of art is to imitate "reality." Beginning with postmodernism— such as Warhol's Brillo pads and Campbell's soup cans—and especially over the past two decades, certain artists have taken this assumption at face value, yielding to the temptation to create exact copies of everyday items of experi- ence—ceramic books, boxes, plumbing fixtures, Dixie cups, and suitcases. Extreme examples are Daniel Dowke's cardboard box bottom that looks ex- actly like a piece of cardboard hanging on the wall and John DeAndrea's and Duane Hanson's convincing replicas of guards and other ordinarily dressed people one would expect to see in a gallery, or their "Art from the Earth" (a few square yards of soil in minute detail) (see Fisher 1990). Only recently, with the exception of trompe l'oeil paintings, have such obvious counterfeits been re- garded as works of art. This so-called art has been loaded down with various modifiers such as "photo-," "super-," "hyper-," and "perfect-realism."[7]

To be sure, the work of "perfect-realism" is an object that is not really "real." In a manner of speaking, it is an illusion of the "real" object, which, one might contend, makes it art. But Macbeth's dagger was supposedly an illusion, though not art; while Zeuxis's grapes are art, and yet an illusion. And Magritte's nonpipe pipe is art revealing the illusion for what it is; hence does it not sepa- rate art from illusion? Where is the line of demarcation? Perhaps it could be said that a counterfeit object is a mere copy of a token, whether that token is a work of art or something "real"; while a replica need not reduplicate any par- ticular token but a type, hence it is a re-creation possibly consisting of the combination of many tokens of the type to which they belong. In this sense, the replicative, "perfectly real" artwork is an arrangement that could easily be taken for the "real" article. In fact, its creator intended that it be so taken, yet it is not "real." The replica is constructed deliberately to fool the eye, and at the same time it is deliberately constructed to be viewed as art when properly contextualized (Fisher 1990). So it must be seen *as* "real" and at the same time *as* art. The onlooker tends to be fooled by the remarkable likeness, but she must realize that it is illusory. In order that she properly view the work, her percep- tion must be booted to the next level, which includes conception as outlined in Chapter Two: she must see *that* the work is *as if* "real," though it is not "real"— the same oscillation of conceptual categories demanded by Magritte's painting. There is thus a glut of contradictory information.

269

Goodman (1976, 131–32) argues that notations—marks, inscriptions, glyphs, letters, ideograms, and auditory distinctive features such as phonemes or notes of music—when reduplicated, can be freely exchanged for one another without any effect on the syntactic arrangement and virtually no change in semantic values, while disjointedness and differentiation are the requirements for distinct notations. The instantiation of a token represents a type, and "true copies" or "replicas" of that token can stand in for the original token without causing any disruption. A necessary condition for replication of a token, then, is character indifference, for a sense of identity must be preserved. At this point, however, we are still short of Baudrillard's third phase of simulacra, with respect to which I turn to Eco (1984, 202–26), who asks whether a mirror image is a sign, and responds with an emphatic no.[8]

Eco grounds his response in the mirror image's inability to pass the entrance examination into the venerable Academy of Signhood. Briefly, a mirror image, unlike a sign, cannot refer back to an absent object; is causally and determinately produced; cannot be used to lie; must refer to the entire content of the object; is incapable of establishing a relationship with a type but only to a token of which it is an image; cannot enjoy independence of its medium or channel; and cannot be interpreted in isolation from its object. According to Eco, if mimetic art at its best were a simple mirroring of the world, then art would not be endowed with semiotic qualities. Actually, the work of art indexically points to something else, whether it be another work or some semiotically real object. This is, in terms of Eco's semiotic imperative, a referring back. Such reference is not causally determined. It is as if the sign were a lie—a lie that the beholder must properly decipher, for if not, she is caught up in the quandary inherent in the bird's-eye view of Zeuxis's grapes.[9] Moreover, a sign's referring back always produces an incomplete portrayal. Though the sign can refer to a type, its artistic value must remain partly independent of the medium it employs, yet, unlike a mirror image, it can always be interpreted in terms of its self-containment, its self-sufficiency.

Elsewhere, Eco (1990, 188) asks whether a fake is a sign, suggesting that if it is related to the original by lines of similarity, it is at least an icon. But, he continues, a fake is put forth with the intention of its being mistaken for the original, in which case the fake ideally reproduces, in the mind of its contemplator, the whole of the original's properties. In such case, it would be a "completely iconic sign," in Morris's (1946, 17) words.[10] But complete iconism is tantamount to Leibnizian indiscernibility, while a bogus icon is only an alleged identity, hence it must be incompletely iconic, if only by the fact that it is not the original, even though both share identical properties. As such, a fake is a sign only insofar as nobody perceives it as something standing for something else to someone in some capacity, and hence everybody would mistake it for the original. It would, nevertheless, be a sign, in view of previous chapters in this inquiry: a radically de-generate sign, a pure icon coterminous with the "real" thing, the authentic signness of the sign having become embedded. It has centripetalated from an iconic representamen as Thirdness to a pure icon, a self-contained monad representing itself and nothing but itself.

Thus mirror images and fakes that manage to fake out their victims appear to be the Ecoan counterpart to Baudrillardian simulacra. The mirror image's incapacity to refer back, to lie, to separate itself from its medium or from its object, characterizes Baudrillard's simulacra, which consist of referenceless signs. And the fake passed off as "real" has become charged with the "hyperreality" intended by the sign producer, while the consumer fails to interpret it as she should ordinarily interpret a sign. In both cases, what is un-real trades its sham wardrobe in for "real" apparel and parades around in ec-static ignorance of the purpose for which the "real" thing was originally put to use. 271

In other words, any aspect of the "real" put to use for some purpose or other by that mere fact becomes semiotically real. It is not that signs, in Baudrillard's view, have displaced the "real," as Borges's planet Tlön displaced and became the earth; rather, different signs are put to use, one semiotic reality becomes another one, and computer thought takes over traditional discourse. The upshot is that whatever semiotic reality we are in is the order of the day, for tomorrow will find us elsewhere. That is, there was never any Baudrillardian "real" in the first place for us, only particular semiotically real domains. Baudrillard's idea of the "real" consists of unwelcome leftovers from positivism's dark and drab banquet of unambiguous signs, properly marinated in the acid of formal language: futile dreams, dismal nostalgia. Thus far it appears that, when placed beside Wheeler and Peirce, Baudrillard's cybernetic vision is embar-rassingly shallow.

Let us try again, then.

Balance: The Balm That Never Was

In *The Ecstasy of Communication* (1988a, 79), Baudrillard writes that simulacra, on passing from the second order to the third order, have brought about a trans-formation from the "dialectic of alienation" to the "giddiness of transparency." The world of alienation at least afforded the surety of a private "inner" world and the public "outer" world, of self and other. This is the world of the detached spectator, a world of surface appearance and depth "reality," of the marvelous, the mysterious, the sublime and divine. There has been an abrupt turnabout in the postmodern world: *"We no longer partake of the drama of alienation, but are in the ecstasy of communication"* (Baudrillard 1988a, 22).

This grave new world is no longer a system of objects. Or better, the object has become a crystal: transparent, everything as surface phenomena, there to be seen by anyone. And the modern subject as the locus of desire, freedom, transgression, and active resistance has become an equally transparent subject of inertia, indifference, conformity, silence, willing servitude. Formerly, "we were haunted by the fear of resembling others, of losing ourselves in a crowd; afraid of conformity, and obsessed with difference. Today, we need a solution to deliver us from resembling others" (Baudrillard 1988a, 40–41). Interchangeability of subjects raises the spectre of transparency in conjunction with the indifference of objects. Simulacra have become equal the world over; value has retreated into the blind alleys; differentiation has reached the nth degree, thus becoming tantamount to continuity. One point is the same as all points, along the line, the sheet, the cube, the hypercube. Balance now rules, for everything consists of symmetrical sameness: pure tedium.

According to modernist preferences and prejudices, we are told, it was important that the artwork in a museum is the original, not a reproduction. Fordist mass production has changed all that. Signs become signs whose indiscernible tokens are interchangeable and can be indefinitely reproduced according to their type. One Warhol soup can or another, one Marilyn Monroe or another: what difference does it make? In museums, original (or fake) works are methodically placed in meticulously reproduced "original" environments, and the onlookers are not concerned over what is "real" and what is not. In zoos "original" animals are given fake habitats that are "real" or more "real"—for us, not them, we must suppose—than that to which their kin are accustomed in Africa, Australia, or Brazil. Baudrillard (1988a, 30–31) recalls a hyperrealist exhibition at Beaubourg

> of flesh-colored, absolutely realistic and naked sculptures, or rather mannequins in unequivocal, banal positions. . . . The reaction of the people was interesting. They leaned over to see something, to look at the texture of the skin, the pubic hair, everything, but there was nothing to see. Some even wanted to touch the bodies to test their reality, but of course that didn't work because everything was already there. The exhibition did not even fool the eye. When one has been visually deceived one takes pleasure in guessing, and even if there is no intent to deceive, to fool, the aesthetic and tactile pleasure produced by certain forms involves a kind of divination. . . . Not even a trace of illusion remains underneath the veracity of the hair.

There is nothing but transparency, technique. No trace of illusion remains beneath the veracity of the surface. It is but a hallucinatory resemblance, an image—or nonimage, as it were—for there is nothing (no-thing) to meet the eye as a sign standing for something to someone in some respect. Like the pure icon, it does not refer to or re-present, nor does it even resemble, anything but itself: it simply *is as it is.* "Giddiness" overtakes those who passively gape at this apparently pure presence in awe, this thing that hides nothing, occupying a shallow space that is at the same time somehow empty. There is no oscillation, according to Baudrillard, between the artistic object qua object and its image, which is not what it represents itself to be. There isn't even any negativity, in the sense of my above comments on perfectly realist art. Nor is there any willing suspension of disbelief, for, like sign processing as a result of knowing *how* and seeing *that,* what is there is all there is, clearly and simply.

In other words, the third-order simulacra of transparency are no longer those of a symbolic order requiring a subject and discourse, with its concomitant arbitrary rules of the game. On the contrary. The game now being played out, an *ars combinatoria* of indiscernibles and quasi-indiscernibles, "is the game of reversibility. It is no longer the desire of the subject, but the destiny of the object, which is at the center of the world" (Baudrillard 1988a, 80). The transformation has been from meaning to information to transparency, from irreversibility to reversibility, from transitivity to reflexivity, from temporality to spatiality. The sign standing in a presumed natural relation to the thing signified is no more. Baudrillard (1988a, 103), as would be expected, concludes *The Ecstasy of Communication* on a dire note:

> And what if reality dissolved before our very eyes? Not into nothingness, but into the more real than real (the triumph of simulacra)? What if the modern universe of communication, of hyper-communication, had plunged us, not into the senseless, but into a tremendous saturation of meaning entirely consumed by its success . . . ?

Yes, what if?

In spite of Baudrillard's slapping the label of reversibility onto the hollow age of simulation—giving rise to atemporality, hyperreality, everything *now,* the "myth of presence"—he apparently implies that the passage from phase-one to phase-three simulacra is an accomplished fact, a singular happening once and forever. Phase one was the grand era of ritual, myth, a mystique of the word. Phase two, which coincided with modernity, separated the sign from its referent, establishing more formal *relata* of abstraction between them—the sign as arbitrary, a tool of reason, having no inherent connection with the meanings it evoked or the things to which it pointed. Yet the modern mind was still confident enough in the sign's power of representation. The link between sign and thing was undeniably shattered with the final phase, we are told. Signs became signs merely of themselves, the hyperreal hyperbolized. And we are thus prepared for the end of history, the individual having been dissolved into the collective mass of humanity. This must be the case, writes Baudrillard, for mass media have neutralized the world—our semiotic world—canceling the possibility of our formulating creative responses to the tide of simulacra that engulfs us, annihilating meaning so as to prohibit our placing in question the contemporary deluge of hollow signs masquerading as "real," the only "reality" with which we, in our inability to differentiate the reigning indifference, can be acquainted.

274   However, it is not merely, Hutcheon (1988a, 132–33) reveals, that meaning and reference have ceased to exist. We cannot—yet, at least—initiate a chant over the demise of the "real" and of the sign as mere sign. Baudrillard's plunge into the seething mass of denuded signs is not that obstinate entropic push toward a lifeless, totally undifferentiated universe of atemporal reversibility. We have not simply dozed off and now find ourselves in a state of soporific bliss, having relegated the problematics of the past to forgetfulness. Life is not so effortless as all that. To be sure, Baudrillard envisions a state free of tension between the pleasure and the reality principles. But actually, according to the new physics of complexity, there must always be tension: conflict, not balance and harmony; dissymmetry, not symmetry; far-from-equilibrium, not equilibrium; irreversibility, not reversibility; a not-quite-exact return with each and every recursive cycle; dissipative structures, fluctuations, perturbations, bifurcations, catastrophes, and fuzzy fractals. Baudrillard himself pays lip service to so much, though the message seems not to have taken effect. If, as he writes, the sign has emancipated itself from the "'archaic' obligation it might have had to designate something" and is "at last free for a structural or combinatory play that succeeds the previous role of determinate equivalence," it does not necessarily follow that these signs, which are now presumably enjoying a life of their own, do not continue to interact with us reciprocally, in good Peircean dialogic fashion, which is in essence a sign-interpreter-interpretant interaction more than a sign-sign interaction (Baudrillard 1984, 54).[11]

For example, Magritte's nonpipe pipe is a model presupposing an original, or an original presupposing a model—prioritization is not clear here. It is a simulacrum that denies its ontologic and a proposition that denies its subject-predicate logic. Yet it is an embodiment of the most rigorous hyperlogic imaginable: a resemblance and a proposition indefinitely oscillating between what *is* and what *is not,* ranging across the depthless canvas, eliminating the original, and offering itself up as a model, which forces a reorientation of sentiment (Firstness), perception (Secondness), and intellection (Thirdness). While modernism was obsessed with thinking the unthinkable and directly perceiving what there *is,* postmodernism is engaged in unthinking thinking and perceiving no more than what *might be.* The modernist move thought it could gravitate toward immediacy, toward Firstness, in the name of *episteme*. Postmodernism, rather than constituting stolid acquiescence, as Baudrillard would have it, reverses—or should reverse—the equation. It should project out from the merely possible to an incessant questioning of any and all efforts to legitimize, authenticate, validate, constitute, reify. Postmodern life is not a meaningless surface open to the phlegmatic, passive contemplator. Rather, in the Peircean sense of there being no indubitable knowledge and no innocent eye, it engages—that is, should engage—in self-reflective, self-conscious criticism, whether it be discursively or through action, by words or by deed, in science or in art.   275

Beyond Dyadophilia

According to Baudrillard, the great simulacra of the West have evolved from "a universe of natural laws to one of force and tensions, and finally, today, to a universe of structures and binary oppositions." The metaphysical isomorphism of this transition is from being and appearance to energy, and from determination to "indeterminacy and the code" (Baudrillard 1988b, 139). Digitality, Leibniz's mystical system of zeros and ones, and DNA, the genesis of simulacra, have finally come into their own, we are told. Following Monod, Baudrillard (1988b, 140) writes:

> Dialectical evolution is over. Now it is the discontinuous indeterminism of the genetic code that regulates life—the *teleonomic* principle. Finality is no longer located at the conclusion; indeed, there is no end, and no determination. The finalities are established in advance, inscribed in the code. In a way, things have not really changed. The system of ends has only ceded to the play of molecules, as has the order of signifieds to the play of infinitesimal signifiers reduced to aleatory commutation.

Digitality has presumably overtaken the world. From the most insignificant disjunctive unities (question/answer, stimulus/response) to the molar systems of alternation that preside over social, political, and economic affairs, and upward to global coexistence, the matrix remains invariant: it is always the binary scansion that self-sufficiently confirms itself as a metastable homeostatic system. Throughout it all, simulations dominate, from the play of differences to polyvalent modes to identity, all of which often come in pairs: the World Trade Center in New York City is Baudrillard's prototype. And it goes on and on.

From a certain modern perspective it might appear that Baudrillard is in tune with the times. Biological reductionists sought an organism-independent theory of organisms; Noam Chomsky, a language-independent theory of language; Lévi-Strauss, a culture-independent theory of culture; and philosophers, a transcendental, knowledge-independent theory of knowledge. These grand designs evoke the image of mathematician David Hilbert's project to found mathematics in a mathematics-independent—i.e., logical—base, which was shattered by Gödel and others. Now we have Baudrillard, who presumably stands beyond simulacra—apparently he thinks he is somehow not caught up in the swamp of freewheeling signs like the rest of us—outside the homogeneous mess, and above a society that has already "transgressed everything," that has already "really gone beyond" (Baudrillard 1990, 71). Baudrillard apparently believes he enjoys a simulacra-independent view of simulacra. Complexity is reduced to the most simple of simples, which, given its very complexity, cannot be fathomed except by Baudrillard's omniscient eye and mind.

But something is amiss in this Leibnizian intoxication, this hyper-Boolean frenzy, this infatuation with computer thought and computerese. It is not actually consonant with the times, for from quantum theory to Prigogine's order out of chaos, Mandelbrot's fractals, and chaos physics, the watchwords are rapidly becoming "non-Boolean," "nonlinear," "dissymmetry," and "irreversibility." This observation applies also to contemporary mind-sets in physiology (after reductionism), linguistics (after Chomskyan algorithmic imperatives), anthropology (after Lévi-Strauss's binary biases), and philosophy (after Cartesian self-help programs). It has even infiltrated AI studies, where researchers are now trying to teach computers soft-minded human frailties such as forgetfulness, fuzzy logic, faulty inferences, and vague images (Campbell 1989). The obvious problem here is that my own critique is itself binary in nature: the postmodern spirit against its decadent predecessor, non-Booleanism against Booleanism, nonlinearity against linearity, and so on. So to save face I must more adequately qualify myself.

Let me begin at the lowest possible point and try to work up. Spencer-Brown, whose work lies at the heart of the rhizome metaphor outlined in Chapter Six, develops, in addition to number, which is traditionally assumed to consist of positive, negative, and zero, another term, "imaginary value"—symbolized by i ($+\sqrt{-1}$, $-\sqrt{-1}$). He demonstrates how the implications of this term are profound in the fields of mathematics, logic, philosophy, and even physics. The imaginary is not zero, nor is it either negative or positive but rather both and neither. It stands between zero—Peirce's "nothingness"—and the mark (or cut). The mark would be the equivalent of the prioritized term, in contrast to the other term according to semiological binarism, which produces marked/unmarked or cut/uncut. Thus from the domain of nothingness there emerges a mark of positive value, implying its mirror image, the unmarked, of negative value. The former is unfolded from the enfolded, a boundary extracted from the unboundaried, a cipher generated from zero. The latter's very existence depends upon the former, and at the same time the former cannot exist without the latter. In order that the mark take on value, there must be acknowledgment of that which it *is not*—an oscillatory pattern. This is the hyperlogic of Magritte's nonpipe pipe: a resemblance and a proposition oscillating between what *is* and what *is not,* a Firstness that tries but cannot quite become Secondness, a Secondness that cannot make up its mind.

Thus, in order that I might not remain entirely false to myself, I must show that the virgule is, in the final analysis, fuzzy. I do so by evoking Varela's (1975) work, who, following from the marked/unmarked or cut/uncut binaries, and in addition to the concept of nothingness, or 0, introduces what he calls a "re-entry" of the Spencer-Brownian form into itself. Varela (1975, 19) suggests that "re-entry," which is derived from Spencer-Brown's imaginary value, is "a self-referential autonomous state which . . . *cannot* be reduced to the laws of the dual domains [of binarism]. If we do not incorporate this . . . domain [of re-entry] explicitly into our field of view, we force ourselves to find ways to avoid it (as has been traditional) and to confront it, when it appears, in paradoxical form." Varela demonstrates that the imaginary value can be reduced to a Boolean oscillation between the *either* and the *or,* but when it reenters itself, its own space, it departs from Booleanism and serves as a basis for a more general form of logic—in Peircean terms, a logic of self-contained Firstness.

Of course, when our natural language of daily affairs reenters its own syntactic and semantic space—becomes self-referential—paradox often raises its ugly Hydra head. This flies in the face of our perennial demand for clear and distinct ideas, for certain and indubitable knowledge. It was the original Platonists, we will recall, who generalized ethical imperatives for certainty into epistemological desires with the rule that knowledge must be given explicit definitions applicable by anybody. What could not be stated outright—intuition, sentiment, knowing *how*—was condemned to the secondary status of belief. However, Plato was not interested exclusively in syntactic (arbitrary, cybernetic, context-free, binary) criteria but also in semantics—which might help account for the aborted Platonist dream of rendering all knowledge explicit, irrespective of contexts and styles of reasoning.

Now Platonism, to be sure, is a lovely ideal. Modern science, following Galileo, did Platonism one better, however. By brushing secondary qualities aside, it would presumably be possible to describe the physical universe in purely formal terms. By extension, "computer thought," upon eliminating all semantic considerations, could introduce purely syntactic (formal) accounts. The faith that such an abstract formulation was possible "came to dominate Western thought, both because it corresponded to a basic moral and intellectual demand and because the success of physical science seemed to imply to sixteenth century philosophers . . . that the demand could be satisfied" (Dreyfus

1971, 106). Leibniz, of course, played hard and fast in his effort to bring the dream to fruition. And the dream has been self-perpetuating. More than twenty years ago, Hubert Dreyfus (1971, 106–7) viewed the scene with considerable trepidation:

> Leibniz only had promises, but now it seems the digital computer has realized his dream and thus Plato's demand. The computer operates according to syntactic rules, on uninterpreted, determinate bits of data, so that there is no question of rules for applying rules; no question of interpretation; no appeal to human intuition and judgment. It is thus entirely appropriate that in his UNESCO address [Heidegger 1969] Heidegger cites cybernetics (not, as formerly, the atom bomb) as the culmination of philosophy.

Nevertheless, Dreyfus has argued vehemently since that time—forging a healthy career for himself in the process—that philosophy and AI studies today are as far from their goal as they ever were.

But actually, insight into the shortcomings of all grand designs pointing toward totalization can be found closer to home, in the mathematicians' own playpens, and using the chess-game analogy to which Saussurean linguistics and Wittgensteinian language games owe a debt. The formal (syntactic) method calls for: an initial list of *abstract symbols* (red and black squares and red and white chess pieces); *formation* (syntactic) *rules* (the arrangement of squares on the board and the limit of one piece per square); *initial formulas* (the beginning array of pieces on the board); and *transformation rules* (for manipulating the pieces). The theorems then correspond to the set of configurations on the board after the game has begun (DeLong 1970, 92–94).

In the spirit of modernist exigencies for control and absolute knowledge, it would appear that all semantic considerations of the chess game (appeal to meanings) are eschewed to make way for purely syntactic (formal) constructs—i.e., chess moves as group operations (Chomskyan generative grammar). As such the game is purely binary, purely a play of Secondness devoid of the equivalent of Firstness (intuition) and Thirdness (interpretation).[12] In order to endow the system with an interpretation, consideration must be given to a set of symbols defined outside the formal system in question. Meanings can then be assigned them in such a manner that the initial formulas—which are now axioms—become true of the new symbols. This set of symbols now becomes a model for the system (with the attendant problems of metalanguages, contradictions, and paradoxes such as the infinite regress of maps within maps). Choice of the model, which is derived from foreign symbols injected into the system, inevitably depends upon a greater or lesser degree of intuition, inclination, preferences, and taste (DeLong 1970, 223–29). Regarding mathematical systems—and, by extension, less formal systems—proof of a particular proposition can be forthcoming by showing

> that such-and-such a formula is a theorem in such-and-such a formal system with such-and-such initial formulas and such-and-such undefined terms using such-and-such transformation rules; and that upon interpretation in such-and-such a specified way, the formula expresses the proposition in question, the initial formulas become axioms accepted by the individual, and the transformation rules become rules of inference similarly accepted by the individual. The proposition is then proved. (DeLong 1970, 93)

279

Thus questions of proof depend upon questions of the acceptability of interpretations. And regarding acceptability, arguments are never final; consensus is always at least a step away, as Peirce tells us. Of course, the chess model of Saussurean linguistics and Wittgensteinian language games is informal and lacks the rigor of mathematics. The same can be said for the "universe ≈ machine" and other metaphor-models. Nevertheless, like mathematics, all metaphors and models must perpetually bring interpretation (interpreter-interpretant interaction) to the fore, which requires self-reflexive, self-returning, self-referential acts of signification, which constantly threaten to end in contradiction, if not out-and-out paradox. This we now know from the limitative theorems, Heisenbergian uncertainty, Bohrian complementarity, and from other circles, whether hermeneutic or otherwise, and whether vicious or virtuous.

Varela, strangely enough, claims to have surmounted this obstacle. He argues that the initiatory, primitive "form," having separated itself from the void, can now, by reentering its own space, maintain a sort of autonomy with respect to its environment, which cancels the necessity of any intercession by outside forms, symbols, or axioms. Hence the paradox of self-reflexive reentry is benign rather than malignant; in fact, Varela tells us that it is entirely vanquished by life's processes—which is somewhat like Peirce's contention that experience overcomes Zeno's formal argument. An individual cell, for example, maintains a Spencer-Brownian distinction between the marked (itself) and the unmarked (everything else), between *this* and *that, inside* and *outside, here* and *there*—binaries all. Yet it is not an island unto itself, not absolutely autonomous. It is open to, and in perpetual interaction with, its surroundings—though it is autonomous and self-sufficient insofar as it contains, within itself, the symbols, rules, and primitive axioms generating the formulas necessary for its survival. Consequently, it exists in a far-from-equilibrium state of dissonance, asymmetry, imbalance, and it constantly expels negentropy in order to sustain life. Thus the cell (representamen-sign) is both producer (interpreter) and produced (interpretant). And when it divides, it is a form reentering its own self and in the process creating a replica (object) of itself. But this reentry is not exactly self-referential in the Gödelian sense: it is merely reentry. And a certain increment of time was necessarily involved—created?—in the operation, making it much like the cycle on the Möbius strip: along the strip, a cipher, upon completion of a 360-degree journey, becomes its enantiomorphic twin, and after repeating the trip, it reenters its own space to become itself. This unfolding and enfolding necessarily occurs in time—a reiterative process that can continue ad infinitum. It also suggests the possibility for constructing self-identity—that is, quiddities from haecceities, the incessant *semiosic* push toward generality.

Over time, the cell can thus be defined as the production of production of production of itself, which further accounts for the recursive self-returning arrows surrounding each sign type in figure 7. In this fashion, the sign determines an interpretant, which becomes the sign; and the interpreter, which is the necessary agent (operant) of the act of reentry, is itself a sign (interpretant) interpreting (reentering) itself while at the same time enabling itself to realize its fullness as a sign on the road toward its becoming enshrouded with a final interpretant—the ultimate stage of generality. By the same token, our interpretations—from the low-level oscillator examples given in the Necker cube to the most exacting of texts, to formal systems, and to the very text of the universe—cannot but be interpretations of interpretations of interpretations. Thus it is a matter not merely of semiologically stringent marked/unmarked values but, in addition, of constant mediation, through Thirdness.

In fact, we, as interpreter-interpretants, having marked the text off from what it *is not* and ourselves off from what we *are not* in our making of the text ourselves and of ourselves the text, repeatedly reenter the text, and hence we reenter our own selves, our own conceptual space. On this road from stark simplicity to numbing complexity—that same road which provides for increasing generality drawn from the sphere of vagueness—signs begin merging with signs in the flow, such that, in the final analysis, differentiation rather than distinction and ultimately, in certain subdomains, homogenization, begins to rule (Varela 1975, 21).

So perhaps, one might wish to conclude, Baudrillard has his head on straight after all. However, contrary to his conception of things, in our finite world there cannot be any gaseous state of random simulacral signs that, at large, are in homeostatic equilibrium. Rather, there is progressive differentiation punctuated with occasional catastrophes, with no end game in sight. This endows the system with increasing richness and increasing breadth, but at the same time with perpetual disharmony, tension, and imbalance. In fact, the introduction of the concepts of imaginary value and reentry, in addition to those of marked/unmarked and nothingness, extends binarism to trinarism, forcing an abandonment of *either-or* and *both-and* thought and inviting a tolerance for incompleteness and inconsistency. It is incompleteness because the sign, which is engaged in constant reentry, is with every recursion something other than what is was: it is a difference that makes a difference. And it is inconsistency because the sign's self-referential nature is tantamount to its saying of itself "I *am not* what I *am.*" The sign is and is not itself, like Magritte's nonpipe pipe. This is the semiotic equivalent of Gödel's self-denying sentence, which is ex- emplified in natural language by the Cretan quandary, "I am lying."

There is actually no calamity here, however. The absence of internal contradiction as a key to the secrets of the universe was the cornerstone of the Platonic edifice, and it presumably remained intact down through the heyday of empirical positivism. From Parmenides and Zeno on the one hand and Heraclitus on the other, we have been exposed to the notion that paralogisms and antinomies invariably foil all attempts to grasp the ultimate nature of the world. Hegel picked up on this view that "reality" is so wily, given its subtle changeability and its deceptive complexity, that all attempts at a comprehensive account of it are destined to end in paradox. Now, with quantum theory, the incomplete and inconsistent nature of the world we found has compelled scientists, logicians, and philosophers alike to look paradoxes in the eye without horror (in general, see Rescher and Brandom 1979).

Paradoxes appear freely, and we resolve them if possible, but if not, we can take playful delight in the insight they may afford, or we can merely ignore them. I speak of a tolerance for local inconsistencies. We cannot hope effectively to cope with global inconsistencies, nor should we even attempt, as does Jameson, to assume a totalizing grasp of the whole. Perhaps the best we can do is do the best we can do and hope for the best (Rorty 1989). After all, if the thesis I am presenting is of any value, sign systems, living systems, and self-consciousness itself are, with respect to their nature as self-reentering entities, sympathetically paradoxical. (And at this juncture, I would hope that the nonlinear, non-Boolean, context-dependent complementarity principles underlying this entire inquiry are taking on greater force.)

With further regard to self-reentering entities, Baudrillard's infatuation with DNA, his model *par excellence* of digitality, hyperinformation, hypercommunication—that is, the dominance of the code—rests on tenuous grounds. Codes and rules must be clarified. Just as the rules of chess define the game of chess, so linguistic rules define the game of language, and so also the rules of genetics define the game played out by DNA. These are not strict mechanisms of linear cause and effect—one element in the syntagmatic string making another one appear. On the contrary, the rules essentially leave the system open to nonlinear development, which always remains incomplete: it is not merely a matter of dice throws or the eternal return of incessant permutations; rather, novelty is the norm.

Such an unbounded system helps explain how an elaborate organism can spring forth from the information in a set of genes. The "text" is not simply read off along a one-dimensional length of the DNA chain but is expressed in various combinations by rules applied recursively to symbols, much like the rules of language governing the combination of words to make up a sentence potentially of infinite length and infinitely more complex than the set of rules or the alphabet composing it. The information content and meaning of a genetic "sentence" cannot be determined by counting the codons in a DNA string any more than a natural-language sentence can be understood by counting the number of words or looking up their meanings in the dictionary. The sentence is not a linear but a hierarchical structure of a potential infinity of nested clauses. DNA, therefore, is a protagonist on the multiply expansive stage of life, not a passenger in a train speeding along its linear fast track (Pattee 1972, 1977, 1986). It is, in short, like an aperiodical crystal striving for perfection without the wherewithal to achieve its chief goal in life.

Baudrillard, in spite of recent trends in mathematics, logic, and the natural sciences, remains captivated by Monod, for whom the universe is a vast probabilistic machine, a Cosmic Computer in which life has hardly any chance of existing. Nevertheless, by some strange quirk, we are told, it exists. It is a mere accident and does not follow directly from the laws of physics, yet it is compatible with them. Evolution is the product of a Cosmic Lottery, the Chairman of the Board is natural selection, and the rank-and-file workers blindly pick occasional winners from numbers drawn at random. Scientific inquirers, as a consequence, are expelled from the cosmos. They are gypsies, living at the margins of an alien world totally indifferent to their hopes and fears, their joys and sorrows. Knowledge, in fact, is their downfall, for in our times, "man knows at last that he is alone in the universe's unfeeling immensity, out of which he emerged only by chance. His destiny is nowhere spelled out, nor is his duty. The kingdom above and the darkness below; it is for him to choose" (Monod 1971, 180). This interpretation of DNA and its consequences is reductionism to the nth degree, certainly the scientific counterpart to high modernism. Monod is steeped both in modern scientific ideals and in the Cartesian tradition. It comes as a surprise, perhaps, that Baudrillard would develop his model of simulacra as Monodian aleatory permutations in the name of postmodernism, and that many observers of the postmodern scene set his works up as testimony to the demise of modernity. The connection is strained, if not ludicrous.

Prigogine, for example, soundly rejects Monod's reductionism. Prigogine's universe is not systematically built up from atomic structure culminating in complex biological organisms, with each successive level encompassing the preceding level like a series of Chinese boxes. It is not built solely from the bottom up but rather by nonlinear interaction and feedback at all levels, with none being able to lay claim to preeminence over any other. No laws or parts of the universe are necessarily any more fundamental than any other. On the contrary, there is an intricate network of laws, processes, and nonlinear cause-effect sequences at all levels of the interacting hierarchy. Moreover, nature's laws are not mechanical but creative, and, as with Wheeler—and Peirce—they evolve (Prigogine and Stengers 1984; Nicolis and Prigogine 1977, 1989).

    In contrast, Baudrillard's one-dimensional serial reduction of everyday life forces the image upon his reader of culture as a cybernetic machine and humans as passive information-processing automata, on the margin and alienated, like Monod's scientist. The individual is no individual at all but an electric conduit through which information networks pass. She has no control over the switch. Quite simply, the "on" button is automatically pushed when the channel is activated. She is a locus of stolid ecstasy, lethargic bliss, media instantaneity, meaningless transparency, and exposure to series after series of mind-stultifying simulacra. She is no interpreter interacting and collaborating with interpretants to generate interpretations of interpretations. She is merely a passive recipient, an object (Secondness) contiguous with other objects in a series parallel with the linear staccato of disembodied signs (Firsts).

    So much for Baudrillard's comatose binarism. Now for a further connection between his simulacral vision and AI.

A Tango for Three

Cybernetics: cyberspace, cyberblitz, cyberpunk, the strange world of glassy-eyed disheveled hackers, Maxwell demons of the megabytes, Turing machinations. These are some of the unrestrained images of cybernetics erroneously conjured up by novice aficionados when introduced to the euphoric, utopian pioneer work in AI.

    From another vantage point, cybernetics is also, we must remember, the last gasp of the mechanistic paradigm. So-called information theory in its inception was purely a mathematical expression, devoid of reference to the sensed world, and AI tends to be a reductionistic "nothing but" enterprise taking the computer to be an immature brain and the brain to be nothing more than today's computer after having advanced a few more links along the evolutionary chain.[13] The cult of information borrows heavily from the mystique of mathematics, presumably a clean kind of thinking unblemished by the messy ways of the world. Information traveling through the microchips acquires ironclad certainty, offering a peek into that crystalline, silicon-based Boolean utopia free of

283

the clutter and imperfections of life known to the organic world. It is not surprising, in this respect, that the "cool" digitality of Baudrillard's cyberuniverse—piloted, governed, and controlled by mechanical principles that maintain homeostatic balance, harmony, order—is viewed from the hot seat of semiological binarist idealism. It is all a matter of the permutability of signifiers (rearrangement of bits), of computability, of pure information.

If we take information theory literally, it boils down to a matter of messages without meaning, and hence without the possibility of interpretation. The strings "A rose is a rose is a rose," "Jesus saves," "$E = MC^2$," "John blocks that Mary's briskly," and "Colorless green ideas sleep furiously" are taken on an equal basis. They are context-free, and their information needs to be encoded for transmission through a channel connecting a source to a receiver, regardless of the semantic content. The strings, whether loaded with meaning or pure nonsense, can be equivalent regarding information theory's "information." Once they have been translated into bits, their qualitative differences are blurred. Clearly, the term "information" was extracted entirely from the context within which it was ordinarily used. It takes on strict mathematical precision, without which it would have no computational value. It is pure syntax (see Roszak 1986). Information transfer is thus no more than a matter of converting a rendition of a *Brandenburg Concerto* into radio waves and back into sound once more. It is like a superanalyst listening to a fugue not in terms of its aesthetic properties but as pure information according to probability equations derived from the musical script's recursive phenomena (much like Hofstadter's conception in *Gödel, Escher, Bach* [1979]). Sound quality is irrelevant; the analyst's task is merely an exercise in structure, composition, technique: there is no meaning, only "information." Admittedly, Baudrillard (1983b, 95) remarks that we are "in a universe where there is more and more information, and less and less meaning," though he does not, in my estimation, go far enough toward highlighting the distinction between "information," as he uses the term, and the change it has suffered in the high-tech computer world.

Another problem stems from Baudrillard's infatuation with DNA and his apparently indiscriminate reference to DNA in conjunction with AI. James Watson and Francis Crick's breaking of the genetic code unfortunately created the image of a tie-in between information theory and biology—thus providing grist for the AI mill. Initially this seemed to confirm Norbert Wiener's (1954) speculation regarding common ground between cybernetics and human beings. A DNA molecule, it was assumed, could be looked upon as a data-computing mechanism, as automation at the molecular level. Optimism had it in the 1960s that not merely the genes but also the brain could be programmed with Boolean "information"—e.g., John Lilly's (1967) human "biocomputer." More recently, as our computer age skips along in helter-skelter fashion, "information" has become a commodity to be consumed, thus threatening to absorb the material consumption of commodity capitalism. Armed with the proper chips and with binary bits merrily dancing in their heads, computer technicians are now mass-producing information the way Detroit once mass-produced cars. Unlike Peirce's concept of information outlined in Chapter Six, there is no more than the promise of context-free consistency, computation without innovation, symbols without value or meaning. God the Great Watchmaker has become God the Hoary Hacker.[14] In this spirit, a turn to human-machine interaction is appropriate, in order better to come to terms with Baudrillard's postmodern world.

285

Sherry Turkle (1984) cites numerous case studies involving human interaction with computers—most particularly video games and hacker play—concluding that a sense of the computer as just another toy gives way to a rather close, intimate feel for the images ("information") on the screen, which in turn gives way to a need to engage in a contest, to prove oneself against the machine, as if it were an opponent. Detachment becomes metaphysics, which is converted into a need to be master. We have, on the one hand, the action-reaction, cause-effect reversibility of pinball machines (Secondness), springing out of mere chance happenings (Firstness); and on the other, the possible—hyperreal?—informational worlds of video games (Thirdness), providing a temporary liberation from the "real world." In this programmed world, this abstract (hyper)space, there seem to be no bounds. Everything is apparently possible. Images flash in and out, gyrate and sporadically move about in Brownian randomness. The unexpected can always occur. And there is not only change but change of change; the game is cumulative, becoming faster paced and more complex as it proceeds.

One of Turkle's informants, Jarish, a twelve-year-old, remarks that when he is interacting with the game,

> you feel sort of cut off. When I play the game, I start getting into it, and you start taking the role of the person . . . and then the game ends. And you have just put all of your energy into it. It doesn't make me angry, more like depressed. You walk out of the arcade and it's a different world. Nothing that you can control. (Turkle 1984, 72)

"Nothing that you can control." This apparently inner need for mastery, common to children and adults—video game addicts and Hackers alike—is a far cry from the popular conception that video games (like TV) turn kids into zombies and adults into dopes and dupes. It is also a giant step removed from the neoaristocratic critique of mass culture as the unfortunate by-product of hyper-democracy—from José Ortega y Gasset's (1965) revolt of the barbarous masses to Guy Debord's (1977) *spectacle* as the caretaker of a somnolent public whose choices are already made by the logic of late capitalism to Daniel Boorstin's (1972) vision of free individuals who just happen to have chosen to live a life of illusion, of simulacra.[15]

According to Turkle's studies, human agents, in their interaction with machines, do not become processed cheese as a result of the omniscient force of modern technological communication. They are anything but passive. They are in their world—a simulated world, no doubt, but a world within which they can exercise a degree of dominion and establish their own parameters of jurisdiction. They engage in the task of empire building with the energy and enthusiasm of the most aggressive corporate executive. Human-machine interaction has been perhaps nowhere more evident than in the game Virtual Reality, which was developed by a throwback to the 1960s, Jaron Lanier, and recently placed on the market. Armed with an electronic glove, the player, by pointing, can enter a room, fly through the ceiling, cause objects to disappear, approach a dinosaur, drive a car, and much more. In the future, a player might be Luke Skywalker, Ronald Reagan, Scarlett O'Hara, Julius Caesar, or whoever. And she might be able to construct a bridge, fly to Mars, go swimming in the nude, or stalk a Bengal tiger. This is high-spirited involvement at its best . . . or perhaps worst, depending upon the ways of the user.[16]

In contrast to Turkle's active agent in a society pervaded by technological communication, Baudrillard's automatized, sterile masses passively tossed about in a sea of simulacra are hopeless, helpless, and faceless atoms among atoms within the aggregate. This frenzy of simulacra is a litany proclaiming death to *mimesis* (*mimetikos*) and everlasting life to *eidesis* (*eidetikos*) while grounding *kinesis* (*kinetikos*) on the sandbar of impossible dreams, given that

> [r]eality no longer has the time to take on the appearance of reality. It no longer surpasses even fiction: it captures every dream even before it takes on the appearance of a dream. Schizophrenic vertigo of these serial signs, for which no counterfeit, no sublimation is possible, immanent in their repetition—who could say what the reality is that these signs simulate? They no longer even repress anything (which is why, if you will, simulations pushes us close to the sphere of psychosis). Even the primary processes are abolished in them. (Baudrillard 1983b, 152)

Quite obviously, Baudrillard's signs are overwhelmingly visual, and if perchance verbal, they are most often accompanied by *eidola*. I am not speaking of the *eidola* (images, copies, representations) outlined by Plato as the distinction between kinesis and mimesis. Eidesis stands between them, neither as mediator nor as moderator but as mummifier, as inducer and displacement of the subject into a trance, *ecstasy* (*ekstasis*)—a pure, unmediated experience of floating signifiers.

These *hyper-eidola,* fleeting unsubstantial impressions on the eye, phantoms without form, meaningless messages made meaninglessly meaningful as a result of their displacement by the media, produce, we are told, a *"hallucinatory resemblance of the real with itself"* (Baudrillard 1983b, 142). Tyler's (1987, 171) statement that "seeing is always mediated by saying" thus becomes *there is nothing but unmediated seeing:* semiological binarist idealism to the hilt. There is, in this strange sphere of existence, neither sign-events nor thought-signs, neither re-presentation nor intellection, neither feeling nor volition, but merely automatism. Baudrillard seems to be saying that since the "hyperreal worlds" of cybernetic media, of pure binary-based information, have become the only "reality," and since it has succeeded in zombifying most of us—but Baudrillard himself remains somehow hyperimmune—our consumption of raw information is measured in terms of quantity, not quality; of data, not ideas; of what happens to be *there* (Secondness), not what *might be* (Firstness) or *would* or *could be* (Thirdness).

In contrast, Turkle's hackers and, to a degree, video game addicts strive to create their own parallel worlds in order to satisfy their will to power, but upon so doing, they also free themselves from the encumbrance of having to deal with people. Business executives, scientists, engineers, and even humanists do the same with spreadsheet manipulations, mock-ups, flow charts, diagrams, figures, and assorted graphics: simulations all. The simulated model, a crisp, obedient, predictable universe, cannot talk back, nor can it ask intimidating questions. But it can potentially force itself onto the mind to the extent that it is preferred over the "real" world. Therein lies the crux of simulacral "reality." Simulacra can become, and do become, I would suggest, the target of one's active escape from the "real," thus providing rejuvenation by the experience rather than their merely stupifying Baudrillard's "silent majority."

Simulation at its most abstract—and Baudrillard is often speaking of abstraction, of precision—consists of hypothetical constructs. It is "computer thought" applicable only to models, or at best, it consists of as-if hypostats to be used, then discarded in good Vaihingerian fashion. Computer simulations, in fact, hypersimplify to the extreme. If a simulation is used to recreate a scientific experiment, the result is a severe abstraction of the original. Like prescission taking a hypercube to a point, simulation might reveal no more than a caricature of that which it simulates—and is in this sense reminiscent of Jameson's "hyperspace." Actual flesh-and-blood scientific experiments present hits and misses, borderline cases, many intermediate stages, contradictory data, and concepts that, fuzzy in the beginning, usually suffer a quick death, with the few survivors taking on clarity only very gradually. With computer simulation, in contrast, there is rarely a shadow of a doubt. An image flashes on the screen, standing straight and tall, with all the clarity and distinction of a legitimate model of the world; but actually, it is no more than "a step away from the disorderly reality around us into the tidy fictions of the computer" (Roszak 1986, 70). In video game simulation, there is, during the give-and-take of the cybernetic world-play, interaction between the physical interpreter and the physi-

cal cybergenerator of signs. But, unfortunately, there may be little to no interaction between the player's own human culture and the forthcoming simulation culture, between slushy meaning and precise rule-driven meaning, between life's uncertain game and the simulated game of necessity. The video player enters an alternate world that may appear to hold little relevance to her semiotically real world "out there." In fact, the two worlds may even be radically incompatible, without recognized points of contact. As such, the simulation does not really simulate at all but enters into competition with the "real."

Thus Baudrillard's contention that simulation culture has absorbed the human culture we once knew is illusive. His third-order simulation culture is a digitalized realm of arbitrary, aleatory signs, while the fact is that the simulation world of "computer thought"—the triumph of nominalism, of binarism— is devoid of indeterminacy except that which has been programmed into the black box, and even then, the indeterminacy is built into the system with the most exacting precision. Whatever constraints there are in simulation culture are severely imposed by the rules of the system that do not necessarily have anything to do with physical reality, morals, ethics, or what the poststructuralist conceives to be a random play of floating signifiers. In the simulated world, everything is possible, yet nothing is left to mere chance, and the rules can rarely be broken at will.

If there is a danger in Baudrillard's notion of contemporary simulation society, like the danger inherent in human-computer interaction, it does not lie in the perils presented by mindless walks through life but in an unbridled, uncritical infatuation with the interaction itself. Baudrillard would call such mindlessness the "ecstasy of communication." But he propagates the idea of a passive, zombielike, almost catatonic ecstasy. In contrast, human-simulacra interaction is generally active; in fact, it is hyperactive, though the activity exists in another world, and the player must enter a somewhat altered state in order to play by the rules. Once having entered the world of simulacra, she is swept away and loses herself in the cataract of signs. A feeling of possession, even of omnipotence, and of manipulation punctuated by surrender may come over her. This need to control renders the computer age a hyperextension of modernity rather than a manifestation of postmodernism. Simulation worlds are more uppers than downers, they stimulate rather than sedate. And if they tend to homogenize their audience, the risk, whether from Baudrillard's view or the alternative presented here, lies in the audience, either because of its passive, ecstatic bliss or because of its bewitchment with the interaction for its own sake, which weakens its inclination toward criticism and self-criticism.

However, in the final analysis, and following from the discussion in chapters Four and Five, the issue at hand is a matter neither simply of modernism's emphasis on formalistic novelty (T. S. Eliot's "making things new") in the arts and unlimited progress in the material world nor of a laid-back pop culture envisioned by some postmodernists. The masses are neither strictly numbed consumers nor judicious citizens constantly at the voting booth determining what is worthy of their attention and what not. There are neither exclusively embedded behavior and uncontrollable responses nor conscious and conscientiously controlled de-embedment of all messages from the powers that be; neither de-generate signs as symptoms of the unthinking comings and goings of clapped-out somnambulists nor a jumble of bright-eyed signs pussy-footing around, dropping a hint of irony here, presenting a reshuffled deck there to create a new combination, and resolving a paradox somewhere else. *Semiosis* allows of no standard *either-or* choice but rather a combination of *both-and* approaches and an uncertain vacillation between alternatives. In both cases, criticism and self-criticism must be the order of the day. In view of the discussion regarding figure 10, when we consider two superposed alternatives, $a \times b$ is foregrounded; when we vacillate between alternatives, a/b is in effect. In whichever case, one sign or compound sign can be weighed against another in order to exercise an inferential judgment, a critical judgment. Only thus can signs be expected properly to *grow*.

Baudrillard, in contrast, sees things moving in one direction only, toward embedment, automatization, de-generacy. This equation is reversible, however: just as a hypercube can de-generate to a point, so also the point can generate back into a hypercube. But whereas Baudrillard sees the present age of simulacra in static, reflexive, symmetrical, nontransitive, reversible terms, in Peircean fashion, the two-way "generacy <-> de-generacy" system, though formally reversible, is always already something other than what it was in a creative, self-organizing, bootstrapping universe, hence it is actually dynamic and irreversible.

Let us relate this observation more closely to the so-called age of information.

The Bits and Nothing but the Bits?

Modernism's drive for control is nowhere more evident than in "computer thought." The problem is that the laws of the universe have always eluded ordinary thought,

289

and as a result of our not having understood them or heeded their warning signs, Mother Nature is apparently now reaping her revenge over our having raped her for centuries: our efforts to control her are now backfiring. "Computer thought," in contrast, appears at the level of rules and of the sign strings generated from them by entirely predictable algorithmic procedures. In the hypernominalist world of computers, the bit (sign-signifier) is all-important. It comes first; meaning, the interpretant, the idea, and understanding trail along later, if at all. This nominalist obsession with bits, with bare-bones information without the flesh of the semiotic object or the interpreter-interpretant, undervalues and undermines both sign-events and thought-signs.[17]

From the perspective of hypernominalism—another name for semiology in its poststructuralist guise—signs engender texts, concepts, (mis)interpretations. But this equation is inverted and misdirected. Interpreter-interpretants create signs (bits, information), not vice versa. In the Peircean sense, the equation must be nonlinear and circular—or better, spiraloid—with priority placed on the Thirdness of the sign, which is what is most important to humans and to life in general, rather than on referenceless, hollow, and shallow signs. Every sign grows from its inception as an interpreter-interpretant; it is a response to a dialogic question concerning what the sign is a sign of and what its significance is for something or someone. But the question can never be given an ultimate answer, especially since signs tend to become so commonplace, so much a part of community consensus, that they are almost as subliminal as grammar.

Like the misguided use of "information" by those who celebrate the computer age or make illicit use of the term "information theory," whether in conjunction with Saussurean semiology or not, obsession with the sign-as-simulacrum (as bit) ignores the value of the interpreter-interpretant. The tendency is to conflate the interpreter-interpretant and the would-be semiotic object into a bare-bones signifier, which, having liberated itself from things and from human beings, is free to do as it pleases. This is like saying there is no essential difference between the blueprint of a hotel, the architect who designed it, the thought that went into its design, and the activity and materials involved in its construction. Everything is reduced to sign play, to mindless, eventless signs as binary, digital bits whose interpretation always depends upon the arbitrary whims of a subjectless interpreter. On the other hand, in light of Peirce's pragmatic maxim, the composite of, and interrelation between, all thoughts, actions, objects, and events with respect to realization of the building's construction reveal the richness of triadic semiotics in contrast to dyadic semiology. Sign determination is real, though it is a receding pot of gold at the end of the rainbow. There is an interpreting subject, though he is just another sign among signs. And the furniture of the world and of the mind exists, though it cannot be more than semiotically real for us.

Take any sentence—for example, the construction engineer's "Bring this wall of the foyer in two and one half feet for structural stability." It relates triadically, through determination of and by interpreter-interpretants, semiotic objects, and other signs (representamina), to the engineer's knowledge, experience, and predispositions, to the range of possible materials that can be used in such a construction, to the procedures and problems of the actual construction, and finally to the vast storehouse of books, documents, articles, and reports on architecture, structural engineering, building codes, and so on. Plus the fact that it implies the entire range of imponderables incorporated in deliberations and questions such as "Is this the best possible site for the hotel?" "Should there not be more rooms?" "Which carpeting should we use?" and so on, in addition perhaps to "Do we want to build this hotel in the first place?" Elusive, free-floating, subjectless, objectless, and interpretantless signs are incapable of accounting for such intangibles.

The shortcomings of emaciated Saussurean signifiers with respect to human *semiosis* and to the production of legisigns in general is exemplified in the dilemma that AI confronts. AI's genius rests in the reduction (prescission) of complex abstract programs to starkly primitive building blocks and Tinker Toy models when making brain-computer analogies and demonstrating what computers can do with things—or conversely, in the elaboration of sophisticated programs from a few essentials when making computer-brain analogies to demonstrate how computers can do things with words. A computer's ability to manipulate a small number of building blocks is predicated on the idea of Boolean simples: *and, or, neither, implies.* They are binaries (the "cool" digitalism of Baudrillard's culture of simulacra), expressible in such sentences as "*This* is the same as *that*," "*This* is not the same as *that*," "Either *this* or *that*," "Neither *this* nor *that*," "If *this* then *that*," and "If *this* then not *that*." The equivalent of such sentences can move nimbly through the channels of the mother board. Theodore Roszak (1986, 121) writes that as a result, "we get a nice three-tiered synergistic sandwich: *effective procedures* (the idea of the program) based upon *binary arithmetic,* based upon the *physical stop-go traffic of electrons* through semiconductors. This is an intriguing interplay that connects humanly useful operations with an invisible substratum of nonhuman physical phenomena."

When a text is densely packed according to programming rules into a long sequence and flashed on the monitor at breakneck speed, it does not look simple at all to the word-munching assistant professor anxious about his tenurability. Yet it is controlled by strict mathematical laws. And its complexity, by and large the product of "computer thought," is hypernominalistic to the extreme. Signs programmed into computers in "computer thought" can be regurgitated in a linear sequence only. Like the mind of Borges's "Funes the Memorious" (1962, 59–66), everything is there all at once and available for linear recall. And, like Funes, "computer thought" knows only particulars. At its most precise behavior, it must generate signs as disconnected atoms; it can hardly abstract, generalize, think on its own. Although a computer can be "taught" to engage in rudimentary forms of generalization, according to AI programs—e.g., ELIZA, LISP, LOGO—its "thought" will still be overwhelmingly nominalistic.[18]

On a more positive note, when constructing alternative microworlds to be programmed into computers, AI researchers have made use of programs developed from Marvin Minsky's (1977) "frames" and Roger Schank's "scripts" (Schank and Abelson 1977). A restaurant "script" might include a sequence of simple operations, each related to a particular item and activities related to it, such as "Go into restaurant," "Find a table," "Go to table," "Sit down." This is naive taxonomization at its most primitive. It substitutes a static microworld of ready-made things in their proper place for a human semiotic world of continuity and change. A restaurant script consisting of simple stories might work fine in an instruction book for introducing Martians to a particular sort of human activity or in a child's reader. But it ignores the complexity, the myriad subtle nuances and variations, necessary for a human to function effectively in a restaurant, which entails knowledge that he has accumulated over the years, knowledge the Martian or child can internalize most adequately only by learning *how* and knowing *how* to behave in a restaurant through actual cultural practices. Attempting to develop "scripts" according to this knowledge would soon become a hopelessly complicated task of formalization. Yet it is in theory possible, so the AI people tell us.

Without taking a stand on the question of whether or not the brain functions holographically—as Karl Pribram (1971, 1981, 1991) would have it—Hubert and Stuart Dreyfus (1986) argue that the human mind's remarkable ability to absorb whole scenes in one perceptual gulp without decomposing them nominalistically into all their features will remain forever beyond the capability of machines. Dreyfus and Dreyfus distinguish between "mechanistic systems" and "holistic systems." A simple screw is a holistic system. Yet a child learns, chiefly by language instruction, about such systems in terms of simple machines that correlate with mechanistic systems. The important distinction is thus lost in our inherited language, which persists in its mechanistic biases. Actually, to know what a screw is in the full sense of a logical and final interpretant, one must be familiar, by experience gathered through the actual use of screws, with the direction of the threads, the type of threads, different sorts of screws and their functions, screwdrivers, drills and bits, the texture of materials that screws are screwed into, and so on. If we once again recall Peirce's pragmatic maxim, in the apparently simple sentences "This is a restaurant" and "This is a screw," the necessary infinite regress of disseminative, corroborating, complementary, contradictory, and supplementary sentences begins to come through. And finally, the holistic import of the maxim—as well as human perception and thought in general—is foregrounded.

In contrast to most scholars who have set out to prove computers cannot do what humans can, John Searle (1984) argues that no matter how "intelligent" machines become, and even if they evolve to the extent that they can do virtually everything humans do, they will still not be able to think. They are destined merely to *simulate* thought. Endowing a machine with the status of an intelligent being is not directly relevant to human behavior, nor is it sufficient that a machine be able to pass the Turing test, which consists of someone connected to a human and a machine in another room and unable to determine which is which. Searle developed an alternative test, his "Chinese Room Experiment." He asks us to imagine that he is placed in a room with piles of papers on which stories are written in Chinese, which he does not understand. He is then given questions on slips of paper, in Chinese, about the stories. He, of course, understands nothing. But fortunately, he is also provided with a set of rules telling him how to match his questions with the marks and squiggles making up the stories and manipulate them to formulate "answers" for his examiners. He soon becomes remarkably adept at this game, manipulating the meaningless signs on paper in a flash. But to the questions Does Searle understand the stories? and Does he employ insight and reason in generating the answers? the response is negative. Searle has simply applied rules given him by a wily programmer. His examiners have not been able to pass the Turing test, for presumably they cannot differentiate between him—answering the questions in machinelike fashion—and a computer. Yet he understood nothing; he was incapable of interpreting anything.

If humans are nimble holistic cogitators, and if digital machines are incapable of such cerebral powers, the fact remains that computers can be programmed to *model—simulate—*holistic systems at primitive levels (Dreyfus and Dreyfus 1986, 90–100).[19] I refer to devices called "distributed associative memory systems." When used to simulate holistic domains, these systems no longer function as symbol-manipulating computational (nominalistic) systems; instead, the computer simulates the entire domain. This has been hailed even by critics of AI as "a monumental step toward a genuine artificial intelligence" (Dreyfus and Dreyfus 1986, 91). Now the question is, Is the simulation of a holistic system—or conceivably of an entire culture—itself that culture, or another culture, a culture of simulation?

And we find ourselves back on Baudrillard's turf. The AI researchers contend that perfect simulation of intelligence is intelligence, and therefore perfect simulation of an entire culture would be that culture. Critics shoot back that there is a distinction of kind between simulation of the "real" and the "real" itself. Are Baudrillard's masses merely simulating thought? If so, are they really automata? Has the distinction between mind and machine dissolved? Are they actually doing no more than simulating simulacra? And if so, is their "thought" therefore not merely the simulation of simulated thought? Is their "reality," in this sense, the simulation of a simulation of the "real," which has, we are told, become more "real" than the "real"? And is this "reality," then, not yet another step removed from the "really real"? A "hyperhyperreality"? If not, if an unbreachable chasm endures between the simulated and the "real," and if simulated intelligence, no matter how complete, is not human intelligence in the form of Baudrillard's mindless silent majority's tacit, nonconscious comings and goings, then does the *"only referent that still functions"* still consist of nothing more than simulacra? Such would appear to be the case, for "the silent majority (or the masses) is an imaginary referent" (Baudrillard 1983b, 19–20).

All this is not to say that Baudrillard's masses do not exist but that *"their representation is no longer possible."* The masses are not referents because they "no longer belong to the order of representation. They don't express themselves, they are surveyed. They don't reflect upon themselves, they are tested" (Baudrillard 1983b, 20). They cannot be re-presented, we are told, because polls, tests, and the media are devices "which no longer belong to the dimension of representations, but to one of simulation. They no longer have a referent in view, but a model" (Baudrillard 1983b, 20).

A nostalgic Baudrillard laments the loss of "revolution in relation to the devices of classical sociality." In the classical view, meaning still flows from entity to referent; dialectic is still possible between the poles. This changes in the culture of simulacra. Now, there is no polarity, no differential term. Society is short-circuited, thus confusing the poles, and the system gyrates endlessly (Baudrillard 1983b, 20–21). The masses remain inaccessible to the schemas of liberation, revolution, and history. Everything flows through the masses; they engulf the social. Thus they can be neither an object of analysis nor the subject of knowledge (Baudrillard 1983b, 30–31). The subject, following poststructuralist tenets, has been displaced, and the object has been replaced by the hyperreal. No subject and no object, only the field of simulacra. "Pataphysics"—or the science of the imaginary (mental, "in here"), the science of hypersimulation—supposedly introduced by the masses, is now destined to replace physics and ultimately "relieve us of all that cumbersome metaphysics of the social" (Baudrillard 1983b, 34). And the masses themselves, a stronger medium than the media, will dominate: a sort of Brownian movement of undifferentiated atoms (Baudrillard 1983b, 37, 44).

Baudrillard's digital randomness taking on embodiment in terms of imaginary filtrates from the cultural sluice of signifiers (as simulacra) smacks of what we might label a nominalism of the subjectless collective mind. There is a primacy of mental sign-things over the process of sign-events "out there" and thought-signs "in here." Hypersimulation goes hand in hand with hyperconformity. The masses as a statistical aggregate envelop and absorb the media. Yet the fact remains that each individual, each atom, behaves in randomly caroming Brownian fashion with no apparent reasoning, rhythming, or rhyming. The trajectory of each simulacrum (icon, de-generate sign) is reversible in the classical sense. There is no differentiable self, no "I," no interpreter-interpretant.

Baudrillard's masses thus remain outside the sphere of signification. And his "real," having been completely displaced by hyperreality, is now entirely out of the picture as well. Hyperreality is no more than an *ars combinatoria* of atoms—commutative, reflexive, but not necessarily transitory atoms—giving rise to the eternal return, a vast tautological system, as Barthes (1974) once put it. There is no meaning, only information, and no interpreters, only disembodied individuals. This is radically different from Peirce's semiotically real as potentially—and hopefully—an approximation to the "real." As stated in the above chapters, a particular semiotically real sphere *is* "real" *for* the community that constructed it. It is context-bound, *Umwelt*-dependent, and inseparable from a human community's worldview and language. But above all, semiotically real spheres of existence depend upon *mind*.

Indeed, Wheeler's maxim "no mind, no world" translates into Peirce's "no self, no interpreter-interpretant; no interpreter-interpretant, no world." The self is not an atom but rather at one with all selves; the interpreter-interpretant coexists with all interpreter-interpretants in their interminable navigation toward that elusive end product; and the sum of all interpreter-interpretants is coequal with the world itself, the particular semiotically real of a given community. Only when we strike such a clear distinction between a holistic and a nominalistic or pluralistic view of signs can we recognize that they pertain to radically different levels of discourse. Yet they are both absolutely essential. Pluralism is essential, for without the particularity of things there would be no differences for us. And holism is essential, for unless we have some sort of global grasp of things, no matter how feeble, fallible, and incomplete, differences will make hardly any difference. There will be no rule against which to gauge this thing *here-now* with respect to that thing *there-then,* and anything *wherever-whenever.* In short, both "computer thought" and wholes of thought

295

are cardinal. The holistic perspective is open-ended. From the whole, in the Peircean sense, there is no mere dice roll, for *semiosis* is ultimately bound by purpose. And there are no hard and fast rules, for they are always subject to change. The entire system is self-organizing, a creative advance. At the same time, particulars still count, for they exist as such only insofar as they are set apart from other particulars. And the individual still counts as a subject set apart from the object, yet in its interaction at one with it and with the entire community of subjects.

The pluralism-holism pair is also relevant to the distinction between a reversible, symmetrical, computer-simulated world in contrast to something like a child's irreversible, asymmetrical, open-ended world of make-believe. The former is a model that, according to Baudrillard, once evinced a resemblance to the "real" but has now become the "real." The latter entails dialogic interaction between the self and its other self and between the self and others. It is role playing ("We'll be the good guys and you be the bad guys." "You be the Daddy, I'll be the Mommy, and she is Uncle Jack"). There is open-endedness, creativity, imagination, conflict and negotiation, antipathy and empathy, fighting and playing, confusion and understanding. A spectrum of possibilities constantly presents itself rather than a mere series of either/or choices. Most importantly, the game is ongoing and irreversible, a system of constantly evolving and involving disequilibria and imbalance rather than homeostatic equilibria and reversibility. The interpreter-interpretant, the self, the entire community, can never hope to regress to square one. Everything is always other than what it was.

In contrast, Baudrillard's signifieds implode into signifiers, an apparently irreversible event as well. But I repeat: in spite of Baudrillard's nostalgia to the contrary, the signifieds never really constituted the "real" in the first place. They were from the beginning the products of denatured illusions and deluded illuminations of modern thought—foundations, faithful representations, control, power, omnipresence. Modernity persists and endures in Baudrillard's signifiers (simulacra) in the sense that, though they may have taken on a different countenance, they continue exercising another, more subliminal form of oppression. For example, Timothy Luke (1989, 19–58) argues that if Baudrillard's hyperreality promotes hyperconformity, then rather than being a response to problems of modernity, it exacerbates them. The artifacts produced by a hyperrealistic simulation, and ultimately a displacement, of "reality" become more potent than classical ideological modes of power and control. Historical modes betray or distort "reality" with signs of deluded or false consciousness. Simulation takes the struggle a giant step further: "reality" is short-circuited by its reduplication such that the very notions of truth and falsity are radically suspended in the fabric of hyperreality. In a cybernetic world of hyperreality, subjectless individuals can do no more than experience a pale reflection or hallucination of the "real," and since there can be no definable subject, it is impossible to pinpoint the locus of power. Power has become yet another elusive abstraction among abstractions.

For Peirce, on the other hand, the subject *is* a sign. There is no short-circuiting of signs as atoms making up, in their aggregate, some chimerical simulated world. Rather, all signs, the subject included, are self-organizing. They require the subject (mind, sign) for the perpetual "becoming" of their elusive "beingness," and the subject requires them to identify its own "beingness," which is perpetually in a state of "becoming." Like the possible sequence of Macbeth's *semiosic* generation outlined in Chapter Seven, signs emerge while consciousness and the self emerge, and both pass away into other signs while leaving a trace of what *was,* and *will have been.* This process is not exclusively linguistic in the semiological, binary sense, but more broadly semiotic, triadic. As such, all signs flow over and under, betwixt and beside, themselves, progressing or regressing, dancing about in circles or madly dashing toward a promising interpretant in the distance: they are always on the go, being transformed and transmuting themselves into more developed or less developed signs.

Every sign having evolved into a symbol is a further determination of an already known sign whose object is a variation of that of the recently arrived symbol. Those signs of lesser evolution or generation are perpetually in the process of founding and grounding themselves in a state of becoming something other than what they were. Likewise, every instantiation of (mediated, deferred) consciousness or the self is always passing on while in the process of bringing signs to their fruition as interpretants, of developing interpreter-interpretants, all of which merge into and collaborate with one another. If, perchance, an icon or model-metaphor is for an instant taken as if it were the authentic item, interpreter-interpretants have backpedaled. No problem, however. What *was* can be once again—though with a difference—and what *will have become* is always something else.

Let us, in this vein, turn more directly to the sign triad.

The Current's Form and Flow

Consider figure 17, a variant of several earlier figures. Diverse parts of this whole have been examined throughout history. Descartes meditated chiefly on the reliability of the mind's re-presentations of the world, highlighting all three corners of the semiotic triangle: subject, object, and language (sign). For Berkeley, the triangle is much too complicated. He defined the world in terms of *our* representation, which consists of the subject and object. Hume simplified matters even further, reducing the subject to its bare-bones re-presentation, primarily

sensations of the object and of the sign: nothing more than relationships between the re-presentations themselves. Other philosophies, and especially some
Hindu thought, take as the only "reality" the subject, whose task is to brush
aside all the illusions finally to get at "reality." And naive realism assumes that
the "real" object simply *is as it is:* what you see is what you get.

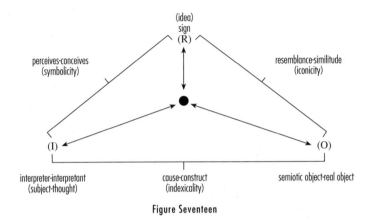

Figure Seventeen

More recently, semiology, of both the structuralist and poststructuralist
varieties, attends chiefly to the sign (signifier plus signified), which, given its
arbitrary nature, remains divorced from "reality" and passes through the
subjectless agent, like water through a conduit, to be taken according to either
convention or idiosyncrasies, depending upon the mode of the taking.
Baudrillard, we have noted, amplifies this skeletal schema to a perceptual cym-
bal crash: there is nothing but simulacra, signs divorced from "reality" and
from any manageable form of convention that are in control of the agent such
that he has no recourse but to bow to the will of a hyperreality totally devoid of
re-presentation. There is no territory; only the map remains, the map of a map
of a map.

What we have here, albeit in a new garment, seems to be the perennial
philosophical problem of showing how appearances (simulacra) have been taken
for the "real." Descartes once thought he discovered that the experience he was
having was indistinguishable from the experience he would have had were he
dreaming instead of awake. Hume once imagined two identical universes, in
one of which everything that happened was a matter of necessity and in the
other everything happened by pure chance: viewed as wholes, however, the
two universes are absolutely indistinguishable. Berkeley's universe is what is
seen, either by us or by God, and since God is eternally hidden from view, there
is no way to know whether what we see is what there is because we see it or

whether it is the same when we do not see it. Spinoza thought that God was coequal with the universe, which throws the possibility of proving his existence indefinitely into limbo. I have already cited Turing's machine, whose output, which is potentially the same as that of a human computer for AI gurus, renders the product of its machinations indistinguishable from the cerebral workings of you or me. Comparable quandaries exist in the sciences, as I have shown in preceding chapters, as well as in the arts. Schrödinger's eigenpussy, the possibility of which was set up by the double-slit experiment, is one of the best among a spate of examples in science. And Marcel Duchamp and later proponents of "found" or "ready-made" art, as well as contemporary "perfect realists," throw the art/nonart distinction into utter confusion. What is appearance and what is "real"? If a distinction between the two is impossible, then are we not, at long last, and in spite of the most dreadful scenarios implied by metaphysicists throughout history, *in* hyperreality? It seems, after all, that Baudrillard persists in having his say.

299

But there is still a difference between the philosophical problems I have very briefly sketched out and Baudrillard. In each philosophical position, the existence of two spheres of influence is presupposed. For Baudrillard, one of them has vanished. This is the difference, Baudrillard points out, between dissimulation and simulation. To dissimulate is "to feign not to have what one has." To simulate is "to feign to have what one hasn't. One implies a presence, the other an absence" (Baudrillard 1983a, 5). The first operation leaves the reality principle in one piece; the second threatens to demolish the very difference between true/false and "real"/"unreal." The dissimulator feigns illness; the simulator produces the symptoms of illness, thus placing in jeopardy any determination of his illness. He *is* ill and *is not* ill—Peirce's vagueness principle—since contradiction has been injected into any consideration of the simulator's condition. Simulation thus breeds inconsistency, or better, sheer undecidability.

On the other hand, Baudrillard's world of simulacra is a strange counterpart to Berkeley's world insofar as neither allows for meaning regarding anything external to our sensations, be they simulacra in the first case or the product of subjective idealism in the second case. And in neither case is there any alienation from "reality," since we cannot set out in good Platonic fashion to compare what we perceive in delusory fashion to the "real" world: appearance and "reality" (hyperreality) are one, and beyond that, there is nothing. This is virtually to say that simulacra, or sensations, are the stuff dreams are made of, which apparently serves to corroborate the idea of Baudrillard's somnambulistic masses.

In this sense, the sleight-of-hand artist who pulls from his coat pocket a fake dove that we take to be "real" is not producing appearance as opposed to "reality." Rather, as far as we can tell, what we see is what there is. In fact, it is hyperreal because it satisfies our expectations and soothes our beliefs. The formula is actually quite simple, and it entails a commonality between ourselves and our neighboring organisms. A frog extrudes his tongue and flicks it at a moving spot because he believes such mobile spots are food. A bat homes in on an echo because she believes it is her form of nourishment. We could simulate a darting black spot or an echo, and frog and bat would fall victim to their own equivalent of hyperreality. All this occurs below the threshold of consciousness, of course, whether speaking of frogs, bats, or Baudrillard's taciturn majority. The difference is that frogs and bats under the right circumstances eventually learn, at some dreamlike level of consciousness, that they were duped, while Baudrillard's masses, it appears, are destined to continue on in ignorant bliss. There is no indication of any turning back.

300

Thus the fitness and advantage of Peirce's conception of the sign, which encompasses *R, O,* and *I* and allows for generacy as well as de-generacy, for the emergence into consciousness of novelty or that which was embedded as well as the inverse submersion into the depths of the mind, for reversibility as well as irreversibility, for sign-events and thought-signs, for *semiosis* and phaneroscopy, for the interplay of possibility, actuality, and potentiality, vagueness and generality, "real" and semiotically real, inconsistency, incompleteness, and complementarity. And thus the possibility, through Peirce's conception, of bridging modernism and postmodernism, retaining some of the best of the former and projecting into the latter, of being inside language yet constantly pushing at the periphery, of stressing the importance of the will yet celebrating will-lessness, of exalting self and other yet dissolving both in the community, of highlighting complementarities between subjectivity and objectivity, idealism and realism, stasis and change, continuity and discontinuity, immediacy and mediacy. And thus the correlation between Peirce and Wheeler, integrating sign, object, and subject (interpreter-interpretant) into an interconnected whole.

But let us not, I must emphasize, assume that Baudrillard's transition from resemblance to re-presentation to simulacral hyperreality, from counterfeit to production to simulation, is merely patterned in something in the order of Peirce's de-generacy (indexicalization and iconization) of signs, which at long last frees them from both the subject and the object to engage in free flights whenever and wherever. The beauty—and the threat—of Peirce's conceptual scheme is that symbols can become *as if* icons with embedment (degeneracy) but also vice versa, with de-embedment (generacy). For "the mind is virtual, not in a series of moments, not capable of existing except in a space of time—nothing so far as it is at any one moment" (CP, 8.248).

Introduction

1. This problem is aggravated by the customary observation that "postmodernism" rejects modernist claims to some privileged insight. But in so doing, postmodernism is caught up in a dilemma of its own making. Rejection of modernist legitimacy assumes a particular shape that reflects the specificities of the context within which that rejection was exercised, which leaves open the question of how postmodern theories—the term must be plural (contextualized specificities breed pluralism)—of contemporary social, cultural, political, and economic life can legitimately relate to the actual practices constituting that selfsame life.

2. In Jameson's (1991, 55) words,

> [w]hen we make some initial inventory of the varied cultural artifacts that might plausibly be characterized as postmodern, the temptation is strong to seek the "family resemblance" of such heterogeneous styles and products not in themselves but in some common high modernist impulse and aesthetic against which they all, in one way or another, stand in relation.

The Wittgensteinian term "family resemblances" is notoriously loose, of course, granting leeway to an overwhelming diversity of interpretations. In the final analysis—and with the risk of knee-jerk reactions from diverse quarters—it might be said that each theorist of the postmodern scene is his/her own measure of all things.

3. But actually, postmodernism has now become "pastmodernism." As Barry Smart (1993, 12) observes of postmodernity, it is no longer a novelty but merely boring now that everybody is doing it.

4. The issue is complex and beyond the scope of this introduction. In brief, I defer to Stanley Rosen's (1987) argument that though the contemporary movements gathered under the umbrella term "postmodernism" are in reality a continuation of the Enlightenment, the belief exists that they are a frontal attack on the twentieth-century culmination of eighteenth-century thought. To complicate matters, hermeneutics, a characteristic obsession of postmodernism, has an intrinsically political thrust that, especially in the United States, has recently been taking on a scholastic and technophile character. In Rosen's (1987, 6) words, "just as Marxists quarrel over whether the postcapitalist epoch is inevitable or is dependent upon human choice, so too it is not clear within postmodernism whether modernity has already and inevitably exhausted itself or whether it requires the continuous stimulus of postmodern rhetoric to hasten it to its grave."

5. There is considerable discord in this respect. For example, Andreas Huyssen (1986, 170), among others, argues that self-reflexivity, indeterminism, immanence, and other such labels customarily attached to postmodernism are no more than a revival of modernist features. I would contend, however—and I trust the following chapters bear me out—that these are specific features of late modernism, in science developed by Niels Bohr and Werner Heisenberg among others, that have generally been incorporated into the postmodernist *mise-en-scène*.

6. For example, it is generally conceived that the postmodern novel and its precursors emphasize the contingent, random, nonlinear, self-reflexive, irrational, nonmechanistic, and subjectivistic experience of time, in contrast to the modern novel's general enslavement to clockwork regularity and chronology, though there are certain trappings of these postmodern characteristics in key works of modernism.

7. However, opinion often has it that to be modern is to break with tradition, to become self-consciously new, which ultimately leads to uncertainty and despair. The confusion lies with the disparate use of terms to qualify modernism-modernity on the one hand and postmodernism-postmodernity on the other. As a case in point, Alan Wilde (1981) uses the terms "fragmentation," "disruption," and "disintegration of form" to characterize postmodernism, yet the same terms are often attached to modernism (see, for example, Berman 1982). They are merely recycled.

8. See Hayles 1991 regarding postmodernist characteristics implicit in chaos theory and the science of complexity.

9. For example, the "new historicism" in de Certeau 1980, 1983, 1988; Darnton 1984; Foucault 1970, 1972; Gutting 1989; Hunt 1989; LaCapra 1985, 1989; Lueders 1989; Sahlins 1985; Scott 1988; and White 1978, 1987. From this view, modernism has generally been accused of ahistoricity, elitism, cultural hermeticism, political conservatism, a deluded search for the transcendental, and alienating notions of the autonomy of art (C. Russell 1981, 8). In contrast, postmodern writing presupposes that both history and fiction are equally discursive, and that the writing of history as a narrative representation of the past is a literary adventure, more what certain events mean for a given culture than what actually happened (Hutcheon 1988a, 89). The shift is from legitimation to pluralist signification, for the past is always already interpreted, and values are inseparable from so-called facts (Derrida 1981, 56; White 1986).

10. Especially Baudrillard 1983a, 1983b, 1988a; Bourdieu 1984a, 1984b; de Certeau 1984; Lyotard 1984.

11. Arac 1986; Bürger 1984; Foster 1983; Hassan 1980, 1987; Hutcheon 1988a; Krauss 1985; Poster 1989; A. Ross 1988; Willis 1984.

12. Feyerabend 1975, 1987; Gutting 1980; M. Kaplan 1984; Kuhn 1970; Polanyi 1958; Toulmin 1982a, 1982b.

13. Bakhtin 1968, 1973, 1981; Holquist 1990; Holquist and Clark 1984; Morson 1986; Morson and Emerson 1989; Stam 1988.

14. Strangely, and perhaps ironically, enough, Berman's conception of modernity via Marx and Engels's "All that is solid melts into air" image from the *Communist Manifesto* is of the sort recently attributed to deconstruction, poststructuralism, and postmodernism (see Rose's [1991, chap. 3] observations on this point).

302

15. Some observers have charged that postmodernism's delirious claim to have subverted the problem of elitism is artificial, for postmodernists are more likely than not impotent bourgeois critics faced with exhaustion (i.e., the "literature of exhaustion" [Barth 1974]), and now seek comfort in mass art and mass media with the illusion that in so doing they are by, with, and for the people (Jameson 1983; Kuspit 1990, 54).

16. However, see biologist Conrad Waddington's (1969) enlightening study of the relationship among quantum physics, relativity, and modern art since cubism (see also Friedman and Donley 1985 on the influence of Einstein on literature, and Gross 1990 on scientific rhetoric in general).

17. T. S. Eliot, among others, strikes a responsive chord in the modernist mind by using form, specifically mythical form along the lines of James Joyce's *Ulysses,* as "a way of controlling, of ordering, of giving a shape and a significance to the immense panorama of futility and anarchy, which is contemporary history" (in Kermode 1975, 177).

18. On the other hand, according to Jameson (1991, 2–3), postmodernists were at the outset rather fascinated by the

> whole "degraded" landscape of schlock and kitsch, of tv series and Reader's Digest culture, of advertising and models, of the late show and the grade-B Hollywood film, of so-called paraliterature, with its airport paperback categories of the gothic and the romance, the popular biography, the murder mystery, and the science fiction or fantasy novel: materials they no longer simply "quote," as a Joyce or a Mahler might have done, but incorporate into their very substance.

19. See G. B. Madison 1982, 20–22 on Peirce's "unmodern" posture in this regard.

20. On the relevance of Peirce to postmodernism, see the recent debate in the *Transactions of the Charles S. Peirce Society* (Liszka 1993; Nielsen 1993; also Alexander 1993). On Peirce's antifoundationalism, a theme common to much discourse on postmodernism, see Delaney 1993; Olshewsky 1993; Rockmore and Singer 1992. Strangely enough, I might add, John Deely (1994) would like to place Peirce within the postmodern current, though he himself continues his relentless search for "foundations" for the study of signs.

21. In this vein, Eugene Rochberg-Halton (1986, 96) writes: "I must acknowledge what seems to me the broad possibilities of semiotics for contributing to 'post modern' culture. But in order for this to occur a radical transformation must take place." Among other transformations, Rochberg-Halton would call for a reform of the "semiotics of Saussure, Morris, and Eco," which "preserve a positivist substratum to which signs do not penetrate, the fictional substratum of nominalism" (Rochberg-Halton 1986, 104–5). While I have high regard for Eco—albeit with some reservations—Rochberg-Halton's case would convince any honest jury regarding Charles Morris's distortion of Peirce and the distinction between Peircean semiotics and Saussurean "semiology," which will be shoved onto center stage in Chapter Eleven (see also Merrell 1991b).

22. However, see Finlay 1990; Greenberg 1973; and Melville 1986 for the concept of modernism precisely as the initiator of this self-critical posture.

Chapter One

1. As, for example, in Boon 1982; Brown 1987; Clifford 1983; Clifford and Marcus 1986; Keesing 1987; Marcus 1980; Marcus and Cushman 1982; Marcus and Fischer 1986; Sahlins 1981; Tyler 1987; and Woolgar 1988. For a brief critique of this view, see Sangren 1988.

2. For example, in Ashley 1990; Douglas 1966, 1970, 1975; Geertz 1983; Polkinghorne 1988; Sperber and Wilson 1986; Turner 1974, 1982, 1986; Tyler 1987. For an argument in favor of literature as knowledge, see Livingston 1988; regarding science as story, Bohm 1988; Ferré 1988; Griffin 1988; Lyotard 1984; McIntyre 1980; and for philosophy as narrative, Bourdieu 1977; de Certeau 1984; Danto 1985; Rorty 1978.

3. Actually, the Vienna school's posture concerning language, meaning, and conceptual schemes, all of which pertain to modernity, was generally—and rather surprisingly—compatible with North American New Criticism, especially concerning the autonomy of artworks and of scientific language, the self-containment of works and of theoretical language, and the crucial importance of language itself (poetic language for the New Critics, theoretical language for the positivists) (Hacking 1983). Nevertheless, the general positivist thesis had it that science is rational, while literature is not; thus science was pigeonholed with epistemological concerns and literature with sentimental, emotional, and subjective expression.

4. Hacking's notion of style of reasoning thus bears on recent debates over rationalism versus irrationalism. From various disciplines, see R. Bernstein 1983; Gellner 1985; Gutting 1980; Hollis and Lukes 1982; Hübner 1983; Jarvie 1984; Krausz 1989; McMullin 1988; Newton-Smith 1981; Rajchman and West 1985; and Wilson 1970.

5. A few years later, however, upon relating "styles of scientific reasoning" to other trendy catchphrases, Hacking (1985, 149) opts for Foucault's "epistemes" and "discourse" over "paradigms." His admiration for Foucault appears to stem from the French historian-philosopher's "willingness quite deliberately" to abandon "nearly all his neologisms as soon as he has put them into currency in a book"—that is, he appears to be capable nimbly of jumping in and out of styles of reasoning while remaining committed to none of them.

6. This notion appears at the outset to be supported by postmodernism's pluralism, fragmentation, and diversity, in contrast to modernism's notion of organic unity, monolithic and univocal meaning, and the positivist's dream of a unified science. As a case in point, Derrida's dismantling of the traditional idea of structure as a totalized and complete whole is in line with postmodernism and makes shambles of the modernist concept of unity and order (see Shusterman 1989, but for an organicist view of "postmodern science," see Bohm 1980; Griffin 1988; Lovelock 1987; Margulis and Sagan 1986; and Wilber 1983).

7. Although he by no means enjoys a monopoly in this respect, John Caputo (1987) effectively demonstrates how Gadamer's hermeneutics was relatively conserva-

tive in comparison to Heidegger's, Derrida's—whom he considers a "radical hermeneut"—and that of other off-the-wall thinkers. While time and space do not permit expatiation on this topic, I refer the reader to Caputo's thought-provoking work.

8. Indeed, the growing attitude among "pure" scientists is that, since the subject cannot but meddle in the affairs of the object under study, focus should be not on *what* there is but on the *nature* of our knowledge of what we *cannot know as it is.* In Heisenberg's (1976, 38) words, natural science "does not simply describe and explain nature; it is a part of the interplay between nature and ourselves."

9. Ironically, Connor (1989, 10) remarks: "What is striking is precisely the degree of consensus in postmodern discourse that there is no longer any possibility of consensus, the authoritative announcements of the disappearance of final authority and the promotion and recirculation of a total and comprehensive narrative of a cultural condition in which totality is no longer thinkable."

10. See Barnes 1985; Barnes and Edge 1985; Bazerman 1988; Bloor 1983; Hanson 1958, 1969; M. Kaplan 1984; Knorr-Cetina 1981; Knorr-Cetina and Mulkay 1983; Latour and Woolgar 1979; Myers 1990; Phillips 1973, 1977; and Polanyi 1958.

11. Lyotard (1984, 60) writes along similar lines that

> [p]ostmodern science—by concerning itself with such things as undecidables, the limits of precise control, conflicts characterized by incomplete information, *"fracta,"* catastrophes, and pragmatic paradoxes—is theorizing its own evolution as discontinuous, catastrophic, nonrectifiable, and paradoxical. It is changing the meaning of the word *knowledge,* while expressing how such a change can take place. It is producing not the known, but the unknown.

Katherine Hayles (1990, 288) criticizes Lyotard, arguing that his characterization of contemporary theories—such as quantum mechanics, fractal geometry, irreversible thermodynamics—as the product of fractionation, of pluralism, is misguided, "for they have not by any means abandoned globalizing concepts." I am not inclined to look upon Lyotard's work with so critical an eye—I am not sure how much globalization, at least in the modernist sense, has been retained—though I readily concede that Lyotard's enthusiasm occasionally gets out of hand (see Merrell 1992, chap. 4).

12. Toulmin (1982b, 254), in fact, goes so far as to posit that "[i]n due course, the change from modern to postmodern science will evidently be matched by corresponding changes in philosophy and theology also; in particular, the 'postmodern' positions and methods that natural scientists are now working out will have implications, also, for a possible reunion of natural science with natural theology."

13. Toulmin also alludes to postmodern science's effort to conceive of the universe as "a single integrated system united by universal principles" (Toulmin 1982b, 224). In order to achieve this task, he calls for a new dialogue among scientists and humanists to dissolve the "two cultures." The conditions for such a postmodern science entail a reinsertion of humanity into nature with the understanding that we cannot continue artificially to set ourselves apart from the world, for we are immanent, not transcendent. On the other hand, and as we shall note throughout this inquiry, Peirce

(re)constitutes the subject as an interactive member in a community of subjects—thus also abandoning the Cartesian autonomous individual who plumbs the depths of her consciousness to attain eternal truths—and in so doing, he inserts humanity into the world of nature. Peirce was, in this respect, more postmodern than many poststructuralists.

The ambitious task that Toulmin envisions appears to contradict postmodern pluralism (see note 6 of this chapter). However, he is not writing about the monolithic, unified-science idea of positivism but about dialogue between citizens with intellectual and artistic interests and about dialogue with nature, in an effort to approximate common understanding of ourselves and our world. Along these lines, Ronald McKinney (1989) argues that although the humanist variety of postmodernism and the emerging scientific (unmodernist) "holism" appear to be incompatible, they share significant territory insofar as both recognize the limitations of discursive reason; are admittedly fallible; must inexorably confront, at the outer edges of their particular styles of reason, paradoxes of the identity of opposites; and are opponents of classical mechanism, reductionism, and determinism. Yet an overriding distinction remains: "holistic" views stress the unity of the universe, while in humanist circles, postmodernism is pluralist, placing emphasis on the many.

14. The disconcerting effects that I speak of are by no means limited to our times. E. H. Gombrich (1960) effectively demonstrates how, throughout the ages, art has been born of art, painting has altered perception and created tastes, and in the process our "reality" has been transformed by aesthetic proclivities rather than the other way around.

15. Feyerabend (1987), in his invectives against metalanguages, argues that worn-out notions of meaning should be thrown out altogether, allowing us to contemplate sentences qua sentences and thus attending to *what* is said and even *how* it is said, not what is meant. Heisenberg is even more poignant:

> We can sometimes by axioms give a precise meaning to words, but still we never know how these precise words correspond to reality, whether they fit reality or not. . . . We have learned that language is a dangerous instrument to use, and this fact will certainly have its repercussions in other fields, but this is a very long process which will last through many decades I should say. (cited in Buckley and Peat 1979, 11–12)

16. If one compares Heisenberg's use of "fire" and "energy" with Gerald Holton's (1973) general "themata" recurrent in the history of scientific thought, I believe the point comes through loud and clear.

17. Jeremy Bernstein (1983, 161) remarks, in this regard, that the crisis of physics can be found in the apparently "'schizophrenic' character of light."

18. See A. Miller 1986 for a history of the struggle during the early days of quantum theory between visualizable and nonvisualizable models of quantum events.

19. James Jeans (1943, 204) puts the matter bluntly: "There is no longer a dualism of mind and matter, but of waves and particles; these seem to be the direct, although almost unrecognizable, descendants of the older mind and matter, the waves replacing mind and the particles matter."

20. Harold Morowitz (1981, 39) points to a comparable "epistemological circle":

> First, the human mind, including consciousness and reflective thought, can be explained by activities of the central nervous system, which, in turn, can be reduced to the biological structure and function of that physiological system. Second, biological phenomena at all levels can be totally understood in terms of atomic physics, that is, through the action and interaction of the component atoms of carbon, nitrogen, oxygen, and so forth. Third and last, atomic physics, which is now understood most fully by means of quantum mechanics, must be formulated with the mind as a primitive component of the system.

21. Augusto Ponzio (1985) cogently elucidates lines of similarity between Bakhtin, whose theory of writing is dialogical, and Peirce's own dialogic—which I will briefly discuss in Chapter Eight.

22. In recent times, Roland Barthes (1972) and Derrida (1978), among other poststructuralists, illustrate that from modernism to postmodernism there has been a progressive trend toward increased abstraction, all signifieds eventually becoming signifiers (or in Peircean terms, icons and indices becoming symbols). The theme is also taken up by Baudrillard (1981) and Jameson (1983, 1984a), which they attribute to the rise of multinational capitalism. However, this "fetishism of the signifier" or of the "abstract" is actually a far cry from Peirce, who, though squarely within the milieu of modernity, was nonetheless in many respects quite "unmodern" (Rochberg-Halton 1986, 72).

23. Morris turns Peirce's "antifoundationalism" inside out in his search for the most scientistic foundations imaginable. Morris's strained division (following Rudolf Carnap) of the branches of his envisioned "science of science" into syntax (science as language), semantics (science as knowledge of the world), and pragmatics (science as method or practice) aided in fostering what is now clearly a false typology. It attempted to wed logical positivism and even behaviorism with *semiosis* rather than following in Peirce's "pragmaticist" footsteps—Roland Posner's (1981, 1986) recent infatuation with Morris notwithstanding.

24. I must point out, before the reader draws a hasty conclusion, that my use of the term "generativity" is not Chomskyan. Rather than attempting to define the term here, I will let it speak for itself in the context of the following chapters.

Chapter Two

1. This notion bears on the Sapir-Whorf hypothesis, according to which a society's organization of the world is linguistically determined. Eleanor Rosch (1974, 1975a, 1975b, 1977) critiques this hypothesis, arguing that "reality" is cut up irrespective of language use, and that we can go beyond ("transcendentalize") language—a rather modernist view, if I might say so. On the other hand, Jakob von Uexküll's *Umwelt* idea, to be discussed in Chapter Three, lies somewhere between Benjamin Whorf's linguistic determinism and Rosch's view. According to Uexküll, we are limited ordinarily by our physiological make-up—i.e., certain perceptual and conceptual modes—rather

than by language, and though we can alter many facets of our language-determined perception and conception of the world, severe limitations remain.

2. However, see Abner Shimony's (1977) critique of Hanson in this regard.

3. In fact, seeing something while one's conscious attention lies elsewhere is to be unaware of the feeling or sensation of a percept, as Wittgenstein (1953, 211e) observes: "I looked at the flower, but was thinking of something else and was not conscious of its color. . . . [I] looked at it without seeing it."

4. See also CP, 5.115–19, 181, 184, 7.643.

5. Comparable views are found in literary studies. For example, Stanley Fish (1980) writes that all statements are interpretations, and that resort to the text in order to get the "facts" straight is itself grounded in an interpretation of one sort or another. These interpretations are community affairs, not subjective in terms of isolated individuals divining meaning from the text. And meanings are culturally available, not inventions *ex nihilo,* generated by single interpreters. It follows that all interpretations, especially those that are presumably free of presuppositions, are possible only on the basis of other interpretations.

6. Goodman's nominalistic "ways of worldmaking" is, of course, largely out of synch with Peirce's "objective idealism." Nonetheless, I suggest that there is a significant conjunction between the two semioticians—and Goodman, it bears stating, is a supreme semiotician in his own right (see Almeder 1980 for Peirce's "objective idealism" and antinominalism).

7. See, for more detailed discussions of the maxim, Almeder 1980; Hookway 1985; and Nesher 1983, 1990.

8. In general CP, 2.296, 5.412, 427, 483, 8.178, 184, 195.

9. In fact, according to Peirce, a totalistic conception of the universe—the totality of all possible worlds—would be unrecognizable for a finite semiotic agent (CP, 5.294).

10. The reference is to Hugh Everett's "many worlds interpretation" of quantum mechanics, according to which all possible worlds are "actualized," only one of which is "our" world, the rest constituting parallel "realities" (for a layperson's account, see Herbert 1985).

11. In passing I briefly cite a few examples. At the outset of the Copernican revolution, Ptolemy's geocentric system was, for practical purposes, empirically more plausible than its heliocentric competitor. But Copernicus and Galileo proved to be rhetorical geniuses, thus eventually gaining the upper hand (Feyerabend 1975). Newton's theory of color won out over Goethe's chiefly because the latter did not dovetail with the accepted scientific framework of the day. Nevertheless, in its own right Goethe's hypothesis presents an attractive and in many ways viable alternative (LeShan and Margenau 1982, 196–204). The phenomenalist Ernst Mach defeated Ludwig Boltzmann in a debate over the latter's probabilistic derivation of the second law of thermodynamics. Boltzmann was beaten, Popper (1974, 157) writes, not because he was wrong but "because he had been too bold"—in other words, Boltzmann miserably failed the litmus test for rhetoric. And finally the Copenhagen interpretation of quantum mechanics ran off with first prize,

chiefly due to Bohr's charisma: young physicists flocked to him like apprentices to their guru (A. Miller 1986). The upshot is, according to Feyerabend's tart rhetoric, that all "worlds" should enjoy at least a little consideration, if not equal time, for the most unlikely of "worlds" can and often have become at one time or another elevated to "reality" status.

12. The unified-science idea, derived from the spirit of positivism, encapsulates the belief that natural science, whose fairy godmother is physics, is the only reliable source of knowledge, and that the philosophy of science is philosophy enough. The philosopher was given the supreme task of applying the formal methods of deduction propounded in Whitehead and Russell's *Principia Mathematica,* and by judicious use of scientific method, meaningful statements would surely become those and only those that were empirically testable. A corollary to the positivist article of faith was the claim that there must be a unity of method between the natural and social sciences, and if the lesser sciences wanted any form or fashion of legitimacy, they would have to learn how to march in step with the brass band of physics.

Chapter Three

1. I appropriate Comfort's use of the term "empathy," which I will further qualify below, while mindful that its traditional use is now looked upon in many circles as worn out. With respect to human communication, theoretical and commonsense methods for getting in tune ("empathizing") with others' forms of life are diverse and subtle, and they continue to remain rather slippery. Such methods include Paul Grice's (1975) formulas regarding how we proceed in conversations, Geertz's (1973) oscillation between *experience-near* and *experience-distant,* Sperber and Wilson's (1986) thesis that we assume that what others say must make some sense and that we act accordingly, Hilary Putnam's (1983) contention that we assign a workable level of ignorance or cleverness to each other's speech, Donald Davidson's (1984) common ground of sharable statements, and Gadamer's (1975) fusion of horizons. The debate, of course, will undoubtedly continue into the foreseeable future. Rather than enter into the problematics of this issue, I choose simply to use the term "empathy," since my focus rests on the difficulty, and perhaps the virtual impossibility, of radical conceptual and perceptual switches, not the methods for exercising such leaps.

2. Indeed, regarding anthropomorphism, François Jacob (1982, 56) tells us: "We ourselves are so deeply entrapped in the representation of the world made possible by our own sense organs and brain, in other words by our genes, that we can barely conceive the possibility of viewing this same world in a different way. We can hardly imagine the world of a fly, an earthworm or a gull." Peirce views such anthropomorphism to be not only inevitable (CP, 1.121, 316, 2.750), but, in addition, ultimately the only route toward viable human knowledge. He writes: "I have after long years of severest examination become fully satisfied that, other things being equal, an anthropomorphic conception, whether it makes the best nucleus for a scientific working hypothesis or not, is far more likely to be approximately true than one that is not anthropomorphic" (CP, 5.47). And this, in spite of Keesing's warning in Chapter One with respect to anthropomorphism in ethnography.

309

3.   Although Jakob von Uexküll (1957) himself offers some remarkable pictures of a living room as seen now by a human, now by a dog, now by a fly, and a boat as perceived by a sea urchin, and other such oddities, one cannot help but sense that these attempts are perhaps more entertaining than instructive, more charming than illuminating. They appear to give little idea what it is like to be a dog, let alone a frog, a fly, a sea urchin, or Nagel's bat.

4.   In the pages that follow, I am concerned in large part with Michael Polanyi's (1958) *focal* and *subsidiary* awareness in relation to Hanson's (1958, 1969) seeing and seeing *as-that* and knowing *how* and knowing *that*—or implicit and explicit knowledge. Regarding habit in this respect, see CP, 2.450, 654, 3.160ff., 4.629, 5.27ff., 268, 440ff., 479, 6.497, 7.34ff. From a general psychological view, see also Calvin 1989; and Langer 1989.

5.   For example, at sixty miles per hour on a crowded expressway you have little time to think about your next move. Your driving has become automatized to the extent that you leave the car and its motion in relation to the other cars nearby to your body, disengaging your mind for other matters, such as projecting your attention further up the road in anticipation of what might occur, daydreaming, or fantasizing about another time and place.

6.   As we shall observe in the two succeeding chapters, while the mind tends toward habituation, new stimuli that contradict that which was expected prod the mind out of its pathways of least semiotic resistance. In Peirce's (CP, 6.301) words:

> Everybody knows that the long continuance of a routine of habit makes us lethargic, while a succession of surprises wonderfully brightens the ideas. Where there is a motion, where history is a-making, there is the focus of mental activity.... A portion of mind, abundantly commissured to other portions, works almost mechanically. It sinks to a condition of a railway function. But a portion of mind almost isolated, a spiritual peninsula, or *cul-de-sac,* is like a railway terminus. Now mental commissures are habits. Where they abound, originality is not needed and is not found; but where they are in defect spontaneity is set free.

7.   Propositional and computational knowledge is embodied chiefly in Hanson's "sentential knowledge" and explicit knowing *that,* discussed in Chapter Two. In this chapter, I include tacit, or nonsentential knowledge—a portion of which can be made explicit—from a more general perspective.

8.   See in this regard Howard Gardner's (1987) review of AI research; see also Johnson-Laird 1987; McGinn 1987; Penrose 1987.

9.   Although this idea apparently conflicts with Hanson's knowledge as largely sentential, one must bear in mind that Hanson refers specifically to explicit knowledge, that which can and is put into language—a somewhat rough counterpart to Popper's (1972) World 3 ("objective knowledge").

10.   Hermann Weyl (1949, 219), in reference to David Hilbert's ambitious program to axiomatize the whole of mathematics and the devastating blow Gödel dealt it, writes:

We are not surprised that a concrete chink of nature taken in its isolated phenomenal existence, challenges our analysis by its inexhaust-
ibility and incompleteness; it is for the sake of completeness, as we
have seen, that physics projects what is given onto the background of
the possible. But it is surprising that a construct created by mind itself,
the sequence of the integers, the simplest and most diaphanous thing
for the constructive mind, assumes a similar aspect of obscurity and
deficiency when viewed from the axiomatic angle.

11.   See also Penrose 1989, where he offers a more developed treatment of
this topic.

311

12.   See Poundstone 1988 for a popular account of the impossibility of a
computer's knowing how; see also, from a "quantum-world" perspective, Penrose 1987,
1989.

13.   Peirce writes: "One of the most remarkable distinctions between the
Instinctive mind of animals and the Rational mind of man is that animals rarely make
mistakes, while the human mind almost invariably blunders at first, and repeatedly,
where it is really exercised in the manner that is distinctive of it" (CP, 7.380; see also
5.480).

14.   The following very brief discussion of abduction is only a preliminary
step, since I shall periodically return to the topic in later chapters.

15.   In general, see also CP, 5.57–58, 312, 417, 512, 6.469; and Chisholm
1952.

16.   I refer the reader especially to Peirce's essays "The Fixation of Belief"
(CP, 5.358–87) and "How to Make Our Ideas Clear" (CP, 5.388–410).

17.   Regarding simian language versus human language within a semiotic
framework, see Sebeok and Rosenthal 1981; Sebeok and Umiker-Sebeok 1980.

18.   See Hanson 1961, 1965 on the logic of discovery; also Nickles 1980a,
1980b, which include studies of both Hanson and Peirce; and Fann 1970 on abduction.

19.   In general, Hanson's work is much in the spirit of Heisenberg (1972,
134), who writes:

When we speak of a picture of nature provided by contemporary exact
science, we do not actually mean any longer a picture of nature, but
rather a picture of our relation to nature. The old compartmentalization
of the world into an objective process in space and time, on the one
hand, and the soul in which this process is mirrored, on the other . . . is
no longer suitable as the starting point for the understanding of modern
science.

20.   Dan Nesher (1983, 1990), for example, focuses almost exclusively on
conscious, logically and rationally controlled semiotic behavior. However, Peirce also
duly acknowledges the tacit component of sign processing, which he attributes to "intention" and "purpose." His words from MS 1476 warrant extended citation in this respect:

Every mental representation, in the widest sense, everything of a cognitive character, is of the nature of a sign. "Representation" and "sign"

are synonyms. Now the purpose of a sign is that it shall be interpreted. The interpretation of it is again a sign. So that the whole purpose of a sign, as such, is to determine a new sign; and the whole purport of a sign lies in the character of its intended interpretation. But in order that a sign should produce another sign, it is necessary that it should in some sense (not necessarily in this or that technical sense, but in some sense) influence or act upon something external to itself. It is only in doing so that it can get itself interpreted. Consequently, the whole purport of any sign lies in the intended character of its external action or influence. This external influence is of different kinds in different cases. Some signs are interpreted or reproduced by a physical force or something analogous to such a force, simply by causing an event; as, sounds spoken into a telephone effect variations of the rate of alternation of an electric current along the wire, as a first interpretation, and these variations again produce new sound vibrations by reinterpretation. Another case is where a sign excites a certain quality of feeling, simple or complex, which quality of feeling is a sign of anything that partakes of it, as the sound of this word "red" may make us imagine the color red.

In this sense, the sign's push for its self-interpretation and for its passing away into another sign is also part and parcel of the sign user's being compelled to intermingle with it, to become one with it, thus leading to a tacitly derived interpretation, which entails seeing *as* and knowing *how.*

Chapter Four

1.   As David Savan (1987–88) observes, Peirce at the outset did not actually mean for the sign to be synonymous with the representamen. Rather, at the most fundamental level, all three components claim equal membership to the category of signhood.

2.   Limited time and space do not allow for detailed explanation of Peirce's sign types, though I will elaborate briefly on them in the following sections, and especially in Chapter Six (see Fisch 1978; Savan 1987–88 for notable introductions to Peirce's system of signs).

3.   See Tursman 1987 for a more detailed treatment of phaneroscopy. Though I disagree with him on certain points, I do not wish to pursue my disagreement here, since it is not relevant to the issue at hand.

4.   This is a giant step toward breaking down the subject/object and body/mind dichotomies, the focus of Peirce's anti-Cartesian posture (see Merrell 1991a, where I give this topic treatment in a context similar to the present).

5.   Peirce (CP, 5.71) used Josiah Royce's map paradox—a map containing the entirety of the territory it maps, therefore containing a replica of itself, ad infinitum—to demonstrate the self-sufficiency, yet in-sufficiency, of the notion of self-consciousness. Regarding phanerons (and signs in general, for that matter) as melding into a continuum, a complementary paradox inheres: if phanerons compose a continuum, then any cut is artificial and unrepresentative of the whole. But we can have nothing else to go on, since the infinite nature of the continuum cannot be interjected into our finitude.

6.   For want of a more adequate term, I will hereafter use *re-presentation*—in contrast to representation—to depict movement, a new beginning with each sign instantiation, something produced rather than the reproduction of some prior model. I would hope the reader will take *re-presentation* to be genuine *kinesis,* as did Peirce, somewhat like Kierkegaard's *repetition* and Derrida's *différance.*

7.   Peirce later virtually abandoned his use of the term "de-generacy," though the general idea remained in his work. See Gorlée 1990 and Buczynska-Garewicz 1979a, 1979b for a more detailed discussion of de-generate signs, and Tursman 1987, who discusses de-generacy within a mathematical context.

8.   According to Peirce,   313

[a]n *Index* or *Seme* is a Representamen whose Representative character consists in its being an individual second. If the Secondness is an
existential relation, the Index is *genuine.* If the Secondness is a reference, the Index is *degenerate.* A genuine Index and its Object must be
existent individuals (whether things or facts), and its immediate
Interpretant must be of the same character. (CP, 2.283)

For a comparison of the three types of signs with regard to genuine signs, see CP, 2.309–10, 4.448.

9.   Peirce writes that genuine signs involve purpose, as in A gives B to C with some intention in mind, which entails Thirdness (CP, 1.366–67). First-degree de-generacy—such as billiard ball 2 hitting 3 and 3 hitting 4 or a brain-numbed drunk bumping into a woman as he leaves a bar—involves Secondness, mere action and reac-tion without conscious intention. An example of second-degree de-generacy is the sen-sation of an orange spot without there (yet) existing any explicit acknowledgment of the color's relation to red on the one side of the spectrum and yellow on the other (CP, 1.473). Nevertheless, Peirce asserts, even the most de-generate forms of Thirdness still have some aspect of mind (CP, 8.331).

10.   Sebeok 1976, 124, defines a symptom (index) as "*a compulsive, auto-matic, nonarbitrary sign, such that the signifier is coupled with the signified in the man-ner of a natural link.* (A syndrome is a rule-governed configuration of symptoms with a stable designatum.)" As we shall note shortly, a symptom as compulsive, obsessive behavior is comparable to Milic Capek's (1961) "Newtonian unconscious," the after-effects of an indexicalization and iconization of the "universe ≈ machine" metaphor-model. In this regard, a symptom is to be taken as any other mental disorder, whose history must be traced in order to discover the events that played a part in its develop-ment. The mental patient suffers from the "figments" of his own imagination, which he takes to be "real"; the "universe ≈ machine" equation was, in the beginning, the "figment" of Descartes's imagination and, over time, became literally construed in Western cul-ture as the way things are.

11.   See, in this respect, Groupe µ's (1981) conceptualization of a metaphor as the combination of two instances of metonymy.

12.   The reader will observe certain lines of similarity between the notion being developed here and Russian formalism and Prague structuralism, according to which the chief function of poetic language is to lay bare the linguistic-poetic device in

order to "de-automatize," "de-familiarize," "de-habitualize" language—in other words, to "make it strange" (see especially Mukarovsky 1964; Shklovsky 1965; Steiner 1984). According to Gerald Graff (1979, 13), the formalist view sees the work of art as autonomous and therefore separate "from objective reality, science, and the world of practical, utilitarian communication and defines it as an autonomous, self-sufficient 'world' or law unto itself, independent of the external world. It is this formalist notion of the self-sufficient work that usually comes to mind when the term 'autonomy' is employed." Regarding the sign in general—and this will become apparent in later chapters—I see composite signs as maintaining a degree of autonomy, yet in another respect they remain open to their environment, hence the literary language/everyday language split becomes problematic.

13. It will become evident in the following chapter that I depart from Tursman's notion of phanerons (and *semiosis*) as "group permutations" in favor of a "matrix model."

14. Indeed, I would by no stretch of the imagination suggest—nor would Peirce if he were alive today, I presume—that a typology of signs could attain the rigor of the typology of the chemical elements.

15. The columns in figure 5 depart from those of Tursman (1987, 42, 49) insofar as I begin phaneronic subdivision with authentic Thirds, the last of which is the first to de-generate to a Second, and I begin *semiosic* generation with Firsts, the first of which is the first to generate a Second.

16. They are "harder to discern" due to embedment. The "error" of falling victim to embedment is potentially revealed when one embraces a trinary view rather than a stringent binary one.

17. This sign activity leads ultimately to Peirce's doctrine of synechism, or continuity, following the notion that signs—or ideas, which is to say the same—"tend to spread continuously and to affect certain others which stand to them in a peculiar relation of affectivity" (CP, 6.104).

18. From a general semiotic perspective, see Merrell 1991a; also, in biology, Jantsch 1980; Pattee 1977, 1986; Varela 1979; in psychology, Bateson 1972; Bruner 1962, 1986; Butler 1913; and from a metaphysical-scientific view, Schrödinger 1967.

19. Savan 1987–88 offers a concise, detailed, and cogent outline of the three types of interpretants.

20. See, from various vantage points, Bertalanffy 1967; Cassirer 1953, 1957; Koestler 1963; Maslow 1966; Matson 1964; Whitehead 1925; Rifkin 1983.

21. See Curd 1980; Merrell 1987, 1992.

22. Cybernetics, a holdover from mechanism (of which more in Chapter Eleven), was in its inception the last gasp of classical mechanics. The cybernetic machine analogy also strangely underlies deconstruction and various and sundry other recent rages (Harvey 1989). Though the thought may be disconcerting, it appears that this analogy is becoming more tolerable, and even acceptable, perhaps ceasing to be a synonym for mere mechanism of the nineteenth-century variety: it has lost its strangeness. For example, we are now quite familiar with the unconscious as a machine producing meanings (Lacan 1966), detective novels as machines for reading (Narcejac 1975), gram-

mars as machines for generating sentences (Chomsky 1957), myths as machines for canceling time (Lévi-Strauss 1964), and even desiring machines (Deleuze and Guattari 1983). I would suggest that in these instances—with perhaps the exception of Deleuze and Guattari—an embedded, automatized form of mechanism perseveres—the vice and the danger of all models (for more on this topic, see Merrell 1991a, 1992).

23. On the other hand, with respect to the interpretation of literary texts, Hans Robert Jauss (1982) suggests an interesting case of potential meaning provided by innovative works that cannot be understood at their time of production because they require conventions and procedures of reading that the public only later develops. That is, actualization of what is embedded in the work as a potential must await de-embedment by more aware and self-aware readers made possible by a different historical context. **315**

Chapter Five

1. Recently, as I pointed out in Chapter Two, this model has been appropriately debunked, perhaps most notably by Rorty.

2. However, see Eco (1990, 23–43) for distinctions between Derrida and Peirce with focus on Peirce's "unlimited semiosis" in terms of successive differentiation. Rather than a mere free play of signifiers, it is a game with purpose, by way of habit, and therefore affords a sense of direction, though at any given point it invariably remains unidentifiable or ill defined.

3. Things can appear otherwise, however. If an interpretant becomes habit, part of one's belief system, then it can appear to be final for the true believer, though this finality is mere illusion. The interpretant, in other words, has become embedded; as such, it is inauthentic. An authentic interpretant must continually subject itself to "a change of habit of conduct." One can understand the meaning of a concept (interpretant) only when one knows how one would modify one's conduct—given one's desires and beliefs—if one came to accept it as true, and accepting an interpretant demands awareness of what one would do in certain circumstances in order to put that interpretant on trial. Hence interpretants can never sit still; they are never stable but continually undergo change (CP, 5.475–76).

4. Ogden and Richards set up a triangular model in which the relation between "symbol" and "referent" is mediated by "thought or reference." Their "symbol" would be comparable to Peirce's representamen, their "thought or reference" to the interpretant, and their "referent" to the "real"—not semiotically real—object.

5. From diverse vantage points, see Berggren 1962–63; Brown 1976; Harré 1970; Leatherdale 1974; McClosky 1964; MacCormac 1985; and Turbayne 1962; for discourse as tropological through and through, see de Man 1981; Derrida 1974; and, from a semiotic perspective, Deely 1990; Johansen 1989, 1992.

Chapter Six

1. In Peirce's words, "A *sign* or *Representamen* is a First which stands in such a genuine triadic relation to a Second called its *Object,* as to be capable of determining a Third, called its *Interpretant,* to assume the same triadic relation to its Object in which it stands itself to the same Object" (CP, 2.274).

2. See Marty 1982 for a discussion of the mathematical implications of this hierarchically and partially ordered lattice structure, especially as depicted in figure 8.

3. Peirce, who is for obvious reasons partly a product of modernist thinking, uses the phrase "modes of being," for which I will generally substitute "signification" to avoid jargon that might be misconstrued as part of essentialist philosophy.

4. The three types of interpretants were briefly introduced in Chapter Four. The object of a sign is a Second, hence it can be subdivided into its immediate and dynamical characteristics. The immediate object exists within the sign; it is immediately present to the interpreting mind, and there is not yet any consciousness of it. The dynamic object is external to the sign; it is the thing or event "out there" determining the nature of the sign and its interpretant. For further details, I refer the reader to Savan's (1987–88) excellent introduction.

5. I should point out that Marty uses the term "functor" in his more rigorously formal exposition.

6. For Peirce, each sign instantiation requires a substrate, a First, and something that is differentiated from it, a Second. Likewise, Derrida (1982) writes regarding *différance* that a sign which cannot be iteratively recognized as such is not a legitimate sign. Such recognizability demands a differential otherness: there is no absolute identity after each reiteration of a sign in the semiotically real world.

7. I cannot overemphasize the very important point that at Spencer-Brown's deepest level of the act of distinction, indication, and assignment of value, a boundary must be crossed for there to be a bona fide sign instantiation, and if it is crossed again, "nothingness" remains. In contrast, in the realm of the semiotically real, a crossing again is never exactly the same as there not having been a crossing, for there invariably remains a difference from one crossing to another, and awareness of this difference, in the most primitive sense, may help to account for the emergence of memory (Spencer-Brown 1979, 62–68). This notion is similar to Kristeva's (1969, 246–77) contention that classical logic, especially the idempotent (in Boolean logic, $xx = x$, or in Spencer-Brown's notation, $\daleth\daleth = \daleth$), does not apply to poetic language—and, by extension, to Peircean semiotics in the most general sense.

8. Bear in mind that Spencer-Brown speaks of the *act* of naming, not the *function* of names or the names *themselves*. This is, in a certain manner of speaking, a *pre-syntax*. The act of naming has virtually nothing to do with the material aspect of a sign or the position of a name within the structure of a sequence of signs in an utterance.

9. See Merrell 1991a, chap. 8, for more specifics regarding the unboundaried or "nothingness," a sort of pre-Firstness.

10. Holophrastic sentences customarily suppress the predicate (icon) in contrast to the hole in Russell's "—— is blue." Johansen (1989) refers to this sort of repression in the Coca-Cola slogan, "Coke is it!" the "it" referring not only to the soft drink in question but also to an indefinite range of commodities, moods, and activities designed to appeal to the citizens of a hedonistic, consumer-oriented society. "Coke!" in other words, is the only necessary component of the phrase, since the predicate is no more than an open set.

316

11. See Schrödinger 1967, where it is postulated, some years before the discovery of DNA, that life begins with the equivalent of an aperiodic crystal (see also Hoffmeyer and Emmeche 1991; Löfgren 1978, 1981a, 1981b, 1984; and Pattee 1969, 1972, 1977 on the idea that language—i.e., *semiosis* in the broader sense—and life itself share common modes of signification) (for further discussion, see Merrell 1994).

12. Brian McHale (1987) argues that the dominant characteristic of modernism is epistemological, revolving around the questions What is to be known? How can I know it? and How is knowledge transmitted? while postmodernism shifts the problems of knowing to problems of modes of being, of ontology. However, I would submit that rather than being ontological, the postmodern world is semiotic to the core. Whatever "beingness" there may be, it is indelibly semiotically real, hence focus lies more properly on modes of signification. For this reason also, I have replaced Peirce's "being" with "signification."

13. Vagueness and generality, which were briefly touched upon above, will be discussed further in Chapter Eight (see also Brock 1979; Goudge 1952; Liszka 1989; Merrell 1991a, 1994; and Nadin 1983).

14. Compare also to Kristeva's (1969) non-Boolean, nonclassical, orthocomplemented logic, the sort that is found in poetic language, especially in such works as Mallarmé's "Un coup de dés."

15. Quantum logic is not funny-farm logic but rather the consequence of quantum observables refusing to follow Boolean distributive rules. Mathematicians generally have no truck with quantum and other bizarre logics, and logicians, for historical reasons, find them difficult pills to swallow. In general, quantum logic is a logic of complementarity. Complementary colors combine in suitable proportions to produce a neutral color, something unlike each of the combined colors in isolation. Complementarity in molecular biology is characterized by the capacity for precise pairing of purine and pyrimidine between strands of DNA such that the structure of one determines the structure of the other; each mutually supplies the other's lack, and together they produce something foreign to both. In quantum theory, there are two types of complementarity: the wave-particle sort, and position-momentum. The first involves fields in contrast to things, while the second involves spatiotemporal descriptions in contrast to velocity-energy descriptions. Regarding the first, Dirac writes that atomic theory takes fields and particles into its purview. Fields and particles "are not two different things. They are two different ways of describing the same thing—two different points of view. We use one or the other according to convenience" (cited in B. Gregory 1988, 155). Bohr tells us that specifying a particle according to space-time coordinates while including causality in the entire picture—both characteristics of classical theory—is impossible in simultaneity. The union of the two characteristics, though in and of themselves classical, must be looked upon "as complementary but exclusive features of the description" (Bohr 1934, 54).

Bohr (1958, 67) emphasizes further that all knowledge "presents itself within a conceptual framework adapted to account for previous experience and that any such frame may prove too narrow to comprehend new experiences." A conceptual scheme that works for one horizon of experience may be inadequate when that experience is met with a set of surprises and becomes inadequate for dealing with the world. When this occurs, the scheme must be modified—if not discarded entirely—by widening it sufficiently so that it can account for the new range of experience. Regarding quantum complementarity, this broader scheme includes both wave and particle, as it does both position and momentum, but these pictures considered independently cannot be held in check simultaneously, since their knowable, describable properties are mutually exclusive. Any logic capable of accounting for two complementary sets of phenomena within a given conceptual scheme must therefore be a *temporal* logic.

Bohr insists that his notion of complementarity does not imply mutual exclusiveness—as it has often been interpreted—but rather the notion of joint completion: two horns are necessary to the whole of the beast; jointly, they are capable of making it what it is. This joint completion, when embedded in the nonclassical, context-dependent logic of complementarity, evinces a diachronic dimension that renders it not exactly incompatible with, but complementary to, classical logic. Thus, quantum logic is an alternative to classical logic in the inclusive, not the exclusive, sense. Hilary Putnam (1969) argues that at the macrolevel, classical logic is intuitively valid, but this validity is not absolutely but approximately true. If Putnam is correct, with good reason quantum logic was originally thought of as a "fictitious logic," though it has gradually changed labels to become, in the conception of many observers, "real" (Dalla Chiara 1986).

16. Very significantly, Bohr wrote that all knowledge presents itself in the form of conceptual frameworks or schemes with which a community can account for its experience of the world. If a conceptual scheme is found to be inadequate over a wide range of phenomena and in a new domain of experience, it need not be categorically rejected but may be modified by increasing its generality. Bohr believed that the failure of a conceptual scheme is not necessarily because its conceptual content and structure is lacking but because it is too rich—i.e., extraordinarily inflexible. Hence, an effort to construct a viable understanding of increasingly broader domains while "recognising that no experience is definable without a logical frame" demands a "widening of the conceptual framework" (Bohr 1958, 82). In terms of definition (1), this entails the broader context of I_2, for example, which is capable of holding both R_1 and O_1 in check, each as a logically coherent sublattice, though they cannot both coexist within the same classical logical space: they are complementary.

17. As Peirce (CP, 7.349) often observed, ideas come in a one-at-a-time sequence. In other words, they are complementary and entertained on the same basis as disconnected singularities. Experience and mediary consciousness, which swim in the space-time continuum, serve to bring them together.

18. Regarding what Herbert dubs "sublattices," for example, the linear progression $R_1 \rightarrow I_2 \rightarrow O_3 \rightarrow I_{f-1}$ is properly Boolean, as are other subdomains within the matrix, but the matrix taken as a whole is non-Boolean.

19. The implicate (enfolded) and explicate (unfolded) orders are used by physicist David Bohm (1980) in the context of quantum interconnectedness. The implicate consists of the range of *possibilia* (Firstness). It is non-Cartesian and non-Boolean. The explicate consists of actuals (Seconds) accountable in terms of Cartesian coordi-

nates. The enfolded is not tantamount to the static, synchronic block universe—a rough equivalent of Saussurean *langue*. Rather, the enfolded and unfolded compose a dynamic, scintillating, trembling *holomovement* (whole movement), a dance of Shiva, so to speak (see Merrell 1991a, 1992, where I trace patterns between Bohm and Peirce).

20. See CP, 7.647, where, instead of the Necker cube, Peirce alludes to "Schroeder's stair," which can be seen either from above or from below.

21. Putnam (1976) proposes that Reimannian geometry : Euclidean geometry :: quantum logic : classical logic. But this presupposes yet a "higher" logic from which vantage point it is possible to account for Putnam's homology. In fact, ultimately, one might surmise, it presupposes the equivalent of Peirce's totalizing "logic of the universe."

22. In this sense, regarding my use of the term "quantum logic," it is not that quantum events are presumed tantamount to sign-events. It is an alternative logic that in a roundabout way can account for complementarity between signs, and in fact, it can potentially account for Peirce's complementary concepts of vagueness and generality. Recall summary remarks in this respect in chapters Three and Five, which will also be taken up further in Chapter Eight.

23. Peirce's asymptote, or his approximation theory of "truth," does not entail a smooth ride to the end of the epistemological rainbow; that is modernist thinking. Rather, somewhat contra Rescher (1978), I would submit that the pathway toward "truth" is discontinuous, and, in accordance with my above comments on Peirce's relation to Popper, we can never know absolutely if we are on the right track or not (see Merrell 1991a for more on this topic).

24. In fact, Barthes (1972, 131) qualifies his position vis-à-vis the import of Sless's critique, admitting to his immanentist posture (see also Goodheart 1984, chap. 3).

25. Thus the oscillating *I*s tend to linearize the matrix, but its nonlinear character can always exercise a certain force.

26. In Peirce's words, a sign "is anything which is related to a Second thing, its *Object*, in respect to a Quality, in such a way as to bring a Third thing, its *Interpretant*, into relation to the same Object, and that in such a way as to bring a Fourth into relation to that Object in the same form, *ad infinitum*" (CP, 2.92).

27. It bears mentioning at this juncture that our complementary matrix could be expanded almost indefinitely to include Peirce's sixty-six classes of signs, and on to his mind-boggling 3^{10} different sign types, though this would undoubtedly prove to be a supreme but numbing exercise in number crunching and, from a broader view, rather "ill advised" (Sanders 1970, 15).

Chapter Seven

1. Admittedly this assumption is problematic, and Peirce was cognizant of this, since he readily conceded that there is no absolute distinction between the "external universe" as a given semiotic agent knows it and his/her "inner world" (CP, 7.438).

2. Regarding Peirce's dialogic, Savan (1987–88, 46) observes: "Since the mind is an interpretant, or a system of interpretants, the development and growth of the mind can come about only through dialogue. Echoing Plato, Peirce said that thought is

an interior dialogue. The utterances of each voice in the dialogue are signs whose interpretants are the utterances of the answering voice. The full meaning of any sign emerges only as the dialogue expands into a conversation in which all the members of a community of interpretants take part." Quite significantly, a dialogic interpretation has been developed for a description of quantum phenomena and their intersection with observers (that is, the proponent [self] and opponent [other] of a dialogue on the verifiability or refutability of a proposition concerning a particular quantum event). This quantum dialogic procedure establishes the "pragmatic foundation of quantum logic" (see Stachow 1979).

320

3. C. W. Spinks has independently appropriated the same Macbeth scene as a paradigm for his unique interpretation of "marginal signs" (i.e., of vagueness, ambiguity, indeterminacy, undecidability) that focuses on the trickster theme (Spinks 1991).

4. Among the myriad interpretations of this scene, some have Macbeth apparently grasping something when he reaches for the weapon, since he has to look at his hand to see that it is empty. In others he seems to be in a dream or sleepwalking, or he rubs his eyes and makes a gesture of casting the illusion away. In still others he even tries to wipe the blood from the weapon. In all cases, some doubt lingers (Rosenberg 1978, 298–312).

5. The three sorts of hallucination mentioned here correspond to three types of Peirce's psychical elements, making up percepts: "qualities of feeling," "their reaction against my will," and "their generalizing or associating element" (CP, 8.144). Peirce uses the example of the inkstand on his desk, which he first sees in a perceptual grasp; then he takes a look at it from another angle to satisfy himself that it exists, whether he wills it or not; and finally he names it an "inkstand" as a generalized percept.

6. Actually, Peirce writes that no percept can be false, for if it is a percept, it is true that it is the "real" or imagined re-presentation of something (CP, 7.658). Moreover, he maintains that there is "no difference between a real perception and a hallucination, taken in themselves" (CP, 7.644). In both cases, what is taken in as a percept is at that moment simply what it is, a percept of something (see also MS 200).

7. Elsewhere Peirce (CP, 7.444, 448) writes that "all psychical actions divide into two great classes, those which are performed under the *uncontrolled* governance of association and those in which by the 'agency' of consciousness,—whatever that may mean,—the actions come under self-criticism and self-control. The latter class of actions may be pronounced *good* or *bad;* the former could not be otherwise than they were. . . . Such inferences are beyond the jurisdiction of criticism. . . . The ordinary business of life is, however, best conducted without too much self-criticism. Respiration, circulation, and digestion are . . . better carried on as they are, without any meddling by Reason; and the countless little inferences we are continually making,—be they ever so defective,—are, at any rate, less ill performed unconsciously than they would be under the regimen of a captious and hypochondriac logic." (In contrast, however, see Chapter Three, note 20; CP, 5.181.)

8. On the other hand, Nesher (1983, 1990) brushes aside the process of mental *semiosis* remaining in the domain of uncontrolled consciousness and proposes that Peirce's concerns lie almost exclusively with self-consciousness, with self-con-

trolled and rationally and logically meaningful cognition. Self-consciousness, Nesher (1990, 2–3) writes, "is identical with the *sign processes*—their development, and operation."

9.   I must insist that this exercise in *semiosic* generation is not a buildup of complex signs from "atomic" simples in grand logical positivist style. In the first place, much or most of the process necessarily remains tacit—limited semiotic animals that we are. In the second place, the process is nonlinear and context-dependent, a generation of signs complementarily interconnected with the entire web constituting Macbeth's background knowledge.

10.   See Merrell 1982 on the concept of boundaried spaces, which is comparable to Peirce's cuts and Spencer-Brown's mark of distinction.

Chapter Eight

1.   Since each sign (thought or cognition) is a determination or interpretant of a previous sign, there can be no sign that is not already interpreted. Peirce's semiotic consequently rules out any intelligible explanation of the relation of signs and their "real-world" referents, the relation of signs and their interpretants, and the fact that signs have the particular interpretants they do. As Peirce puts it,

> there is no moment at which there is a thought belonging to this series
> [of signs, thoughts, cognitions], subsequently to which there is not a
> thought which interprets or repeats it. There is no exception, therefore,
> to the law that every thought-sign is translated or interpreted in a sub-
> sequent one, unless it be that all thought comes to an abrupt and final
> end in death. (CP, 5.284)

Peirce's admission, "unless it be that all thought comes to an abrupt and final end in death," reveals his recognition that the process must have some natural beginning and finality, which would imply that there is, after all, an interpretant of a sign that is not itself a sign for some other interpretant. The inaccessibility of this final interpretant for a finite community, however, reveals the incompatibility of finitude and the infinite, though it does not do away with the lingering quandary remaining at the heart of Peirce's cosmology. In the final analysis, perhaps such quandaries cannot be avoided.

2.   In Merrell 1985b I developed the idea of a *parallel processing* of the Saussurean-Jakobsonian paradigmatic and syntagmatic axes, which is still a giant step removed from the nondistributive "dialectical" model I put forth here.

3.   See Merrell 1991a, 1994 on *semiosic* nonlinearity regarding chaos physics and dissipative structures.

4.   Nesher's work, which focuses on conscious self-control, is only one side of the picture. Tacit knowledge invariably exercises its force, as evidenced by Peirce's nonconscious immediacy of Firstness, Polanyi's tacit knowing, Wittgenstein's language games, and Hanson's mediated seeing *as-that*, to mention only a few cases.

5.   If there must be notation for "nothingness," the 0, topologically speaking, fits the bill quite well. As a sign among signs, and unlike the vast majority of signs, 0 signifies *no*-thing (Rotman 1987). It is the void that Hermann Weyl (1949, 75) envisioned when he qualified the Cartesian coordinates (0,0) with 0 at the midpoint between

positive and negative integers as the "necessary residue of ego extinction." At this point, the ego is collapsed into the continuum such that distinctions that were there are simply *no more*. Nevertheless, 0 is still not exactly "nothingness," as I use the term, for there is still a residue, a *noticed absence*, ∅.

6.   See Merrell 1985a, 1991a for further treatment of this topic.

7.   See, in a complementary vein, Merrell 1991a, 1992 on Bohm's explanation of the "smoothing" of quanta in experience, from micro- to macrophysical levels.

8.   For the implications of such experiments, see Goodman 1978; Kolers 1972; Pöppel 1972, 1988; Wiener 1948.

9.   The moiré effect on the senses is as if everything were held in check, or in imaginary time—a standing wave pattern—like the holographic model, each part of which reduplicates the whole (see Comfort 1984; Merrell 1991a; Pribram 1991; Pribram et al. 1974).

10.   These relationships are diagrammed by what is called an Argand circle, which incorporates the function of the imaginary number, i ($\sqrt{-1}$), in the two-dimensional Cartesian plot, where the y axis is represented by $+\sqrt{-1}$ (i.e., i) and $-\sqrt{-1}$ (i.e., $-i$), and the x axis by -1 and +1.

11.   See Merrell 1991b for detailed study of Borges along similar lines.

12.   What I have dubbed "history" (linear sequence) is not the multiply interconnected, nonlinear unfolding of the universe as propounded in this inquiry but rather a radically simplified metaphor of becoming, in contrast to the ensemble ("block," "being").

13.   Peirce struggled for more than fifty years to lay bare the device for generating new ideas. He put forth the claim that abduction, at times termed "retroduction" or "hypothesis," represents the most general sort of reasoning. It is the basis of pragmatism (CP, 5.196), which is essential to the first stage of all inquiry (CP, 6.469), and a necessary component of perception (CP, 5.181) and meaning (CP, 2.625). In explaining abduction, Peirce first observed that it is the only logical operation which introduces novelty. It is originary in the sense that it presents an assumption in the premise similar to something proposed in the conclusion, which could well be true without the latter being true and yet go unrecognized as such. The conclusion is not asserted positively; there is no more than an inclination toward it inasmuch as it represents that assumption in the premise iconically. For example, Kepler discovered the likeness between the observed longitude of Mars and an elliptical orbit modeling its movement. He did not, however, immediately conclude from this that the orbit of Mars is actually an ellipse, "but it did incline him to that idea so much as to decide him to undertake to ascertain whether virtual predications about the latitudes and parallaxes based on this hypothesis would be verified or not" (CP, 2.96). Preliminary adoption of an abduction or hypothesis must necessarily be probational until after a period of testing, an inductive procedure, can be carried out. An abduction, in this sense, is originary regarding its "being the only kind of argument which starts a new idea" (CP, 2.96).

14.   See, in this context, catastrophe theory (Thom 1975, 1983), dissipative structures (Prigogine 1980), and their counterparts in biology (Abraham and Shaw 1982; Jantsch 1980; Gould 1979, 1983) and, regarding society at large, Kuhn 1970.

15. Along similar lines, see Prigogine and Stengers 1984; Wheeler 1980a; and Merrell 1991a, 1994, where I briefly link Prigogine's view to semiotics.

Chapter Nine

1. I have developed this theme in Merrell 1994, following Schrödinger's notion that signs, and life itself, are patterned by way of an exceedingly complex "aperiodic crystal."

2. The circularity of this notion, depending as it does on musement, is equally obvious. In spite of its drawbacks, it nevertheless represents a gallant attempt on Peirce's part to account for the intangibles tying thought to feeling, reason to belief, objectivity to subjectivity, necessity to contingency, or in a manner of speaking, Thirdness to Firstness.

3. A comparable model using a Chinese box is appropriated by J. W. Dunne (1934) and Ignacio Matte Blanco (1975) in developing their concept of consciousness as infinite sets that, like a hologram, are such that every part contains the whole (see also CP, 1.169 for the notion of consciousness as an infinite regress).

4. On a similar note, Freeman Dyson (1980, 376) reports Richard Feynman as having once remarked: "The electron does anything it likes. . . . It goes in any direction at any speed, forward or backward in time, however it likes, and then you add up the amplitudes and it gives you the wave function."

5. Of course, Maxwell's notorious demon, given his phenomenal reflexes, is presumably capable of bringing order to an aggregate at the molecular level, thus creating negentropy. In the process, *molecular* indeterminacy is rendered mechanically rather than statistically determinate at the *molar* level.

6. The distinction alluded to here is Bohm's (1980) non-Cartesian implicate order (the enfolded, Firstness) and the Cartesian explicate order (the unfolded, Secondness), the former irreducible to classical formalisms, and the latter not. I leave open the question of so-called hidden variables, upon which Bohm's hypothesis is predicated and which can purportedly account for the inadequacies (incompleteness, due to the limitations of alternate complementary perspectives) of the Copenhagen interpretation (for further, see Hübner 1983).

7. As Spencer-Brown (1979, 104–5) puts it:

Let us . . . consider for a moment, the world as described by the physicist. It consists of a number of fundamental particles which, if shot through their own space, appear as waves, and are thus of the same laminated structure as pearls or onions, and other wave forms called electromagnetic which it is convenient, by Occam's razor, to consider as travelling through space with a standard velocity. All these appear bound by certain natural laws which indicate the form of their relationship.

Now, the physicist himself, who describes all this, is, in his own account, himself constructed of it. He is, in short, made of a conglomeration of the very particles he describes, no more, no less, bound together by and obeying the general laws as he himself has managed to find and to record.

Thus we cannot escape the fact that the world we know is constructed in order (and thus in such a way as to be able) to see itself.

8. See Gribbin 1984 for a layperson's account. In Merrell 1991b, I briefly discuss Schrödinger's cat in the context of Borges and the new physics.

9. Julian Jaynes (1976) argues that consciousness did not exist even in humans until recent times, since they did not previously have a self-referential notion of mind. On the other hand, perhaps the Geiger counter, the apparatus that records the decayed particle, or even the cat, which are all devoid of self-referential consciousness, should be construed as the observer. This is Wheeler's contention, as we shall note shortly.

10. With respect to literary texts, Hutcheon (1985, 23) similarly argues that there must be a reader; if not, the text qua text has not been properly actualized. She continues:

> Today's theories of intertextuality are structural in focus, . . . but depend upon an implied theory of reading or decoding. It is not just a matter of the text's somehow parthenogenetic or magical absorption and transformation of others texts. . . . Texts do not generate anything— until they are perceived and interpreted. For instance, without the implied existence of a reader, written texts remain collections of black marks on white pages.

11. More recently, Wigner (1967), Walker (1970), Walker and Herbert (1977), and Wolf (1986, 1988) have developed elaborate mathematical models that purport to demonstrate the crucial role of consciousness in bringing about the actualization of the physical world.

12. Reliance on recursive, self-referential consciousness to account for the collapse of a wave function creates problems with respect to different observers presumably making the same observation. Suppose, for example, two physicists decide to observe Schrödinger's system "simultaneously," each taking a photograph of the cat from equal distances at a 90-degree angle from one another. Then they travel to distinct galaxies at the same velocity. Exactly one year later, and now outside each other's "light cone," they develop their film. According to relativity theory, given its nonsimultaneity principle, there will be a frame of reference in which the first observer developed his film first, and hence collapsed the wave function, and another frame of reference in which the second observer developed her film first and collapsed her wave function. There are two distinct states, but there is no guarantee, from the frame of reference of each observer, that the two photographs coincide. The only way the two photographers can compare their results is to travel at the same velocity to their starting point and place their photographs side by side. In other words, given distant and distinct frames of reference, there can be no Cartesian immediacy of observation. There is no simultaneity, only what is for them time-bound mediacy (see Barrow and Tipler 1988, 469).

13. In this regard, Peirce writes: "Signs, the only things with which a human being can, without derogation, consent to have any transaction, being a sign himself, are triadic; since a sign denotes a subject, and signifies a form of fact, which latter

it brings into connexion with the former. 'But what,' some listener, not you, dear Reader, may say, 'are we not to occupy ourselves at all with earthquakes, droughts, and pestilence?' To which I reply, if those earthquakes, droughts, and pestilences are subject to *laws,* those laws being of the nature of signs, then, no doubt being signs of those laws they are thereby made worthy of human attention; but if they be mere arbitrary brute interruptions of our course of life, let us wrap our cloaks about us, and endure them as we may; for they cannot injure us, though they may strike us down" (CP, 6.344).

14. This is not to say that Wheeler's "joint product" or Peirce's community consensus can be in tune with the one and only "real" world. Peirce's individual, the locus of ignorance and error, is capable potentially of rising above his limitations, with community backing, of course. And the community, which is only slightly less finite than the individual, still remains fallible. In fact, there is no guarantee that the community is at a given time and place any less fallible than an individual within that community. Habermas's (1975, 105) vision of a transparent, fully communicative society whose citizens, engaged in practical discourse, test the claims of norms and, to the extent that they accept them with reasons, arrive at the conviction that in the given circumstances the proposed norms are "right," implies a unity of experience that simply cannot be. Moreover, Habermas's (1971) criticism of Peirce on the grounds that he reduces the process of inquiry to purely logical grounds while circumventing the role of dialogue within the community is unfounded (Merrell 1992, chap. 4). Interaction between individuals is the key to development of communal knowledge. And what each individual can eventually believe is the long-term agreement of the community; that is, it depends upon public language, shared conventions, and a particular form of life. So the individual collaborates with all individuals potentially—but never actually—to bring about a consensus, which by and large determines what the individual believes if he is in step with the collective march. This is admittedly a circular bootstrap operation, but it is virtuously, not viciously, circular.

15. Very much unlike Peirce, however, Wheeler maintains that the concept of continuous space-time is no more than an idealization. He notes that

> cloth shows nowhere more conspicuous than at a selvedge that it is not a continuous medium, but woven out of thread. Space-time . . . often considered to be the ultimate continuum of physics, evidences nowhere more strikingly than at big bang and collapse that it cannot be a continuum.
>
> There is an additional indication that space cannot be a continuum. Quantum fluctuations of geometry and quantum jumps of topology are estimated and calculated to pervade all space at the Planck scale [10^{-33} cm.] of distances and to give it a foamlike structure. (Wheeler 1980a, 350)

For Peirce, time and space are continuous because they embody conditions of possibility, and since the possible is general, and generality is continuity, they are two names for the same absence of distinction. This failure on the part of Peirce to anticipate quantization in physics was a grave error, Charles Hartshorne (1973) writes—though this should actually be no surprise, for after all, the most eminent physicists of the nineteenth century failed in this respect as well.

16.   Peirce writes that an inscription that is never interpreted by any semiotic agent will never become more than a variegated grouping of dreamy squiggles, an index testifying to the fact that some organism of some sort or other had been there, but without communicating anything or being able to communicate anything in the absence of an addressee (NE 4, 256; see also CP, 1.422, on the "real" when not put to use).

17.   J. Fisher Solomon (1988, 41) refers to Aristotle's notion that the logical difference between the writing of history and the writing of poetry consists in the first relating what happened and the second relating what may happen. In this sense, history would correspond to the Secondness of actual events, and poetry to Firstness, the possibility of events not yet actualized. Wheeler, in contrast, would view history more as Thirdness, that is, from a conditional and even past anterior vantage point.

18.   See Merrell 1994 for the concept of signs as living process.

19.   Wheeler has also engaged in a verbal sparring match with Popper, that most stalwart of realists. However, Wheeler does follow Popper's interpretation of Bohr's version of quantum mechanics, according to which an observation is not an observation at the quantum level until there has been an irreversible act of amplification, which thus adds a pragmatic note to the equation. Like Wheeler, I cannot overemphasize that the phenomenon must be a *recorded* phenomenon: nothing has happened until it is acknowledged as a happening. Although a particle recorded "now" by a physicist might only have begun its life's journey a millionth of a second before, the physicist could equally well have directed his attention to a particle that began billions of years ago, before there was any form of life as we know it. In such case, the same rule applies: until the "now" of the particle's recording, it has not really "happened."

20.   This situation is reminiscent of Borges's (1962, 19–29) remark in "The Garden of Forking Paths" that the only prohibited word in a riddle is the answer to the riddle. Riddles generally contain an inherent contradiction (e.g., "What is black and white and *red* all over?"), and their answers reveal a hidden ambiguity that clarifies the contradiction ("A newspaper is black and white and *read* all over"). The answer was implicitly there, yet it wasn't there. It had to be teased out of the riddle from within, and when it was forthcoming from within, it entailed a conceptual or semantic push to broaden the frame such that it could contain both sides of the ambiguity.

21.   Of interest, in this respect, is Derrida's (1984, 20) apparently strange syntax in his statement regarding the nuclear age: *"At the beginning there will have been speed,"* giving the reader to believe that the mad race toward war exists in a timeless orb, that all societies have experienced it in their own way. That is, the nuclear age was somehow preordained from the very inception of culture.

22.   Regarding this problem, John Barrow and Frank Tipler comment on what they dub the "Everett's Friend Paradox," so named after Hugh Everett, creator of the "many-worlds interpretation" of quantum mechanics. "Everett," they observe, pointed out that

> if it is considered problematic whether a single observer A with consciousness can collapse a wave function of a quantum system Q, then

it is equally problematic whether another observer B can collapse the wave function corresponding to the system A + Q, and whether a *third* observer C can collapse the wave function of the system B + C + Q, and so on for an infinite series of observers. There seem to be only five ways to avoid this quandary. First, solipsism, which, as Wigner emphasizes, any physicist would reject out of hand. Second, any being with consciousness can collapse wave functions by observations. Third, a "community" of such beings can collectively collapse wave functions. Fourth, there is some sort of Ultimate Observer who is responsible for the collapse of wave functions. Fifth, wave functions *never* collapse. (Barrow and Tipler 1988, 468)

Barrow and Tipler go on to write that the third and fourth possibilities have not been explored to any extent, though Wheeler

has been intrigued by the notion of collapse by intersubjective agreement, but he confesses that he does not see any way to make this idea mathematically precise. What really interests him about possibility three is that it would be a mechanism of bringing the entire Universe into existence! In the opinion of Heisenberg and von Weizsäcker, the Copenhagen Interpretation implies that properties of objects do not exist until they are observed; the properties are "latent" but are not "actual" before the observation. (Barrow and Tipler 1988, 469)

This "mechanism of bringing the entire Universe into existence" would require a final or ultimate observer collapsing the universe as a cosmic electron, a monad—which has actually been the object of some speculation regarding the "many-worlds interpretation"—to yield the "Ultimate Interpretant," the universe as an "Argument," a "Cosmic Poem," as Peirce has put it (CP, 5.119).

23. It is noteworthy that, with respect to semiotic objects in contrast to "real" objects, Robert Almeder (1980, 151–52) writes, in a vein reminiscent of Wheeler:

Real objects must be considered to exist in two ways. On the one hand, a real object must exist with its existence not so causally dependent upon the noetic act as to imply that knowledge is creative of the being of objects. On the other hand, since it is essential to the definition of real objects that it be knowable, it could not exist as an object of knowledge apart from a relationship to the mind. In short, the being of real objects is not constituted by the noetic act, but these objects cannot be considered of as having no relationship whatsoever to mind for otherwise they could not be known and we would be committed to a realm of unknowable things-in-themselves.

Chapter Ten

1. However, one must be careful when referring to "physical laws." According to Wheeler, a selection *here-now* can have an irreversible influence on what one *will want to say* about the past, about what *will have happened.* Yet selection and distinction

determine an *already present future*. The question, then, arises, Is strict causality, set in motion by some active agent, operating here? The very idea suggests a chain reaction leading to alterations of tremendous magnitude. To cite one of Wheeler's (1980b, 165) numerous examples, tobacco in a pipe is ignited on a ship steaming through the hot mass of unstable air lying over the Indian Ocean. The rising air current produced from the heat triggers a set of "perturbations," leading ultimately to a grand-scale "bifurcation" (in Prigogine's terms—recall the above example), and a typhoon results. Can this typhoon be traced back to the atom initially causing the set of reactions involved in lighting the match? Did that primitive act of amplification lead to a typhoon? Such questions regarding the "physics of chaos" are left unanswered, and they are most likely unanswerable in the classical language of causality. Yet ultimately, Wheeler suggests, the question revolves around the quantum theory of observation, of measurement, and of recorded phenomena (that is, phenomena made meaningful) (see also Wheeler 1982, 1986).

328

In this light, if we tune in on the idea of multiple semiotic realities and drop the bull-headed belief that somehow we can know "actual reality," we will realize that the elixirs of ancient alchemists, phlogiston, ether, atoms, quarks, and naked singularities are all semiotically real. And they are "fictions," as Nietzsche realized at a time when rampant optimism ruled regarding cognizability of the "actually real." Each semiotically real interpretant began humbly, as an act of *semiosic* amplification, with the potential to become charged with ever greater signifying power. As interpretants pile upon interpretants—ultimately to generate myths—sentences about semiotically real worlds may become capable of moving mountains.

2. Recall especially Eddington's "common ground," comparable to Wheeler's "joint product," which was discussed briefly at the beginning of Chapter Two.

3. For a similar view from another slant, see Rorty's (1988) "contingency" of language, of selfhood, and of community.

4. That which is selected and actualized at a given instant must be considered relatively infinitesimal with respect to the total number of possibilities. Significantly, in this regard, Peirce once wrote that the actual does not "constitute one trillionth of one *per cent* of what might be and would be under supposible conditions" (CP, 6.327).

5. With respect to the beginning of things, Sebeok (1983, 4–5), without referring to Wheeler, frames the essence of his hypothesis nicely in Peircean terms while alluding to the strange world of quanta. The remark merits full citation:

> We can say essentially nothing about the existence of the universe prior to about 20 billion years ago, save that, when it began in a singularity—equivalent to Peirce's Firstness— when any two points in the observable universe were arbitrarily close together, and the density of matter was infinite, we were past possibility and already in the realm of actuality (alias Secondness). In the opening millisecond, the universe was filled with primordial quarks. These fundamental particles, the basic building blocks from which all elementary particles are constituted, can best be grasped as signs, for as we learn from the physics

of our day, "Quarks had never been seen. . . . Most physicists today believe that quarks will never be seen . . ." (Pagels 1982, 231). As the universal expansion proceeded, temperatures fell to around 12^{27} K, the simple natural law that obtained in the infancy of this Cosmos unfolded into the three interactions now known as gravitation, the electroweak force, and the strong (Hadronic) force that binds the particles of the nucleus in the atom. The evolution—Thirdness—of these forces, in a single mathematical framework, as hoped for in the Grand Unified Theory, marks the appearance of Peirce's "law," which would explain the universal preference for matter over antimatter, as well as provide a solution for the so-called horizon problem (i.e., for the homogeneity of the universe) and the flatness problem (having to do with its mass density).

329

6.   See Merrell 1991a; Merrell and Anderson 1989.

7.   Wheeler's (1982, 22) equation, $0 = 0$, seems to abolish time altogether. In this respect, he often gives his reader the impression that from the perspective of the universe as a whole, time is an Einsteinian illusion, in contrast to Prigogine, for whom time is a real and irreversible process. Prigogine initially accepted Boltzmann's conclusion that, viewed as a totality, the universe's processes are reversible. Far-from-equilibrium studies later led him to conclude that nature performs a constructive, self-organizing, time-irreversible role. We, all of life, and even inorganic dissipative structures are living proof of order irreversibly generated out of chaos. Time is real, says Prigogine. It is no mere illusion.

8.   However, see Turley 1977 for some problems in Peirce's evolutionary cosmology and his concept of "nothingness."

9.   It is interesting to note that Rupert Sheldrake (1988, 80) compares his hypothesis of "morphic fields" to Peirce's notion of habit.

10.   J. T. Fraser (1982) gives this "time" the label of "prototemporal time," that is, "time" without direction or purpose.

11.   I refer to the experiment by Alain Aspect that points toward a quantum interconnectedness of the universe (Herbert 1985, 226–27). However, see Horwich 1987 and Mellor 1981 for detailed philosophical arguments against backward causation. While Horwich's and Mellor's arguments do not necessarily discount Wheeler's hypothesis, they reveal how our commonsensical notions balk at the very idea.

12.   See Murphey 1961, 379–90, for Peirce's lack of clarity on time.

13.   See Turley 1977 for the problematics inherent in Peirce's thought on this topic.

14.   For a popular account of symmetry-breaking in quantum physics, see Davies 1988; Pagels 1982.

15.   This "postmodern" view strikes at the very roots of mathematics, as John Kadvany (1989, 162) observes: "It is simply a basic feature of contemporary foundations of mathematics that from the theoretical perspective provided by mathematical logic, mathematics as a whole is as fragmented and bifurcated a mode of intellectual activity as one might find in the imagination of the most redoubtable postmodernist."

Chapter Eleven

1. Note, however, that Charles Jencks (1986) might label Jameson's conception and terminology part and parcel of late modernism rather than postmodernism.

2. In his development of his three orders of simulacra and the transitions between them, Baudrillard is influenced by Foucault's "epistemic shifts," via Gaston Bachelard. His conception of simulacra also seems similar to Morris's (1946, 23) "pure" iconic sign, which must be a duplicity, a reproduction, a replica. The problem is that Baudrillard's masses do not conceive simulacra as such but to all appearances take them in as if they were Peirce's "pure" icons, which—contra Morris—are mere quality, possibility, and unrelated to anything else as such, be it that of which it is a model, or whatever.

3. In fact, Baudrillard argues, even the most hostile of antagonisms—capitalism and socialism—are annulled by the natural dependence of one upon the other. Consequently, they are free to open themselves up to cooperation and collaboration, as we have witnessed over the past few years.

4. "Hyperspace," in Jameson's conception, is closely related to Baudrillard's "hyperreality" and "hyperspace." As Jameson puts it, a "certain spatial turn has often seemed to offer one of the more productive ways of distinguishing post-modernism from modernism proper, whose experience of temporality—existential time, along with deep memory—it is henceforth conventional to see as a dominant of the high modern" (Jameson 1991, 154; see also Rose 1991, chap. 3).

5. In McLuhanesque fashion, Baudrillard tells us that the "cool" cybernetic universe of "digitality" has engulfed the world. In other words, metaphor and metonymy—that is, the principle of simulation—"wins out over the reality principle just as over the principle of pleasure" (Baudrillard 1983a, 152). It all appears to be a matter of substituting signs of the "real" for the "real" itself such that it no longer needs to be perceived, conceptualized, and produced. The hyperreal is sheltered from the imaginary and from any distinction between the "real" and the imaginary, leaving room only for the orbital occurrence of model-signs and the simulated generation of difference (Baudrillard 1983a, 4).

6. Armed with his "hyperlogic"—which is plagued by illusive and elusive transparencies—Baudrillard argues that the "real" world for the masses is a sham world, the "actually real" world having long since receded beyond reach. Rather than a poststructuralist differential logic, there remains merely a logic of the immediate object *as if* it were the "reality," that is, not a re-presentation of "reality" (see also Pefanis 1991, chap. 4).

7. There might be some bizarre sense in all this. Paintings have become trophies or the source of quick profits among the insanely rich of the world. The ecstasies and agonies of Vincent van Gogh, one might protest, are surely worth more than so many junk bonds. And ironically, in a way they are, for they are now being made available to a larger audience—albeit as counterfeits.

8. Eco (1984, 217), however, writes: "Mirror images are not signs and signs are not mirror images. And yet there are cases when mirrors are used to produce processes which can be defined as semiotic."

9. However, when dealing with fakes and forgeries, we are not directly concerned with lies but with mistaking something for what it *is not* (Eco 1990, 177).

10. According to Eco (1990, 191–92), one must authenticate the original, not denigrate the fake because it is not the same as the original. The problem is that we cannot verify, only falsify, so to speak, for the absolutely authentic sign would be a sign of itself—i.e., the consummate symbol, unlike de-generate signs. It would be complete and consistent, precise and unambiguous, and as such we would be able to know it only approximately.

11. In this sense, Peirce stands Lewis Carroll's Humpty-Dumpty on his head:

331

> Man makes the word, and the word means nothing which the man has
> not made it mean, and that only to some man. But since men can think
> only by means of words or other external symbols, these might turn
> round and say: "You mean nothing which we have not taught you, and
> then only so far as you address some word as the interpretant of your
> thought." In fact, therefore, men and words reciprocally educate each
> other; each increase of a man's information involves and is involved
> by, a corresponding increase of a word's information. (CP, 5.313)

12. And here, once again, the danger of Morris's syntax/semantics/pragmatics triad comes into view. Just as syntax does not correspond specifically to Firstness, so also pragmatics does not correspond to Thirdness, for both rely on implicit intuition, abduction, knowing how, and seeing as-that, in addition to that which is made explicit.

13. See H. Dreyfus 1979, where AI is appropriately dubbed "alchemy"; see also Dreyfus and Dreyfus 1986; Boden 1977; McCorduck 1979; and in philosophy, Dennett 1987; Sloman 1979.

14. See Wright 1988 for an enlightening insight into the thought of Edward Fredkin, for whom the universe is nothing but a massive computer—the ultimate extension of the machine model-metaphor.

15. Some observers of the "postmodern" scene, for example John Fiske (1989a, 1989b, 1993) and Barry Smart (1993), have articulated, contra Baudrillard, their faith in the self-consciousness of the "masses" and their efforts to exercise a degree of control over their destiny. In fact, Roy Porter (1993) goes so far as to argue that Baudrillard's proclamations are not limited to our contemporary cultures at all but, from his particular perspective, could be addressed to a host of past cultures as well.

16. As of this writing, Virtual Reality has captivated the imagination of, and has been appropriated by, the advertising media, the video industry, and it has found its way into such films as *The Lawnmower Man* and *Total Recall*. According to reports from recent computer fairs, it appears that offshoots from Virtual Reality programs are soon to be made accessible to the BMW-penthouse crowd (for recent discussions, speculations, occasional euphoria, and a few warning signs regarding Virtual Reality, see Heim 1993; Helsel and Roth 1991; Levy 1990; Rheingold 1991; Wooley 1992).

17. On the notion of the "loss of meaning" in postmodernism, see Kellner 1989, 118; Pefanis 1991, 11.

18. Hubert Dreyfus and others, however, are prone to admit that computers have been taught rudimentary forms of generalization, abstraction, and various "fuzzy" logics of very basic sorts.

19. "Neural-network" research has injected a new note of optimism. Neural-network software, now being marketed for use with Windows at a cost of up to $795, can presumably serve educational purposes and host "real-world" applications—as if educational purposes were out of tune with the "real world." The claim has it that neural-networks will learn to recognize increasingly more sophisticated patterns and ultimately be capable of conceptualizing in terms of generalizations of the human sort (see Johnson 1992).

References

Abraham, Ralph, and Christopher D. Shaw. 1982. *Dynamics: The Geometry of Behavior.* Santa Cruz, Calif.: Arial Press.   **333**

Agassi, Joseph. 1975. *Science in Flux.* Dordrecht: D. Reidel.

———. 1981. *Science and Society: Studies in the Sociology of Science.* Dordrecht: D. Reidel.

Alexander, Thomas M. 1993. "John Dewey and the Moral Imagination: Beyond Putnam and Rorty toward a Postmodern Ethics." *Transactions of the Charles S. Peirce Society* 29 (3): 369–400.

Almeder, Robert. 1980. *The Philosophy of Charles S. Peirce: A Critical Introduction.* Totowa, N.J.: Rowman and Littlefield.

———. 1983. "Peirce on Meaning." In *The Relevance of Charles Peirce,* edited by E. Freeman, 328–47. LaSalle, Ill.: Monist Library of Philosophers.

Appel, Alfred. 1967. "An Interview with Nabokov." *Wisconsin Studies in Contemporary Literature* 8:140–41.

Arac, Jonathan, ed. 1986. *Postmodernism and Politics.* Minneapolis: University of Minnesota Press.

Ashley, Kathleen M., ed. 1990. *Victor Turner and the Construction of Cultural Criticism: Between Literature and Anthropology.* Bloomington: Indiana University Press.

Baer, Eugen. 1988. *Medical Semiotics.* Lanham, Md.: University Press of America.

Baker, Lynn Rudder. 1987. *Saving Belief: A Critique of Physicalism.* Princeton, N.J.: Princeton University Press.

Bakhtin, Mikhail. 1968. *Rabelais and His World.* Trans. H. Iswolsky. Cambridge, Mass.: MIT Press.

——— [V. N. Voloshinov]. 1973. *Marxism and the Philosophy of Language.* Trans. L. Matejka and I. R. Titunik. New York: Seminar Press.

———. 1981. *The Dialogic Imagination: Four Essays.* Trans. C. Emerson and M. Holquist. Austin: University of Texas Press.

Barnes, Barry. 1985. *About Science.* Oxford: Basil Blackwell.

Barnes, Barry, and David Edge, eds. 1985. *Science in Context: Readings in the Sociology of Science.* Cambridge, Mass.: MIT Press.

Barrow, John D. 1990. *The World within the World.* Oxford: Oxford University Press.

Barrow, John D., and Joseph Silk. 1983. *The Left Hand of Creation.* New York: Basic Books.

Barrow, John D., and Frank Tipler. 1988. *The Anthropic Cosmological Principle.* Oxford: Oxford University Press.

Barth, John. 1974. *The Literature of Exhaustion*. Durham, N.C.: Duke University Press.

Barthes, Roland. 1972. *Mythologies*. Trans. A. Lavers. New York: Hill and Wang.

———. 1974. *Critical Essays*. Trans. R. Howard. Evanston, Ill.: Northwestern University Press.

Bateson, Gregory. 1972. *Steps to an Ecology of Mind*. New York: Chandler.

Baudrillard, Jean. 1981. *For a Critique of the Political Economy of the Sign*. Trans. C. Levin. St. Louis, Mo.: Telos.

———. 1983a. *In the Shadow of the Silent Majorities*. Trans. P. Foss, J. Johnston, and P. Patton. New York: Semiotext(e).

———. 1983b. *Simulations*. New York: Semiotext(e).

———. 1984. "The Structural Law of Value and the Order of Simulacra." In *The Structural Allegory: Reconstructive Encounters with the New French Thought*, edited by J. Fekete, 54–73. Minneapolis: University of Minnesota Press.

———. 1988a. *The Ecstasy of Communication*. Trans. B. Schutze and C. Schutze. New York: Semiotext(e).

———. 1988b. *America*. London: Verso.

———. 1990. *Fatal Strategies*. New York: Semiotext(e).

Bazerman, Charles. 1988. *Shaping Written Knowledge: The Genre and Activity of the Experimental Article in Science*. Madison: University of Wisconsin Press.

Bense, Max. 1969. *Einführung in die informationstheoretische Aesthetik*. Hamburg: Rowohlt Taschenbuch Verlag.

Berger, Arthur Asa. 1989. *Signs in Contemporary Culture: An Introduction to Semiotics*. Salem, Wis.: Sheffield.

Berggren, D. 1962/63. "The Use and Abuse of Metaphor I," "The Use and Abuse of Metaphor II." *Review of Metaphysics* 16:236–58, 450–72.

Berman, Marshall. 1982. *All That Is Solid Melts into Air: The Experience of Modernity*. New York: Viking.

Bernstein, Jeremy. 1983. *Einstein*. Glasgow: Fontana.

Bernstein, Richard. 1983. *Beyond Objectivity and Relativism: Science, Hermeneutics, and Praxis*. Philadelphia: University of Pennsylvania Press.

———. 1988. "The Rage against Reason." In *Construction and Constraint: The Shaping of Scientific Rationality*, edited by E. McMullin, 189–221. Notre Dame, Ind.: University of Notre Dame Press.

Bertalanffy, Ludwig von. 1967. *Robots, Men, and Minds*. New York: George Braziller.

Black, Max. 1962. *Models and Metaphors: Studies in Language and Philosophy*. Ithaca, N.Y.: Cornell University Press.

Bloor, David. 1983. *Wittgenstein: A Social Theory of Knowledge*. New York: Columbia University Press.

Blonsky, Marshall, ed. 1985. *On Signs*. Baltimore, Md.: Johns Hopkins University Press.

Boden, Margaret. 1977. *Artificial Intelligence and Natural Man*. New York: Basic Books.

———. 1984. "Animal Perception from an Artificial Intelligence Viewpoint." In *Minds, Machines and Evolution: Philosophical Studies*, edited by C. Hookway, 153–74. Cambridge: Cambridge University Press.

Bohm, David. 1980. *Wholeness and the Implicate Order*. London: Routledge and Kegan Paul.

———. 1988. "Postmodern Science and a Postmodern World." In *The Reenchantment of Science,* edited by D. R. Griffin, 57–68. Albany: State University of New York Press.

Bohr, Niels. 1934. *Atomic Physics and the Description of Nature.* Cambridge: Cambridge University Press.

———. 1958. *Atomic Physics and Human Knowledge.* New York: John Wiley.

Boler, John P. 1964. "Habits of Thought." In *Studies in the Philosophy of Charles Sanders Peirce,* edited by E. C. Moore and R. S. Robin, 382–400. Amherst: University of Massachusetts Press.

Bolter, J. David. 1984. *Turing's Man: Western Culture in the Computer Age.* Chapel Hill: University of North Carolina Press.

Boon, James A. 1982. *Other Tribes, Other Scribes: Symbolic Anthropology in the Comparative Study of Cultures, Histories, Religions and Texts.* Cambridge: Cambridge University Press.

Bourdieu, Pierre. 1977. *Outline of a Theory of Practice.* Cambridge: Cambridge University Press.

———. 1984a. *Distinction.* Cambridge, Mass.: Harvard University Press.

———. 1984b. *Homo Academicus.* Paris: Editions de Minuit.

Boorstin, Daniel. 1972. *The Image: A Guide to Pseudo-events in America.* New York: Atheneum.

Borges, Jorge Luis. 1962. *Labyrinths, Selected Stories and Other Writings.* Ed. D. A. Yates and J. E. Irby. New York: New Directions.

———. 1964. *Other Inquisitions, 1937–1952.* Trans. R. L. C. Simms. Austin: University of Texas Press.

———. 1978. *The Book of Sand.* Trans. N. T. di Giovanni. New York: E. P. Dutton.

Broad, C. D. 1938. *An Examination of McTaggart's Philosophy.* Vol. 2, part 1. Cambridge: Cambridge University Press.

Brock, Jarrett E. 1979. "Principle Themes in Peirce's Logic of Vagueness." In *Peirce's Semiotic Studies,* no. 1, edited by J. E. Brock et al., 41–50. Lubbock, Tex.: Institute for Studies in Pragmaticism.

Broglie, Louis de. 1939. *Matter and Light: The New Physics.* Trans. W. H. Johnston. New York: W. W. Norton.

———. 1953. *The Revolution in Physics.* New York: Noonday.

Bronowski, Jacob. 1978. *The Origins of Knowledge and Imagination.* New Haven, Conn.: Yale University Press.

Brown, Richard Harvey. 1976. "Social Theory as Metaphor: On the Logic of Discovery for the Sciences of Conduct." *Theory and Society* 3 (2): 169–97.

———. 1987. *Society as Text.* Chicago, Ill.: University of Chicago Press.

Bruner, Jerome. 1957. "Going beyond the Information Given." In *Contemporary Approaches in Cognition: A Symposium Held at the University of Colorado,* 41–69. Cambridge, Mass.: Harvard University Press.

———. 1962. *The Process of Education.* Cambridge, Mass.: Harvard University Press.

———. 1986. *Actual Minds, Possible Worlds.* Cambridge, Mass.: Harvard University Press.

Buchler, Justus. 1952. "What Is the Pragmaticist Theory of Meaning?" In *Studies in the Philosophy of Charles Sanders Peirce,* edited by P. P. Wiener and F. H. Young, 21–32. Cambridge, Mass.: Harvard University Press.

Buckley, Paul, and F. David Peat, eds. 1979. *A Question of Physics: Conversations in Physics and Biology.* Toronto: University of Toronto Press.

Buczynska-Garewicz, Hanna. 1979a. "The Degenerate Sign." *Semiosis,* no. 13, 5–16.

———. 1979b. "The Degenerate Sign." In *Semiotics Unfolding (Proceedings of the Second Congress of the International Association for Semiotic Studies),* edited by Tasso Borbé, 1:43–50. Berlin: Mouton de Gruyter.

Bürger, Peter. 1984. *The Theory of the Avant-Garde.* Minneapolis: University of Minnesota Press.

Burks, Arthur W. 1980. "Man: Sign or Algorithm? A Rhetorical Analysis of Peirce's Semiotics." *Transactions of the Charles S. Peirce Society* 16 (4): 279–92.

Butler, Samuel. 1913. *Life and Habit.* London: Jonathan Cape.

Calvin, William H. 1989. *The Cerebral Symphony: Seashore Reflections on the Structure of Consciousness.* New York: Bantam.

Campbell, Jeremy. 1982. *Grammatical Man: Information, Entropy, Language, and Life.* New York: Simon and Schuster.

———. 1989. *The Improbable Machine.* New York: Simon and Schuster.

Capek, Milic. 1961. *The Philosophical Impact of Contemporary Physics.* New York: American Book.

———. 1965. "The Myth of the Frozen Passage: The Status of Becoming in the Physical World." In *Boston Studies in the Philosophy of Science. Proceedings of the Boston Colloquium for the Philosophy of Science, 1962–64,* edited by R. S. Cohen and M. W. Wartofsky, 2:441–61. Dordrecht: D. Reidel.

Caputo, John D. 1987. *Radical Hermeneutics: Repetition, Deconstruction and the Hermeneutical Project.* Bloomington: Indiana University Press.

Cascardi, Anthony J. 1988. "History, Theory, (Post)Modernity." In *Ethics/Aesthetics: PostModern Positions,* edited by R. Merrill, 27–46. Washington, D.C.: Maisonneuve.

Cassirer, Ernst. 1953. *Language.* Vol. 1 of *The Philosophy of Symbolic Forms.* Trans. R. Manheim. New Haven, Conn.: Yale University Press.

———. 1957. *The Phenomenology of Knowledge.* Vol. 3 of *The Philosophy of Symbolic Forms.* Trans. R. Manheim. New Haven, Conn.: Yale University Press.

Casti, John. 1989. *Paradigms Lost: Images of Man in the Mirror of Science.* New York: William Morrow.

Certeau, Michel de. 1980. "Writing vs. Time: History and Anthropology in the Works of Lafitau." *Yale French Studies* 59:37–64.

———. 1983. "History: Ethics, Science, and Fiction." In *Social Science as Moral Inquiry,* edited by N. Hahn et al., 173–209. New York: Columbia University Press.

———. 1984. *The Practice of Everyday Life.* Trans. S. Randall. Berkeley and Los Angeles: University of California Press.

———. 1986. *Heterologies: Discourse of the Other.* Minneapolis: University of Minnesota Press.

336

————. 1988. *The Writing of History*. New York: Columbia University Press.

Charon, Jean E. 1987. "The Real and the Imaginary in Complex Relativity." In *The Real and the Imaginary: A New Approach to Physics,* edited by J. E. Charon, 47–68. New York: Paragon House.

Chisholm, Roderick M. 1952. "Falliblism and Belief." In *Studies in the Philosophy of Charles Sanders Peirce,* edited by P. P. Wiener and F. H. Young, 93–120. Cambridge, Mass.: Harvard University Press.

Chomsky, Noam. 1957. *Syntactic Structures.* The Hague: Mouton.

Clifford, James. 1983. "On Ethnographic Authority." *Representations* 1:118–46.

Clifford, J., and George E. Marcus, eds. 1986. *Writing Culture: The Poetics and Politics of Ethnography.* Berkeley and Los Angeles: University of California Press.

Collins, Jim. 1989. *Uncommon Cultures: Popular Culture and Postmodernism.* New York: Routledge.

Comfort, Alex. 1984. *Reality and Empathy: Physics, Mind, and Science in the Twenty-first Century.* Albany: State University of New York Press.

Connolly, John M., and Thomas Keutner, eds. 1988. *Hermeneutics versus Science? Three German Views.* Notre Dame, Ind.: University of Notre Dame Press.

Connor, Steve. 1989. *Postmodern Culture: An Introduction to Theories of the Contemporary.* Oxford: Basil Blackwell.

Count, Earl W. 1969. "Animal Communication in Man-Science: An Essay in Perspective." In *Approaches to Animal Communication,* edited by T. Sebeok, 77–130. The Hague: Mouton.

Craik, Kenneth J. 1943. *The Nature of Explanation.* Cambridge: Cambridge University Press.

Curd, Martin. 1980. "The Logic of Discovery: An Analysis of Three Approaches." In *Scientific Discovery, Logic, and Rationality,* edited by T. Nickles, 201–20. Dordrecht: D. Reidel.

Dalla Chiara, Maria Luisa. 1986. "Quantum Logic." In *Alternatives in Classical Logic,* 427–69. Vol. 3 of *Handbook of Philosophical Logic,* edited by D. Gabbay and F. Guenthner. Dordrecht: D. Reidel.

Danto, Arthur C. 1985. "Philosophy as/and/of Literature." In *Post-Analytic Philosophy,* edited by J. Rajchman and C. West, 63–83. New York: Columbia University Press.

Dantzig, Tobias. 1930. *Number: The Language of Science.* 4th ed. New York: Free Press.

Darnton, Robert. 1984. *The Great Cat Massacre and Other Episodes in French Cultural History.* New York: Basic Books.

Davidson, Donald. 1984. *Inquiries into Truth and Interpretation.* Oxford: Clarendon Press.

Davies, Paul. 1988. *The Cosmic Blueprint.* New York: Simon and Schuster.

Debord, Guy. 1977. *The Society of the Spectacle.* Detroit, Mich.: Red and Black.

Deely, John. 1982. *Introducing Semiotic.* Bloomington: Indiana University Press.

————. 1990. *Basics of Semiotics.* Bloomington: Indiana University Press.

————. 1994. *The Human Use of Signs, Or, Elements of Anthroposemiosis.* Lanham, Md.: Rowman and Littlefield.

337

Delaney, C. F. 1993. *Science, Knowledge, and Mind: A Study in the Philosophy of C. S. Peirce.* Notre Dame, Ind.: University of Notre Dame Press.

Deleuze, Gilles. 1968. *Différence et répétition.* Paris: PUF.

————. 1983. *Nietzsche and Philosophy.* Trans. H. Tomlinson. New York: Columbia University Press.

Deleuze, Gilles, and Félix Guattari. 1983. *Anti-Oedipus.* Trans. R. Hurley et al. Vol. 1 of *Capitalism and Schizophrenia.* Minneapolis: University of Minnesota Press.

————. 1987. *A Thousand Plateaus.* Trans. B. Massumi. Vol. 2 of *Capitalism and Schizophrenia.* Minneapolis: University of Minnesota Press.

DeLong, Howard. 1970. *A Profile of Mathematical Logic.* New York: Addison-Wesley.

Dennett, David. 1987. *The Intentional Stance.* Cambridge, Mass.: MIT Press.

Derrida, Jacques. 1973. *Speech and Phenomena, and Other Essays on Husserl's Theory of Signs.* Trans. D. B. Allison. Evanston, Ill.: Northwestern University Press.

————. 1974. *Of Grammatology.* Trans. G. C. Spivak. Baltimore, Md.: Johns Hopkins University Press.

————. 1978. *Writing and Difference.* Trans. A. Bass. Chicago, Ill.: University of Chicago Press.

————. 1981. *Positions.* Trans. A. Bass. Chicago, Ill.: University of Chicago Press.

————. 1982. *Margins of Philosophy.* Trans. A. Bass. Chicago, Ill.: University of Chicago Press.

————. 1984. "No Apocalypse, Not Now: Full Speed Ahead, Seven Missiles, Seven Missives." *Diacritics* 14 (2): 20–31.

Descartes, René. 1983. *Principles of Philosphy.* Vol. 4. Trans. V. R. Miller and R. P. Miller. Dordrecht: D. Reidel.

Dewey, John. 1925. *Experience and Nature.* Chicago, Ill.: Open Court.

————. 1929. *The Quest for Certainty: A Study of the Relation of Knowledge and Action.* New York: Minton, Balch.

DeWitt, Bryce S. 1968. "Reversion of the 2-Sphere." In *Battelle rencontres,* edited by C. M. DeWitt and J. A. Wheeler, 546–57. New York: W. A. Benjamin.

Dirac, Paul A. C. 1963. "The Physicists's Picture of Nature." *Scientific American* 208 (5): 45–53.

Dobbs, H. A. C. 1972. "The Dimensions of the Sensible Present." In *The Study of Time,* edited by J. T. Fraser, F. C. Haber, and G. H. Miller, 274–92. New York: Springer-Verlag.

Donougho, Martin. 1989. "Postmodern Jameson." In *Post-modernism, Jameson, Critique,* edited by D. Kellner, 75–95. Washington, D.C.: Maisonneuve.

Douglas, Mary. 1966. *Purity and Danger.* London: Routledge and Kegan Paul.

————. 1970. *Natural Symbols.* New York: Bantam.

Douglas, Mary, ed. 1975. *Implicit Meanings.* London: Routledge and Kegan Paul.

Dozoretz, Jerry. 1979. "The Internally Real, the Fictitious, and the Indubitable." In *Studies in Peirce's Semiotic,* no. 1, edited by J. E. Brock et al., 77–87. Lubbock, Tex.: Institute for Studies in Pragmaticism.

Dreyfus, Hubert L. 1971. "The Critique of Artificial Reason." In *Interpretations of Life and Mind,* edited by M. Grene, 99–116. New York: Humanities Press.

338

————. 1979. *What Computers Can't Do: The Limits of Artificial Intelligence*. 2d ed. New York: Harper and Row.

Dreyfus, Hubert L., and Stuart E. Dreyfus. 1986. *Mind over Machine: The Power of Human Intuition and Expertise in the Era of the Computer*. New York: Free Press.

Duhem, Pierre. 1954. *The Aim and Structure of Physical Theory*. Princeton, N.J.: Princeton University Press.

Dunne, J. W. 1934. *An Experiment with Time*. London: Faber.

Dyson, Freeman. 1980. "Comment on the Topic 'Beyond the Black Hole.'" In *Some Strangeness in the Proportion: A Centennial Symposium to Celebrate the Achievement of Albert Einstein*, edited by H. Wolff, 376–80. Reading, Mass.: Addison-Wesley.

Eagleton, Terry. 1985. "Capitalism, Modernism and Postmodernism." *New Left Review*, no. 152, 60–73.

————. 1987. "Awakening from Modernity." *Times Literary Supplement*, 20 Feb., p. 9.

Eco, Umberto. 1976. *A Theory of Semiotics*. Bloomington: Indiana University Press.

————. 1984. *Semiotics and the Philosophy of Language*. Bloomington: Indiana University Press.

————. 1990. *The Limits of Interpretation*. Bloomington: Indiana University Press.

Eco, Umberto, and Thomas A. Sebeok, eds. 1983. *The Sign of Three: Dupin, Holmes, Peirce*. Bloomington: Indiana University Press.

Eddington, Arthur S. 1920. *Space, Time, and Gravitation: An Outline of General Relativity*. Cambridge: Cambridge University Press.

————. 1935. *New Pathways in Science*. Cambridge: Cambridge University Press.

————. 1946. *Fundamental Theory*. Cambridge: Cambridge University Press.

————. 1958a. *The Nature of the Physical World*. Ann Arbor: University of Michigan Press.

————. 1958b. *The Philosophy of Physical Science*. Ann Arbor: University of Michigan Press.

Eigen, Manfred. 1971. "Self-organization of Matter and the Evolution of Biological Macromolecules." *Naturwissenschaften* 58:465–523.

Eigen, Manfred, and Peter Schuster. 1979. *The Hypercycle: A Principle of Natural Self-organization*. New York: Springer-Verlag.

Einstein, Albert. 1949a. "Autobiographical Notes." In *Albert Einstein: Philosopher-Scientist*, edited by P. A. Schilpp, 1–94. LaSalle, Ill.: Open Court.

————. 1949b. "Reply to Criticisms." In *Albert Einstein: Philosopher-Scientist*, edited by P. A. Schilpp, 665–88. LaSalle, Ill.: Open Court.

————. 1950. *Out of My Later Years*. New York: Philosophical Library.

Ellis, Keith. 1978. *Number Power*. New York: St. Martin's Press.

Escher, Maurits C. 1971. "Approaches to Infinity." In *The World of M. C. Escher*, edited by J. L. Locher, 15–16. New York: Harry N. Abrams.

Fairbanks, Matthew J. 1976. "Peirce on Man as a Language: A Textual Interpretation." *Transactions of the Charles S. Peirce Society* 12 (1): 18–32.

Fann, K. T. 1970. *Peirce's Theory of Abduction*. The Hague: Martinus Nijhoff.

Ferré, Frederick. 1988. "Religious World Modeling and Postmodern Science." In *The Reenchantment of Science: Postmodern Proposals,* edited by D. R. Griffin, 87–97. Albany: State University of New York Press.

Feyerabend, Paul K. 1958. "Complementarity." *Proceedings of the Aristotelian Society Supplement* 32:75–104.

———. 1975. *Against Method.* London: NLB.

———. 1987. *Farewell to Reason.* London: NLB.

Fiedler, Leslie. 1975. "Cross the Border—Close the Gap: Post-Modernism." In *American Literature since 1900,* edited by M. Concliff, 344–67. London: Sphere.

Findlay, J. 1942. "Gödelian Sentences, a Non-numerical Approach." *Mind* 51:259–65.

Finkelstein, David. 1969. "Matter, Space, and Logic." In *Boston Studies in the Philosophy of Science. Proceedings of the Boston Colloquium for Philosophy of Science 1966/1968,* edited by M. Wartofsky and R. Cohen, 5:199–215. New York: Humanities Press.

Finlay, Marike. 1990. *The Potential of Modern Discourse: Musil, Peirce, and Perturbation.* Bloomington: Indiana University Press.

Fisch, Max. 1978. "Peirce's General Theory of Signs." In *Sight, Sound and Sense,* edited by T. Sèbeok, 31–70. Bloomington: Indiana University Press.

———. 1986. *Peirce, Semeiotic, and Pragmatism.* Bloomington: Indiana University Press.

Fish, Stanley. 1980. *Is There a Text in This Class? The Authority of Interpretive Communities.* Cambridge, Mass.: Harvard University Press.

Fisher, John Andrew. 1990. "The Very Idea of Perfect Realism." *Philosophical Forum* 22 (1): 49–62.

Fiske, John. 1989a. *Reading the Popular.* London: Routledge.

———. 1989b. *Understanding Popular Culture.* Boston, Mass.: Unwin Hyman.

———. 1993. *Power Plays, Power Works.* London: Verso.

Fodor, J., and Zenon Pylyshyn. 1981. "How Direct Is Visual Perception: Some Reflections on Gibson's 'Ecological Approach.'" *Cognition* 9:139–96.

Foerster, 1983. "On Constructing a Reality." In *The Invented Reality,* edited by P. Watzlawick, 41–61. New York: W. W. Norton.

Foster, Hal, ed. 1983. *The Anti-aesthetic: Essays on Postmodern Culture.* Port Townsend, Wash.: Bay Press.

———. 1985. *Recodings: Art, Spectacle, Cultural Politics.* Port Townsend, Wash.: Bay Press.

Foucault, Michel. 1970. *The Order of Things: An Archaeology of the Human Sciences.* New York: Pantheon.

———. 1972. *The Archaeology of Knowledge.* London: Tavistock.

———. 1983. *This Is Not a Pipe.* Trans. James Harkness. Berkeley and Los Angeles: University of California Press.

Fraser, J. T. 1982. *The Genesis and Evolution of Time: A Critique of Interpretation in Physics.* Amherst: University of Massachusetts Press.

Franz, Marie Luise von. 1974. *Number and Time.* Trans. A. Dykes. Evanston, Ill.: Northwestern University Press.

Frege, Gottlob. 1970. "On Sense and Meaning." In *Translations from the Philosophical Writings of Gottlob Frege.* Trans. P. Geach and M. Black. Oxford: Basil Blackwell.

Friedman, Alan J., and Carol C. Donley. 1985. *Einstein as Myth and Muse.* Cambridge: Cambridge University Press.

Gadamer, Hans-Georg. 1975. *Truth and Method.* New York: Crossroads.

Gardner, Howard. 1987. *The Mind's New Science: A History of the Cognitive Revolution.* 2d ed. New York: Basic Books.

Gardner, Martin. 1964. *The Ambidextrous Universe: Mirror Asymmetry and the Time-Reversed Worlds.* New York: Charles Scribner's Sons.

———. 1968. *Logic Machines, Diagrams and Boolean Algebra.* New York: Dover.

Geertz, Clifford. 1973. *The Interpretation of Cultures.* New York: Basic Books.

———. 1983. *Local Knowledge: Further Essays in Interpretive Anthropology.* New York: Basic Books.

Gellner, Ernest. 1985. *Relativism and the Social Sciences.* Cambridge: Cambridge University Press.

Genette, Gérard. 1982. *Figures of Literary Discourse.* New York: Columbia University Press.

Gentry, George. 1952. "Habit and the Logical Interpretant." In *Studies in the Philosophy of Charles Sanders Peirce,* edited by P. P. Wiener and F. H. Young, 75–92. Cambridge, Mass.: Harvard University Press.

Gibson, J. J. 1950. *The Perception of the Visual World.* Boston: Houghton-Mifflin.

———. 1966. *The Senses Considered as Perceptual Systems.* Boston: Houghton-Mifflin.

———. 1979. *The Ecological Approach to Visual Perception.* Boston: Houghton-Mifflin.

Giraud, Pierre. 1975. *Semiology.* Trans. G. Gross. London: Routledge and Kegan Paul.

Gombrich, Ernst H. 1960. *Art and Illusion.* Princeton, N.J.: Princeton University Press.

Goodheart, Eugene. 1984. *The Skeptic Disposition in Contemporary Criticism.* Princeton, N.J.: Princeton University Press.

Goodman, Nelson. 1976. *Languages of Art.* Indianapolis, Ind.: Hackett.

———. 1978. *Ways of Worldmaking.* Indianapolis, Ind.: Hackett.

———. 1984. *Of Mind and Other Matters.* Cambridge, Mass.: Harvard University Press.

Gorlée, Dinda L. 1990. "Degeneracy: A Reading of Peirce's Writing." *Semiotica* 81 (1/2): 71–92.

Goudge, Thomas A. 1952. "Peirce's Theory of Abstraction." In *Studies in the Philosophy of Charles Sanders Peirce,* edited by P. P. Wiener and F. H. Young, 323–41. Cambridge, Mass.: Harvard University Press.

Gould, Stephen J. 1979. *Ever since Darwin.* New York: W. W. Norton.

———. 1983. *Hen's Teeth and Horses' Toes.* New York: W. W. Norton.

Graff, Gerald. 1979. *Literature against Itself: Literary Ideas in Modern Society.* Chicago, Ill.: University of Chicago Press.

Granet, Marcel. 1968. *La pensée chinoise.* Paris: Albin Michel.

Greenberg, Clement. 1973. "Modern Painting." In *The New Art,* edited by G. Battcock, 66–77. New York: E. P. Dutton.

Gregory, Bruce. 1988. *Inventing Reality: Physics as Language.* New York: John Wiley.

341

Gregory, Richard L. 1966. *Eye and Brain: The Psychology of Seeing.* New York: McGraw-Hill.

———. 1970. *The Intelligent Eye.* New York: McGraw-Hill.

———. 1972. "Seeing as Thinking: An Active Theory of Perception." *Times Literary Supplement,* 23 June, 707–8.

———. 1981. *Mind in Science: A History of Explanations in Psychology and Physics.* Cambridge: Cambridge University Press.

Greimas, A. J., and J. Courtès. 1982. *Semiotics and Language: An Analytical Dictionary.* Trans. L. Crist et al. Bloomington: Indiana University Press.

Gribbin, John. 1984. *In Search of Schrödinger's Cat: Quantum Physics and Reality.* New York: Bantam Books.

Grice, Paul H. 1975. "Logic and Conversation." In *Speech Acts, Syntax and Semantics,* edited by P. Cole and J. Morgan, 3:41–58. New York: Academic Press.

Griffin, David Ray. 1988. "Introduction: The Reenchantment of Science." In *The Reenchantment of Science: Postmodern Proposals,* edited by D. R. Griffin, 1–46. Albany: State University of New York Press.

Gross, Alan G. 1990. *The Rhetoric of Science.* Cambridge, Mass.: Harvard University Press.

Groupe μ. 1981. *A General Rhetoric.* Trans. P. B. Burrell and E. M. Slotkin. Baltimore, Md.: Johns Hopkins University Press.

Gutting, Gary, ed. 1980. *Paradigms and Revolutions.* Notre Dame, Ind.: University of Notre Dame Press.

———. 1989. *Michel Foucault's Archaeology of Scientific Reason.* Cambridge: Cambridge University Press.

Habermas, Jürgen. 1971. *Knowledge and Human Interests.* Trans. J. J. Shapiro. Boston: Beacon Press.

———. 1975. *Legitimation Crisis.* Trans. T. McCarthy. Boston: Beacon Press.

———. 1983. "Modernity—An Incomplete Project." In *The Anti-aesthetic: Essays on Postmodern Culture,* edited by H. Foster, 192–216. Port Townsend, Wash.: Bay Press.

———. 1985. "Neoconservative Cultural Criticism in the United States and West Germany: An Intellectual Movement in Two Political Cultures." In *Habermas and Modernity,* edited by R. Bernstein, 78–94. Cambridge, Mass.: MIT Press.

———. 1987. *The Philosophical Discourse of Modernity.* Trans. F. Lawrence. Cambridge, Mass.: MIT Press.

Hacking, Ian. 1982. "Language, Truth and Reason." In *Rationality and Relativism,* edited by M. Hollis and S. Lukes, 48–66. Cambridge, Mass.: MIT Press.

———. 1983. *Representing and Intervening: Introductory Topics in the Philosophy of Natural Science.* Cambridge: Cambridge University Press.

———. 1985. "Styles of Scientific Reasoning." In *Post-analytic Philosophy,* edited by J. Rajchman and C. West, 145–65. New York: Columbia University Press.

Hanson, Norwood R. 1958. *Patterns of Discovery.* Cambridge: Cambridge University Press.

———. 1961. "Is There a Logic of Discovery?" In *Current Issues in Philosophy of Science,* edited by H. Feigl and G. Maxwell, 1:20–35. New York: Holt, Reinhart and Winston.

———. 1965. "Notes toward a Logic of Discovery." In *Perspectives on Peirce,* edited by R. J. Bernstein, 42–65. New Haven, Conn.: Yale University Press.

———. 1969. *Perception and Discovery.* San Francisco, Calif.: Freeman, Cooper.

———. 1971. *What I Do Not Believe, and Other Essays.* Dordrecht: D. Reidel.

Hardwick, Charles S., ed. 1977. *Semiotics and Significs: The Correspondence between Charles S. Peirce and Victoria Lady Welby.* Bloomington: Indiana University Press.

Harré, Rom. 1970. *The Principles of Scientific Thinking.* New York: MacMillan.

Hartshorne, Charles. 1952. "The Relativity of Nonrelativity: Some Reflections on Firstness." In *Studies in the Philosophy of Charles Sanders Peirce,* edited by P. P. Wiener and F. H. Young, 215–24. Cambridge, Mass.: Harvard University Press.

———. 1970. *Creative Synthesis and Philosophic Method.* LaSalle, Ill.: Open Court.

———. 1973. "Charles Peirce and Quantum Mechanics." *Transactions of the Charles S. Peirce Society* 9 (4): 191–201.

Harvey, David. 1989. *The Condition of Postmodernity: An Enquiry into the Origins of Cultural Change.* Oxford: Basil Blackwell.

Hassan, Ihab. 1980. *The Right Promethean Fire: Imagination, Science, and Cultural Change.* Urbana: University of Illinois Press.

———. 1982. *The Dismemberment of Orpheus: Toward a Postmodern Literature.* 2d ed. Madison: University of Wisconsin Press.

———. 1987. *The Postmodern Turn: Essays in Postmodern Theory and Culture.* Columbus: The Ohio State University Press.

Hausman, Carl R. 1975. *A Discourse on Novelty and Creation.* The Hague: Martinus Nijhoff.

Hawkes, Terence. 1977. *Structuralism and Semiotics.* Berkeley and Los Angeles: University of California Press.

Hawles, Terry. 1974. "Structural Realism, Coalitions, and the Relationship of Gibsonian, Constructivist, and Buddhist Theories of Perception." In *Cognition and Symbolic Processes,* edited by W. B. Weimer and D. S. Palermo, 367–83. Hillsdale, N.J.: Lawrence Erlbaum.

Hayles, N. Katherine. 1990. *Chaos Bound: Orderly Disorder in Contemporary Literature and Science.* Ithaca, N.Y.: Cornell University Press.

Hayles, N. Katherine, ed. 1991. *Chaos and Order: Complex Dynamics in Literature and Science.* Chicago, Ill.: University of Chicago Press.

Heelan, Patrick. 1970. "Complementarity, Context-Dependence, and Quantum Logic." *Foundations of Physics* 1 (2): 95–100.

———. 1971. "Logic of Framework Transpositions." *International Philosophical Quarterly* 11:314–34.

———. 1983. *Space-Perception and the Philosophy of Science.* Berkeley and Los Angeles: University of California Press.

Heidegger, Martin. 1969. "Das Ende der Philosophie und die Aufgabe des Denkens." In *Zur Sache des Denkens,* 61–84. Tübingen: Max Niemeyer.

Heim, Michael. 1993. *The Metaphysics of Virtual Reality.* Oxford: Oxford University Press.

Heisenberg, Werner. 1958. *Physics and Philosophy.* New York: John Wiley.

———. 1971. *Physics and Beyond: Encounters and Conversations.* New York: Harper and Row.

———. 1972. "The Representation of Nature in Contemporary Physics." In *The Discontinuous Universe: Selected Writings in Contemporary Consciousness,* edited by S. Sears and G. W. Lord, 122–35. New York: Basic Books.

———. 1976. "The Nature of Elementary Particles." *Physics Today* 29 (3): 32–39.

Helsel, Sandra K., and Judith P. Roth. 1991. *Virtual Reality: Theory, Practice, and Promise.* Westport, Wash.: Meckler Corp.

Hempel, Carl G. 1945. "Studies in the Logic of Confirmation." *Mind* 54:1–26, 97–121.

Herbert, Nick. 1985. *Quantum Reality: Beyond the New Physics.* Garden City, N.Y.: Anchor.

Hesse, Mary B. 1966. *Models and Analogies in Science.* Notre Dame, Ind.: University of Notre Dame Press.

———. 1980. *Revolutions and Reconstructions in the Philosophy of Science.* Bloomington: Indiana University Press.

Hesse, Mary B., and Michael A. Arbib. 1986. *The Construction of Reality.* Cambridge: Cambridge University Press.

Hinton, C. H. 1887. *What Is the Fourth Dimension?* London: Allen and Unwin.

———. 1904. *The Fourth Dimension.* London: Sonnenschein.

Hoffmeyer, Jesper, and Claus Emmeche. 1991. "Code-Duality and the Semiotics of Nature." In *On Semiotic Modeling,* edited by M. Anderson and F. Merrell, 117–66. Berlin: Mouton de Gruyter.

Hofstadter, Douglas R. 1979. *Gödel, Escher, Bach: An Eternal Golden Braid.* New York: Basic Books.

Hollis, Martin, and Steven Lukes, eds. 1982. *Rationality and Relativism.* Cambridge, Mass.: MIT Press.

Holquist, Michael. 1990. *Dialogism: Bakhtin and His World.* London: Routledge.

Holquist, Michael, and Katrina Clark, eds. 1984. *Mikhail Bakhtin.* Cambridge, Mass.: Harvard University Press.

Holton, Gerald. 1973. *Thematic Origins of Scientific Thought.* Cambridge, Mass.: Harvard University Press.

Hookway, Christopher. 1985. *Peirce.* London: Routledge and Kegan Paul.

Horwich, Paul. 1987. *Asymmetries in Time: Problems in the Philosophy of Science.* Cambridge, Mass.: MIT Press.

Howe, Irving. 1970. *The Decline of the New.* New York: Harcourt, Brace, and World.

Hübner, Kurt. 1983. *Critique of Scientific Reason.* Trans. P. R. Dixon, Jr., and H. M. Dixon. Chicago, Ill.: University of Chicago Press.

Hunt, Lynn, ed. 1989. *The New Cultural History.* Berkeley and Los Angeles: University of California Press.

Hutcheon, Linda. 1985. *A Theory of Parody: The Teachings of Twentieth-Century Art Forms.* London: Methuen.

———. 1988a. *A Poetics of Postmodernism: History, Theory, Fiction.* New York: Routledge.

———. 1988b. "A Postmodern Problematics." In *Ethics/Aesthetics: PostModern Positions,* edited by R. Merrill, 1–10. Washington, D.C.: Maisonneuve.

Huyssen, Andreas. 1986. *After the Great Divide: Modernism, Mass Culture, Postmodernism.* Bloomington: Indiana University Press.

Ihde, Don. 1977. *Experimental Phenomenology.* New York: G. P. Putnam's Sons.

Jacob, François. 1982. *The Possible and the Actual.* New York: Pantheon Books.

Jakobson, Roman. 1960. "Linguistics and Poetics." In *Style and Language,* edited by T. Sebeok, 350–77. Cambridge, Mass.: MIT Press.

———. 1972. "Verbal Communication." In *Communication,* 39–42. A Scientific American Book. San Francisco, Calif.: W. H. Freeman.

James, William. 1950. *The Principles of Psychology.* 2 vols. New York: Dover.

———. 1977. *A Pluralist Universe.* Cambridge, Mass.: Harvard University Press.

Jameson, Fredric. 1979. "Reification and Utopia in Mass Culture." *Social Text* 1:130–48.

———. 1983. "Postmodernism and Consumerist Society." In *The Anti-aesthetic: Essays on Postmodern Culture,* edited by H. Foster, 111–25. Port Townsend, Wash.: Bay Press.

———. 1984a. "Postmodernism, Or The Cultural Logic of Late Capitalism." *New Left Review,* no. 146, 53–92.

———. 1984b. "Periodizing the 60s." In *The 60s without Apology,* edited by S. Sayres et al., 194–201. Minneapolis: University of Minnesota Press.

———. 1988. "Cognitive Mapping." In *Marxism and the Interpretation of Culture,* edited by C. Nelson and L. Grossberg, 347–60. Urbana: University of Illinois Press.

———. 1991. *Postmodernism: Or, The Cultural Logic of Late Capitalism.* Durham, N.C.: Duke University Press.

Jantsch, Erich. 1975. *Design for Evolution.* New York: George Braziller.

———. 1980. *The Self-organizing Universe: Scientific and Human Implications of the Emergent Paradigm of Evolution.* Oxford: Pergamon.

Jarvie, I. C. 1984. *Rationality and Relativism: In Search of a Philosophy and History of Anthropology.* London: Routledge and Kegan Paul.

Jauss, Hans Robert. 1982. *Towards an Aesthetic of Reception.* Trans. T. Bahti. Minneapolis: University of Minnesota Press.

Jaynes, Julian. 1976. *The Origin of Consciousness in the Breakdown of the Bicameral Mind.* Boston: Houghton-Mifflin.

Jeans, James. 1930. *The Mysterious Universe.* New York: Macmillan.

———. 1943. *Physics and Philosophy.* New York: Macmillan.

Jencks, Charles. 1977. *The Language of Postmodern Architecture.* New York: Rizzoli.

———. 1986. *What Is Post-modernism?* London: Academy Editions.

Jerison, Harry. 1973. *Evolution of the Brain and Intelligence.* New York: Academic Press.

Johansen, Jørgen Dines. 1989. "Semiotics of Rhetoric: The 'Consumption of Fantasy.'" In *The Semiotic Web 1988,* edited by T. A Sebeok and J. Umiker-Sebeok, 301–32. Berlin: Mouton de Gruyter.

———. 1993. *Dialogic Semiosis.* Bloomington: Indiana University Press.

Johnson, R. Colin, ed. 1992. *The Cognizer Almanac: Neural Networks, Fuzzy Logic, Genetic Algorithms, Virtual Reality.* Vancouver: Frontline Strategies.

Johnson-Laird, Philip. 1987. "How Could Consciousness Arrive from the Computations of the Brain?" In *Mindwaves: Thoughts on Intelligence, Identity and Consciousness,* edited by C. Blakemore and S. Greenfield, 247–57. Oxford: Basil Blackwell.

Kadvany, John. 1989. "Reflections on the Legacy of Kurt Gödel: Mathematics, Skepticism, Postmodernism." *Philosophical Forum* 20 (3): 161–81.

Kant, Immanuel. 1929. *Critique of Pure Reason.* Trans. N. K. Smith. London: Macmillan.

Kaplan, E. Ann, ed. 1988. *Postmodernism and Its Discontents: Theories, Practices.* London: Verso.

Kaplan, Morton A. 1984. *Science, Language and the Human Condition.* New York: Paragon.

Kauffman, Louis H. 1986. "Self Reference and Recursive Forms." *Journal of Social Biological Structure* 9:1–21.

Kauffman, Louis H., and Francisco J. Varela. 1980. "Form Dynamics." *Journal of Social Biological Structure* 3:171–216.

Keesing, Roger M. 1987. "Anthropology as Interpretive Quest." *Current Anthropology* 28 (2): 161–76.

Kellner, Douglas. 1989. *Jean Baudrillard: From Marxism to Postmodernism and Beyond.* Stanford, Calif.: Stanford University Press.

Kenner, Hugh. 1972. *The Pound Era.* London: Faber and Faber.

Kermode, Frank, ed. 1975. *Selected Prose of T. S. Eliot.* New York: Harcourt, Brace, Jovanovich/Farrar, Straus and Giroux.

Kline, Morris. 1980. *Mathematics: The Loss of Certainty.* Oxford: Oxford University Press.

Knorr-Cetina, Karin. 1981. *The Manufacture of Knowledge: An Essay on the Constructivist and Social Nature of Science.* Oxford: Pergamon.

Knorr-Cetina, Karin, and Michael Mulkay, eds. 1983. *Science Observed: Perspectives on the Social Study of Science.* Beverly Hills, Calif.: Sage.

Koestler, Arthur. 1963. *The Sleepwalkers.* New York: Grosset and Dunlap.

Kolers, Paul. 1972. *Aspects of Motion Perception.* New York: Pergamon Press.

Krauss, Rosalind E. 1985. *The Originality of the Avant-Garde and Other Modernist Myths.* Cambridge, Mass.: MIT Press.

Krausz, Michael, ed. 1989. *Relativism: Interpretation and Confrontation.* Notre Dame, Ind.: University of Notre Dame Press.

Kristeva, Julia. 1969. *Sémeiotiké: Recherches pour une sémanalyse.* Paris: Seuil.

———. 1984. *Revolution in Poetic Language.* New York: Columbia University Press.

Kroker, Arthur. 1987. "Panic Value: Bacon, Colville, Baudrillard and the Aesthetics of Deprivation." In *Life after Post-modernism: Essays on Value and Culture,* edited by J. Fekete, 181–93. New York: St. Martin's Press.

346

Kroker, Arthur, and David Cook. 1986. *The Postmodern Scene: Culture and Hyper-Aesthetics.* New York: St. Martin's Press.

Kuhn, Thomas S. 1970. *The Structure of Scientific Revolutions.* Chicago, Ill.: University of Chicago Press.

———. 1977. *The Essential Tension.* Chicago, Ill.: University of Chicago Press.

Kuspit, Donald. 1990. "The Contradictory Character of Post-modernism." In *Postmodernism—Philosophy and the Arts,* edited by H. J. Silverman, 53–68. New York: Routledge.

Lacan, Jacques. 1966. *Ecrits.* Paris: Seuil.

LaCapra, Dominick. 1985. *Rethinking Intellectual History: Texts, Contexts, Language.* Ithaca, N.Y.: Cornell University Press.

———. 1989. *Soundings in Critical Theory.* Ithaca, N.Y.: Cornell University Press.

Laclau, Ernesto. 1988. "Politics and the Limits of Modernity." In *Universal Abandon? The Politics of Postmodernism,* edited by A. Ross, 63–82. Minneapolis: University of Minnesota Press.

Landon, R., and E. Bauer. 1939. *La théorie de l'observation en mécanique quantique.* Paris: Hermann.

Langer, Ellen J. 1989. *Mindfulness.* Reading, Mass.: Addison-Wesley.

Laszlo, Ervin. 1972. *Introduction to Systems Philosophy: Toward a New Paradigm of Contemporary Thought.* New York: Gordon and Breach.

———. 1987. *Evolution: The Grand Synthesis.* Boulder, Colo.: Shambhala.

Latour, Bruno, and Steve Woolgar. 1979. *Laboratory Life: The Social Construction of Scientific Facts.* Beverly Hills, Calif.: Sage.

Laurentis, Theresa de. 1985. "Gaudy Rose: Eco and Narcissism." *Sub-Stance* 47:13–29.

Layzer, David. 1990. *Cosmogenesis: The Growth of Order in the Universe.* Oxford: Oxford University Press.

Leatherdale, W. H. 1974. *The Role of Analogy, Model and Metaphor in Science.* Amsterdam: North-Holland.

LeShan, Lawrence, and Henry Margenau. 1982. *Einstein's Space and van Gogh's Sky: Physical Reality and Beyond.* New York: Macmillan.

Lévi-Strauss, Claude. 1964. *Le cru et le cuit: Mythologiques,* vol. 1. Paris: Plon.

———. 1966. *The Savage Mind.* Chicago, Ill.: University of Chicago Press.

Levy, Steven. 1990. "Brave New Worlds." *Rolling Stone,* 14 June, 580, 92–103.

Lilly, John C. 1967. *Programming and Metaprogramming in the Human Biocomputer.* New York: Julian Press.

Liszka, James J. 1989. *The Semiotic of Myth: A Critical Study of the Symbol.* Bloomington: Indiana University Press.

———. 1993. "Good and Bad Foundationalism: A Response to Nielsen." *Transactions of the Charles S. Peirce Society* 29 (4): 573–79.

Livingston, Paisley. 1988. *Literary Knowledge: Humanistic Inquiry and the Philosophy of Science.* Ithaca, N.Y.: Cornell University Press.

Löfgren, Lars. 1978. "Some Foundational Views on General Systems and the Hempel Paradox." *International Journal of General Systems* 4:243–53.

———. 1981a. "Knowledge of Evolution and Evolution of Knowledge." In *The Evolutionary Vision,* edited by E. Jantsch, 129–51. Boulder, Colo.: Westview.

347

Löfgren, Lars. 1981b. "Life as Autolinguistic Phenomenon." In *Autopoiesis: A Theory of Living Organization,* edited by M. Zeleny, 236–49. New York: North-Holland.

———. 1984. "Autology of Time." *International Journal of General Systems* 10:5–14.

Lovelock, James E. 1987. *Gaia: A New Look at Life on Earth.* Oxford: Oxford University Press.

Lueders, Edward, ed. 1989. *Writing Natural History.* Salt Lake City: University of Utah Press.

Luke, Timothy W. 1989. *Screens of Power: Ideology, Domination, and Resistance in Informational Society.* Urbana: University of Illinois Press.

Lyotard, Jean-François. 1983. *Le différend.* Paris: Editions de Minuit.

———. 1984. *The Postmodern Condition: A Report on Knowledge.* Trans. G. Bennington and B. Massumi. Minneapolis: University of Minnesota Press.

MacCannell, Dean, and Juliet Flower MacCannell. 1982. *The Time of the Sign.* Bloomington: Indiana University Press.

McClosky, M. 1964. "Metaphors." *Mind* 73:215–33.

McCorduck, Pamela. 1979. *Machines Who Think.* San Francisco, Calif.: W. H. Freeman.

MacCormac, Earl R. 1985. *A Cognitive Theory of Metaphor.* Cambridge, Mass.: MIT Press.

McCulloch, Warren Sturgis. 1965. *Embodiments of Mind.* Cambridge, Mass.: MIT Press.

McFarland, David. 1985. *Animal Behaviour.* Menlo Park, Calif.: Benjamin/Cummings.

McGinn, Colin. 1987. "Could a Machine Be Conscious?" In *Mindwaves: Thoughts on Intelligence, Identity and Consciousness,* edited by C. Blakemore and S. Greenfield, 279–91. Oxford: Basil Blackwell.

McHale, Brian. 1987. *Postmodernist Fiction.* New York: Methuen.

McIntyre, Alasdair. 1980. "Epistemplogical Crises, Dramatic Narrative, and the Philosophy of Science." In *Paradigms and Revolutions,* edited by G. Gutting, 39–53. Notre Dame, Ind.: University of Notre Dame Press.

McKinney, Ronald H. 1989. "Towards the Resolution of Paradigm Conflict: Holism versus Postmodernism." *Philosophy Today* 32 (4): 299–311.

McMullin, Ernan, ed. 1988. *Construction and Constraint: The Shaping of Scientific Rationality.* Notre Dame, Ind.: University of Notre Dame Press.

McTaggart, J. M. E. 1927. *The Nature of Existence.* Vol. 2. Cambridge: Cambridge University Press.

Madison, G. B. 1982. *Understanding: A Phenomenological-Pragmatic Analysis.* Westport, Conn.: Greenwood.

Malcolm, Norman. 1959. *Dreaming.* London: Routledge and Kegan Paul.

Man, Paul de. 1981. *Allegory and Representation.* Baltimore, Md.: Johns Hopkins University Press.

Marcus, George E. 1980. "Rhetoric and the Ethnographic Genre in Anthropological Research." *Current Anthropology* 21 (4): 507–10.

Marcus, G. E., and Dick Cushman. 1982. "Ethnographies as Texts." *Annual Review of Anthropology* 11:25–69.

Marcus, G. E., and Michael M. J. Fischer, eds. 1986. *Anthropology as Cultural Critique: An Experimental Moment in the Human Sciences.* Chicago, Ill.: University of Chicago Press.

Margulis, Lynn, and Dorian Sagan. 1986. *Microcosmos: Four Billion Years of Evolution from our Microbial Ancestors*. New York: Summit Books.

Marr, David. 1979. "Representing and Computing Visual Information." In *Artificial Intelligence: An MIT Perspective*. Vol. 2, edited by P. H. Winston and R. H. Brown, 17–80. Cambridge, Mass.: MIT Press.

———. 1982. *Vision: A Computational Investigation into the Human Representation and Processing of Visual Information*. San Francisco, Calif.: W. H. Freeman.

Marty, Robert. 1980. "Sur la réduction triadique." *Semiosis*, no. 17/18, 5–9.

———. 1982. "C. S. Peirce's Phaneroscopy and Semiotics." *Semiotica* 41 (1/4): 169–81.

Maslow, Abraham H. 1966. *The Psychology of Science*. New York: Harper and Row.

Matson, Floyd. 1964. *The Broken Image: Man, Science, Society*. New York: Doubleday.

Matte Blanco, Ignacio. 1975. *The Unconscious as Infinite Sets: An Essay in Bi-Logic*. London: Duckworth.

Maturana, Humberto, and Francisco Varela. 1980. *Autopoiesis and Cognition: The Realization of the Living*. Dordrecht: D. Reidel.

———. 1987. *The Tree of Knowledge: The Biological Roots of Human Understanding*. Boston, Mass.: Shambhala.

Mellor, D. H. 1981. *Real Time*. Cambridge: Cambridge University Press.

Melville, Stephen W. 1986. *Philosophy beside Itself: On Deconstruction and Modernism*. Minneapolis: University of Minnesota Press.

Merrell, Floyd. 1982. *Semiotic Foundations: Steps toward an Epistemology of Written Texts*. Bloomington: Indiana University Press.

———. 1983. *Pararealities: The Nature of Our Fictions and How We Know Them*. Amsterdam: John Benjamins.

———. 1985a. *Deconstruction Reframed*. West Lafayette, Ind: Purdue University Press.

———. 1985b. *A Semiotic Theory of Texts*. Berlin: Mouton de Gruyter.

———. 1987. "Of Position Papers, Paradigms, and Paradoxes." *Semiotica* 65 (3/4): 191–223.

———. 1991a. *Signs Becoming Signs: Our Perfusive, Pervasive Universe*. Bloomington: Indiana University Press.

———. 1991b. *Unthinking Thinking: Jorge Luis Borges, Mathematics, and the New Physics*. West Lafayette, Ind: Purdue University Press.

———. 1991c. "Model, World, Semiotic Reality." In *On Semiotic Modeling*, edited by M. Anderson and F. Merrell, 247–84. Berlin: Mouton de Gruyter.

———. 1992. *Sign, Textuality, World*. Bloomington: Indiana University Press.

———. 1994. *Signs Grow: Semiosis and Life Processes*. Toronto: University of Toronto Press (forthcoming).

Merrell, Floyd, and Myrdene Anderson. 1989. "Shifting Worlds, Semiotic Modeling." Fourth World Congress of the International Association for Semiotic Studies, Barcelona, Spain, 30 March.

Miller, Arthur I. 1986. *Imagery in Scientific Thought*. Cambridge, Mass.: MIT Press.

Miller, George A., and P. N. Johnson-Laird. 1976. *Language and Perception*. Cambridge: Belknap Press of Harvard University Press.

Minsky, Marvin. 1977. "Frame System Theory." In *Thinking: Readings in Cognitive Science*, edited by P. N. Johnson-Laird and P. C. Wason, 355–76. Cambridge: Cambridge University Press.

349

Minsky, Marvin. 1980. "Decentralized Minds." *Behavioral and Brain Sciences* 3:439–40.

Monod, Jacques. 1971. *Chance and Necessity*. Trans. A. Wainhouse. New York: Random House.

Morowitz, Harold J. 1981. "Rediscovering the Mind." In *The Mind's I*, edited by D. Hofstadter and D. Dennett, 34–42. New York: Basic Books.

Morris, Charles. 1938. *Foundations of the Theory of Signs*. Chicago, Ill.: University of Chicago Press.

———. 1946. *Signs, Language, and Behavior*. New York: Prentice-Hall.

Morson, Gary Saul, ed. 1986. *Bakhtin: Essays and Dialogues on His Work*. Chicago, Ill.: University of Chicago Press.

Morson, Gary Saul, and Caryl Emerson, eds. 1989. *Rethinking Bakhtin: Extensions and Challenges*. Evanston, Ill.: Northwestern University Press.

Mukarovsky, Jan. 1964. "Standard Language and Poetic Language." In *A Prague School Reader on Esthetics, Literary Structure, and Style*, edited by P. Garvin, 31–69. Washington, D.C.: Georgetown University Press.

Murdoch, Dugald. 1987. *Niels Bohr's Philosophy of Physics*. Cambridge: Cambridge University Press.

Murphey, Murray G. 1961. *The Development of Peirce's Philosophy*. Cambridge, Mass.: Harvard University Press.

Myers, Greg. 1990. *Writing Biology: Texts in the Social Construction of Scientific Knowledge*. Madison: University of Wisconsin Press.

Nadin, Mihai. 1983. "The Logic of Vagueness and the Category of Synechism." In *The Relevance of Charles Peirce*, edited by E. Freeman, 154–66. LaSalle, Ill.: Monist Library of Philosophers.

Nagel, Thomas. 1974. "What Is It Like to Be a Bat?" *Philosophical Review* 83:435–51.

Narcejac, T. 1975. *Une machine à lire: Le roman policier*. Paris: Denoel/Gonthier.

Neisser, Ulric. 1967. *Cognitive Psychology*. New York: Appleton-Century-Crofts.

———. 1980. "The Limits of Cognition." In *The Nature of Thought: Essays in Honor of D. O. Hebb*, edited by P. W. Jusczyk and R. M. Klein, 115–32. Hillsdale, N.J.: Lawrence Erlbaum.

Nesher, Dan. 1983. "A Pragmatic Theory of Meaning: A Note on Peirce's 'Last' Formulation of the Pragmatic Maxim and Its Interpretation." *Semiotica* 44 (3/4): 203–57.

———. 1990. "Understanding Sign Semiosis as Cognition and as Self-conscious Process: A Reconstruction of Some Basic Concepts of Peirce's Semiotics." *Semiotica* 79 (1/2): 1–49.

Newman, Charles. 1985. *The Post-modern Aura: The Act of Fiction in an Age of Inflation*. Evanston, Ill.: Northwestern University Press.

Newton-Smith, W. H. 1981. *The Rationality of Science*. London: Routledge and Kegan Paul.

Nickles, Thomas, ed. 1980a. *Scientific Discovery: Case Studies*. Dordrecht: D. Reidel.

———. 1980b. *Scientific Discovery, Logic, and Rationality*. Dordrecht: D. Reidel.

Nicolis, Grégoire, and Ilya Prigogine. 1977. *Self-organization in Non-equilibrium Systems: From Dissipative Structures to Order through Fluctuations*. New York: John Wiley.

———. 1989. *Exploring Complexity: An Introduction.* New York: W. H. Freeman.

Nielsen, Kai. 1993. "Peirce, Pragmatism and the Challenge of Postmodernism." *Transactions of the Charles S. Peirce Society* 29 (4): 513–60.

Nietzsche, Friedrich. 1968a. *Twilight of the Gods and the Anti-Christ.* Trans. R. J. Hollingdale. Middlesex: Penguin Books.

———. 1968b. *The Will to Power.* Trans. W. Kaufmann and R. J. Hollingdale. New York: Vintage Books.

———. 1969. *Selected Letters of Friedrich Nietzsche.* Trans. C. Middleton. Chicago, Ill.: University of Chicago Press.

Noble, G. B. 1969. *Applied Linear Algebra.* Englewood Cliffs, N.J.: Prentice-Hall.

Ogden, C. K., and I. A. Richards. 1923. *The Meaning of Meaning.* New York: Harcourt, Brace, and World.

Olshewsky, Thomas. 1993. "Peirce's Antifoundationalism." *Transactions of the Charles S. Peirce Society* 29 (3): 401–9.

Ortega y Gasset, José. 1985. *The Revolt of the Masses.* Trans. A. Kerrigan. Notre Dame, Ind.: University of Notre Dame Press.

Owens, Craig. 1983. "The Discourse of Others: Feminists and Post-modernism." In *The Anti-aesthetic: Essays in Postmodern Culture,* edited by H. Foster, 57–82. Port Townsend, Wash.: Bay Press.

Pagels, Heinz R. 1982. *The Cosmic Code: Quantum Physics as the Language of Nature.* New York: Simon and Schuster.

Pattee, Howard H. 1969. "How Does a Molecule Become a Message?" *Developmental Biology,* supplement 3, 227–33.

———. 1972. "Laws and Constraints, Symbols and Languages." In *Towards a Theoretical Biology,* edited by C. H. Waddington, 4:248–58. Edinburgh: University of Edinburgh Press.

———. 1977. "Dynamic and Linguistic Modes of Complex Systems." *International Journal of General Systems* 3:259–66.

———. 1986. "Universal Principles of Measurement and Language Functions in Evolving Systems." In *Complexity, Language, and Life: Mathematical Approaches,* edited by J. L. Casti and A. Karlqvist, 268–81. New York: Springer-Verlag.

Pauli, Wolfgang, ed. 1955. *Niels Bohr and the Development of Physics.* New York: McGraw-Hill.

Pefanis, Julian. 1991. *Heterology and the Postmodern: Bataille, Baudrillard, and Lyotard.* Durham, N.C.: Duke University Press.

Peirce, Charles S. 1931–35. *Collected Papers of Charles Sanders Peirce.* Ed. Hartshorne and P. Weiss. Vols. 1–6. Cambridge, Mass.: Harvard University Press. [Reference to Peirce's papers will be designated CP.]

———. 1958. *Collected Papers of Charles Sanders Peirce.* Ed. A. W. Burks. Vols 7–8. Cambridge, Mass.: Harvard University Press. [Reference to Peirce's papers will be designated CP.]

———. 1976. *The New Elements of Mathematics.* Ed. C. Eisele. 4 vols. The Hague: Mouton. [Reference to this book will be designated NE.]

———. MS refers to Peirce's unpublished manuscripts.

Penrose, Roger. 1986. "Big Bangs, Black Holes and Time's Arrow." In *The Nature of Time,* edited by R. Flood and M. Lockwood, 36–62. Oxford: Blackwell.

———. 1987. "Minds, Machines and Mathematics." In *Mindwaves: Thoughts on Intelligence, Identity and Consciousness,* edited by C. Blakemore and S. Greenfield, 259–76. London: Basil Blackwell.

———. 1989. *The New Emperor's Mind: Concerning Computers, Minds, and the Laws of Physics.* Oxford: Oxford University Press.

Petersen, A. 1963. "The Philosophy of Niels Bohr." *Bulletin of Atomic Scientists* 19:8–14.

Phillips, Derek C. 1973. *Abandoning Method.* San Francisco, Calif.: Jossey-Bass.

———. 1977. *Wittgenstein and Scientific Knowledge: A Sociological Perspective.* Totowa, N.J.: Rowman and Littlefield.

Piaget, Jean. 1971. *Biology and Knowledge.* Trans. B. Walsh. Chicago, Ill.: University of Chicago Press.

Poincaré, Henri. 1913. "Mathematical Creation." In *The Foundations of Science,* 383–95. Trans. G. B. Holstead. New York: The Science Press.

———. 1914. *Science and Mind.* Trans. F. Maitland. London: Thomas Nelson.

———. 1952. *Science and Hypothesis.* Trans. F. Maitland. New York: Dover.

Polanyi, Michael. 1958. *Personal Knowledge.* Chicago, Ill.: University of Chicago Press.

Polkinghorne, Donald E. 1988. *Narrative Knowing and the Human Sciences.* Albany: State University of New York Press.

Ponzio, Augusto. 1985. "Semiotics between Peirce and Bakhtin." *Kodikas/Code* 8 (1/2): 11–28.

Pöppel, Ernst. 1972. "Oscillators as Possible Basis for Time Perception." In *The Study of Time,* edited by J. T. Fraser, F. C. Haber, and G. H. Miller, 219–41. New York: Springer-Verlag.

———. 1988. *Mindworks: Time and Conscious Experience.* Boston: Harcourt, Brace, Jovanovich.

Popper, Karl R. 1959. *The Logic of Scientific Discovery.* New York: Harper and Row.

———. 1963. *Conjectures and Refutations: The Growth of Scientific Knowledge.* Oxford: Clarendon.

———. 1972. *Objective Knowledge.* Oxford: Oxford University Press.

———. 1974. *Unended Quest: An Intellectual Autobiography.* LaSalle, Ill.: Open Court.

Porter, Roy. 1993. "Baudrillard: History, Hysteria and Consumption." In *Forget Baudrillard?* edited by C. Rojek and B. S. Turner, 1–21. London: Routledge.

Posner, Roland. 1981. "Charles Morris and the Behavioral Foundations of Semiotics." In *Classics of Semiotics,* edited by M. Krampen et al., 23–57. New York: Plenum.

———. 1986. "Morris, Charles William." In *Encyclopedic Dictionary of Semiotics,* edited by T. A. Sebeok, 565–71. Berlin: Mouton de Gruyter.

Poster, Mark, ed. 1989. *Critical Theory and Poststructuralism: In Search of a Context.* Ithaca, N.Y.: Cornell University Press.

Poundstone, William. 1988. *Labyrinths of Reason: Paradox, Puzzles, and the Frailty of Knowledge.* New York: Doubleday.

Pribram, Karl H. 1971. *Languages of the Brain: Experimental Paradoxes and Principles of Neuropsychology.* Englewood Cliffs, N.J.: Prentice-Hall.

———. 1981. "The Distributed Nature of the Memory Store and the Localization of Linguistic Competencies." In *The Neurological Basis of Signs in Communicational Processes,* edited by P. Perron, 127–82. Toronto Semiotic Circle Monographs, Working Papers and Prepublications, vols. 2–3. Toronto: Victoria University.

———. 1991. *Brain and Perception: Holonomy and Structure in Figural Processing.* Hillsdale, N.J.: Lawrence Erlbaum.

Pribram, Karl H., Marc Newer, and Robert Baron. 1974. "The Holographic Hypothesis of Memory Structure in Brain Function and Perception." In *Contemporary Developments in Mathematical Psychology: Measurement, Psychophysics, and Neural Information Processing,* edited by R. C. Atkinson et al., 416–57. San Francisco, Calif.: W. H. Freeman.

Prigogine, Ilya. 1980. *From Being to Becoming: Time and Complexity in the Physical Sciences.* San Francisco, Calif.: W. H. Freeman.

Prigogine, Ilya, and Isabelle Stengers. 1984. *Order out of Chaos: Man's New Dialogue with Nature.* New York: Bantam.

Pugmire, David. 1989. "Bat or Batman?" *Philosophy* 64 (28): 207–17.

Putnam, Hilary. 1969. "Is Logic Empirical?" In *Boston Studies in the Philosophy of Science. Proceedings of the Boston Colloquium for Philosophy of Science 1966/1968,* edited by R. S. Cohen and M. W. Wartofsky, 5:216–41. Dordrecht: D. Reidel.

———. 1976. "How to Think Quantum-Logically." In *Logic and Probability in Quantum Mechanics,* edited by P. Suppes, 47–53. Dordrecht: D. Reidel.

———. 1983. "Is There a Fact of the Matter about Fiction?" *Poetics Today* 4 (1): 77–82.

Quine, Willard van Orman. 1953. *From a Logical Point of View.* New York: Harper and Row.

———. 1966. *The Ways of Paradox, and Other Essays.* New York: Random House.

———. 1969. *Ontological Relativity, and Other Essays.* New York: Columbia University Press.

Rajchman, John, and Cornell West, eds. 1985. *Post-analytic Philosophy.* New York: Columbia University Press.

Ransdell, Joseph. 1979. "The Epistemic Function of Iconicity in Perception." In *Studies in Peirce's Semiotic,* no. 1, edited by J. E. Brock et al., 51–66. Lubbock, Tex.: Institute for Studies in Pragmaticism.

Rashevsky, N. 1956. "Is the Concept of the Organism as a Machine a Useful One?" In *The Validation of Scientific Theories,* edited by P. G. Frank, 142–48. Boston, Mass.: Beacon.

Rescher, Nicholas. 1978. *Peirce's Philosophy of Science.* Notre Dame, Ind.: University of Notre Dame Press.

Rescher, Nicholas, and Robert Brandom. 1979. *The Logic of Inconsistency: A Study of Non-standard Possible World Semantics and Ontology.* Totowa, N.J.: Rowman and Littlefield.

Rheingold, Howard. 1991. *Virtual Reality.* New York: Simon and Schuster.

Rifkin, Jeremy. 1983. *Algeny.* New York: Viking.

Rochberg-Halton, Eugene. 1986. *Meaning and Modernity: Social Theory in the Pragmatic Attitude.* Chicago, Ill.: University of Chicago Press.

Rock, Irvin. 1983. *The Logic of Perception.* Cambridge, Mass.: MIT Press.

Rockmore, T., and B. J. Singer, eds. 1992. *Antifoundationalism Old and New.* Philadelphia, Pa.: Temple University Press.

Romanyshyn, Robert D. 1989. *Technology as Symptom and Dream.* London: Routledge.

Rorty, Richard. 1978. "Philosophy as a Kind of Writing: An Essay on Derrida." *New Literary History* 10 (1): 141–60.

———. 1979. *Philosophy and the Mirror of Nature.* Princeton, N.J.: Princeton University Press.

———. 1982. *Consequences of Pragmatism.* Minneapolis: University of Minnesota Press.

———. 1988. "Is Natural Science a Natural Kind?" In *Construction and Constraint: The Shaping of Scientific Rationality,* edited by E. McMullin, 49–74. Notre Dame, Ind.: University of Notre Dame Press.

———. 1989. "Two Meanings of 'Logocentrism': A Reply to Norris." In *Redrawing the Lines: Analytic Philosophy, Deconstruction, and Literary Theory,* edited by R. W. Dasenbrock, 204–16. Minneapolis: University of Minnesota Press.

———. 1991a. *Objectivity, Relativity, and Truth.* Vol. 1 of *Philosophical Papers.* Cambridge: Cambridge University Press.

———. 1991b. *Essays on Heidegger and Others.* Vol. 2 of *Philosophical Papers.* Cambridge: Cambridge University Press.

Rosch, Eleanor, ed. 1974. "Linguistic Relativity." In *Human Communication: Theoretical Explorations,* edited by A. Silverstein, 95–121. New York: Halsted Press.

———. 1975a. "Cognitive Representations of Semantic Categories." *Journal of Experimental Psychology: General* 104:192–233.

———. 1975b. "Universals and Cultural Specifics in Human Categorization." In *Cross-cultural Perspectives on Learning,* edited by R. Brislin, S. Bochner, and W. Lonner, 177–206. New York: Halsted Press.

———. 1977. "Human Categorization." In *Studies in Cross-cultural Psychology,* edited by N. Warren, 1:3–49. London: Academic Press.

Rose, Margaret A. 1991. *The Post-modern and the Post-industrial: A Critical Analysis.* Cambridge: Cambridge University Press.

Rosen, Stanley. 1987. *Hermeneutics as Politics.* Oxford: Oxford University Press.

Rosenberg, Marvin. 1978. *The Masks of Macbeth.* Berkeley and Los Angeles: University of California Press.

Ross, Andrew, ed. 1988. *Universal Abandon? The Politics of Postmodernism.* Minneapolis: University of Minnesota Press.

Roszak, Theodore. 1986. *The Cult of Information: The Folklore of Computers and the True Art of Thinking.* New York: Pantheon.

Rotman, Brian. 1987. *Signifying Nothing: The Semiotics of Zero.* New York: St. Martin's.

Russell, Charles, ed. 1981. *The Avant-Garde Today: An International Anthology.* Urbana: University of Illinois Press.

Russell, Bertrand. 1905. "On Denoting." *Mind* 14:479–93.

Sábato, Ernesto. 1945. "Borges: Geometrización de la novela." In his *Uno y el universo,* 104–10. Buenos Aires: Editorial Sudamericana.

Sahlins, Marshall. 1981. *Historical Metaphors and Mythical Realities: Structure in the Early History of the Sandwich Islands Kingdom.* ASAI Special Publication, no. 1. Ann Arbor: University of Michigan Press.

———. 1985. *Islands of History.* Chicago, Ill.: University of Chicago Press.

Sanders, Gary. 1970. "Peirce's Sixty-six Signs?" *Transactions of the Charles S. Peirce Society* 6 (1): 3–16.

Sangren, P. Steven. 1988. "Rhetoric and the Authority of Ethnography." *Current Anthropology* 29 (3): 405–35.

Savan, David. 1952. "On the Origins of Peirce's Phenomenology." In *Studies in the Philosophy of Charles Sanders Peirce,* edited by P. P. Wiener and F. H. Young, 185–94. Cambridge, Mass.: Harvard University Press.

———. 1987–88. *An Introduction to C. S. Peirce's Full System of Semeiotic.* Monograph Series of the Toronto Semiotic Circle, vol. 1. Toronto: Victoria College.

Schank, Roger, and Robert Abelson. 1977. *Scripts, Plans, Goals and Understanding.* Hillsdale, N.J.: Lawrence Erlbaum.

Schneider, Herbert W. 1952. "Fourthness." In *Studies in the Philosophy of Charles Sanders Peirce,* edited by P. P. Wiener and F. H. Young, 209–14. Cambridge, Mass.: Harvard University Press.

Schrag, Calvin O. 1986. *Communicative Praxis and the Space of Subjectivity.* Bloomington: Indiana University Press.

Schrödinger, Erwin. 1967. *What Is Life?* and *Matter and Mind.* Cambridge: Cambridge University Press.

Schwartz, Sanford. 1985. *The Matrix of Modernism.* Princeton, N.J.: Princeton University Press.

Scott, Charles E. 1990. "Postmodern Language." In *Postmodernism—Philosophy and the Arts,* edited by H. J. Silverman, 33–52. New York: Routledge.

Scott, John Wallach. 1988. *Gender and the Politics of History.* New York: Columbia University Press.

Searle, John. 1984. *Minds, Brains and Science.* Cambridge, Mass.: Harvard University Press.

Sebeok, Thomas A. 1976. *Contributions to the Doctrine of Signs,* 143–47. Bloomington: Indiana University/Peter de Ridder.

———. 1979. *The Sign and Its Masters.* Austin: University of Texas Press.

———. 1983. "One, Two, Three Spells Uberty." In *The Sign of Three: Dupin, Holmes, Peirce,* edited by U. Eco and T. A. Sebeok, 1–10. Bloomington: Indiana University Press.

Sebeok, Thomas A., and Robert Rosenthal, eds. 1981. *The Clever Hans Phenomenon: Communication with Horses, Whales, Apes, and People.* New York: Academy of Science.

Sebeok, Thomas A., and Jean Umiker-Sebeok, eds. 1980. *Speaking of Apes: A Critical Anthology of Two-Way Communication with Man.* New York: Plenum.

Shakespeare, William. 1939. *The Tragedy of Macbeth.* Ed. G. L. Kittredge. Boston, Mass.: Ginn.

Sheldrake, Rupert. 1988. "The Laws of Nature as Habits: A Postmodern Basis for Science." In *The Reenchantment of Science: Postmodern Proposals,* edited by D. R. Griffin, 79–86. Albany: State University of New York Press.

Shimony, Abner. 1977. "Is Observation Theory-laden? A Problem in Naturalistic Epistemology." In *Logic, Laws, and Life: Some Philosophical Complications,* edited by R. G. Colodny, 6:185–208. Pittsburgh, Pa.: University of Pittsburgh Press.

Shklovsky, Victor. 1965. "Art as Technique." In *Russian Formalism: Four Essays,* edited by L. T. Lemon and M. J. Reis, 3–24. Lincoln: University of Nebraska Press.

Short, T. L. 1982. "Life among the Legisigns." *Transactions of the Charles S. Peirce Society* 18 (4): 285–310.

Shusterman, Richard. 1989. "Organic Unity: Analysis and Deconstruction." In *Redrawing the Lines: Analytic Philosophy, Deconstruction, and Literary Theory,* edited by R. W. Dasenbrock, 92–115. Minneapolis: University of Minnesota Press.

Sless, David. 1986. *In Search of Semiotics.* New York: Barnes and Noble.

Sloman, Aaron. 1979. *The Computer Revolution in Philosophy.* Brighton: Harvester.

Smart, Barry. 1993. *Postmodernity.* London: Routledge.

Smith, David Woodruff. 1983. "Is This a Dagger I See before Me?" *Synthese* 54:95–114.

Smith, John E. 1965. "Community and Reality." In *Perspectives on Peirce,* edited by R. J. Bernstein, 92–119. New Haven, Conn.: Yale University Press.

Solomon, J. Fisher. 1988. *Discourse and Reference in the Nuclear Age.* Norman: University of Oklahoma Press.

Solomon, Jack [J. Fisher] 1988. *The Signs of Our Times.* Los Angeles, Calif.: Jeremy P. Tarchner.

Spencer-Brown, G. 1979. *Laws of Form.* New York: E. P. Dutton.

Sperber, Dan, and Deirdre Wilson. 1986. *Relevance: Communication and Cognition.* Cambridge, Mass.: Harvard University Press.

Sperry, Roger W. 1956. "The Eye and the Brain." *Scientific American* 194 (5): 48–52.

Spinks, C. W. 1991. *Semiosis, Marginal Signs, and Trickster: A Dagger of the Mind.* London: Macmillan.

Stachow, Ernest-Walther. 1979. "Completeness of Quantum Logic." In *Physical Theory as Logico-operational Structure,* edited by C. A. Hooker, 203–44. Dordrecht: D. Reidel.

Stam, Robert. 1988. "Mikhail Bakhtin and Left Cultural Critique." In *Postmodernism and Its Discontents: Theories, Practices,* edited by E. A. Kaplan, 116–45. London: Verso.

Stearns, Isabel. 1952. "Firstness, Secondness, and Thirdness." In *Studies in the Philosophy of Charles Sanders Peirce,* edited by P. P. Wiener and F. H. Young, 195–208. Cambridge, Mass.: Harvard University Press.

Steiner, Peter. 1984. *Russian Formalism: A Metapoetics.* Ithaca, N.Y.: Cornell University Press.

Stephanson, Anders. 1988. "Regarding Postmodernism—A Conversation with Fredric Jameson." In *Universal Abandon? The Politics of Postmodernism,* edited by A. Ross, 3–30. Minneapolis: University of Minnesota Press.

Stuhr, John J. 1993. "Can Pragmatism Appropriate the Resources of Postmodernism? A Response to Nielsen." *Transactions of the Charles S. Peirce Society* 29 (4): 561–72.

Tarski, Alfred. 1956. *Logic, Semantics, Metamathematics.* Oxford: Clarendon.

Taylor, Charles. 1980. "Understanding in the Human Sciences." *Review of Metaphysics* 34 (1): 25–38.

Thom, René. 1975. *Structural Stability and Morphogenesis.* Trans. D. H. Fowler. Reading, Mass.: W. A. Benjamin.

———. 1983. *Mathematical Models of Morphogenesis.* Trans. W. M. Brooks and D. Rand. West Sussex: Ellis Horwood.

Tilghman, B. R. 1991. "What Is It Like to Be an Aardvark?" *Philosophy* 66:325–38.

Toulmin, Stephen. 1982a. "The Construal of Reality: Criticism in Postmodern Science." In *The Politics of Interpretation,* edited by W. J. T. Mitchell, 99–117. Chicago, Ill.: University of Chicago Press.

———. 1982b. *The Return to Cosmology: Postmodern Science and the Theology of Nature.* Berkeley and Los Angeles: University of California Press.

Toynbee, Arnold. 1954. *A Study of History.* Vol. 9. London: Oxford University Press.

Turbayne, Colin. 1962. *The Myth of Metaphor.* New Haven, Conn.: Yale University Press.

Turkle, Sherry. 1984. *The Second Self: Computer and the Human Spirit.* New York: Simon and Schuster.

Turley, Peter T. 1977. *Peirce's Cosmology.* New York: Philosophical Library.

Turner, Victor. 1974. *Dramas, Fields and Metaphors: Symbolic Action in Human Society.* Ithaca, N.Y.: Cornell University Press.

———. 1982. *From Ritual to Theater: The Human Seriousness of Play.* New York: Performing Arts Journal Publications.

———. 1986. *The Anthropology of Performance.* New York: Performing Arts Journal Publications.

Tursman, Richard. 1987. *Peirce's Theory of Scientific Discovery: A System of Logic Conceived as Semiotic.* Bloomington: Indiana University Press.

Tyler, Stephen. 1987. *The Unspeakable: Discourse, Dialogue, and Rhetoric in the Postmodern World.* Madison: University of Wisconsin Press.

Uexküll, Jakob von. 1957. "A Stroll through the Worlds of Animals and Men: A Picture Book of Invisible Worlds." In *Instinctive Behavior: The Development of a Modern Concept,* edited by C. H. Scholler, 5–80. New York: International Universities Press.

Uexküll, Thure von. 1982. "Jakob von Uexküll's The Theory of Meaning." *Semiotica* 42 (1): 1–87.

———. 1989. "Jakob von Uexküll's Theory." In *The Semiotic Web 1988,* edited by T. A. Sebeok and J. Umiker-Sebeok, 129–58. Berlin: Mouton de Gruyter.

357

Ullman, Shimon. 1979. *The Interpretation of Visual Motion.* Cambridge, Mass.: MIT Press.

———. 1980. "Against Direct Perception." *Behavioural and Brain Sciences* 3:373–81.

Ulmer, Gregory. 1985. *Applied Grammatology: Post(e)-Pedagogy from Jacques Derrida to Joseph Beuys.* Baltimore, Md.: Johns Hopkins University Press.

Vaihinger, Hans. 1935. *The Philosophy of "As If": A System of the Theoretical, Practical and Religious Fictions of Mankind.* Trans. C. K. Ogden. London: Kegan, Paul, Trench, Trubner.

Varela, Francisco J. 1975. "A Calculus for Self-reference." *International Journal of General Systems* 2:5–24.

———. 1979. *Principles of Biological Autonomy.* Amsterdam: North-Holland.

Vygotsky, Lev Semenovich. 1962. *Thought and Language.* Trans. E. Hanfmann and G. Vakar. Cambridge, Mass.: MIT Press.

Waddington, Conrad H. 1969. *Behind Appearances: A Study of the Relations between Paintings and the Natural Sciences in This Century.* Cambridge, Mass.: MIT Press.

Waismann, Friedrich. 1952. "Analytic-Synthetic." *Analysis* 13:1–14, 73–89.

Walker, Evan Harris. 1970. "The Nature of Consciousness." *Mathematical Biosciences* 7:138–78.

Walker, Evan Harris, and Nick Herbert. 1977. "Hidden Variables: Where Physics and Paranormal Meet." In *Future Science,* edited by J. White and S. Krippner, 279–94. New York: Doubleday.

Warnock, Mary. 1978. "Nietzsche's Conception of Truth." In *Nietzsche: Imagery and Thought,* edited by M. Pasley, 33–63. Berkeley and Los Angeles: University of California Press.

Weinsheimer, Joel D. 1985. *Gadamer's Hermeneutics: A Reading of Truth and Method.* New Haven, Conn.: Yale University Press.

Weizsäcker, C. F. von. 1971. "The Unity of Physics." In *Quantum Theory and Beyond,* edited by T. Bastin, 229–62. Cambridge: Cambridge University Press.

———. 1980. *The Unity of Nature.* Trans. F. J. Zucker. New York: Farrar, Strauss, Giroux.

Weyl, Hermann. 1921. *Space, Time, Matter.* New York: E. P. Dutton.

———. 1949. *Philosophy of Mathematics and Natural Science.* New York: Atheneum.

Wheeler, John Archibald. 1979. *Frontiers of Time.* Amsterdam: North-Holland.

———. 1980a. "Beyond the Black Hole." In *Some Strangeness in the Proportion: A Centennial Symposium to Celebrate the Achievement of Albert Einstein,* edited by H. Woolf, 341–75. Reading, Mass.: Addison-Wesley.

———. 1980b. "Law without Law." In *Structure in Science and Art,* edited by P. Medawar and J. H. Shelley, 132–68. Amsterdam: Excerpta Medica.

———. 1982. "Bohr, Einstein, and the Strange Lesson of the Quantum." In *Mind in Nature,* edited by R. Q. Elvee, 1–23. New York: Harper and Row.

———. 1984. "Bits, Quanta, Meaning." In *Theoretical Physics Meeting,* 121–34. Naples: Edizioni Scientifiche Italiane.

White, Hayden. 1978. *Tropics of Discourse: Essays in Cultural Criticism.* Baltimore, Md.: Johns Hopkins University Press.

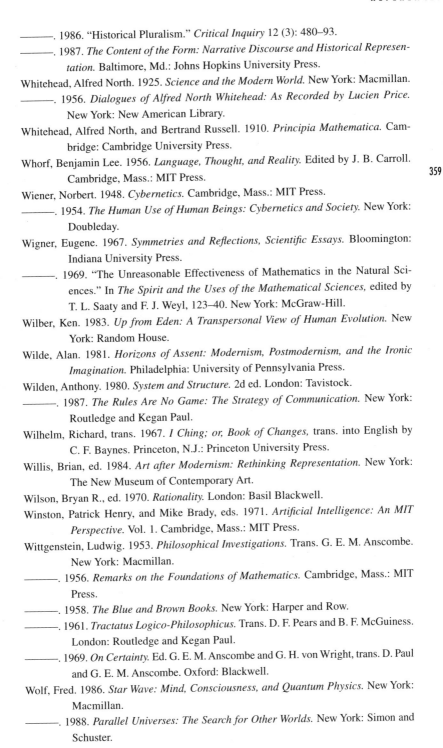

———. 1986. "Historical Pluralism." *Critical Inquiry* 12 (3): 480–93.

———. 1987. *The Content of the Form: Narrative Discourse and Historical Representation.* Baltimore, Md.: Johns Hopkins University Press.

Whitehead, Alfred North. 1925. *Science and the Modern World.* New York: Macmillan.

———. 1956. *Dialogues of Alfred North Whitehead: As Recorded by Lucien Price.* New York: New American Library.

Whitehead, Alfred North, and Bertrand Russell. 1910. *Principia Mathematica.* Cambridge: Cambridge University Press.

Whorf, Benjamin Lee. 1956. *Language, Thought, and Reality.* Edited by J. B. Carroll. Cambridge, Mass.: MIT Press.

Wiener, Norbert. 1948. *Cybernetics.* Cambridge, Mass.: MIT Press.

———. 1954. *The Human Use of Human Beings: Cybernetics and Society.* New York: Doubleday.

Wigner, Eugene. 1967. *Symmetries and Reflections, Scientific Essays.* Bloomington: Indiana University Press.

———. 1969. "The Unreasonable Effectiveness of Mathematics in the Natural Sciences." In *The Spirit and the Uses of the Mathematical Sciences,* edited by T. L. Saaty and F. J. Weyl, 123–40. New York: McGraw-Hill.

Wilber, Ken. 1983. *Up from Eden: A Transpersonal View of Human Evolution.* New York: Random House.

Wilde, Alan. 1981. *Horizons of Assent: Modernism, Postmodernism, and the Ironic Imagination.* Philadelphia: University of Pennsylvania Press.

Wilden, Anthony. 1980. *System and Structure.* 2d ed. London: Tavistock.

———. 1987. *The Rules Are No Game: The Strategy of Communication.* New York: Routledge and Kegan Paul.

Wilhelm, Richard, trans. 1967. *I Ching; or, Book of Changes,* trans. into English by C. F. Baynes. Princeton, N.J.: Princeton University Press.

Willis, Brian, ed. 1984. *Art after Modernism: Rethinking Representation.* New York: The New Museum of Contemporary Art.

Wilson, Bryan R., ed. 1970. *Rationality.* London: Basil Blackwell.

Winston, Patrick Henry, and Mike Brady, eds. 1971. *Artificial Intelligence: An MIT Perspective.* Vol. 1. Cambridge, Mass.: MIT Press.

Wittgenstein, Ludwig. 1953. *Philosophical Investigations.* Trans. G. E. M. Anscombe. New York: Macmillan.

———. 1956. *Remarks on the Foundations of Mathematics.* Cambridge, Mass.: MIT Press.

———. 1958. *The Blue and Brown Books.* New York: Harper and Row.

———. 1961. *Tractatus Logico-Philosophicus.* Trans. D. F. Pears and B. F. McGuiness. London: Routledge and Kegan Paul.

———. 1969. *On Certainty.* Ed. G. E. M. Anscombe and G. H. von Wright, trans. D. Paul and G. E. M. Anscombe. Oxford: Blackwell.

Wolf, Fred. 1986. *Star Wave: Mind, Consciousness, and Quantum Physics.* New York: Macmillan.

———. 1988. *Parallel Universes: The Search for Other Worlds.* New York: Simon and Schuster.

Wooley, Benjamin. 1992. *Virtual Reality: A Journey in Hype and Hyperreality.* Oxford: Blackwell.

Woolgar, Steve. 1988. "Reflexivity Is the Ethnographer of the Text." In *Knowledge and Reflexivity: New Frontiers in the Sociology of Knowledge,* edited by S. Woolgar, 14–34. London: Sage.

Wright, Robert. 1988. *Three Scientists and Their Gods.* New York: Harper and Row.

Young, John Z. 1978. *Programs of the Brain.* Oxford: Oxford University Press.

Zohar, Danah. 1990. *The Quantum Self: A Revolutionary View of Human Nature and Consciousness Rooted in the New Physics.* New York: Morrow.

Index

365